THE NONVIOLENT GOD

THE NONVIOLENT GOD

J. Denny Weaver

WILLIAM B. EERDMANS PUBLISHING COMPANY

GRAND RAPIDS, MICHIGAN / CAMBRIDGE, U.K.

Published 2013 by

Wm. B. Eerdmans Publishing Co.

2140 Oak Industrial Drive N.E., Grand Rapids, Michigan 49505 /
P.O. Box 163, Cambridge CB3 9PU U.K.

www.eerdmans.com

Printed in the United States of America

19 18 17 16 15 14 13   7 6 5 4 3 2 1

Library of Congress Cataloging-in-Publication Data

Weaver, J. Denny, 1941-
     The nonviolent God / J. Denny Weaver.
         pages   cm
     Includes bibliographical references and index.
     ISBN 978-0-8028-6923-4 (pbk.: alk. paper)
     1. Atonement.   2. Nonviolence — Religious aspects — Christianity.
     3. Jesus Christ.   4. Bible. New Testament — Criticism, interpretation, etc.
     I. Title.

     BT265.3.W44   2013
     232′.3 — dc23

                                                              2013010382

Unless otherwise noted, the Scripture quotations in this publication are from the
New Revised Standard Version of the Bible, copyright © 1989 by the Division of
Christian Education of the National Council of Churches of Christ in the U.S.A.,
and used by permission.

For Gerald J. Mast,
    Friend
        Colleague
            Conversation Partner

Contents

Preface

The formal beginning of this book was the lecture I prepared in 2006 on the concept of a nonviolent God with the support of the C. Henry Smith Trust fund. Before this lecture the idea that we should understand God with nonviolent images was not the focus, but it was certainly a conclusion drawn already from the first edition of *The Nonviolent Atonement,* published in 2001. And before that I came to see this book on a nonviolent God as the current stage of the quest that emerged from my first year of college teaching in 1974, namely to understand what Jesus' rejection of the sword and violence might imply for and how it might become more visible in our theology about Jesus.

Along the way, many informal conversations as well as responses to lectures have provided valuable assistance. Supporting comments whether in informal settings or in response to lectures contribute inspiration to continue while challenges expose weakness or gaps in the argument and allow for corrections. I am grateful for all such feedback in whatever form it came.

I single out some names for recognition in full awareness that I have likely omitted others. People with whom I had significant conversations or who responded to sections of the manuscript at some point in its development include J. R. Burkholder, Robert Enright, Larry George, Hannah Heinzekehr, Justin Heinzekehr, Caleb Heppner, Gregory Jones, Donald Kraybill, Steven Nolt, Jonathan Sauder, Neff Serrano, Karen Serrano, David W. Shenk, and Todd Warren. I have had many enlightening conversations over the years with colleagues Ray Gingerich, Ted Grimsrud, and Earl

Zimmerman. Along with thanks to the C. Henry Trust Fund that sponsored the lecture on the nonviolent God, I am grateful to Larry Eby, who arranged for a series of subsequent lectures at the Portland (Oregon) Mennonite Church, and to Larry Wilson, who sponsored a lecture series at First Mennonite Church of Urbana-Champaign, Illinois and to Robert McKim, who invited a lecture for the Work in Progress Series, sponsored by the Religious Studies Program of the University of Illinois at Urbana-Champaign. Scott Anderson and Ken Penning arranged for a lecture series under the auspices of the Wisconsin Council of Churches. I am grateful to Suzanne Lind and the Mennonite Central Committee office in Kinshasa for arranging a series of lectures in university and church settings in the Congo that provided an opportunity to test ideas in a cultural setting much different from the United States, and to Fernando Enns, who arranged a series of lectures in university and ecumenical church settings in Germany that allowed testing in yet another foreign context. I have enjoyed email interaction with Fulco van Hulst, who sought me out from the Netherlands and has posed thoughtful questions and comments from afar. Loren Johns, Laura Brenneman, and Mark Fretz each suggested literature that has contributed to my argument. Ron Adams, widely read pastor and theologian at Madison (Wisconsin) Mennonite Church, read a draft of the entire manuscript and offered many helpful suggestions from both pastoral and theological perspectives. C. L. Nash read four chapters and provided numerous insightful comments and suggestions. If I have not made sufficient use of such a wealth of experiences and proffered wisdom, the fault is, as is often said, entirely mine.

This book would not exist without the support of my wife Mary. On occasion she has to remind me that life consists of more than writing, but she nonetheless understands my need to write.

Last for thanks is Gerald J. Mast, my colleague for many years, friend, frequent collaborator, and ongoing conversation partner. He has long urged me to write a book on the order of this one, and his efforts contribute to this book in more ways than I can enumerate. In gratitude for that relationship, I dedicate this book to Gerald.

J. DENNY WEAVER
Madison, Wisconsin

Introduction

Christian faith begins with a narrative — the story of Jesus Christ. Christian theology, literally our words about the God of Jesus Christ, emerges as reflections on that story and its meaning. Those reflections on the narrative began already in the New Testament. The earliest such reflections — theologizing on the narrative of Jesus — occur in the writings of Paul. Two of Paul's short reflections frame the theologizing of the book in hand.

Paul wrote: "in Christ God was reconciling the world to himself, not counting their trespasses against them, and entrusting the message of reconciliation to us" (2 Cor. 5:19). Paul's words can serve as a summary of this book's depiction of the saving message of Jesus Christ and of the acts and the character of the God who is fully revealed in Jesus.

Paul also wrote: "I worked harder than any of them — though it was not I, but the grace of God that is with me" (1 Cor. 15:10). This statement extends the work of Jesus Christ by linking it to our working in the world. This working requires our personal responsibility and engagement, but at the same time this statement indicates that it cannot be accomplished on our initiative alone; it happens only through the grace of God. The theologizing to follow about extending the work of Jesus in the world is an expansion of Paul's statement of the paradox of grace: actions that humans engage in but that God enables.

Each of Paul's comments introduces one of this book's two major parts. The first text concerns the action of God in Christ. This book's Part I deals with the character and activity of the God who is revealed in the life, teaching, death, and resurrection of Jesus Christ. Since Christian theology is our words about the God revealed in Jesus Christ, it is important to note that the discussion begins in Chapter 1 with a brief, thematic résumé of the narrative of Jesus. In a reprise of the atonement discussion from my earlier book *The Nonviolent Atonement,* the argument shows that this presentation of Jesus' story can also serve as the atonement image that I have called "narrative Christus Victor." As its name indicates, this motif emerges specifically from a reading of the New Testament's narrative of Jesus. The comparisons of narrative Christus Victor with the classic theories of atonement in Chapter 3 then focus on the activity of God, with particular attention paid to the violence implied in the traditional images. One result of the comparisons is to show that atonement imagery is less about the death of Jesus and more an understanding of the character of God and how God works in the world. Discussion of atonement thus leads to a discussion of the character of God.

Since the narrative of Jesus in the New Testament pictures Jesus' rejection of violence and his refusal to use the sword, the traditional confession that God is revealed in this story calls for understanding God in terms of nonviolent images. That God should be understood with nonviolent images constitutes the major thesis of this book. In this discussion, narrative Christus Victor emerges as an atonement motif that not only contrasts with the classic motifs but, most significantly, shows that the important differences concern their contrasting images of God. Whereas the God of the classic atonement motifs uses or sanctions violence as God's modus operandi in the world, the God of narrative Christus Victor is a God who saves through the power of resurrection and the restoration of life. For this reason, narrative Christus Victor is described as a nonviolent atonement image.

Part II builds on and extends the profession that God is revealed in the life, teaching, death, and resurrection of Jesus. In Jesus, the character of God and the reign of God on earth become visible. Those who seek to know the God of Jesus will thus live in the story of Jesus, in which God is revealed. In the second text quoted above, Paul mentioned his own working but then attributed that effort to the working of God — the grace of God — that was within him. By implication, Paul's statement extends that grace to the life of every Christian, and through the narrative of Jesus it involves God in the life of every Christian. Christians continue the mission of Jesus, and their lives thus witness to the presence of the reign of God on earth. Part II provides additional material from the life of Jesus as a picture of God's reign in the world. This sketch becomes the basis for a description of the church of Jesus Christ and outlines some suggestions for what the reign of God made visible in Jesus looks like for both individuals and structures in our contemporary time and contexts. Issues addressed in Chapters 7 through 10 include baptism, the nature of the church and its relationship to civil religion and the "Christian society," nonviolent activism, forgiveness, responses to sexism and racism, economic issues, the Lord's Supper, creation, and suffering.

Stated another way, this book presents a theology for living, a theology that is lived. Being identified as "Christian" involves a way of living, a way of life that is identified by the story of Jesus. The theologizing of the book in hand draws on the narrative of Jesus. To describe the life of Jesus (or the nature of the reign of God made visible in Jesus) is to describe the basis of the Christian life. Conversely, to ask how one identified by Christ — a *Christian* — should live requires a description of the life of Jesus. It is drawing on the narrative of Jesus as the basis of theology that gives this theology for living its distinct character. With the reference to the life of Jesus, it could be called a discipleship theology or a theology for disciples of Jesus.

Being Christian is a commitment to the living Christ, a commitment to live in his story. Theology or doctrine are the words by which we describe the Jesus of that commitment. Ethics or the Christian life is the lived version of that commitment. The words of the book in hand display this kind of theology. Alongside the written theology, the Christian life provides a living picture of the continuing presence of Jesus in the world.[1] This lived version and the accompanying written and oral version — theology — are inseparable. To do theology with words is to provide the basis for living the Christian life, and without the lived version the theology in words devolves into mere abstractions. This volume is an attempt to sketch the theology that is lived as a commitment to the risen Christ.

The theologizing in this book speaks to three sets of questions. The

---

1. Monika Hellwig makes a similar comment. It may be argued, she wrote, that the "real sources" of Christology are "the person and event of Jesus Christ seen in context; and the continuing experience of living the Christian life in community." As a Christological image for our time she suggests "the compassion of God," which includes both concrete efforts to achieve justice in this world and reconciliation to God in individual lives. Monika K. Hellwig, *Jesus: The Compassion of God* (Wilmington: Michael Glazier, 1983), quoting pp. 43 and 122. Robert Krieg uses a biography of Dorothy Day as an example of extending the narrative of Jesus Christ in the world today. Robert A. Krieg, *Story-Shaped Christology: The Role of Narratives in Identifying Jesus Christ* (New York: Paulist, 1988).

first is, "How is the story of Jesus a saving story?" That is, "What is the meaning of salvation and how is it found in this story?" This question leads into a second, "How does the salvation found in the saving story of Jesus impact contemporary lives, our lives today, as Christians?" That is, "How are the lives we live as Christians changed by virtue of finding salvation in the story of Jesus?" Readers will discover that answers to these two questions are inseparable — experiencing salvation and living as a Christian are each an expression of the other. To experience salvation is to live as a Christian.

In these two answers one discovers the presence of God in the story of Jesus. It is a story of salvation because God is in this story, and the discussion of how it is a saving story points to the relationship of God to Jesus Christ. With the discussion of Jesus' relationship to God, we enter the realm of one of the classic theological concerns in the early centuries of the church, namely how Jesus relates to God. The answer that emerged in the early church was the profession that God is truly or fully present and revealed in Jesus Christ.

I agree with the profession from the early church that God was fully present and revealed in Jesus, which leads to the third question addressed by this book. It concerns God, and more specifically, the character of God. "What is the character of the God revealed in Jesus Christ?" Discussing the character of God is perhaps the most crucial issue of all. The answer impacts one's view of reality as a whole, or what John Howard Yoder famously called "the grain of the universe."[2]

Theologizing that starts from the narrative of Jesus rather than as reflections shaped by the classic formulas does produce some alternative images. The basis of that argument appears in Chapter 6. As will become clear in several sections of the book, the narrative of Jesus is virtually absent from the classic formulas and confessions of theology, namely Christology and Trinity as well as the classic atonement images. In contrast, the new formulations based specifically on the narrative reflect Jesus' rejection of violence. Of course, the classic formulations are also theologizing on what the New Testament says about Jesus. Using biblical material and from within their particular context, the authors of the classic statements identify Jesus with God or deity and with humanity as categories. However,

---

2. John H. Yoder, "Armaments and Eschatology," *Studies in Christian Ethics* 1 (1988): 58. It is "grain of the cosmos" in John Howard Yoder, *The Politics of Jesus: Vicit Agnus Noster* (2d ed.; Grand Rapids: William B. Eerdmans, 1994), 246.

these formulations provide little that puts the specifics of Jesus' life as a man on display. The new formulations (or the efforts to produce new formulations) thus reveal the extent to which theology that treats the classic images of Christology as the unquestioned norm can accommodate violence, and display how the classic atonement theories model violence and innocent, passive submission to violence.

Discussion of these issues appears in several sections of this book. Coming to see the importance of understanding God with nonviolent images and what that view implies for other questions is a developing, multi-layered discussion. One result is that the classic images also emerge as a theology for living, but a quite different version of Christian living than that projected by the book in hand. The pages to follow will put on display the extent to which images of God are mirrored in Christian practice, whether those of a violent or a nonviolent God.

That God was revealed in the story of Jesus, and that the image of God reflects the nature of reality and produces alternative images thus leads directly to a challenge to the common perception that an all-powerful God acts in the world with violence. It seems to me that one of the great and longest-running distortions in Christian theology has been the attribution of violence and violent intent to the will and activity of God. But if God is truly revealed in Jesus Christ, and if Jesus rejected violence, as is almost universally believed, then the God revealed in Jesus Christ should be pictured in nonviolent images. If God is truly revealed in the nonviolent Christ, then God should not be described as a God who sanctions and employs violence. Part I of this book develops the argument for the nonviolence of God, which emerges from the discussion of atonement imagery and is itself a way of talking about the narrative of Jesus as a saving story. Part II then sketches some implication of living in the narrative of Jesus that reveals this understanding of God.

The statement that God is truly revealed in Jesus needs a brief explanation. Since human minds can make no claim to know everything about an infinite God, it is not a claim that by looking at the narrative of Jesus one can know everything about God. The phrase does mean something important however. It means that whatever we might say or think about God should not be contradicted by what is revealed about God in the narrative of Jesus. In this sense the character of God is fully revealed in Jesus. Thus the argument to follow disputes those efforts to defend the violence of God by claiming that, because we cannot know everything about God, the full character of God was not revealed in the incarnation. This claim allows for divine violence as God's prerogative in manifestations of God outside of the incarnation.

Advocating a nonviolent image of God requires responding to a number of challenges from the received tradition. These challenges include the seeming violent imagery of Revelation, the longstanding assumption that Paul's writings undergird classic satisfaction atonement imagery, and the efforts of many writers to hold all the classic atonement images together as parts of a greater whole. Chapters 2 and 3 respond to these challenges. Perhaps the most important challenge to the idea of a nonviolent God is the extensive material from the Old Testament along with some material in the New Testament that pictures a God who uses violence and who even commands the people of God to use violence and to conduct massacres. This material is laid out in Chapter 4 and responded to in Chapter 5.

The book begins in Chapter 1 with a discussion of Jesus. That conversation uses the New Testament's earliest statements about Jesus, namely the narratives and sermons that identify Jesus in the book of Acts. Although Acts was written some decades after the sermons reported, these recorded statements in Acts show how the Apostles were identifying Jesus in the weeks immediately after his death and resurrection. The brief narrative identification of Jesus in Acts is then expanded via a discussion of material primarily from the Gospel of Luke, but with some additional references. The following discussion of the book of Revelation in Chapter 2 reveals that the imagery of this book conveys the same message as that found in the Gospels. As a story of salvation, these images from the Gospels and Revelation can be construed as an atonement image. Comparing that image with the traditional atonement images reveals the extent to which the traditional images feature a God who sanctions violence.

In contrast, the atonement image sketched in this book has a nonviolent image of God, and is also a saving message of life in the living Christ. In developing the atonement image from Revelation, the discussion displays the image of a nonviolent God in Revelation. It is thus a response to one important challenge to the idea of God's nonviolence, namely the claim that Revelation pictures both Jesus and God exercising great violence in final judgment.

The effort to produce a theology for living results in a distinct if not quite unique theology. And it will become evident that the line between the narrative of Jesus and the meaning of the narrative, that is theology, is often rather indistinct. At times one moves almost imperceptibly from the narrative to the meaning of the narrative. The approach also shows that the line between theology and ethics is also indistinct. To talk about the story and its meaning is also to talk about ethics, that is, about the foundation of the *Christ*ian life and what it means for a Christian to live in the life of Jesus.

The theology developed in this book is not defined by doctrine claimed to be universally correct, as in the several Christian creedal traditions, both Catholic and Protestant, although the presence of this volume obviously puts on display that I take doctrine very seriously. Neither is this version of Christian theology defined by a particular kind of experience or spirituality, as occurs in various forms of pietism, both early and contemporary, although those who live in the theological outlook developed here obviously have an experience of the risen Christ. Since the theology developed here does not fit within these two traditional methodologies, it will appear to some readers as a "third way" of doing theology. That designation is acceptable in the particular, narrow context of distinguishing theology for living from both doctrinal and experiential theologies.

However, "third way" only defines this theology in terms of other theologies. The theology presented in this book is not properly understood or defined by holding up what it is not, namely not defined either by creedalism or a specific kind of experience. Rather, it should be understood in terms of what it is. True to its stated beginning point, the theology of this book aims to be "specific to Jesus." Theology that is specific to Jesus does not reject the creedal definitions as false. In fact, it recognizes the truth of the creedal formulas in their historic context, but it can also express the meaning of Jesus in other ways in our contemporary context. Similarly, it does not specify a particular kind of experience, as some traditions have done, but is open to a variety of ways to give existential expression to the presence of Jesus today.

In presenting this theology for living, the imprint of John Howard Yoder is clear. It appears both in the specifics of the chapter on Christology that leads off Part II as well as in the methodology as a whole, which identifies the narrative of the man Jesus as the beginning point for Christian theology and ethics. However, I make no claim that this book represents a mere extension of Yoder's work or that he would have approved the moves made in this book. In fact, even though his imprint is clear, this book may have made him a bit nervous. He once told me, "If you write a systematic theology, you will end up defending the system rather than Jesus." And this book does have some attributes of a systematic theology in that it identifies an atonement image and then applies it to a number of other issues.

But in a specific nod to Yoder, Chapter 6 on Christology follows Yoder's approach: he displayed the multiple images by which the New Testament writers expressed in differing contexts the truth that God was in Christ, and he used that description as a call for the church today to engage in a continual process of asking how to express the meaning of Jesus in its current contexts. This book is one such effort. It does not pretend to produce an eternally valid statement about Jesus Christ that transcends culture, but is rather an effort to state the truth of the gospel in and for our world of the early twenty-first century.

Finally, there is yet another way of identifying the theological trajectory of this book. It is inspired by but not dependent on sixteenth-century Anabaptism. Perhaps the most important impulse of that historical movement is to identify Jesus Christ as the foundation of our existence as Christians. Anabaptism returns us to the New Testament to discover our center and our norm, Jesus Christ. The sixteenth-century movement provides examples of that return to the New Testament, and some examples of beginning the kind of theologizing that is developed in this volume as theology specific to Jesus.[3] Some readers will find this historical reference useful and informative. At the same time, other readers new to Anabaptism will be relieved to know that one can read and embrace this book's message about the gospel of Jesus Christ without any dependence on or knowledge of the sixteenth-century Anabaptist tradition.

Although the theology to follow does pose some alternative images to and alongside the classic formulations, it is established on an ecumenical foundation. After all, every Christian tradition in some way claims the New Testament's story of Jesus. Thus theology for living that extracts meaning from the narrative of Jesus claims a common foundation with each and every Christian tradition. It thus invites every Christian to join the conversation engaged by this book about what it means to be specific to Jesus.

As a statement of theology that develops from reflections on a narrative claimed by all Christians, this book engages conversation with a range of audiences. It might appeal to certain skeptics who have contemplated leaving or have recently abandoned Christian faith. These skeptics and

3. The coauthored book *Defenseless Christianity* develops a model for understanding historic Anabaptism as the beginning of the contemporary peace church specific to Jesus with some brief indications of theology. The volume in hand develops this theology. See Gerald J. Mast and J. Denny Weaver, *Defenseless Christianity: Anabaptism for a Nonviolent Church* (Telford: Cascadia/Herald, 2009).

doubters would be represented by the numerous conversations I have had with people who told me, "Your book *The Nonviolent Atonement* persuaded me to give the church one more chance." Such speakers include pastors who told me that salvation based on an atonement image of God punishing Jesus never made sense, "but now your book enables me to preach again on Easter." The book may appeal to those who have been turned off by the church's too easy accommodation of national violence and by the injustice perpetrated by empire and global capitalism under the guise of Christian civilization. Further, the book will appeal to those who have long been skeptical of a violent God, a God who commands war and natural disasters as punishment, or has a "secret plan" whereby a beloved wife dies of cancer or a long-desired baby dies at birth or a brother is killed by a drunken driver. Pacifists of many stripes may find this book attractive. In advocating nonviolence, it goes beyond mere appeal to the authority of Jesus. It establishes a wide-ranging theological framework for nonviolence that is compatible with and can lend support to many forms of pacifism. It points the way for Christians to support activities of very different groups when there is an intersection of interests in a particular justice concern. This theology for living intersects with the interests of those concerned with justice issues not addressed specifically by the classical theology. These issues include sexism and patriarchy addressed by feminists and womanists, the racism addressed by womanists and black theology, and issues of economics and poverty also addressed by womanists and black theology and some feminists. Further, this theology for living will find support and fellow travelers among those who represent what some observers have called the "emergent church," represented by figures such as Brian McLaren, and among the "postconservative evangelicals" identified by Roger Olson.[4] These categories cut across traditional denominational lines. In principle, this theology for living can engage persons from any denominational perspective. I have had supportive conversations on issues addressed in this book with people ranging from Roman Catholics and across the Protestant spectrum to Old Order Amish.

Now, as the beginning of a theology specific to Jesus, we turn to the earliest New Testament statements that identify Jesus.

---

4. See Roger E. Olson, *Reformed and Always Reforming: The Postconservative Approach to Evangelical Theology* (Grand Rapids: Baker Academic, 2007).

I The God of Jesus

1   *Jesus in Acts and the Gospels*

The Earliest Statements: Acts

The earliest recorded statements about Jesus appear in the sermons and orations preserved in the book of Acts. Although Acts was written a generation after the events in question, it preserves the Apostles' statements about Jesus in the first weeks and months after he was no longer with them bodily.

Six such statements occur: Acts 2:14-39; 3:13-26; 4:10-12; 5:30-32; 10:36-43; 13:17-41. Five are addressed to audiences in Jerusalem and one to those in attendance at the synagogue of Antioch in Pisidia. The orations and sermons follow a clear outline. They begin with a statement that, in the fullness of God's time or as a continuation of the history of God's people Israel, Jesus came and lived among them. In Jerusalem the audience is told "you crucified and killed [him] by the hands of those outside the law" (2:23) while in Antioch Paul says that "residents of Jerusalem . . . asked Pilate to have him killed" (13:27-28). The accounts then report that God raised Jesus from the dead, and the speaker includes himself in the story by listing himself as a witness to the events. Finally, there is a statement of response to the oration — people join or sins are forgiven or salvation is part of the story. Along with these common elements appear several other, lesser mentioned statements — details of Israel's history, performance of signs and wonders by Jesus, Jesus' burial, or various mentions of the work or presence of the Spirit.

These sermons and orations in Acts tell a story. It is the story that identifies Jesus. When the Apostles were asked in whose name they spoke or in whose authority they dared to act, they replied by telling this story about Jesus. At this juncture, early in our theologizing, it is important to observe that the Apostles identified Jesus in terms of a narrative. That it is a narrative takes on added significance in the course of the argument to follow.

Expanded Statements: The Gospels

The Gospels expand the narrative outline from Acts. As the eyewitnesses to the events of Jesus' life, death, and resurrection began to disappear from the scene, it became important to preserve the memories of the story. The New Testament contains four of these expanded accounts, the four Gospels. The following sketch of the narrative of Jesus uses most often the Gospel of Luke, with assistance from other Gospels on occasion. This sketch displays the challenges and confrontations that Jesus' message and movement posed to the institutions of his time as well as the nonviolent character of those challenges and confrontations. The theologizing of the book in hand develops as reflections on this narrative.

Jesus began his public ministry with an appearance in the synagogue in Nazareth when he read from Isaiah 61:1-2. His words signaled that his ministry had a strong social component, bringing "good news to the poor," "release to the captives and recovery of sight to the blind," freeing of oppressed people, and "proclaim[ing] the year of the Lord's favor" (Luke 4:18-19). Throughout Jesus' ministry, his actions give visibility to its social element. Jesus went out of his way to minister to outcasts like lepers and prostitutes. He paid attention to widows, orphans, and strangers — those without representation in the patriarchal society of first-century Palestine. In a society in which a woman's legal status was dependent on a property-owning man, a widow, an orphan, or a stranger — perhaps today's equivalent of an undocumented alien — had no legal spokesman or representative.

Comparing the text Jesus quoted with the full text Isaiah 61:1-2 shows an early indication of the nonviolent character of Jesus' mission. Jesus stopped after the line about proclaiming the year of the Lord's favor. Isaiah's text completes the thought with an additional phrase about proclaiming "the day of vengeance of our God." That Jesus omitted this phrase indicates his nonviolent orientation.[1]

---

1. Jack Nelson-Pallmeyer points out that the Gospel writers put both violent and nonviolent images of God in the sayings of Jesus. He uses the omission of the vengeance phrase

With this social mission, Jesus was performing what the prophets anticipated, namely radical social change, the bringing down of the mighty and the lifting up of the lowly. One sees that expectation of social change in the words attributed to Mary in celebration of her pregnancy:[2]

> He has shown strength with his arm;
>   he has scattered the proud in the thoughts of their hearts.
> He has brought down the powerful from their thrones,
>   and lifted up the lowly;
> he has filled the hungry with good things,
>   and sent the rich away empty. (Luke 1:51-53)

It may be that these words were borrowed from a Maccabean revolutionary poem, and they hold up expectation of a social revolution. However, the difference between Jesus and other "messiahs" and social revolutionaries in attempting to enact this social revolution is that Jesus carried out his social program without violence.

As the Gospels tell the story, Jesus carried on an activist mission whose purpose was to make the rule of God visible. His mission was to live and teach in ways that displayed the reign of God. This ministry had confrontational components. He challenged the religious practices taught by the Pharisees. He plucked grain on the Sabbath (Luke 6:1-5), healed on the Sabbath (Luke 6:6-11; 13:10-17), traveled through Samaria and interacted with a Samaritan woman (John 4:1-38), freed rather than stoning the woman caught in adultery (John 8:1-11), disputed with the Pharisees, cleansed the temple (Luke 19:45-47), and more.

These actions display an element of deliberate confrontation,[3] which

---

from Isaiah as one indication that Jesus intended to challenge the idea of a violent God who directed vengeance on God's enemies. Jack Nelson-Pallmeyer, *Jesus against Christianity: Reclaiming the Missing Jesus* (Harrisburg: Trinity, 2001), 321. Specific discussion of these contradictory sayings attributed to Jesus will come in Chapter 4.

2. John Howard Yoder, *The Politics of Jesus: Vicit Agnus Noster* (2d ed.; Grand Rapids: William B. Eerdmans, 1994), 21-22.

3. No contradiction exists between the statement that the purpose of Jesus' ministry was to "make the rule of God visible" and the claim that his ministry had "an element of deliberate confrontation." When the social situation is economically and politically unjust, making God's rule visible will indeed expose that injustice, and that exposure will make its perpetrators uncomfortable. Confrontation is the inevitable result of pointing out injustice. Richard Horsley develops Jesus' ministry to make the reign of God visible as a confrontation of rulers, which included the Roman occupiers of Palestine and their client rulers — King

is easily seen in the account of healing the man with the withered hand in Luke 6. Because of Jesus' previous activity, the scribes and Pharisees recognized that the setting was right for a Sabbath healing. He knew they were watching, hoping to catch him in a violation of Sabbath restrictions. Certainly some voices around Jesus had suggested that he postpone such activity until the following day when it would not give offense (as in 13:14-15). Most certainly Jesus did not wait. He invited the man to come and stand where all could see (6:8). Then he posed the question, "Is it lawful to do good or to do harm on the sabbath, to save life or to destroy it?" (v. 9). Finally he looked around at all of them (v. 10) — a dramatic pause for effect in which he made eye contact with the crowd. Only after everyone was watching did he give the command, "Stretch out your hand" (v. 10). This episode was a deliberate and public breaking of Sabbath holy laws.

In his encounter with the Samaritan woman at Sychar, Jesus confronted prevailing standards in more than one way (John 4:1-38). He had already violated the strict purity expectations by traveling through rather than around Samaria. For the strict Pharisees, Samaritans were a mixed race, and therefore inferior and unclean. People who wanted to travel from Judea (in the south) to Galilee (in the north) without contaminating themselves with the supposed low-class Samaritans walked extra miles to the east side of the Jordan River. They walked north on the east side of the Jordan and then crossed back to the west bank when they reached Galilee. It could add 30 or 40 extra kilometers to the journey. Jesus had already violated that purity standard just by being in Samaria. And then he surprised the woman at the well by his willingness, as a Jew, to accept a drink from her, a Samaritan. The purity code forbade contact with a menstruating woman. Since one could never be certain that a woman was not in the un-

---

Herod, followed by his son Herod Antipas in Galilee, and the high priestly rulers of the temple appointed by Pilate. As Horsley wrote concerning the parable of the vineyard and the wicked tenants in Mark 12:1-9: "The high priests are hardly 'Jewish leaders.' Mark has just demonstrated that they have no authority whatever among the people as leaders. Neither in this episode nor in Mark as a whole is there any suggestion of the replacement of 'Judaism' by 'Christianity.' Mark has Jesus direct the parable in 12:1-8 and the rhetorical question in 12:9 pointedly at the high priests, scribes, and elders (11:27; 12:12). Moreover, they immediately recognize that they are implicated and resolve to arrest Jesus, but are afraid of the crowd. Here, as throughout Mark's story, the fundamental conflict lies between rulers and ruled, not 'Judaism' and 'Christianity.'" Richard A. Horsley, "Ethics and Exegesis: 'Love Your Enemies' and the Doctrine of Nonviolence," in *The Love of Enemy and Nonretaliation in the New Testament*, ed. Willard Swartley (Louisville: Westminster/John Knox, 1992), 93.

clean state, the practice was to assume that she was unclean, a condition which also extended to any vessel that she touched.[4] In their turn, the disciples were equally surprised that he spoke to a woman (v. 27), and on top of that a Samaritan woman.

This account displays Jesus crossing barriers of class and race. It also illustrates how his interactions with women frequently raised their standing and broke the conventions of a patriarchal society. His acts of healing on the Sabbath and his encounters with women are integral dimensions of his mission to make the reign of God visible over against conditions of discrimination and oppression in the social order.

With such actions, Jesus confronted the purity code taught by the religious leadership. These confrontations display vividly in the context of that day the difference between the purity code and the rule of God that Jesus' actions make present. The reign of God valued women equally with men, valued the despised Samaritans as much as the supposed pure ethnic group, sought restoration of relationships rather than punishment, and more.

Jesus healed people and he cast out demons — actions which show that the reign of God encompasses the created order. He sent out the twelve (Luke 9:1-6) and then seventy (10:1-17) to "proclaim the kingdom of God" (9:2) and to say that "the kingdom of God has come near you" (10:9). The reign of God was near because in his person Jesus made the reign of God present. His acts, such as confronting the purity code, his healings, and his teaching, such as the Sermon on the Mount (Matthew 5–7), showed the comprehensive character of the reign of God for those who would live within it.

One of the important texts displaying the nonviolence of Jesus occurs in the Sermon on the Mount, in which he tells his followers not to resist an evildoer, to turn the other cheek, to give the cloak with the coat, to go the second mile, and to love enemies (Matt. 5:38-48). Since there is a long tradition of interpreting these injunctions as passive nonresistance, it is important to examine them again in order to see that they too reflect Jesus' nonviolent but assertive ministry.

The command commonly understood as a passive statement of nonresistance to evil — "do not resist an evildoer" (5:39) — actually conveys a different message. Rather than constituting a command not to resist, it

---

4. C. K. Barrett, *The Gospel According to St. John: An Introduction with Commentary and Notes on the Greek Text* (New York: Macmillan, 1962), 194.

counsels not to resist evil with more evil, that is, not to respond in a way that mirrors evil.[5] Jesus then provided three examples of how to resist without mirroring evil: turning the other cheek, giving the inner garment with the outer garment, and going the second mile.

Matthew specifies not responding to a strike on the "right cheek." Since the left hand was the unclean hand and not used in public, a strike on the "right" cheek can only be a backhand slap. Such a slap is not intended to injure; it is a way to rebuke and humiliate a social inferior. By turning the other cheek, the person of lesser status has acted in a way that refuses humiliation and asserts equal humanity. The aggressor has failed in the effort to humiliate. If the aggressor follows up by striking with a fist on the now open left cheek, which cannot be conveniently reached by another backhand slap, the blow with a fist acknowledges equality. Either outcome raises the status of the person slapped vis-à-vis the aggressor.

The context for the coat statement is an often exploitative debtors' court. Debtors were called to court to give security. Often the poor person's last item of value was the coat he slept in. The debtor was called to surrender the coat in the morning, but could retrieve it at night for sleeping. To expose the greed of wealthy debt holders in an oppressive system, Jesus suggests that when the poor debtor must surrender the coat as security in court, he should hand over his inner garment along with the outer garment and then walk around naked for the day. Since the shame of nakedness in that society fell not on the naked person but on the one who caused the nakedness, the nakedness of the debtor would embarrass and display the greed of the exploitative debt holder.

Finally, rules for the Roman army of occupation allowed a soldier to compel a citizen to carry the soldier's pack. However, as relatively enlightened occupiers, to lessen resentment against the forces of occupation, Roman army regulations permitted only one mile of this forced service at a time from any one citizen. Going a second mile would thus transform the citizen from coerced laborer into the decision maker. More significantly, it put the soldier in violation of his own regulations, and he would risk discipline from his commander. One can even envision a complete reversal of requests, with the soldier begging the citizen to put down the pack before the soldier gets in trouble.

5. The interpretation here of Matt. 5:38-42 follows Walter Wink, *Engaging the Powers: Discernment and Resistance in a World of Domination* (The Powers, 3; Minneapolis: Fortress, 1992), 175-84.

This brief analysis of the three injunctions aligns them with the assertive view of Jesus visible in other stories as well. In each case, these are strategies by which a person without power can resist and turn the tables on a more powerful superior.

In discussion of the nonviolence of Jesus, the story usually called "the cleansing of the temple" requires particular comment. Some writers have argued that this story displays Jesus using violence and thus places Jesus in support of the use of violence by Christians. I reject that conclusion. First, I simply point to the prior description of Jesus' assertive but nonviolent actions and teaching. Throughout the Gospels there is a pattern of assertive or confrontational but nonviolent actions by Jesus. Second, there are several things to notice about the story itself. One is obvious but nonetheless bears pointing out: Jesus did not kill anyone. He used a whip; whips make noise. He used the noise of a whip to chase animals out of the temple. He also dumped over the tables of the money changers. This was an aggressive act, but the surprised money changers would not necessarily even lose any money from overturned tables — although they certainly could end up in embarrassing positions to retrieve it. Jesus clearly caused embarrassment and discomfort to some moneyed people and disrupted a system that greatly enriched the priestly rulers, but he did not launch a terrorist attack and he did not kill anyone. The so-called "cleansing of the temple" was not an act of violence. It is another event that follows the pattern of Jesus' actions that gave visible and assertive or confrontational witnesses to the rule of God in contrast to the conditions around him.[6]

The high priests who ruled the temple were not leaders of the Jewish people.[7] In this action in the temple, Jesus was not confronting Judaism. He was confronting an exploitative system of domination that involved both Romans and their clients, the high priests. The priests as temple rulers were appointed by the Romans and served at the pleasure of the Roman occupiers. This system imposed double taxation on the populace, who had

6. Equivalent actions today might be entering an Air Force base to hammer on missiles and bombers to act out "turning swords into plowshares," African Americans occupying lunch counter seats designated by law as "whites only," or Gandhi's campaign in India to make illegal salt.

7. The following analysis of the cleansing of the temple follows Richard Horsley and Jack Nelson-Pallmeyer and their descriptions of the temple system and Jesus' confrontation of it. See Richard A. Horsley, *Jesus and Empire: The Kingdom of God and the New World Disorder* (Minneapolis: Fortress, 2003), especially 91-93, and Nelson-Pallmeyer, *Jesus against Christianity*, especially chapters 16 and 17.

to pay taxes to Rome as well as to the temple rulers. Further, the priests claimed divine authority to control access to the temple rituals of forgiveness and access to God, which compelled the populace to spend money in the temple. The people suffered from this system while the priests enriched themselves with Roman backing. This was the system that Jesus' "temple cleansing" confronted.

Jesus' actions were a condemnation of the temple rulers as client appointees of the Romans, and a disruption of their normal activity. In his protest, Jesus stood in the prophetic tradition of both Isaiah and Jeremiah. With "'My house shall be a house of prayer'; but you have made it a den of robbers" (Luke 19:46), Jesus was citing Isaiah 56:7 and Jeremiah 7:11. Each prophet had also engaged in a symbolic action: Isaiah walked naked for three years to symbolize the way the Assyrian empire would lead away captive the Egyptians, with whom the Judean monarchy wanted to make an alliance (Isaiah 20), and Jeremiah wore yokes of wood and then iron to act out the call for the Judean monarchy to submit to Babylon (Jeremiah 27–28). As Richard Horsley wrote, "Jesus was thus symbolically acting out a new prophetic condemnation not just of the building but of the Temple system, because of its oppression of the people, as indicated in the reference to Jeremiah's original condemnation of the Temple system." Jesus' protest of this system precipitated a plot to have him arrested and killed. From this point on, the temple authorities looked to kill him, "just as the earlier officers of the Temple sought to lynch Jeremiah after his oracle pronouncing God's judgment against the Temple (Jeremiah 26)."[8]

Details of his arrest and trial indicate Jesus' principled rejection of violence and armed resistance. At his arrest, he forbade his companions to defend him with swords, rebuked Peter for using his sword, and healed the damage Peter had caused (Luke 22:49-51; John 18:10-11). Apparently Jesus scolded those who arrested him for thinking that they even needed swords and clubs: "Have you come out with swords and clubs as if I were a bandit?" He had been teaching every day in the temple, he said, where it was obvious that he could be taken without weapons (Luke 22:52-53).

An even clearer indication of his principled rejection of the option of violent resistance becomes visible in his conversation with Pilate. When questioned about his mission, Jesus told Pilate: "My kingdom is not from this world. If my kingdom were from this world, my followers would be fighting to keep me from being handed over to the Jews. But as it is, my

---

8. Horsley, *Jesus and Empire*, 91-93, quoting 93.

kingdom is not from here" (John 18:36). A kingdom "not from this world, . . . not from here" cannot be an inner, spiritual kingdom as has been frequently suggested. Jesus' entire mission had external components and a social agenda, beginning with the announcement of the mission in the synagogue in Nazareth. The statement about a kingdom "not of this world . . . not from here" concerns the source of the orientation that gave shape and visibility to the kingdom preached by Jesus. Those values and the orientation they produced were different from the violence-based system that stemmed from Rome and which Pilate administered.

These observations all indicate that rejection of violence belonged intrinsically to Jesus' witness to and making present of the reign of God. Thus nonviolence is an intrinsic dimension of *how* Jesus identified with and pursued justice for the suffering and oppressed.

Jesus was tried, condemned, and, with the connivance of the religious leadership, executed by the Romans, the highest political authority of the day. But three days later God raised him from the dead. The story of Jesus in the Gospels culminates with his resurrection from the dead and his appearances to witnesses. The resurrection and the witnesses to the risen Jesus constitute the climax of the narrative from the Gospels as well as the culminating point of the sermon outline from Acts.

This account describes Jesus' rejection of violence as intrinsic to his teaching and to the way he carried out his mission. Following chapters have additional analysis of the nonviolence of Jesus and its implications for our understanding of God. Meanwhile, the discussion here emphasizes the resurrection. It is the resurrection that identifies God with Jesus' life, including his rejection of violence. Thus Jesus' life makes visible the character of God and the reign of God.

A number of contemporary theologians representing several theological perspectives support the move to include Jesus' life in theologizing and thereby put on display the nonviolent character of the reign of God that Jesus embodied. John Dominic Crossan witnesses the Bible's conversation between violent and nonviolent images of God (described in detail in Chapter 4 of the book in hand) and writes, "It is not the violent but the nonviolent God who is revealed to Christian faith in Jesus of Nazareth and announced to Christian faith by Paul of Tarsus." In the Epilogue to *God and Empire* Crossan states, "It is the radicality of God's justice and not the normalcy of civilization's injustice that, as a Christian, I find incarnate in Jesus of Nazareth."

Jack Nelson-Pallmeyer also depicts contradictory images of God in both Old and New Testaments. To understand the character of God in the midst of these contradictions, Nelson-Pallmeyer writes, "I believe the historical Jesus offers Christians the best example of what God is like." In dealing with the contradictions "Jesus fundamentally challenges many of the images of God on which both the faltering old theology [of a violent, punishing God] and its apocalyptic alternatives were founded."

Eugene Peterson is quite clear about the rejection of violence by Jesus. He depicts Jesus in contrast to the Zealot parties, who advocated violent resistance to the Roman occupation. These parties enjoyed popularity among the populace. Since Jesus' message concerned the inauguration of a new kingdom, some people thought that he perhaps sounded like a Zealot. But he was not. "He blessed the poor in spirit, commanded love for enemies, approved paying taxes to Caesar, collected all kinds of people around him who would be of absolutely no use in a war." For Peterson, "The final and convincing proof that Jesus was not a Zealot was that after his crucifixion there was no revolt, no violence. No looting. No killing. Nothing."

Gregory Boyd contrasts the "power over" domination enforced by the sword of the kingdoms of the world to the "power under" rule of the kingdom of God made visible in Jesus. "The character and rule of God is manifested when instead of employing violence against his enemies to crush them, Jesus loves his enemies in order to redeem them."

Brian McLaren suggests new metaphors for displaying Jesus' embodiment of God in the world. It can be described as a "divine peace insurgency" or "God's unterror movement" or again, "the new global love economy." And in contrast to Rome's motto of peace through destructions of enemies, McLaren writes, "for Jesus the motto is peace through nonviolent justice, peace through the forgiveness of enemies, peace through reconciliation, peace through embrace and grace."[9] The story of Jesus is much more than a murder plot that culminates with resurrection. And the resurrection is not merely the final act of the story. It is the event that certifies the importance of what has come before.

9. John Dominic Crossan, *God and Empire: Jesus against Rome, Then and Now* (New York: HarperCollins, 2007), 95, 238; Nelson-Pallmeyer, *Jesus against Christianity*, 84, 136; Eugene H. Peterson, *The Jesus Way: A Conversation on the Ways That Jesus Is the Way* (Grand Rapids: William B. Eerdmans, 2007), 246-47; Gregory A. Boyd, *The Myth of a Christian Nation: How the Quest for Political Power Is Destroying the Church* (Grand Rapids: Zondervan, 2005), chapter 2, quoting 34; Brian D. McLaren, *Everything Must Change: Jesus, Global Crises, and a Revolution of Hope* (Nashville: Thomas Nelson, 2007), 128-30, 159.

The Significance of the Resurrection

Some of the theological implications of resurrection emerge from the writings of Paul, whose initial theologizing on the narrative of Jesus deals with the resurrection. The sermon outline visible in Acts appears again in 1 Corinthians 15:3-9, where Paul reminds his readers of the "good news" that he proclaimed and that they received (v. 1). The "good news" is the narrative outline found in the sermons in Acts and expanded in the Gospels. It features the event of Jesus as an act of the God of Israel, and Jesus' death and burial, God's resurrection of Jesus, and finally a list of witnesses that testify to the truth of the account.

In this text, however, Paul goes beyond identifying Jesus by means of the narrative. The narrative identification of Jesus becomes the basis for making a new assertion about the resurrection. Although the narrative outline says nothing about a general resurrection, in vv. 12-20 Paul argues that believing in the resurrection of Jesus requires belief in a general resurrection of all dead. This claim makes sense only if Paul makes a prior assumption, namely that what happens to Jesus also applies to all human beings.[10] On the basis of this assumption, Paul extends the meaning of the story to include an implication derived from the original story. Here is an example of the beginning of theologizing that occurs already in the New Testament. The point is that theologizing about Jesus, that is, deriving meaning from the narrative beyond what the narrative says explicitly, was practiced already by the Apostle Paul. The church has engaged in the practice ever since.

The resurrection is important for a number of reasons.[11] It is because of the resurrection that Christians proclaim Jesus as Lord and claim immediate access to Jesus today. In classic theological language, the resurrection testifies to the incarnation, the presence of God in the flesh. Paul wrote to the Romans that Jesus was "declared Son of God with power . . . by resurrection from the dead" (1:4) That God raised Jesus from the dead is

10. John Howard Yoder called this "the logic of solidarity." The description here of the beginning of theologizing in Paul follows Yoder in his *Preface to Theology: Christology and Theological Method* (Grand Rapids: Brazos, 2002), 95-97, quoting 96.

11. The primary focus of N. T. Wright's major work on the resurrection was to make a case for the historicity of Jesus' bodily resurrection. However, his discussion of the meaning of the resurrection is echoed in the following discussion. See N. T. Wright, *The Resurrection of the Son of God* (Christian Origins and the Question of God, 3; Minneapolis: Fortress, 2003), 723-36.

the evidence that God was present in the life of Jesus. Only Jesus was raised and still lives. Other features follow from this beginning point.

If resurrection indicates the presence of God in the life of Jesus, then the life of Jesus becomes important for our theology and our lives as Christians.[12] It is there, in Jesus' acts and his teaching, that one sees the character of the reign of God and what it looks like in human form. In examining the acts and teaching of Jesus, one sees that the reign of God embraces and has concern for the powerless — those without advocates in a given society. These include widows who have no one to speak for them in a male-oriented, hierarchal society; Samaritans who experience discrimination because of their ethnicity; poor people who own no property in a society where power depends on ownership; and people oppressed by military occupation.

Stated another way, that God is present in the life of Jesus means that the fulfillment of the reign of God involves people, their relationships to each other, and the form of their structures on earth and in human history. N. T. Wright wrote that death is the ultimate weapon of the tyrant. Resurrection overcomes death, and thereby "is the ultimate affirmation that creation matters, that embodied human beings matter. That is why resurrection has always had an inescapable political meaning."[13]

Equally important as whom Jesus identified with in making the reign of God visible is *how* he identified with them, and *how* he confronted the injustices they faced. In confronting injustice and uplifting the poor and oppressed, Jesus rejected the option of violence as a way to alleviate suffering. Rather than mirror violence with more violence, Jesus taught ways for the powerless to turn the tables on social superiors, and his life illustrated nonviolent confrontation of injustices. This rejection of violence is intrinsic to the story of Jesus and to his work as it will be developed in following chapters. Jesus' rejection of violence — his nonviolence — along with his nonviolent efforts to confront evil and to change the situation comes back repeatedly throughout the remainder of this book.

A fourth point is obvious, which is perhaps why it is so often missed. When the reign of God is made present in Jesus, that story tells us about the character of God. Theologizing about God emerges from the narrative

---

12. This point and the point in the two preceding paragraphs are similar to statements by Stanley J. Grenz, *Theology for the Community of God* (Nashville: Broadman Holman, 1994), 334, 366.

13. Wright, *Resurrection*, 730.

of Jesus. It is from this narrative in which God is truly or fully revealed that one sees on display the nonviolent character of God and thus the need to counter the many images of a God who uses or sanctions violence. That the character of God is known through God's revelation in Jesus Christ is a frequently missed point in much theologizing. This emphasis on the non-violent character of God will also return repeatedly throughout the remainder of this book.

A fifth dimension of resurrection is that it constitutes an invitation. It invites us to experience the reign of God by living in the story of Jesus. Since God is present in the story of Jesus, to live in the story of Jesus is to experience God in human history. Living in Jesus is living in and with God.

The invitation posed by the resurrection returns us to the life of Jesus. To live in his story is to join with and follow Jesus in his mission of witnessing to the gospel, the peaceable reign of God. This is a life of disciple-ship, namely making the story of Jesus a norm for our lives. Living in his story is how we are *Christ*ian. Living in his way is what it means to be *Christ*ian, to be identified by and with Christ. And to be *Christ*ian means to witness to the reign of God in the same *manner* that Jesus did. The reign of God becomes visible in the world when Christians — people identified with and by Jesus Christ — continue to live in Jesus so that the reign of God becomes visible. The Christian calling — the mission of the church — is to carry on Jesus' mission of witnessing to and making present the reign of God in human history.

Thus this invitation posed by the resurrection honors and hallows our work as Christians and gives it a social and political dimension. Paul concluded the discussion of resurrection in 1 Corinthians 15 not with an injunction to wait patiently for heaven but with an injunction to work seriously. "Therefore, my beloved, be steadfast, immovable, always excelling in the work of the Lord, because you know that in the Lord your labor is not in vain" (15:58). For N. T. Wright this means "that what we do in the present by way of justice and mercy and grace and forgiveness and healing and liberation and all the rest of it, all that is done in the name of Christ and in the power of the Spirit, will not be lost but will be part of the eventual kingdom that God will make."[14] And as he said in another place, "It is . . . only with the bodily resurrection of Jesus, demonstrating that his death dealt the decisive blow to evil, that we can find the proper ground for

---

14. Robert B. Stewart, ed., *The Resurrection of Jesus: John Dominic Crossan and N. T. Wright in Dialogue* (Minneapolis: Fortress, 2006), 42.

working to call the kingdoms of the earth to submit to the kingdom of God." This "deeply orthodox" view of the resurrection "is the proper seedbed of radical politics."[15]

Putting together all these statements about the importance of resurrection brings us to the most important point of all. Resurrection means that the narrative of Jesus, the one in whose story we are invited to live, is a saving story, a story of *salvation*. With the resurrection, God has demonstrated that the last enemy, namely death, is overcome. Jesus did not save by dying. His death reveals that killing is the ultimate tool employed by the opponents of the reign of God. Resurrection constitutes God's response to death, revealing that death is not the final answer. Resurrection is God's victory over death and the vindication of Jesus as the presence of the reign of God in our history, and thus it is a witness to the character of God. The resurrection is the real saving act of God, and Christians share in it through identification with the living Christ. Or as Brian McLaren stated so graphically, "Jesus' quiet but real resurrection validated to his disciples that the liberating king was not defeated, . . . that Caesar's whips and nails and crosses couldn't overcome God's way of love and reconciliation. . . . So in the shadow of Caesar's ruthless kingdom, witnesses of Jesus' resurrection . . . chose to live in the framing story of a new Lord, . . . they chose to believe Jesus' wild, untamed good-news story about the kingdom of God — as a story of hope that could frame and transform a better future."[16]

The narrative outlined in Acts and expanded in the Gospels is a saving message because what happens to Jesus will one day happen to us. Paul's point in 1 Corinthians 15:3-8 as he rehearses the narrative of Jesus by which the Apostles identified Jesus (in Acts) and which was expanded in the Gospels is that one cannot believe in the resurrection of Jesus, with which the story culminates, without also believing in a future general resurrection, and that to deny a future general resurrection is equivalent to denying the resurrection of Jesus. This means, I suggest, that the real saving message of Jesus consists of the resurrection. And the resurrection is then God's invitation to live in the story of Jesus and thereby to participate in the future reign of God that is already present in part whenever and wherever people live in the life of Jesus.

Resurrection as invitation means that our individual responsibility, via a decision, is engaged in experiencing salvation. To experience salva-

---

15. Stewart, ed., *Resurrection of Jesus*, 23.
16. McLaren, *Everything Must Change*, 272.

tion in the reign of God requires a decision to change sides in the struggle between the reign of God and the rule of Satan. "Changing sides" functions as a metaphor for accepting Jesus or experiencing salvation in the reign of God. Changing sides is more than a mere change in status before God. It is an actual transfer of loyalty and allegiance and a taking on of the task of learning a new way to live. Taking this new way means becoming a disciple of Jesus, whose life and teaching made present the reign of God in human history. One cannot experience this salvation without actually changing loyalty and taking up a new way of life any more than one can switch from being a football player to basketball player without actually going to basketball practice and learning the game.

God created all human beings with a free will, which makes us responsible for our actions. We thus make a conscious choice to leave a sinful way of life and to join and live by the reign of God that is witnessed to and made present in the life of Jesus. That free choice and individual responsibility appear clearly visible when Jesus told Peter and Andrew and Matthew, "Follow me." In the language of Anabaptism, this is a call to discipleship. Discipleship means that we are responsible for the choices that align our actions with structures and powers of the rule of Satan. We have to make a choice to reject those powers and to become a disciple of Jesus — to move to the side of God and to join the reign of God in opposition to the defeated rule of evil that still struggles. For some people, this change may begin with an emotional or decisive and monumental decision at a particular point in time; for others it is a process of gradual growth over an extended period of time in learning a new way to live. But for all, it becomes a lifelong engagement and a daily choice to continue to live within and by the narrative of Jesus as that which shapes our lives according to the rule of God. In this conceptualization, human beings are responsible and an understanding of salvation and Christian faith distinct from living as a disciple of Jesus is inconceivable.

On the other hand, sinful human beings cannot save themselves. Under their own power and authority, sinful human beings cannot overcome the rule of Satan. Change to the side of God can occur only under the call and the power of God. Without God's transforming power, the change of sides is impossible. Sinful human beings cannot undo their participation with the powers that killed Jesus — they can only beg forgiveness. And God incorporates them onto the side of God in spite of what they have done. God incorporates them onto the side of the reign of God without those sinful human beings having any capacity to return anything to God in compensation for their participation in the death of Jesus. As Paul wrote, "He has rescued us from the power of darkness and transferred us into the kingdom of his beloved Son, in whom we have redemption, the forgiveness of sins" (Col. 1:13-14). Participating in the salvation of the reign of God is therefore an experience of grace — it is unearned and unmerited and happens through God's call, which accomplishes in sinners what they cannot accomplish through their own power. In this conceptualization, the life of discipleship is a life of grace. To experience salvation distinct from living as a disciple of Jesus is inconceivable. But most importantly, living as a disciple depends on grace. Without grace it is inconceivable. As Paul wrote to the Romans, it is "Jesus Christ our Lord" through whom we receive "grace and apostleship to bring about the obedience of faith among all the Gentiles for the sake of his name" (1:4-5).

The ideas in these last paragraphs present a genuine paradox — two contradictory statements that are both true. We do choose and exercise responsibility, but it is the grace of God that inspires that choice. This telling of the narrative of Jesus with the image of "choosing sides" makes visible this "paradox of grace." Paul wrote about it. It is expressed in his statement: "I worked harder than any of them — though it was not I, but the grace of God that is with me" (1 Corinthians 15:10).

In language used at the beginning of this chapter, I have sketched the narrative of Jesus as a theology for living. To understand the story of Jesus as a story of salvation means to live in that story. The version articulated with words and the version expressed by living are inseparable. It is also important to note that this lived theology speaks to the classic question of the early Christian centuries, namely how Jesus is related to God. The story told here makes clear that God is fully present in this story. That God resurrected Jesus from the dead is the evidence that God was present in the story. Resurrection is also what vouchsafes Jesus' teaching and life as the presence of God and the reign of God in human history. Resurrection constitutes our invitation to live in the reign of God.

The discussion now turns to another level of theologizing from the narrative of Jesus the Christ.

Narrative Christus Victor: Round One

To this point the focus has been on the narrative of Jesus in the New Testament and the description of that narrative as a story of salvation. Another kind of theologizing on the basis of that biblical narrative intersects with traditional discussions of the meaning of Jesus as Savior. In conventional language, this is the discussion of theories of atonement.

The Story as Atonement Motif

Thus far, the discussion has identified the narrative of Jesus as a story of salvation. In the history of doctrine, conventional usage employs the term "atonement" to describe the saving work of Jesus Christ. And in common usage, atonement doctrine is frequently assumed to answer the question, "Why did Jesus have to die?" with "atonement" then frequently used synonymously with the satisfaction image. The focus on resurrection in the current analysis shifts the focus away from death and thus displays the way in which the question focused on the death of Jesus misses the culmination of the story. Since the dominant satisfaction atonement images focus on Jesus' death, the description here of the narrative of Jesus as a story of salvation, with God's resurrection of Jesus as the salvific act, could proceed without identifying resurrection as an atonement image. However, for ease of reference and to make clear the particular conversation in which the discussion engages, I have continued to describe my discussion of the "work of Christ" via the image of narrative Christus Victor as an "atonement" motif. In terms of Jesus' work, this motif responds to the question, "How does the life, teaching, death, and resurrection of Jesus save?"

When expounded as an atonement image, the narrative of Jesus just depicted fits under the general category of Christus Victor images. As will become apparent, there are both similarities and differences between the form just rehearsed and the classic images of Christus Victor. The earliest or classic images of Christus Victor, found in the writings of the early church fathers, feature a cosmic conflict between the forces of God and forces of Satan or the devil. In this conflict, sinful human beings have given themselves over to Satan, who holds their souls captive, and Jesus the Son of God is killed, an apparent defeat for the reign of God. However, the defeat is temporary. Three days later God raises Jesus from the dead. With the resurrection of Jesus, God has defeated the devil, and sinners are freed from his power. This cosmic victory reveals what was always the case, namely that God reigns as ultimate ruler of the cosmos. With Satan defeated, sinners escape Satan's clutches and become free to return to fellowship with God.

This early classic image existed in multiple versions. It is associated with Irenaeus (c. 130-c. 200), who depicted the life of Jesus as a recapitulation of the entire history of humanity, from the fall of Adam, through restoration of humanity by performance of the obedience Adam lacked, to victory over Satan in the resurrection of Christ, and finally the restoration of humankind to fellowship with God. Irenaeus and others, including Origen (c. 185-254), Gregory of Nyssa (c. 330-c. 395), Augustine (354-430), and Gregory I (c. 540-604) wrote of Jesus' death as a ransom payment to the devil to secure the release of captive souls, with resurrection the defeat of Satan. The defeat of Satan could involve trickery, which was depicted in rather humorous images such as the humanity of Jesus functioning like the bait that lures a mouse into a trap or hiding the deity that defeated Satan as bait hides a fish hook.[17]

It is readily apparent that the narrative just sketched shares some features with the classic versions of Christus Victor. For one, the story presented the image of conflict between reign of God made visible by Jesus and rule of Satan, present in all the forces that opposed Jesus and ultimately executed him. Further, resurrection is indispensable to the image: without resurrection there is no victory by God or of the reign of God.

However, this narrative also differs in important ways from the classic Christus Victor, and, similarities notwithstanding, the differences carry the most significance. First, since the story recited here comes from the Gospels, the version of Christus Victor based on this narrative is prior to any statement of the classic images. Thus the narrative of this account is neither dependent on nor derived from the classic versions. Further, to state the obvious, this depiction makes use of — actually depends on — the narrative of Jesus. This narrative for the most part is absent from the classic versions. To emphasize its dependence on the New Testament narrative as well as to distinguish this version from the classic edition, this version is called *narrative* Christus Victor.[18]

The narrative does more than designate a form of Christus Victor. As

17. Descriptions of these images and their meanings appear in many volumes on the history of doctrine. See for example Robert S. Paul, *The Atonement and the Sacraments: The Relation of the Atonement to the Sacraments of Baptism and the Lord's Supper* (New York: Abingdon, 1960), 53-56; Jaroslav Pelikan, *The Emergence of the Catholic Tradition (100-600)* (The Christian Tradition: A History of the Development of Doctrine, 1; Chicago: University of Chicago Press, 1971), 148-49; J. N. D. Kelly, *Early Christian Doctrines* (rev. ed.; New York: Harper and Row, 1978), 393; H. D. McDonald, *The Atonement of the Death of Christ in Faith, Revelation, and History* (Grand Rapids: Baker, 1985), 143.

18. The atonement image *narrative Christus Victor* was first developed in *The Nonviolent Atonement*, now in its second edition. See J. Denny Weaver, *The Nonviolent Atonement* (2d ed.; Grand Rapids: Wm. B. Eerdmans, 2011). The book in hand extends the discussion of narrative Christus Victor in a variety of ways.

was apparent from its first description, the narrative supplies the basis for living in Jesus and experiencing communion with God that comes through living in the story of Jesus. When Christians live in this story, they participate in the confrontation of evil by the reign of God that was made visible in the life of Jesus.

Thus the narrative displays the confrontation of God's reign and Satan's rule on earth, in human history. It is the accumulation of human evil that killed Jesus in opposition to the reign of God. Since the reign of God has not yet come in its fullness, that evil still abounds in the world. All human beings are subject to that evil. It can be said that all human beings, including ourselves today, participate in the evil that killed Jesus. The narrative dimension involves every individual. And given the pervasive presence of evil and injustice in the world, it is more than obvious that evil has not been vanquished. Although the resurrection of Jesus constitutes victory over evil, evil is still present and active in the world. It takes faith in the resurrected Jesus to proclaim that victory.

What makes this story good news is that through living in the story of the resurrected Jesus, believers participate in the victory of the reign of God over the rule of evil. Living in that story is what gives visibility to the victory as a living reality in the world, even if much of the world fails to recognize it. This brings the discussion once again to a juncture that affirms the theology proposed here as theology for living.

Locating the confrontation on earth in human history is in no way a denial of the cosmic dimension of the confrontation and victory. However, locating the narrative in history endows the confrontation with a reality and relevance in this world that is lacking when it concerns only or primarily the cosmic, ahistorical confrontation of the classic images.

Characteristics of Narrative Christus Victor

It is important to evaluate narrative Christus Victor with relation to the three questions posed in the Introduction, namely how the story of Jesus is a saving story, how this saving story impacts lives today, and what the character is of the God revealed in the story of Jesus Christ. The fact that individuals who live in the narrative of Jesus participate in the victory of the resurrection makes clear that this narrative is a saving story and that narrative Christus Victor is an image that depicts salvation. Narrative Christus Victor is theology for living. It is a depiction of the saving message of Jesus, but stated in a way that draws the hearer into the story and invites people to live in the story and experience the salvation that it describes. This theology most certainly has a lived version. Quite clearly the salvific quality of the story is related to the impact of the story on the life of believers. One cannot believe this saving story of Jesus without living in the story, and one cannot live in the story without believing the story. Experiencing salvation and living as a Christian truly are inseparable. The way one lives demonstrates whether one truly believes the story of Jesus.

That God is truly in this story reveals the power of God to overcome death. Killing, denying people their existence, is the ultimate exercise of evil. The story of Jesus reveals that God can overcome death, the worst evil that human beings can accomplish. And according to Paul's argument in 1 Corinthians 15, that overcoming of death is an invitation and a promise to each of us.

The narrative of Jesus makes clear that he rejected the option of the sword: he engaged in nonviolent confrontation and witness. Since Jesus' story makes God's rule visible, Jesus' rejection of the sword makes a statement about the God who is revealed in Jesus. The God revealed in Jesus would not employ violent or destructive means. Any images of God that picture a God who employs violence or who orders death via natural or man-made disasters stand in sharp contrast with the image of God that is revealed in the nonviolent narrative of Jesus.

Chapter 3 will have an extended discussion of atonement motifs and the nonviolence of God. In anticipation of that discussion, it is sufficient here to state that in narrative Christus Victor in no way is the death of Jesus aimed at God or in any way needed by God. Jesus' death does not impact God or "satisfy" God. Neither does God arrange the death of Jesus or require it to meet a divine, cosmic need. On the contrary, dealing death to Jesus is a blow against the reign of God, and, through the saving action of resurrection, God responds to the death-dealing blow by giving life.

Further, God's overcoming of death puts on sharp display the contrast between God's modus operandi and that of the forces of evil. Whereas the forces of evil employ death-dealing as the solution to their supposed problems, God's answer and response is the overcoming of death, the restoration of life. God saves, not by taking life but by restoring life.[19] From this

---

19. Craig Carter rejects the view articulated here, instead arguing that the resurrection requires a death, which appears to make God responsible for the death of Jesus, similar to the various satisfaction theories. See Craig A. Carter, "The Liberal Reading of Yoder: The

discussion about the presence of the reign of God in the life of Jesus and the role of God in Jesus' resurrection, it is apparent that narrative Christus Victor is appropriately described as a nonviolent atonement image.

In these observations about the rejection of violence on display in the narrative of Jesus followed by a statement about the nonviolence of God, it is important to emphasize that rejection of violence was derived from the story itself. The affirmation about the nonviolence of God follows from the prior belief that God is fully revealed in the person and life of Jesus and is true only if God is fully or truly revealed in Jesus.

To this point the account has pursued theology that develops as a drawing out of the significance of the narrative of Jesus. This theology concerns a story located in human history, with a beginning and an end — a future culmination. It locates Jesus as the decisive midpoint in this linear history; the event of Jesus more than any other makes visible the end point of history. This eschatological perspective becomes most visible in the book of Revelation, to which the discussion now turns.

Problem of Yoder Reception and the Need for a Comprehensive Christian Witness," in *Radical Ecumenicity: Pursuing Unity and Continuity after John Howard Yoder,* ed. John C. Nugent (Abilene: Abilene Christian University Press, 2010), 89-93. Carter's understanding fails at two points. For one, he does not recognize that resurrection as God's overcoming of death is most meaningful if God did not engineer Jesus' death. The meaning of resurrection is most profound if it is God's response to human freedom's efforts to do its worst, namely to deny life. Further, Carter's argument that God is behind the death of Jesus in narrative Christus Victor in the same way as in the satisfaction theories fails to acknowledge the profound difference in these images. For the satisfaction theories, the death is aimed at God, it satisfies God's honor or the requirement of God's law, and without the death God's honor or God's law is not satisfied. In contrast, in narrative Christus Victor, the death is not aimed at God, it does not impact God, and it accomplishes nothing in the economy of God. Instead, death — killing Jesus — is what those desire who opposed the will of God. Tom Neufeld also seems to desire to preserve the hand of God in atonement imagery, including Jesus' death as satisfaction to God. That intent would lie behind his critique when he writes that although I am correct in developing the story of Jesus through to the resurrection, "Weaver is wrong, however, to leave God out of it when it comes to this darkest, most violent hour. Evangelists and apostles alike insist that it was *God* who retrieved from the event of the death of Jesus the means of reconciliation precisely with those who killed him." Thomas R. Yoder Neufeld, *Killing Enmity: Violence and the New Testament* (Grand Rapids: Baker Academic, 2011), 94. However, I have not left God out. Instead, I have pictured God as the one who raised Jesus from that violent hour, which then constitutes the invitation to participate in the reign of God, rather than seeing God as the one who engineered Jesus' death as the means of "reconciliation . . . with those who killed him."

2 *Jesus in Revelation and Paul*

At the opposite end of the New Testament from the Gospels sits one of the most misunderstood books of the Bible, namely the Apocalypse of John, frequently called Revelation. Revelation uses apocalyptic language to present the same message about Jesus Christ that one finds in the Gospels. This chapter demonstrates that thesis and then situates the writings of the Apostle Paul between the two symbolic bookends of the New Testament.

In the book of Revelation, the line between the narrative of Jesus and theology about Jesus is not always distinct. Revelation deals with the Jesus of history. But in dealing with Jesus, it conveys answers to the questions that frame this book. In Revelation one reads the meaning of Jesus as a story of salvation. And as will become apparent, it gives the meaning of the resurrection in celebratory fashion, presents the relationship of Jesus to God, and gives important clues to the character of God, and does so in a way that describes both Jesus and a theology for living.

In contrast to the common assumption that Revelation presents a violent God who wreaks future, violent vengeance on evil people and an evil world,[1] this chapter emphasizes the nonviolent theology of Revelation —

1. One of the latest examples of such interpretations is the well-known Left Behind series written by Tim LaHaye and Jerry Jenkins. One reviewer writes that of authors who have imagined the return of Jesus, "few have portrayed him wreaking more carnage on the unbelieving world than Tim LaHaye and Jerry B. Jenkins. . . . Jesus eviscerates the flesh of millions of unbelievers merely by speaking," as if superheated blood was bursting through skin, eyes were melting, and tongues disintegrating. David D. Kirkpatrick, "The Return of the Warrior Jesus," *New York Times*, April 4, 2004, 4, p. 1. Although LaHaye and Jenkins have

the nonviolence of God, the victory of the reign of God through resurrection, and the church as the earthly manifestation of the reign of God made visible in the life, death, and resurrection of Jesus.

Revelation

Reading Revelation

It is important to clarify some interpretative methodology before entering Revelation itself. Locating the meaning and message of Revelation in the life, death, and resurrection of Jesus is a direct challenge to the common assumption that Revelation predicts the events of the end times, with some of those events already occurring in the present time of the interpreter. The widely popular novels of the Left Behind Series constitute only the latest of many versions of this predictive approach. The previous generation was enthralled by the writings of Hal Lindsey, who famously predicted that the end-time events supposedly identified in Revelation as precursors to the second coming of Jesus would occur "within forty years or so of 1948."[2] Obviously Lindsey was wrong, just as wrong as the widely publicized and much lampooned claim by Harold Camping for the end on May 21, 2011, which was then pushed forward to October 21, 2011 and then abandoned entirely. In fact, there is a long history of such failed predictions, stretching far back into medieval history. The failure rate is 100 percent.

Such efforts at predicting the future from Revelation fail because it is not a book of predictions. An unarticulated but nonetheless real assumption of the predictive approach is that the symbols in Revelation refer to things in the present context of the modern reader — the late twentieth and early twenty-first century for the Left Behind series and Harold Camping, the 1960s and 1970s for Hal Lindsey, and earlier times for previ-

---

produced a particularly violent account, many writers on Revelation assume that Revelation pictures a God of violent judgment and Jesus who returns wielding a violent sword. An example is Jack Nelson-Pallmeyer. He argues that the nonviolence of Jesus reveals a nonviolent God, which means rejecting the violent images of God in the Bible. In his view Revelation presents such a violent image: "The New Testament ends with Christ terminating history as an apocalyptic judge in the book of Revelation." Jack Nelson-Pallmeyer, *Jesus against Christianity: Reclaiming the Missing Jesus* (Harrisburg: Trinity, 2001), 143. The chapter in hand counters all such assumptions concerning the book of Revelation.

2. Hal Lindsey, *The Late Great Planet Earth* (Grand Rapids: Zondervan, 1970), 43.

ous predictors. But this predictive approach ignores a simple premise. If Revelation was to be understood by its first readers, the seven churches in Asia Minor addressed in chs. 2 and 3, then the symbols must refer to things within the time frame and fields of experience of those first readers. If Revelation refers to, that is, predicts, items in our present time — modern technology including electricity and computers, the international banking and credit card system, recent political alliances in Europe, the United Nations with headquarters on a continent unknown in the first century, and much more — then Revelation was completely inaccessible and meaningless to the first readers, for whom these modern developments were entirely outside their frame of reference. Thus the following develops the message of Revelation based on the assumption that its meaning for modern readers is derived from a message that the first-century readers could understand.

The Message of Revelation

The first clue, a very strong clue, to the content of Revelation occurs in the first two verses of the first chapter: "The revelation of Jesus Christ, which God gave him to show his servants what must soon take place; he made it known by sending his angel to his servant John, who testified to the word of God and to the testimony of Jesus Christ, even to all that he saw." The content of Revelation is Jesus Christ — of him, from him, about him.

These first two verses are the real title to the book and unfold with circular logic, beginning and ending with Jesus Christ. In between, this revelation is said to come from God, be given to Jesus, made known by sending an angel to John, who then testified to the word of God — another reference to Jesus Christ — and to the testimony of Jesus Christ, with which the sentence began. This circular sentence contains several ambiguities. "Revelation of Jesus Christ" could be either a message given by Jesus or a message about Jesus. That ambiguity need not be resolved in order to follow the logic of the sentence — in either meaning the revelation of Jesus is from God. Further, the antecedent of "he" in the second phrase is unclear. While the "he" could refer to either Jesus Christ or God as the one who made the revelation known by sending an angel, the most likely antecedent is God — but again in either case, the content of the revelation is Jesus Christ. The import of this title sentence, including its ambiguous references, is to establish quite unambiguously that the book is about Jesus

Christ, who is the author, the messenger, and the content of God's revelation. So the rest of the book consists of theology about Jesus.

This observation about the Jesus-focused or christocentric orientation of Revelation is a component of the argument that the symbols of Revelation be located in the historical context of first-century readers. Obviously, Jesus was known to the readers of this book written at the end of the first Christian century. Further, it serves to show that the book deals with the meaning of Jesus rather than predictions about the distant future.

At first glance, the phrase "what must soon take place" might appear to establish Revelation as a book of predictions and thus to pose a challenge to a contemporary historical, nonpredictive interpretation. But that challenge is easily answered. If the author John was writing what he thought were predictions soon to happen, he was obviously wrong — and Revelation as a predictive book is already discredited. More properly, "soon" locates events in finite human history in contrast to God's time, which is infinite. As will become clear, Revelation concerns the ultimate and cosmic significance of Jesus, and, regardless of how long human history endures before its culmination in Christ, that length of human history is "soon" when compared with the never ending expanse of God's time.

But, most significantly, establishing that Revelation focuses on the meaning of Jesus establishes the perspective from which to discuss whether the book espouses violence or nonviolence. By virtually all accounts, Jesus rejected the sword, he taught that one should not retaliate against evil or violence with more evil or violence, and he both taught and illustrated strategies of nonviolence resistance. If then Revelation is truly about Jesus Christ, one should anticipate that the book reflects a perspective of Christian nonviolence. And since Jesus Christ is said to be the content of God's revelation, if in fact Jesus truly is of God, then the nonviolence of Jesus comes from God and reflects the character of God.

These observations mean then that one need read no further than the first two verses of Revelation to encounter an expectation that the book reflects and espouses a nonviolent, Christian worldview. If one truly looks to Revelation as a book about Jesus Christ, the surprising thing ought to be that one would find Jesus exercising the sword or that God would act violently or countenance violence. And the awareness that Jesus, whose life and teaching exhibit the rejection of violence, is the subject of Revelation provides an interpretative key for reading the symbols in the book. The following discussion applies that interpretive key to major passages of Revelation that are important for understanding its nonviolent image or that appear in discussions about the supposed violence of the images of Revelation.

The Seven Seals

The well-known image of the seven seals in Revelation 6 is an important text both to observe a christocentric hermeneutic and to illustrate the importance of finding the antecedents of symbols in the experience of first-century readers. I analyze the meaning of the seals in the context of the textual unit 4:1–8:1. Of particular import will be the interpretation of the symbols of astronomical breakdown and earthly chaos and destruction in the sixth seal, which are frequently taken as a picture of the end of the world.

Ch. 4 contains a vision of the heavenly throne room. There is God, the "one seated on the throne," surrounded by four "living creatures" as an honor guard with eyes in every direction, and twenty-four elders with gold crowns and white robes. The four living creatures and the twenty-four elders engage in perpetual worship, the creatures singing "holy, holy, holy, the Lord God the Almighty, who was and is and is to come," which envisions God over all of time, while the elders proclaim "glory and honor and power" to the God who created and is the source of all things.

With "the one seated on the throne" encompassing all time and all things, the element of curiosity appears in 5:1, when the reader encounters the right hand of God holding the scroll sealed with seven seals. A sealed message means a secret message. That secret immediately piques the curiosity of the reader via the narrator John, who weeps loudly and shamelessly at the fact that no one "in heaven or on earth or under the earth" — a three-layered reality depicting the entire cosmology of the time — is worthy to open the scroll. The narrator's distress draws a response from an elder, who tells him not to worry, that the conquering "Lion of the tribe of Judah" (v. 5) has won the right to open the scroll.

But it is not a conquering lion that opens the scroll. The lion turns out to be the Lamb "standing as if it had been slaughtered" (v. 6), who proceeds to open the seals of the scroll. Since it is a living Lamb with marks of slaughter, it is evident that the Lamb symbolizes the resurrected Jesus. If any doubt exists about the symbolic character of this image, one should note that this living, resurrected Lamb resembles no real, biological animal since it has "seven horns and seven eyes" (v. 6). Having the slain and resurrected Lamb open the seals — the secret message of God — presents Jesus as the key to God. If one wants to know the message of God, one must look at Jesus. This message appears in the obvious symbol of having the Lamb open the scroll, but it appears in more subtle ways as well. After it was said that "no one" in the known universe could open the scroll, the Lamb appeared as one who can open the scroll. That capability points to the uniqueness of Jesus, who is unlike every other being in the universe and is the associate of God and the source through which one learns God's message.

The uniqueness of Jesus in his association with "the one seated on the throne" also appears in the worship music of the twenty-four elders. After proclaiming that it was his death which earned him the right to open the seals of the scroll, they lead a choir of tens of thousands of angels in proclaiming the Lamb worthy "to receive power and wealth and wisdom and might and honor and glory and blessing" (v. 12), and then repeat that refrain for the one seated on the throne and the Lamb together. The one seated on the throne and the Lamb — God and resurrected Jesus — appear as equals, with Jesus as the means of God's revelation. And what establishes Jesus as the equal is his death and resurrection: the living Lamb with marks of slaughter — the resurrected Jesus — receives the heavenly praise that also comes to God. Death and resurrection have earned the scarred but living Lamb the right to open the scroll. And from the side of God, the death and resurrection of Jesus constitute the ultimate display of God's power and authority in the cosmos. The most authoritative divine event is not future: it has already happened in the death and resurrection of Jesus. Astute readers will anticipate finding this authority and the character of this victory of God in the message of the seven seals in Revelation 6 and 7.

Following the principle of discovering the antecedents of Revelation's symbols in the context of the first century, I align the seven seals with the seven imperial regimes between the crucifixion of Jesus under Emperor Tiberius (14-37 CE) and the reign of Domitian (81-96), during whose rule the book likely was written.[3] Each seal contains a symbolic reference to an event that occurred during the reign of the corresponding emperor. Understanding the response to these events will make quite clear the nonviolent orientation of the book of Revelation.

---

3. For a detailed discussion of the seals and references to the first-century events symbolized, see J. Denny Weaver, *The Nonviolent Atonement* (2d ed.; Grand Rapids: Wm. B. Eerdmans, 2011), 20-28.

Seal one says that a rider came out "conquering and to conquer." This phrase is a subtle reference, I suggest, to the crucifixion and resurrection of Jesus. From Rome's perspective, removing Jesus from the scene would seem to be a victory, but the resurrection overcame that momentary triumph by the forces of evil. Thus the rider's attempt to conquer does not succeed, and the language of v. 2 expresses an unactualized intent to conquer. In the following seals the connection of the symbol to a corresponding emperor becomes increasingly distinct.

In seal two, the red — for blood — horse, the threat to take peace from the earth, and the great sword represent a military threat to Jerusalem during the reign of Emperor Caligula (37-41 CE). Caligula commissioned a statue of himself in the form of Zeus and ordered an army commanded by Petronius to occupy Jerusalem and to install the statue on the high altar of the temple. As the army marched through northern Palestine, in response to appeals from the Jewish population Petronius halted the advance of the army and sent a messenger to ask permission to cancel the mission. Caligula commanded the messenger to return and kill Petronius and keep the army marching. However, Caligula died before that order was carried out, and the army was halted and Jerusalem spared.

Seal three has symbols of famine, which was widespread under emperor Claudius (41-54 CE). Acts 11:28-29 describes this famine and the collection by disciples in Antioch for relief of the believers in Judea.

The symbols of seal four point to multiple means of misery. The ugly double riders and the spreading of death and destruction by sword, famine, disease, and wild beasts in the arena certainly reflect Emperor Nero (54-68 CE), whose cruelty remains legendary.[4]

The vision of the heavenly altar in seal five corresponds to a break in the succession of emperors. During an eighteen-month interval in 68-69 CE, three rivals — Galba, Otho, and Vitellius — claimed the imperial crown, but none of them survived long enough to consolidate power and rule as emperor.

That brings the reader to seal six, whose imagery of astronomical collapse and earthly chaos and devastation has been frequently interpreted as

---

4. Some years ago, a radio commercial that touted the long-lasting flavor of a brand of chewing gum played off the cruelty of Nero and the supposed burning of Rome that Nero blamed on Christians. The listener heard violin music, supposedly played by Nero, who was also chewing gum. A voiced announced that Rome was burning. When the violin music continued unabated, a voice said, "He's not talking while the flavor lasts," followed by another voice saying "All Rome could burn by then."

a description of the end of the world. It is not. This imagery depicts an actual, historical, mundane event, but one that seemed like the end of the world to those who experienced it. In 70 CE, in response to a zealot rebellion, an army commanded by Titus, son of the reigning Emperor Vespasian (69-79 CE), invaded Jerusalem and sacked the city. Virtually no stone remained unturned. Images of celestial chaos — the sun going black, the moon becoming like blood, stars falling, the sky rolling up — accompanied by earthquakes and terrestrial pandemonium as the wealthy and powerful along with the poor and enslaved flee and hide together, symbolize the breakdown of order and the feelings of total loss and utter devastation when the army of the occupiers utterly destroyed Jerusalem and its sacred temple. In terms of the sequence of bad things happening during the reigns of Roman emperors, the imagery of the sixth seal makes clear that destruction of Jerusalem was by far the worst.

The seventh seal is not opened until chapter eight. When it is, there is "silence in heaven for about half an hour." Here ends the sequence of emperors. Following Vespasian, his son Titus (79-81 CE) had a short reign as emperor. Domitian followed, ruling from 81 to 96 CE. Since the sequence of emperors ends here, it indicates that Revelation was most likely written during the reign of Domitian, with little of note occurring during the rule of Titus.

For interpreting the symbolism of the seals, the significant observation is that the worst of all human, mundane events in the first century — namely the sack of Jerusalem in 70 CE — is not the end of the story. The entirety of ch. 7 also belongs to the sixth seal, and it is here that one most clearly perceives the nonviolent orientation of the textual unit from 4:1 to 8:1. The first paragraph of ch. 7 portrays four angels holding back the winds so that nothing is damaged and the angel with the seal of God staying the hands of the other four angels until all the servants of God are marked on their foreheads. Here is the beginning of a statement that regardless of what has happened in the earthly realm, such as the dastardly deeds of emperors chronicled in ch. 6, ultimately God is in control, and the fate of the people of God resides with God.

Then follows the renowned image of the 144,000, constituted of 12,000 from each of the twelve tribes of Israel. The first point is to recognize that 144,000 is a symbolic number, not intended to be taken as enumerating a precise number one greater than 143,999. Twelves resound here. Since twelve is the number of tribes of Israel, twelve signifies God's people Israel. One thousand is also a symbolic number, used in the Bible to designate a very large number. One thousand would have seemed much larger to a first-century reader than to us in the twenty-first-century computer age, where we routinely encounter extremely large numbers. One thousand is no more a number of mathematical precision than is the statement of a busy person who proclaims that she has "a million things to do today." The number 144,000 is constituted from 12 × 12 × 1000. By squaring 12, which symbolizes Israel, and then multiplying by the large number of 1000, the author has provided a symbolic way to display two characteristics of God's people: they are in continuity with Israel and their number is excessively large.[5]

The vignette of the exceedingly large number of God's people descended from Israel is followed immediately by another "great multitude that no one could count" (v. 9). People that make up this multitude come from every conceivable nation and tribe and language of the earth. When one understands the symbolic nature of the 144,000, it becomes apparent that the two multitudes are comparable in size — each one depicting the people of God as a huge throng, with one image emphasizing continuity with Israel and the other stressing that no ethnic or national group is excluded from the people of God. The second group is clothed in white and stands before the throne of God and the Lamb. They proclaim that "salvation belongs to our God who is seated on the throne, and to the Lamb" (v. 10). In v. 14 the reader learns that this white-robed throng has "come out of the great ordeal" — that is, they are martyrs for God, whose robes have been washed "white in the blood of the Lamb" (v. 14). The reference may be to martyrdom generally. A likely understanding, however, indicated by the foregoing analysis, is that "the great ordeal" refers to the destruction of Jerusalem and perhaps also to all the ongoing damage done to the people by Rome. This multitude, which can also include the 144,000, is pictured as worshiping God "day and night" as he shelters them, while "the Lamb at the center of the throne" guides them "to springs of the water of life," and God wipes away their tears (vv. 15-17). Because the seventh seal is not opened until 8:1, the vignette of the worshiping throngs belongs to the sixth seal and stands juxtaposed with the devastation displayed in the first scene of seal six. What does such positioning mean?

That chapter 7 is four times longer than the scene of devastation indicates relative importance. Even more significantly, the juxtaposition of the

5. M. Eugene Boring, *Revelation* (Interpretation: A Bible Commentary for Teaching and Preaching; Louisville: John Knox, 1989), 129-30.

scenes of devastation and celebration portrays the rule of God, which is revealed triumphant in the death and resurrection of Jesus, as overcoming and overwhelming the worst imaginable devastation meted out by the forces of evil in the world. With eyes on the resurrected Jesus as the living and embodied representative of God, those who have come through the ordeal of Rome, including the human mayhem and material destruction of Jerusalem, can celebrate life in the reign of God, in which salvation is found.

This text makes a profound statement about God — God has triumphed over the forces of evil. In fact, that ultimate triumph has already occurred in the death and resurrection of Jesus. And it is precisely at the point of seeing the means through which the reign of God has triumphed that one sees the intrinsically nonviolent character of God as revealed in this textual unit. The nonviolence of God and the intrinsically nonviolent character of the reign of God are not stated explicitly. However, the development of thought of the unit from 4:1 through 8:1 pictures the triumph of God over the forces of evil through the death and resurrection of Jesus. The several presentations of the living Lamb and God as equals on the throne make abundantly clear that Jesus' triumph is the victory of the reign of God and that Jesus' method of triumph is God's method. God is in the event of Jesus. Thus 4:1–8:1 pictures the reign of God, made visible in Jesus, as having an intrinsically nonviolent character.

Locating antecedents in the time of the first-century readers makes a significant contribution to the conclusion that 4:1–8:1 poses a nonviolent image of God. Identifying the historical antecedents underscores that the violence and destruction pictured in the seals, and in particular seal six, originate with humans on earth and are in no way an act of violent judgment by God at the end of earthly time. And to readers, whether in the first or the twenty-first century, this is a message of salvation. Salvation is at hand through identification with the living, resurrected Jesus, in whom God is present.

Beautiful Woman versus Dragon

Interpretation of a second vignette arrives at a similar set of conclusions. The symbolic confrontations in Revelation 12 of a beautiful, pregnant woman and an ugly dragon, and then between the forces of archangel Michael and of the dragon, also portray the intrinsic nonviolence observed in the image of the seven seals. The pregnant woman in labor stands on the sun, clothed with the moon and wearing a crown of twelve stars. A dragon with seven heads, ten horns, and seven crowns waits to grab the baby as the woman delivers it. But when the baby boy is born, he is snatched up to the throne of God while the woman flees into the wilderness. In heaven war breaks out between Michael and his angels and the dragon and his angels. The dragon, now called "the Devil and Satan," is defeated and thrown down to earth along with his angels.

This confrontation of Michael and the dragon is called "war," and Michael and his angels "fought" and the dragon and his angels "fought back." But it is not really a "war." This is an intrinsically nonviolent image of the triumph of the reign of God through the death and resurrection of Jesus. A key word in making this point is the "Now" that begins the announcement from the heavenly voice. As the defeated dragon is thrown down to earth, the voice from heaven proclaims:

> *Now* have come the salvation and the power
>   and the kingdom of our God
>   and the authority of his Messiah,
> for the accuser of our comrades has been thrown down,
>   who accuses them day and night before our God.
>
> (12:10, emphasis added)

This speech makes clear that the decisive event, the defeat of the dragon, has already occurred — thus the term "now." The ultimate defeat of the dragon is a past rather than a future event.

The next verse explains the means by which the reign of God triumphed.

> But they have conquered him by the blood of the Lamb
>   and by the word of their testimony,
> for they did not cling to life even in the face of death. (v. 11)

The defeat of the dragon has two components, and those whom the dragon accused share in the victory. One component is "the blood of the Lamb," an obvious reference to Jesus' death. The other component of the victory is the testimony of martyrs, whose deaths testify that the reign of God has higher authority than anything that the dragon could demand and ultimately conquers any damage that the dragon metes out. It seems quite clear that the "war" that defeated the dragon was really the death and resurrection of Jesus, the snatching up of the baby to heaven. The reign of God triumphs through death and resurrection, not through superior violence and military might.

The nonviolent character of the dragon's defeat comes into even sharper focus when the woman and the dragon are identified more precisely. The seven-headed dragon seems a rather transparent reference to imperial Rome, which according to legend was built on seven hills. Scanning the list of emperors given above from the time of the death of Jesus to the date of Revelation's composition reveals seven names — Tiberius, Caligula, Claudius, Nero, Vespasian, Titus, and Domitian — which correspond to the seven crowns. Then to that seven add the names of the three claimants during the interregnum — Galba, Otho, and Vitellius — to get ten, the number of horns on the dragon. The crown of twelve stars identifies the woman with Israel, which produced the Messiah, Jesus Christ, and, after the resurrection, the church as well. Identifying these antecedents of the symbols brings the confrontation down from the cosmos and locates it on earth, in history. The confrontation of woman and dragon becomes the confrontation in first-century human history between Jesus with his church and the Roman Empire. And from the side of the church, that struggle is nonviolent. As the church's "weapons" in the "war," Revelation 12:11 identifies two: the death and resurrection of Jesus and the testimony of martyrs.

Like the images of heavenly throne room and opening of the seven seals, the vignette of woman, dragon, and celestial combat portrays the victory of the reign of God over the forces of evil through the death and resurrection of Jesus. The image is of a God who conquers without resorting to the violence employed by the opponents of the reign of God. The two sections of the book present different versions of the confrontation, but in both the victory comes through resurrection — the overcoming of violence by restoring life — rather than through greater violence by God to eliminate the world's violence.

In each case, the church appears as the earthly manifestation of the reign of God that confronts the Roman Empire, which is pictured as the earthly manifestation of the reign of Satan. In Revelation 7, in the face of the evil meted out by the empire, the church celebrates the victory of the living Lamb, who is pictured as the equal of God. Ch. 12 makes it clear that the church participates in the victory. The dragon, a symbol of Roman Empire, is defeated by "the blood of the Lamb" and by the "testimony" of those the dragon accuses. Reminiscent of Paul's "I, . . . though it was not I, but the grace of God that is with me" (1 Cor. 15:10), the victory is both by God in Christ and by the witness of the martyrs. Here is a message of salvation through identification with the victorious Christ. Salvation is extended to the still living church in 12:13-17, as the earth opens its mouth to consume the water that the dragon poured out against the woman, a figure of the church. In the face of potential hostility from the world, ultimate salvation is found with Christ, whom God has raised from the dead.

The vignettes in Revelation use apocalyptic language to portray the saving message that was observed in the Gospels. God is in the story of Jesus. God's saving act is the resurrection of Jesus. The apocalyptic imagery of Revelation invites readers to share in the victory of the resurrection. Believers experience the saving work of Jesus Christ through identification with Jesus, which puts them in fellowship with the God of Jesus Christ. Believers will one day experience resurrection, as Paul asserted in 1 Corinthians 15. God's saving action, the resurrection of Jesus, portends the resurrection of all people in Jesus Christ.

Preliminary Conclusion

As a message of salvation, a statement about the work of Christ, these vignettes in Revelation lend themselves to the development of the narrative Christus Victor atonement image, described in the previous chapter on the basis of the narrative of Jesus from the Gospels. Since Revelation uses apocalyptic language to restate the same message as the Gospels, discovering narrative Christus Victor in Revelation ought not surprise.

In Revelation 12 the war of Satan and his angels against Michael and his angels is the specific image of cosmic Christus Victor, with the forces of the rule of God victorious in the resurrection of Jesus. At the same time, identifying the dragon with the Roman Empire, the woman with Israel and the church, and the baby with Jesus brings the confrontation down to earth. With the antecedents of the symbols in view, it is clear that the "war" is not an event in the cosmos. Rather the symbols picture the cosmic significance of a very earthly event — the death and resurrection of Jesus.

Another picture of this confrontation between forces of God and forces of evil appears in the symbols of imperial evil depicted in seals one through six juxtaposed with the celebrating throngs in the second scene of seal six. Again the reader finds an image of victory over evil in the earthly, historical realm through God's resurrection of Jesus.

It bears repeating that the image of God in these vignettes of narrative Christus Victor is that observed in the version from the Gospels: a God who triumphs not by destroying evil and violence with greater violence but by restoring life. And with the worshiping throngs in Revelation, the resurrection invites believers to join in worship of the God who raised Jesus and in worship of Jesus the Lord, whom God raised. Again we see a theology for living.

Other texts in Revelation complement these conclusions.

Wrath, Judgment, and Divine Violence

I have argued that the narrative of Jesus from the Gospels and the two vignettes in Revelation displays a God whose nonviolence is visible in the resurrection of Jesus, God's ultimate saving act. It is in the resurrection that believers share in the work of Christ and are reconciled to God. However, on first reading, other texts and images in Revelation seem to contradict the idea of an intrinsically nonviolent message and nonviolent God. These texts appear to describe a God who expresses wrath and who judges and eliminates evil violently. The argument about the intrinsically nonviolent character of God necessitates dealing with such texts.

Examples of violent language abound. For example, in the song of the seventh trumpet the twenty-four elders sing to God:

> The nations raged,
>> but your wrath has come,
>> and the time for judging the dead,
> for rewarding your servants, the prophets
>> and saints and all who fear your name,
>> both small and great,
> and for destroying those who destroy the earth. (11:18)

Farther along, the angel declares that those who worship the beast "will also drink the wine of God's wrath, poured unmixed into the cup of his anger, and they will be tormented with fire and sulfur in the presence of the holy angels and in the presence of the Lamb" (14:10). The focus in the sequence of pouring out of the contents of the seven bowls concerns the wrath of God (15:7; 16:1-21). And then there are the rider on the white horse in ch. 19 and the supposed battle of Armageddon in 19:17-21. These texts all seem, at first glance, to portray the capacity of an angry God to use violence, a quite different image than the God who triumphs without violence through the death and resurrection of Jesus in the images of the seven seals and the woman and the dragon. How does one reconcile these statements of wrath and violence with the nonviolence of God in Christ observed thus far?

First of all, note that the wrath and violence of God pose a problem only if one accepts the profession that God is fully revealed in Jesus, that what is revealed in Jesus is the very character of God. To anticipate a discussion in Chapter 6, note that John Howard Yoder argued that positing a violent characteristic of God that is not visible in Jesus is counter to the standard understanding of the Trinity.[6] According to this view, each person of the Trinity is fully God, so that nothing can reside in God that is not present in each person of the Trinity, and no person of the Trinity can have an essential divine characteristic that is not part of Godself.[7] Following this expectation, if Jesus is nonviolent one ought not seek to discover or to justify violence as a characteristic of God. The hermeneutical question becomes one of addressing the texts in Revelation that seem to posit divine violence when other imagery of God as well as the narrative of Jesus reveal that God's response to violence is not greater violence but the death and resurrection of Jesus.

In his discussion of atonement imagery, Raymund Schwager suggests a helpful argument that lends itself to addressing the seeming violent images and language of Revelation. Schwager discussed the supposed violence of God in texts of Paul that speak of Christ's death as a condemnation of sin, in which case those who acted to kill Jesus and thus punish sin

---

6. John Howard Yoder, "How H. Richard Niebuhr Reasoned: A Critique of *Christ and Culture*," in *Authentic Transformation: A New Vision of Christ and Culture*, by Glen H. Stassen, D. M. Yeager, and John Howard Yoder (Nashville: Abingdon, 1996), 61-65. See also Yoder's *The Politics of Jesus: Vicit Agnus Noster* (2d ed.; Grand Rapids: William B. Eerdmans, 1994), 17-18, and *For the Nations: Essays Public and Evangelical* (Grand Rapids: William B. Eerdmans, 1997), 242.

7. This point is already implied in the Nicene Creed's statement that Jesus is *homoousios* or "one substance with the Father" and is underscored in the so-called Athanasian Creed of the fifth or sixth century, which proclaims "Such as the Father is, such is the Son, such also the Holy Spirit," and then lists the characteristics of "increate," "infinite," "eternal," "almighty," "God," and "Lord." "And in this Trinity there is nothing before or after, nothing greater or less, but all three persons are coeternal with each other and coequal." "The Athanasian Creed: Quicunque vult, 5th-6th c," in *Creeds and Confessions of Faith in the Christian Tradition* 1, ed. Jaroslav Pelikan and Valerie Hotchkiss (New Haven: Yale University Press, 2003), 676-77.

would be following at least indirectly the will of God. But as Schwager said, "since the message and surrender of Jesus (nonviolence, love of enemies, holding back from finally judging anyone) and the actions of his enemies stood in contradictory opposition, both cannot point to God under the same aspect, for in that way a contradictory opposition would arise in the idea of God, which would cancel itself."[8] That is, when applied to atonement doctrine, it is a self-contradiction to have Jesus doing the will of God and those who kill Jesus to punish sin also doing the will of God.

Schwager's solution involves a different understanding of how God's wrath or anger is expressed and made known. Sin originates with humankind, not with God, but the omnipotence of God "necessarily included the idea of allowing sin." Thus Schwager argues that comments by Paul about divine wrath or divine punishment of sin are really statements about handing sinners over to the consequences of their own sin and violence. "Sinners are now entirely handed over to and victims both of the passions which have thus arisen and of the overpowering pictures of a thought process which has lost all foundation. Their life with God, their dealings with their fellow humans, and the way they relate to themselves and to the good things of this world are ruined: for this they punish themselves (mutually)."[9] In other words, statements of sin and declarations of divine violence are recognition of a cycle of violence that engulfs its participants. Violence begets more violence. Proclamations of judgment on that sin, including divine judgment, are statements that allow and thus condemn sinners to remain in the cycle to reap its rewards.

A similar argument appears in popular form throughout Rob Bell's book *Love Wins*. His argument that God is loving is essentially a parallel to the argument that God should be understood in nonviolent images. Bell argues that it is an unhealthy image of God if a loving God offers an open invitation to sinners throughout an individual's life, but at the instant of death becomes a vindictive God who condemns the sinner to unending torturous punishment. Bell argues that God does not change character or conduct at the instant of an individual's death. Rather, as Schwager has argued, Bell says that statements of divine wrath and punishment that appear throughout the Bible are actually statements of God turning evildoers over to the consequences of their own choices to do evil. In effect, those

8. Raymund Schwager, *Jesus in the Drama of Salvation* (New York: Crossroad, 1999), 163.

9. Schwager, *Jesus in the Drama of Salvation*, 165.

who choose to continue in the path of evil create their own "hell." God's character does not change. God is always loving but respects the choice of evildoers to continue in their evil ways, thus condemning themselves to a "hell" of their own making.[10]

N. T. Wright offers a parallel argument that sin produces its own reward of self-judgment. People become what they worship, whether God or an idol such as money, sex, power, or other forms of idolatry. After death, those who have chosen to worship what is not God "become at last, by their own effective choice, *beings that once were human but now are not,* creatures that have ceased to bear the divine image at all." For these beings there is no "concentration camp in the beautiful countryside, no torture chamber in the palace of delight," which God has in store for them. Wright acknowledges that we know exceedingly little about life after resurrection, but suggests that these "creatures [will] still exist in an ex-human state, no longer reflecting their making in any meaningful sense."[11]

The arguments of Schwager, Bell, and Wright are applicable to Revelation. Understanding that statements of divine wrath and judgment involve turning human sin over to reap its own rewards provides a solution to the seeming contradiction in Revelation, where the God revealed in Jesus conquers through death and resurrection but also appears to conquer and judge with power and violence. The cosmic imagery of the seven bowls, for example, displays the ultimate consequences of sinful humans who continually choose to reside outside the reign of God. This answer maintains the intrinsic nonviolence of God's reign, the integrity of the text of Revelation, and the idea of a final judgment. I return to the theme of divine violence and judgment in Chapter 5.

The Rider on the White Horse and Armageddon

Given the frequent appeals to the image of the rider on the white horse and the supposed battle of Armageddon in Revelation 19:11-21 as evidence for violent divine vengeance and a conquering Jesus who in the end finally defeats evil with the sword, the nonviolent character of these images needs

---

10. Aspects of this argument appear throughout Rob Bell, *Love Wins: A Book about Heaven, Hell, and the Fate of Every Person Who Ever Lived* (New York: HarperOne, 2011).

11. N. T. Wright, *Surprised by Hope: Rethinking Heaven, the Resurrection, and the Mission of the Church* (New York: HarperCollins, 2008), 182, 183.

specific treatment. First, recall that the supposed "war" in heaven in ch. 12 was not a war — it was imagery to depict the cosmic significance of the resurrection of Jesus for events on earth in human history. That interpretation should prepare a reader to look for the nonviolent character of the supposed battle in ch. 19.

Here a rider on a white horse defeats the kings of the earth and their armies.[12] They are "killed by the sword of the rider on the horse, the sword that came from his mouth" (19:21). It is apparent, however, that no actual battle takes place. The rider is called "Faithful and True" (v. 11) and "The Word of God" (v. 13) and is clothed with a robe dipped in blood *before* the supposed battle (v. 13). The rider is obviously a resurrected, victorious Christ. His weapon is a sword that extends from his mouth, which makes it the word of God. Ephesians 6:17 and Hebrews 4:12 also use a two-edged sword as an image of the Word of God. And note that the text does not even have a battle image. It says that armies of the beast and the kings of the earth "gathered to make war against the rider on the horse and against his army," but no battle occurs. No battle is described nor imaged. The text passes directly to its conclusion — "the beast was captured" (Rev. 19:20).

In the segment of 19:11-21, the beast and the kings and their armies are defeated not by violence and military might. They are undone — defeated — by the Word of God. This passage is another symbolic representation of the victory of the reign of God over the forces of evil that has already occurred with the death and resurrection of Jesus. It is by proclamation of the Word, not by armies and military might, that God's judgment occurs.[13]

Millennium and Great White Throne

In an interpretation that will surprise some readers, a vignette of the victory of the reign of God through resurrection also occurs in Revelation 20. Here one encounters the renowned millennium or "thousand years" for which the "Devil and Satan" are "bound."[14] This set of images, I propose,

12. An earlier version of this discussion of the rider and Armageddon appeared in Weaver, *Nonviolent Atonement, 34.*

13. On 19:11-21 see Richard B. Hays, *The Moral Vision of the New Testament: Community, Cross, New Creation: A Contemporary Introduction to New Testament Ethics* (New York: HarperCollins, 1996), 175; Boring, *Revelation,* 195-200.

14. An earlier version of this discussion of the millennium appeared in Weaver, *Nonviolent Atonement,* 29-31.

uses symbols of time to picture human and divine perspectives on earth's history and to contrast the reign of God and the rule of evil. Recall that *thousand* is a symbolic figure that primarily means an exceedingly large number. This expanse of years contrasts sharply with the forty-two months or 1260 days that the woman (the church) spends in the wilderness under God's protection (12:6), that the nations will trample over the holy city and the court outside the temple (11:2-3), and that the first beast is allowed to exercise authority (13:5).

Forty-two months is three and one-half years, half of a seven-year period. In Revelation the number seven frequently has divine connotations. The book is addressed to seven churches. Seven lamp stands surround the figure of the resurrected Jesus, who holds seven stars in his hand (1:12, 16). In 3:1, Christ as messenger has "the seven spirits of God and the seven stars." In the subsequent vision of heavenly worship, in front of the divine throne burn "seven flaming torches, which are the seven spirits of God" (4:5). The Lamb standing by the throne who has the marks of slaughter and opens the seals on the scroll has "seven horns and seven eyes, which are the seven spirits of God sent into all the earth" (5:6). Half of the divine seven is a "broken seven,"[15] the number used to identify the time of those who oppose the reign of God and the living Lamb. A thousand years and three-and-a-half years are symbolic figures of time that contrast the finite length of earth's human history to the infinite length of God's time.

The binding of Satan is not a new event, encountered only here for the first time in Revelation. What "binds" Satan is the resurrection of Jesus, which is the triumph of the reign of God over the evil perpetrated by the Roman Empire. Binding Satan for "one thousand years" symbolically portrays the victorious rule of God for the unlimited expanse of God's time in contrast to the limited time — the broken seven of Rome's time in human history or "a little while" in the language of 20:3. The binding of Satan refers to the same phenomenon as the defeat of the dragon in 12:9-10 and the victory of God and the Lamb in 7:10-12, namely, the resurrection of Jesus.

The "millennium" of Revelation 20, which occupies only a small space in the book and appears nowhere else in the Bible, does not refer to a spe-

---

15. The term "broken seven" is from Vernard Eller, *The Most Revealing Book in the Bible: Making Sense of Revelation* (Grand Rapids: William B. Eerdmans, 1974), 117. Mitchell G. Reddish suggests that the three and a half years is taken from the "time, two times, and half a time" of Dan. 7:25 and 12:7, but also suggests that it represents half of the perfect number seven. Mitchell G. Reddish, *Revelation* (Smyth and Helwys Bible Commentary; Macon: Smyth and Helwys, 2001), 209.

cific, future period of history yet to be inaugurated. It affirms symbolically that regardless of the apparent power of evil abroad in the world in the first century as well as today, those who live in the resurrection of Jesus know that evil has been ultimately overcome and that its power is already limited. When one considers the power of Satan from the perspective of the reign of God, Satan's power is indeed limited — "a little while," three and a half years — within the vast scope — a "thousand years" — of God's time.

The contrast in times — one vastly expansive, the other quite limited — emphasizes the limited and defeated power of the earthly representatives of Satan when seen in light of the resurrection of Jesus. During the symbolic three-and-a-half years, God limits Satan's power by preparing a place in the wilderness where the woman can be nourished and protected (12:14-17), or limits the time in which the holy city will be trampled (11:2-3), or limits the time of the first beast (13:5). Since the dragon represents Rome, the "millennium" text of ch. 20 proclaims yet another version of the message of the conquering Lamb and of the ultimate limitation on the power of evil from the seven seals motif in chs. 5–7 and the woman and dragon of ch. 12. It is a message of encouragement to Christians who confront the power of the Roman Empire or are tempted to forget that a seemingly benevolent empire really is the "beast." Revelation displays transcendent reality as actual reality, which differs from the perceived reality of human history in earthly perspective. Christians therefore need not ultimately fear the suffering and destruction meted out by Rome, the earthly manifestation of Satan.

The supposed battle that follows the supposed release of Satan after the millennium (20:8-9) then constitutes yet one more image of the ultimate defeat of evil. The "battle" was already won in the resurrection of Jesus, and the enemies of the rule of God are defeated by the Word of God. The following text of judgment at the "great white throne" (vv. 11-15) shows that the choice between living in the reign of God and under the rule of evil has consequences. It is a choice of one's ultimate destiny. Surely after seeing the many images through Revelation of the victory of the reign of God in the resurrection of Jesus, any aware reader of Revelation will choose the side of the reign of God.[16]

16. The image of Jesus as a nonviolent victor through the Word of God poses a sharp contrast to the explicit dependence on violence in the common dispensational premillennial reading of Revelation. See n. 1 above. Since the dispensational scheme requires an actual bat-

Narrative Christus Victor: Round Two

The book of Revelation uses apocalyptic language in contrast to the narrative form of the Gospels. Nonetheless, when the reader discovers the antecedents of Revelation's symbols in Jesus' death and resurrection and in the earthly powers that opposed the church, it becomes apparent that these symbols convey a message similar to that of the Gospels. In either case, one reads that in the life of Jesus the reign of God confronted the rule of evil in the world. Jesus was killed in that struggle, but God raised him from the dead.

Like the Gospels, Revelation's imagery of the victory of the reign of God reveals a nonviolent God, who conquers evil and violence via resurrection — the restoration of life — in contrast to the death-dealing forces of evil symbolized by the dragon as empire. This restoration of life in the face of violence constitutes the ultimate victory of the reign of God over the forces of evil. The resurrection is thus an invitation to all people to identify with Jesus and to share in the victory of the resurrection.

This complex of images from Revelation constitutes another version of narrative Christus Victor, which appears in multiple forms. As an invitation to experience God's saving grace through identification with the story of Jesus, this is theology for living.

Gregory Boyd sketches an approach to a Christus Victor image of atonement that has many similarities with the image of narrative Christus Victor, beginning with his assertion that a Christus Victor model of atonement is the "unifying framework" that best brings together multiple dimensions of the saving work of Christ and deals with the entire scope of biblical material.[17] Boyd's version of Christus Victor, interpreted as "spiritual warfare," emphasizes Christ's cosmic victory over Satan and the powers of evil. He supports that emphasis with references from the Gospels and throughout the New Testament. Boyd then incorporates the life of Jesus in this confrontation of the powers. His approach is an attractive up-

---

tle at Armageddon with earthly armies wielding nuclear weapons before Satan is finally defeated, in dispensationalism the resurrection of Jesus cannot be the ultimately decisive event depicted in Revelation as well as throughout the writings of Paul. Further, the dispensationalist scheme presumes the image of a violent and vengeful god that is entirely different from the God revealed in the narrative of Jesus Christ. Thus dispensationalism's view of God runs afoul of the traditional trinitarian doctrine, as described above and in Chapter 6.

17. Gregory A. Boyd, "Christus Victor View," in *The Nature of the Atonement: Four Views*, ed. James Beilby and Paul R. Eddy (Downers Grove: InterVarsity, 2006), 24.

dating of the ancient theories of the early church fathers. In contrast to this updating, the development of narrative Christus Victor from the narrative of Jesus provides novelty in the approach of the volume in hand. Beginning with this narrative locates the confrontation of evil fully within the historical world. The cosmic dimension is then added by way of analysis of the book of Revelation, although the antecedents of Revelation's symbols are also located in the world of history.

The variations between the approaches of Boyd and the view in this book consist of differing but compatible and complementary emphases. I agree with Boyd that "every aspect of Jesus' life" was an act of "warfare" against the powers of evil "for every aspect of his life reflects Calvary-like love." These acts of "warfare" against evil include "exposing the systemic evil that fuels religious legalism and oppression," crossing "racial lines, fellowshipping and speaking highly of Samaritans and Gentiles," treating women with "dignity and respect" in a patriarchal culture, and extending mercy to people who deserved judgment. In short, the Christus Victor model of atonement "sees every aspect of Christ's life — from his incarnation to his resurrection — as being most fundamentally *about one thing:* victoriously manifesting the loving kingdom of God over and against the destructive, oppressive kingdom of Satan." Boyd is certainly correct that "the central call of every disciple is to imitate *this* life, manifest *this* kingdom, and thereby engage in *this* warfare." In accord with the approach of this book, in the imitation of Jesus' life Boyd specifically includes "expressing Calvary-like love *to our worst enemies*" and the active but nonviolent resistance of Matthew 5:39, in which Jesus forbids responding to violence with more violence.[18]

The description in Chapters 1 and 2 of the victory of the reign of God and the sketch of an atonement motif are constructed with biblical materials from each end of the New Testament. The motif depends on a narrative whose culmination is the resurrection of Jesus, which is the ultimate saving act of God. The motif makes use of the specific narrative of Jesus as the basis for the life the Christian lives in response to the invitation of the resurrection to live as a disciple of Jesus.

There remains one other important complex of New Testament material to consider in the discussion of atonement, namely the writings of the Apostle Paul. The following section will compare narrative Christus Victor with the traditional and prevailing atonement images. As will become

18. Boyd, "Christus Victor," 39-41, emphasis original.

clear from that comparison, narrative Christus Victor differs in significant ways from the traditional images, and in particular from the various forms of satisfaction atonement. Where the satisfaction images identify the death of Jesus as the salvific element of atonement, narrative Christus Victor focuses on the resurrection as the salvific moment with attention to the entire life, teachings, death, and resurrection of Jesus. Since it has been long assumed that Paul supports the traditional atonement motif, it is important to consider the writings of Paul and the extent to which they support narrative Christus Victor.

Narrative Christus Victor: Round Three

The Writings of Paul

No doubt exists that the writings of Paul have been appealed to in support of the received and prevalent satisfaction and substitutionary atonement motifs. And of course, if one accepts these images of satisfaction atonement as unquestioned givens, one can find texts from Paul which can be interpreted as compatible with the satisfaction or substitutionary motifs. However, the question to consider is whether such interpretations are the only or the necessary interpretation of Paul's writings. Several modern scholars now believe that Paul does not support satisfaction atonement or the idea that Jesus' death in some way impacted God or was necessary to God or satisfied a divine penalty. Literature on Paul is voluminous. For the discussion here, I illustrate this literature by means of a brief summary of material from David Brondos's book *Paul on the Cross*.[19] Brondos presents a comprehensive analysis of Paul that dovetails with the discussion in hand of the narrative of Jesus, and that fits Paul easily into narrative Christus Victor.

It is Brondos's thesis that Paul's understanding of the role of Christ's death is fundamentally different from that which has been attributed to him in any of the standard theories of atonement. The death of Jesus has no salvific impact in and of itself, and as an isolated entity it has no "effect" on God or on sinful humans. Rather the death of Jesus "is salvific and redemptive only in that it forms part of a story." Different from that which appears in the standard atonement theories, Jesus' death was not salvific

19. David A. Brondos, *Paul on the Cross: Reconstructing the Apostle's Story of Redemption* (Minneapolis: Fortress, 2006).

because it met a divine need or mechanically filled a slot in a divine equation. Rather "Paul understood Jesus' death primarily as the consequence of his dedication and faithfulness to his mission of serving as God's instrument to bring about the awaited redemption of Israel, which would also include Gentiles throughout the world. . . . [Jesus' death] is salvific because God responded to Jesus' faithfulness unto death in seeking the redemption of others by raising him so that all the divine promises of salvation might now be fulfilled through him."[20]

As depicted by Brondos, the story of redemption known to Paul is the story contained in the Synoptic Gospels and Acts, which is a continuation of the story of Israel in the Old Testament. Brondos's recitation of the story resembles that of narrative Christus Victor, but with some differing emphases. Brondos interprets Paul as though Paul is expanding on this narrative. Quite specifically, in 1 Corinthians 15:3-7 Paul repeats the outline of the story found in Acts. And Paul's mission to bring the gospel to the Gentiles was a part of the divine plan from the beginning.[21] When Jesus is "delivered up," that does not mean that Jesus' death satisfied a need in a cosmic equation but that God did not intervene in Jesus' death and allowed Jesus to die in fulfillment of his mission to bring redemption to all people.[22] When Paul says that Jesus gave himself up for others, this means that Jesus was willing to give his life for the cause of his mission; it is not a reference to death as an isolated entity that impacted God.[23] For Paul, the ultimate purpose for which Jesus gave up his life in obedience to God was the redemption of God's people, of whom both Jews and Gentiles were a part. But this was the goal, not only of Jesus' death, but also of his coming and his ministry before his death and of his resurrection after his death.[24] Because he has been raised from the dead, Jesus can return someday to make the promised redemption a reality.[25] "This means

20. Brondos, *Paul on the Cross*, xi. Among other treatments that dispute or reject an Anselmian or satisfaction reading of Paul, see J. Christiaan Beker's argument for an eschatological orientation in Paul in which resurrection is both victory over evil and death in the old order and the beginning of the transformation of fallen creation in the new order (J. Christiaan Beker, *Paul the Apostle: The Triumph of God in Life and Thought* [Philadelphia: Fortress, 1980], chapter 8), and the Girardian-influenced interpretation of Raymund Schwager, who rejects any idea of God punishing sin in Jesus or of God as the agent of Jesus' death (Schwager, *Jesus in the Drama of Salvation*, 162-69).

21. Brondos, *Paul on the Cross*, 70.

22. Brondos, *Paul on the Cross*, 71.

23. Brondos, *Paul on the Cross*, 72.

24. Brondos, *Paul on the Cross*, 74.

25. Brondos, *Paul on the Cross*, 75.

that for Paul, Jesus' coming, ministry, death, and resurrection are a unified whole and had a single objective: the redemption of God's people."[26]

Since in Brondos's analysis Paul knew and built on the story from the Synoptics and Acts, it does not surprise that his version of Paul's story of redemption differs from the standard theories of atonement. The standard atonement theories focus on the death of Jesus, whereas for Paul it is not Jesus' death but the whole event of Jesus that saves, or the whole event of Jesus' ministry, death, and resurrection through which God saves. In and of itself, Jesus' death does not effect anything or produce any kind of change in the situation of believers or humanity as a whole.[27] "What Jesus died for is the same thing that he lived for." When Paul refers repeatedly to the cross, that is not a statement that the cross itself is salvific, but rather a statement that the cross represents everything that Jesus lived and died for, the ultimate expression of the grace and love of God manifested in all that God has done and continues to do through Jesus. "Jesus willingly endured suffering so that the promises made by God to his people might come to pass through him, as they now certainly will."[28]

Brondos argues that when Paul said that Jesus died "for us," or "for our sins," these phrases should not be understood in terms of penal substitution. The phrase more accurately means "on our behalf" or "for our sake." Brondos summarizes how Jesus' death is then understood "for us": "he dedicated his life to the kingdom of God and to laying the foundation for a new covenant to come about, and he refused to put an end to that activity when threatened with death, thus suffering the consequences of his activity for others and by giving up his life in faithfulness to that mission, he obtained what he had sought for others when God raised him from the dead."[29] Stated briefly, Jesus died carrying out his mission "for us."

Jesus' Death as a Sacrifice

In some versions of traditional satisfaction atonement, Jesus' death is called a sacrifice offered to God to absolve sinners of their sins. This use of sacrifice is based in part on a false understanding of sacrifices in the Old

---

26. Brondos, *Paul on the Cross*, 76.
27. Brondos, *Paul on the Cross*, 76.
28. Brondos, *Paul on the Cross*, 77.
29. Brondos, *Paul on the Cross*, 110.

Testament. It is possible to retain the idea of Jesus' death as a "sacrifice" in narrative Christus Victor, but sacrifice of a different kind.

The first eight chapters of Leviticus outline procedures for a number of ritual sacrifices — burnt offerings, offerings of well-being, cereal offerings, sin offerings, guilt offerings. These ritual sacrifices are performed in times of celebration and thanksgiving (such as the peace offering, Lev. 7:12, 15) and in times of unwitting sin, both when restitution is impossible and when restoration can be made (as in sin and guilt offerings, Lev. 4:1–6:7). In these varying circumstances, the ritual sacrifice is virtually the same. The worshiper — the individual making the sacrifice — brings a perfect and healthy animal to the priest from the herd or flock, a bull, goat, sheep, turtle doves or pigeons, or even grain for those with the fewest resources. The worshiper places his or her hands on the head of the animal. It is then killed by the priest, who scatters the animal's blood on and around the altar. Portions of the animal are then burned on the alter, with the smoke and odor rising from the fire, going "up" where God is. For the cereal offering, oil and frankincense are poured on the flour and it is burned, "a pleasing odor to the Lord." These sacrifices make "atonement" for the worshiper (Lev. 1:4; 4:20, 26, 31, 35; 5:6, 10, 13, 16, 18; 6:7; 7:7).

An initial point concerns the circumstances in which the ritual sacrifice occurred. Since the ritual was performed in times of rejoicing and thanksgiving as well as in times of sin, it cannot be a simple matter of a ritualized blood payment as satisfaction of a legal debt owed to the law.

Further, in the understanding of these Hebrews, the life of an animal was in its blood (Lev. 17:11; Gen. 9:4: Deut. 12:23). Since an animal that lost its blood would die, from within their understanding of biology it was natural to conclude that the life of any creature was in its blood. Through the laying on of hands the worshiper became symbolically identified with the animal. When the priest then placed the blood — the life — of the animal on the horns of the altar where God was said to reside, it was a ritual self-dedication and self-giving of the worshiper to God. This ritual was not a killing of an animal in place of killing the person as the deserved punishment for sin. Rather, in presenting the blood on the altar before God, the worshiper was enacting a ritual of giving himself or herself to God. The animal's blood goes to God, "representing the life of the person who will henceforth live for God."[30] Brondos called these sacrifices "acts of prayer,"

---

30. John Howard Yoder, *Preface to Theology: Christology and Theological Method* (Grand Rapids: Brazos, 2002), 300.

which makes the temple the "house of prayer."[31] This ritual rededication or prayer of the worshiper to God was appropriately practiced at any juncture of life, whether joyous or sorrowful. As a rededication, however, it should not be appropriated as an image of satisfaction atonement in which the blood or death is thought to satisfy a legal penalty imposed as the price of sin.[32] It is rather a blood ritual of self-dedication to God.

Still further, note that the sins dealt with in this ritual rededication are primarily sins committed inadvertently and unintentionally (Lev. 4:2, 13, 22, 27; 5:2, 14, 17; exceptions to the inadvertent sins are noted in 5:1 and 6:2-4). For the most serious and comprehensive sins, blood is not even involved. Leviticus 16 describes the ritual whereby the scapegoat bearing "all the iniquities of the people of Israel, and all their transgressions, all their sins," is driven away into the wilderness, "bear[ing] on itself all their iniquities to a barren region" (16:20-22). It is of note that the scapegoat is not killed; rather it bears the sins away into the wilderness.

The motif of sacrifice can of course be appropriated as an image for the death of Jesus. However, these observations concerning the practice of sacrifice make clear that the element of satisfying a legal penalty was not a dimension of the Hebrew ritual sacrifice. Thus the appearance or use of sacrificial terminology or imagery in and of itself should not be construed as evidence for satisfaction atonement.

In Brondos's depiction of Jesus' death as a sacrifice, he emphasizes Jesus' voluntary submission to death on the cross. Jesus chose not to defend himself and voluntarily surrendered to death. However, this surrender to death is not a death wish, nor is it a death directed toward a need in the divine economy as in satisfaction atonement theories. Rather, Jesus' voluntary surrender to death on the cross must be seen in the context of his intent to carry out his God-given mission. His death was the result of fulfilling his God-given mission. For a mundane analogy, we can say that a parent who turns down opportunities to work overtime on weekends has voluntarily sacrificed extra income in order to spend time with his or her family. This is a sacrifice on behalf of a higher goal. As Brondos says, "What was sacrificial about Jesus' death was not just his willingness to *die*

---

31. Brondos, *Paul on the Cross,* 24.

32. In addition to the reference to John Howard Yoder in n. 30 above, see Donald Joseph Selby and James King West, *Introduction to the Bible* (New York: Macmillan, 1971), 153-55; Timothy Gorringe, *God's Just Vengeance: Crime, Violence and the Rhetoric of Salvation* (Cambridge Studies in Ideology and Religion 9; Cambridge: Cambridge University Press, 1996), 34-57; Schwager, *Jesus in the Drama of Salvation,* 177-82; Brondos, *Paul on the Cross,* 170-71.

for others but his unbending commitment to *live* for others, doing his Father's will in seeking to bring God's blessing into the lives of others and save them from their sins through his teaching and healing activity."[33]

Language from the Last Supper of "body given for you" should be understood in this context. Death is the result of Jesus' mission to make present the reign of God. Since his life was lived for others — to bring the redemption and salvation of the reign of God to them — his death as a sacrifice is a continuation of that ministry. In the image of prayer mentioned above, his sacrificial death is a prayer offered to God that what he had lived for might become a reality through his death. "In effect, by raising and exalting him, God had accepted Jesus' sacrifice, responding favorably to Jesus' petition on behalf of others by granting him the power and authority to bring about what he had sought someday in the future."[34]

In Brondos's analysis, the death and resurrection of Jesus established a new way of relating to God. Previously God was present for healing and redemption in the temple in Jerusalem, but "God would now make himself present through the risen Jesus and the community around him." In contrast to the blood sacrifices in the temple, "in this new covenant the sacrifice would be that of Jesus himself." Sins would "now be cleansed by Jesus' own blood." And in light of his allusion to his body in the accounts of the Lord's Supper, it appears that in offering himself up, "Jesus was constituting himself or his body as the new temple for others."[35]

The material from Paul as outlined by Brondos aligns Paul with the motif I have called narrative Christus Victor. More importantly, it preserves the image of the God who is revealed in the life of Jesus, which is a God who does not sanction or require violence to accomplish salvation. It is the God who offers salvation through resurrection, through giving life, and through restoration of life.

These points all differ from the view of atonement that has dominated Western theology for something like eight hundred years. One facet of the development of a new theological paradigm is to provide some analysis of the received paradigm in order to indicate why I advocate a new theological direction. Since the discussion of the narrative of Jesus as a story of salvation is most importantly a statement about our understanding of God, the discussion of standard atonement images will highlight their image of God.

---

33. Brondos, *Paul on the Cross*, 42, emphasis original.
34. Brondos, *Paul on the Cross*, 42.
35. Brondos, *Paul on the Cross*, 42.

3 Engaging the Atonement Tradition

Following the development of narrative Christus Victor, this chapter sketches the history of the unfolding of atonement doctrines and suggests what the changes through this history can tell us about appropriate atonement images for Christians in the twenty-first century.

Traditional Atonement Images

For some eight hundred years, one version or another of satisfaction atonement has been the dominant motif in the western theological tradition. But satisfaction is not the oldest motif.

In the history of doctrine, the earliest atonement motif was Christus Victor. The previous chapter has already pointed out one important difference between the classic version and narrative Christus Victor. Narrative Christus Victor situates the confrontation of the reign of God with the powers of evil on earth in the person of Jesus rather than in a cosmic battle. An additional important difference concerns the role of God. In the ransom version of the classic version of Christus Victor, God either makes a deal with Satan to pay Jesus as a ransom in exchange for release of the souls of humankind, or tricks the devil — hiding Jesus' deity under his humanity — so that the devil is "caught" when he kills Jesus. In either case, God appears as the Father who sacrifices one of God's children for the sake of the remainder of God's children. It is the image of a God who sanctions violence to accomplish a divine goal. *Narrative Christus Victor*, in contrast, which lays responsibility for the death of Jesus on the Romans and other human beings, involves nothing about the death as a ransom or as a ploy by God to benefit sinners.

Classic Christus Victor visualized sinful human beings captured by and responsible to the devil, through either inadvertent or willful acts. That picture changed entirely with Anselm of Canterbury's *Cur Deus Homo,* published in 1098.[1] Anselm (c. 1033-1109) specifically rejected the ideas that Satan held the souls of humankind captive and that Jesus' death was a ransom paid to free them. Anselm argued that Satan has no rights over sinful human beings and that God would not stoop to making any kind of bargain with Satan. He simply removed Satan from the salvific equation and made sinners responsible directly to God. That is, in Anselm's view humans sinned against God, which offended the honor of God and thus disturbed order in the universe. Human salvation then depended on some act from the side of humanity to placate God. On behalf of humankind, the death of Jesus as a human being was then necessary to satisfy God's honor and restore order in the universe.

In a recent book, *Christ and Empire,* Joerg Rieger shows that Anselm's original depiction of satisfaction can be understood only in terms of the organization of the Norman feudal empire, which was a given for Anselm. Anselm saw society as a hierarchy and a pyramid with pope and emperor at the top, followed by king and archbishop, each a "coruler" with God of the "Christian realm." Vassals swore allegiance to their lords, who in turn swore allegiance to the king. While those below the lord had varying kinds of status in the hierarchy (knights, laborers, monks), the emphasis always fell on their submission to the will of the lord higher up in the hierarchy.[2]

"Peace, justice, and the unity of the empire rest on the maintaining of this order." A violation of honor offended not merely the personal honor of the lord, but threatened his authority and thus the relationship of ruler to ruled on which the system depended. An offense to honor required either punishment by the lord or an act of satisfaction to the lord in order to preserve the system. Forgiveness of an offense without either punishment or satisfaction would undermine the authority of the ruler and thus undermine the order of society and open the door to disorder.[3]

---

1. Anselm of Canterbury, "Why God Became Man," in *The Major Works,* ed. Brian Davies and G. R. Evans (Oxford: Oxford University Press, 1998), 260-356.

2. Joerg Rieger, *Christ and Empire: From Paul to Postcolonial Times* (Minneapolis: Fortress, 2007), 123, 127, 138; R. W. Southern, *Saint Anselm: A Portrait in a Landscape* (Cambridge: Cambridge University Press, 1990), 221-27.

3. Rieger, *Christ and Empire,* 136.

Anselm pictured the relationship of God to humanity in terms of this feudal hierarchy. He did not portray God as a private "person" — the impassability of God meant that God's personal honor could not be taken away. Human sin was not primarily about an insult to God personally, "but about the destruction of order in the world." Restoration of the created order required satisfaction of God's honor. For God to forgive without either satisfaction or punishment would allow disorder to continue in the cosmos.[4] Anselm claimed to be arguing for the necessity of the incarnation on the basis of "reason alone." Actually he was arguing on the basis of what made sense according to the assumptions of a feudal hierarchy, with the image of a feudal lord projected onto God in the divine realm. We no longer have that feudal empire, but an atonement image founded on and based in the retribution assumed by feudalism is still the dominant motif. This atonement motif that emphasizes retribution, namely satisfaction atonement, is echoed in the criminal justice systems of many nations.

With the devil removed from the equation, God remains the sole agent with power. Most certainly, sinful human beings cannot save themselves and cannot with their own power or authority arrange to satisfy the offended honor of God. God is the only actor with agency, who can effect the salvation of sinners. As such, God arranges for Jesus to die to satisfy the debt. It appears that God has Jesus killed — that God arranges for the death of Jesus — in order to pay the debt to God's honor. Sinful human beings cannot save themselves by repaying God on their own. Thus it is merely an extension of the interior logic of Anselm's own move that leads to the conclusion that God is responsible for Jesus' death. With Satan taken out of the picture, God is the only one left to orchestrate the death of Jesus in order to pay the debt owed to God's honor.

In the motif of penal substitution, the evolution of the satisfaction model that emerged with the Protestant Reformation, the image shifts slightly. For penal substitution, the image is that of God punishing Jesus in place of punishing us — sinners — with death. In this motif, it is God's law rather than God's honor that receives the necessary death that is demanded for justice. Since sinners could not pay their own debt, God is the one who arranged to provide Jesus' death as the means to satisfy the penalty required by the divine law. In a sarcastic rendition of this view, Brian McLaren has Jesus addressing sinners, "If you want to be

4. Rieger, *Christ and Empire*, 136-37.

among those specifically qualified to escape being forever punished for your sins in hell, you must repent of your individual sins and believe that my Father punished me on the cross so that he won't have to punish you in hell."[5]

One might ask, Weren't the devil or the mob or the Romans responsible for killing Jesus? Of course they were. But answering "yes" to that question within the framework of satisfaction atonement points to a strange juxtaposition. Jesus, who is innocent and does the will of God, becomes sin, subject to punishment. And the evil powers — however understood — who oppose the reign of God by killing Jesus are actually assisting the will of God by killing Jesus to provide the debt payment that God's honor or God's law demands. The strange implication is that both Jesus and those who kill Jesus would be carrying out or working with the will of God. Asserting both claims results in nonsense. Avoiding the implications of such mutually contradictory claims by cloaking them in a category such as mystery, or by claiming that the acts of God are too big for our categories to contain, renders meaningless any attempt to use theology to express or clarify understandings of God in Christian faith.

Focusing on the violence of retribution in satisfaction atonement, that is, the need to balance sin on one side with an act done to sinners on the other, along with the responsibility of God in the death of Jesus, brings to the fore the issue of the *image of God*. The logic of satisfaction atonement leads to a violent image of God. God emerges as the chief avenger or the chief punisher. God is in charge of retribution. This vengeful image of God led Peter Abelard (1089-1142) to reject the idea that Jesus' death was a payment to God's honor and to suggest that God giving up Jesus to death was an act through which God showed love for sinners. This image has been called the moral influence theory of atonement. But even though the image changes, the moral influence theory still pictures a God who sanctions violence. God is the Father who offers the Son's death as an example of the Father's love for the rest of God's children. Classic Christus Victor also has a violent image of God, the Father who hands over the Son to Satan as a ransom payment for the rest of God's children.

In the worst case scenario, these images of the God from the classic satisfaction, moral influence, and Christus Victor atonement motifs por-

---

5. Brian D. McLaren, *Everything Must Change: Jesus, Global Crises, and a Revolution of Hope* (Nashville: Nelson, 2007), 79.

tray God as a divine child abuser. As feminist and womanist theologians have pointed out, these are all images of a Father who abuses one child for the benefit of other children. Among these, the satisfaction images are judged the most offensive.

Along with the violent image of God in the classic atonement images, consider the model of Jesus in these images. In satisfaction atonement, Jesus is a model of voluntary submission to innocent suffering. The Father needs the death of Jesus to satisfy divine honor; as innocent victim Jesus voluntarily agrees to submit to that death needed by the honor of God. Or as innocent victim Jesus voluntarily agrees to undergo the punishment deserved by sinful humankind in order to meet the demand of divine justice. Because Jesus' death is needed in these motifs, Jesus models being a voluntary, passive, and innocent victim, who suffers for the good of another. A similar critique applies to the moral theory and classic Christus Victor.

It is important to underscore that these images can foster injustice. For people who live in some kind of unjust status quo, the idea of "being like Jesus" as modeled by satisfaction atonement means to submit passively and to endure that injustice. There are many examples. Feminists and womanists have said that God the Father in atonement theology projects an image of divine child abuse. This image, along with the image of Jesus as innocent and passive victim, is an unhealthy model for a woman abused by her husband or a child violated by her father. They constitute double jeopardy when attached to hierarchical theology that asserts male headship.[6] A model of passive, innocent suffering poses an obstacle for people who encounter conditions of systemic injustice or an unjust status quo produced by the power structure. Examples might be the legally segregated American South prior to the civil rights movement; global marketization that favors big business and disadvantages peasant farmers;[7]

---

6. Joanne Carlson Brown and Rebecca Parker, "For God So Loved the World?" in *Christianity, Patriarchy and Abuse: A Feminist Critique*, ed. Joanne Carlson Brown and Carole R. Bohn (New York: Pilgrim, 1989), 1-30; Julie M. Hopkins, *Towards a Feminist Christology: Jesus of Nazareth, European Women, and the Christological Crisis* (Grand Rapids: William B. Eerdmans, 1995), 50-52; Rita Nakashima Brock, *Journeys by Heart: A Christology of Erotic Power* (New York: Crossroad, 1988), 55-57; Carter Heyward, *Saving Jesus from Those Who Are Right: Rethinking What It Means to Be Christian* (Minneapolis: Fortress, 1999), 151; Delores S. Williams, *Sisters in the Wilderness: The Challenge of Womanist God-Talk* (Maryknoll: Orbis, 1993), 161-67.

7. James M. Harder, "The Violence of Global Marketization," in *Teaching Peace: Nonvi-*

and military-backed occupation, under which land is confiscated and indigenous residents crowded into enclosed territories, called "reservations" in North America and "bantustans" in South Africa and "autonomous areas" in Palestine. James Cone linked substitutionary atonement specifically to defenses of slavery and colonial oppression.[8] After depicting numerous ways in which black women were forced into a variety of surrogacy roles for white men and women and black men, womanist Delores Williams says that to accept satisfaction or substitutionary atonement and its image of Jesus — the "ultimate surrogate figure" — is to validate all the unjust surrogacy to which black women have been and still are submitted.[9]

The satisfaction motif countenances violence in another area of social practice as well, in the criminal justice system. The various versions of satisfaction atonement function with the assumption that doing justice or righting wrongs depends on retribution or payback or satisfaction of a divine requirement. Sin creates imbalance or debt. "Pain" against God, understood as sin, must be balanced by "pain" done to humans, called punishment. Resolving that imbalance or debt requires satisfaction, which is provided by Jesus' death. That is, Jesus steps in to endure the punishment, that is the retribution against human sin, in the place of humans.

In the human realm the criminal justice system of many countries — and certainly in the United States where we live — assumes that justice depends on retribution or payback. This payback is punishment, satisfying a legal requirement. To do justice means to enact retribution — balancing pain caused by an offender with equivalent pain — that is, punishment as payback — enacted on the offender. The theory is that pain balances pain. The scales of justice are balanced when the pain experienced by the victim is equal to pain administered to the offender.

Stanley Grenz does not deal with the problem of violence in atonement imagery. Nonetheless, his description of the correlation of the penal atonement image with the philosophy of criminal justice supports this analysis. He writes that with "the demise of the feudal system and the rise of nations, the law of the state replaced the honor of the ruler as the foun-

---

olence and the Liberal Arts, ed. J. Denny Weaver and Gerald Biesecker-Mast (Lanham: Rowman & Littlefield, 2003), 179-93.

8. James H. Cone, *God of the Oppressed* (rev. ed.; Maryknoll: Orbis, 1997), 211-12.

9. Williams, *Sisters in the Wilderness,* 60-83, 161-67, 178-99.

dation for social order. In response, theologians came to view sin as the transgression of the codified law of civil government and to understand government as the upholder and the avenger of the civil law."[10]

This philosophy of criminal justice and the several versions of satisfaction atonement all make the same assumption, namely that doing justice means to balance the pain experienced by the victim with pain or violence or punishment exacted on the offender or his substitute. Offenders in the criminal justice system experience punishment. Sinners avoid punishment under the atonement schemes, but the structure of the atonement motifs is nonetheless based on the assumption that satisfaction or punishment is necessary to balance the offense against God. God can forgive sinners without exacting a penalty or punishment on them because the penalty or payback required by God's justice was previously satisfied or paid back by the death of Jesus. In each case, whether it concerns the criminal justice system or any of the versions of satisfaction atonement, the underlying assumption is that the system depends on payback, as satisfaction, whose ultimate expression is violent death. The discussion of forgiveness in Chapter 8 below develops additional dimensions of satisfaction atonement imagery and the practice of criminal justice.

A replacement for these images of a God who models and sanctions violence, and for the model of Jesus that submits to unjust suffering for the good of another, comes from the atonement motif of narrative Christus Victor and the construction of a theology for living that grows out of the narrative of Jesus. Part II of this book displays that theology for living in an image of the church as the extension of Christ's presence in the world.

But first, if this nonviolent theology for living genuinely reflects the biblical story of Jesus, as I believe it does, where did it go? How did Christian faith evolve from an understanding that the resurrection constituted the saving act of God and a call to nonviolent discipleship to a view that focused on the death of Jesus accompanied by an image of a God who uses and who sanctions violence? The following describes two moves that contribute to those changes. One explains the demise of the biblical motif here called narrative Christus Victor. The second chronicles the development of the motif that took its place.

---

10. Stanley J. Grenz, *Theology for the Community of God* (Nashville: Broadman and Holman, 1994), 450.

From Narrative Christus Victor to Satisfaction Atonement[11]

The Demise of Narrative Christus Victor

The demise of narrative Christus Victor corresponds to the evolving status of Christianity within the Roman Empire. Over a period of several centuries, Christianity's social status evolved from a minority religion harassed and persecuted by the empire to the religion favored by emperors and then established as the imperial religion. As the structure making Christian faith visible, the church evolved from an institution that opposed or challenged the empire to a structure in which competing officials sought imperial support for their side in theological arguments. Stated most succinctly, over the course of several centuries the church passed from dissident minority to favored majority status.

As an atonement motif, narrative Christus Victor also poses an image of ecclesiology. The likely historical antecedents pointed out in Chapter 2 for the symbolism of Revelation locate this telling of the biblical narrative in history and show clearly that the narrative concerns the church of the first century. According to this biblical construction, the church was the earthly instrument that continued Jesus' mission of making visible the reign of God. Since the empire of the first century did not acknowledge the reign of God or confess Jesus as Messiah, it is hardly surprising that the church differed from the empire. One of the most easily perceived differences concerned the use of the sword. Whereas the empire had armies and emperors consolidated their authority with military power, in the teaching and example of Jesus and in the church depicted in Revelation there is a clear rejection of use of the sword.

It is the social relationship of early church to empire that corresponds to the image of narrative Christus Victor. Revelation clearly pictures the church standing over against the empire. In this confrontation, the reign of God triumphs through resurrection. The church participates in this victory through identification with the story of Jesus and by continuing to resist the allure of Rome even in the face of danger. As a motif derived from the narrative of Jesus and from Revelation, narrative Christus Victor makes sense of and depends on this social context.

---

11. This account of the demise of narrative Christus Victor and the rise of alternatives borrows in part from J. Denny Weaver, *The Nonviolent Atonement* (2d ed.; Grand Rapids: Wm. B. Eerdmans, 2011).

Beginning in mid-second century and continuing for several centuries thereafter, the church underwent a series of changes that had far-reaching consequences.[12] The evolutionary character of the changes does not belie

12. For the story of these changes and Emperor Constantine's role in them, see H. A. Drake, *Constantine and the Bishops: The Politics of Intolerance* (Baltimore: Johns Hopkins University Press, 2000); James Carroll, *Constantine's Sword: The Church and the Jews: A History* (New York: Houghton Mifflin, 2001). The following description of the theological significance of these changes is shaped by John Howard Yoder, "The Constantinian Sources of Western Social Ethics," in *The Priestly Kingdom: Social Ethics as Gospel* (Notre Dame: University of Notre Dame, 1984), 135-47; idem, "The Otherness of the Church," in *The Royal Priesthood: Essays Ecclesiological and Ecumenical* (Grand Rapids: Wm. B. Eerdmans, 1994), 53-64.

Recent scholarship, such as Drake, *Constantine*, has revised significantly the picture of Constantine and the era of what Yoder called the Constantinian shift. This changed historiography has led some to question the viability of Yoder's description of the theological import of the shift he used Constantine's name to symbolize. For example, see J. Alexander Sider, "Constantinianism before and after Nicea: Issues in Restitutionist Historiography," in *A Mind Patient and Untamed: Assessing John Howard Yoder's Contributions to Theology, Ethics, and Peacemaking*, ed. Ben C. Ollenburger and Gayle Gerber Koontz (Telford: Cascadia, 2004), 126-44.

Peter Leithart published a full-blown defense of Constantine and challenge to Yoder's historiography. Leithart's argument that no fundamental change occurred from Jesus to Constantine and after starts with the argument that neither Jesus nor the New Testament is clear on rejection of the sword. Thus he can depict Constantine's wars and cruelty without acknowledging a fundamental change in the attitude of the church toward use of the sword or its embrace of the social order. Peter J. Leithart, *Defending Constantine: The Twilight of an Empire and the Dawn of Christendom* (Downers Grove: InterVarsity, 2010). For detailed responses to Leithart's arguments, see John C. Nugent, "A Yoderian Rejoinder to Peter J. Leithart's *Defending Constantine*," and Alan Kreider, "'Converted' but Not Baptized: Peter Leithart's Constantine Project," *Mennonite Quarterly Review* 85 (2011): 551-73 and 575-617. These two items are part of a symposium on Leithart in *Mennonite Quarterly Review* 85.4 and will be published with other material in John D. Roth, ed., *Constantine Revisited* (Telford: Cascade, 2013). Further, the book in hand provides ample evidence to dispute and reject Leithart's contention that neither Jesus nor the New Testament has a convincing position on rejection of the sword.

In addition, it is my contention that the objections of Leithart and Sider to Yoder's use of history concern the details and the particulars of the shift while Yoder was concerned more with the significance of the contrast between the beginning and the end of the process, a contrast many historians recognize. A changing picture of the details of the shift does not undo Yoder's analysis of the theological significance of the shift. Lastly, Leithart contends that for Yoder's argument to be true, the New Testament church had to be fully unanimous on the sword and its rejection of empire. However, contrary to Leithart, Yoder's view of a shift does not depend on an absolute beginning point. The description of the shift concerns priorities, and the shift in priorities has been acknowledged by many scholars as the church

their significance. Because of Emperor Constantine's legalization of Christianity with the Edict of Milan (313 CE), his own adoption of Christianity, and his apparent favoring of Christianity in his policies, his name is often used to symbolize the new status of the church. However, Constantine did not so much cause as reflect and react to the direction in which the situation was evolving. The changes had begun before him and the new status was fully achieved only after him. A level of culmination was reached in 380 when Emperor Theodosius declared a particular formulation of Trinity doctrine to be "the official doctrine of the Roman Empire," and the following year decreed that the form of the Nicene Creed promulgated by the Council of Constantinople (381) was "the official religion" of the empire.[13]

The end result of these changes was that the church came to identify with the social order and to make use of and express itself through the institutions of the social order. Through its institutions, the empire became identified with the cause of Christianity, and the success (or failure) of the political structures became associated with the success (or failure) of Christianity. Rather than posing a contrast or a challenge to the social order, church officials could now appeal to imperial structures as allies, if the political authorities sided with the particular religious officials on the issue in question. And of course they opposed them when the political authorities disagreed with them. This linking of political and religious interests appears clearly when sections of the empire opposed each other for control. These confrontations reflected the assumption that there was one Christian faith to be established for the entire empire, even as there was vigorous debate about the identity of that faith.[14] Although church and government officials continued to engage in disputes, Christianity (or the church) was no longer a minority, oppressed structure. The fact that church and civil authorities also opposed each other sharply on occasion does not challenge the fact that all sides assumed that both civil authorities and churchly authorities had roles in ecclesiastical affairs; their disagreements concerned the manner of intervention and which of the competing

---

evolved from a position outside the social and political order to one that embraced the social and political order.

13. R. P. C. Hanson, *The Search for the Christian Doctrine of God: The Arian Controversy 318-381* (Edinburgh: T. & T. Clark, 1988), 804, 821.

14. For a description of these interlocking political and religious interests in the centuries after the council of Chalcedon, see Philip Jenkins, *Jesus Wars: How Four Patriarchs, Three Queens, and Two Emperors Decided What Christians Would Believe for the Next 1,500 Years* (New York: HarperOne, 2010).

authorities had power over the other rather than being an argument about the principle per se of civil intervention in church affairs, or of churchly officials appealing to civil authorities. With emperors and lesser political officials now taking sides in theological disputes and backing the decrees of church councils, the church saw itself as encompassing the social order as a whole. This fusion of church and social order is what has been called a "Christian society."

The exercise of the sword shows most clearly the change in the status of the church from contrast to accommodation of the social order. Whereas before, as was on display in Revelation, Christians did not wield the sword and pagans did, now Christians wielded the sword in the name of Christ. The claim was that "Christian" concerns required use of the sword in order to defend the society and the empire, which is now a defender of church and Christian faith. In a manner of speaking, *not* applying the teaching of Jesus became the "Christian" thing to do.

While one could indicate a number of other changes,[15] the important point for the present discussion concerns the change in the church's relationship to its surrounding society. The church's social status changed from a position outside of society to a position within society. It shifted from a stance of estrangement and confrontation to one of support for the social order and its governing structures.[16]

As the church ceased to confront empire, the historical antecedents of Revelation and connotations of Christus Victor imagery were lost or forgotten. However, the motif of Jesus' defeat of the devil survived until Anselm of Canterbury could refute it in *Cur Deus Homo*. Although not immediately accepted, versions of the satisfaction motif that Anselm put in place of Christus Victor eventually became the dominant atonement motif, with Peter Abelard's "moral influence" theory as the primary alternative. The traditional reasons given for the demise of Christus Victor are

---

15. See John Howard Yoder, "Constantinian Sources."

16. In the centuries following these changes, kingdoms and empires declined and others arose. A common theme in medieval church history is conflicts between civil authorities and church authorities for control in their territories. Each office, civil or ecclesiastical, claimed divine authorization to appoint or invest the other with the authority of its office. Which actually exercised more authority in these conflicts and the extent to which they submitted to each other varied from region to region and from one epoch to another. But common to all participants in these struggles was the assumption that church coincided with and encompassed civil society or the social order. The conflicts between civil and ecclesial authorities did not challenge that assumption.

several: objections to the idea that God would either recognize certain rights of the devil or stoop to overcoming the devil through trickery, objections to its dualistic worldview, the seeming lack of evidence of the victory of the reign of God in the historical realm in which we live, incompatibility of the imagery of cosmic battle with our modern worldview, and distaste for the battle imagery. None of those reasons is adequate.

With reference to atonement images, the important point is that narrative Christus Victor is an atonement motif that assumes — even depends on — an imagery of confrontation, a church that witnesses to the social order.[17] In fact, it does not make sense without it. At the level of cosmic imagery, the forces of God confront the forces of Satan. In its demythologized and historicized form, the confrontation occurs between the social structure created by Jesus and extended by his followers on the one hand, and the structures of the first-century social order and Roman Empire on the other. The real reason that narrative Christus Victor fell out of the theological matrix was, I believe, not so much its imagery of demons or objections to tricking the devil, but the church's loss of its sense of confrontation with the empire and the social order. One element of this shift from confrontation to accommodation was that the church lost track of the possible historical antecedents of the symbolism in the book of Revelation.[18] With the church no longer confronting the empire but accepting

17. Hans Boersma has written that this dependence on "a situation of confrontation between Church and state is simply not borne out by the facts." Hans Boersma, *Violence, Hospitality and the Cross: Reappropriating the Atonement Tradition* (Grand Rapids: Baker Academic, 2004), 158. Boersma's misunderstanding results from his failure to distinguish narrative Christus Victor from classic Christus Victor, which did lose touch with history.

18. In his discussion of the canonization of Revelation Eugene Boring notes varying attempts at interpretation that already in the second century did not tie it to first-century historical figures and events. M. Eugene Boring, *Revelation* (Interpretation: A Bible Commentary for Teaching and Preaching; Louisville: John Knox, 1989), 2-5. That the church lost track of such historical antecedents of Revelation by the third century ought not surprise. For a contemporary example, note the historical symbolism of Negro spirituals forgotten in a shorter period of time and recovered in James H. Cone, "Black Spirituals: A Theological Interpretation," *Theology Today* 29 (1972): 54-69; idem, *The Spirituals and the Blues: An Interpretation* (Maryknoll: Orbis, 1992). As an informal example, I can recount my own experience with students. To illustrate the use of symbols to depict historical figures, for a contemporary parallel to Revelation's four horsemen, I often described a number of figures on horseback — a headless rider, one with a large scar on a potbelly, one who falls off his horse, and one with a big grin wearing a Los Angeles Angels' baseball cap. My twenty-year-old students needed explanations before recognizing allusions to U.S. presidents Kennedy, Johnson, Nixon, and Carter.

the intervention of political authorities in churchly affairs and also looking to political authorities for support and protection, the actual historical, social situation of church-state cooperation and fusion of church and social order no longer matched the cosmic imagery of confrontation between church and social order. And when the cosmic imagery of Revelation no longer matched the historical context, it lost much of its meaning. And the meaning behind what I call an atonement motif that used such imagery could be refuted and abandoned.

This shift in the social context for atonement imagery took place gradually. It was not the case that the theologians of the time perceived immediately a new ecclesiology and then set out to develop a different theory of atonement to match it. Rather the change in ecclesiology happened gradually, in an evolutionary manner. The shift in atonement images also happened gradually. The idea that God defeated the devil through trickery was still prominent enough to be specifically refuted by Anselm in *Cur Deus Homo* in 1098 and continued, since Anselm's view was not immediately accepted.[19] But although the change was gradual, there did come a time when discussing atonement in terms that assumed confrontation between church and social order no longer made sense. Narrative Christus Victor disappeared from the picture when the church came to support the world's social order, to accept the intervention of political authorities in churchly affairs, and to look to political authorities for support and protection.

Resurrection to Death: The Emergence of Satisfaction

The theological developments that produced the replacement for the emphases of narrative Christus Victor culminated with Anselm of Canterbury's *Cur Deus Homo*. In this trajectory the emphasis shifted from Jesus' resurrection to his death. Research by Rita Nakashima Brock and Rebecca Ann Parker traces this evolution in iconography of Jesus. Images in the early centuries feature a resurrected Jesus, with the image of a dead Jesus appearing in Europe only after 960-70.[20] Brock notes that until the end of

19. Gustaf Aulén, *Christus Victor: A Historical Study of the Three Main Types of the Idea of Atonement* (New York: Macmillan, 1969), 38-39; J. N. D. Kelly, *Early Christian Doctrines* (rev. ed.; New York: Harper & Row, 1978), 375-89; Darby Kathleen Ray, *Deceiving the Devil: Atonement, Abuse, and Ransom* (Cleveland: Pilgrim, 1998), 123-25; Southern, *Saint Anselm,* 210-11.

20. Rita Nakashima Brock and Rebecca Ann Parker, *Saving Paradise: How Christianity*

the tenth century, a period she christened the Anastasic Era (from *anastasis* or resurrection), "incarnation, transfiguration, miracles, and resurrection of Jesus were the central focus of Christian faith and art." The predominant focus was "on Jesus' victory over death."[21]

Already with Jewish writers, affirming belief in the resurrection was an act of defiance — denying ultimate authority and power to imperial violence. Christians pictured the departed faithful "in a place of honor and protection, imaged variously as heaven, as celestial Jerusalem, or as a zone of earthly paradise inhabited by the righteous." By the third century, this haven where Satan could not enter "had become a place of beauty and peace," an "earthly paradise." From this realm, the departed saints comforted and protected the living, and the living felt the presence of the departed.[22] It was believed that the righteous dead lived in peace and harmony in this paradise until the distant future when God would transport them to the far-off heaven.

N. T. Wright offers a similar view. He pointed to the importance of resurrection in the early centuries. "The early Christian future hope centered firmly on resurrection." And Wright identified paradise as the intermediate state on earth described by Brock and Parker. When Jesus told the brigand crucified with him that he would join him in paradise that very day, paradise was not their ultimate destination. "Paradise is rather, the blissful garden where God's people rest prior to the resurrection." When Jesus mentioned the many dwelling places in his father's house, the term for dwelling place indicated a "temporary lodging." Similarly, Wright says, Paul was thinking of this place of bliss immediately after death when he wrote that "to depart and be with Christ . . . is far better" than continuing alive (Phil. 1:23).[23]

Within this picture, death was not to be feared. It was the transition into this paradise. Martyrs were not seen as victims, "but as people who manifested the power of God." Since they had already experienced para-

---

Traded Love of This World for Crucifixion and Empire (Boston: Beacon, 2008), ix, 223. Findings of this book are summarized in Rita Nakashima Brock, "The Cross of Resurrection and Communal Redemption," in *Cross Examinations: Readings on the Meaning of the Cross Today*, ed. Marit Trelstad (Minneapolis: Augsburg Fortress, 2006), 241-51. The summary in hand of Brock and Parker's findings is taken from my *The Nonviolent Atonement*, 109-14.

21. Brock, "The Cross," 242.

22. Brock and Parker, *Saving Paradise*, 58-59.

23. N. T. Wright, *Surprised by Hope: Rethinking Heaven, the Resurrection, and the Mission of the Church* (New York: HarperCollins, 2008), 40-51, quoting p. 41.

dise in their earthly lives, they knew that a martyr's death could not separate them from paradise. "In refusing to submit to unjust power, the martyr witnessed to the true power that generated paradise on earth."[24] The living experienced the earthly beginning of paradise in the church, whose "social practices and spiritual training" constituted "its most concrete, realized form."[25] The pathway to paradise and eternal life began with baptism. It "was the portal to paradise. Through this ritual, Christians gained entrance into the garden of God, which stood beyond the open doors of every church."[26] The Eucharist celebrated the risen Christ and "enacted the community's communion with the presence of the risen Christ and departed saints."[27] The practices of the Eucharist opened recipients to the beauty of "*this* world, unveiled as paradise," and they departed from the church sanctuary strengthened in their resistance to the violence and exploitation of the principalities and power of the world. "In this spirit, the early church avoided focusing on the Crucifixion, not only in its art, but also in its Eucharist."[28]

Both art and architecture expressed this paradise. In art depicting this earthly paradise, Jesus appeared frequently in the image of the Good Shepherd — a sharp and clear contrast to imperial authority. In lush pastoral scenes, sheep represent the apostles while deer and doves represent the risen dead. Other times "saints, martyrs, virgins, and the heavenly cities of Jerusalem and Bethlehem stood in paradisiacal landscapes."[29] Church architecture developed to depict a "three-tiered sacred cosmos" of the heavens, paradise, and earth. On the highest tier, the dome featured a starry sky or multi-colored clouds representing the heavens, with "the hand of God" emerging to "bless the world" while celestial beings hovered in the skies. On the second level, above eye-height to the worshipers, appeared images of paradise, the realm between heaven and earth. Here "the living Christ presided," with images of the living saints inhabiting the meadows of paradise with him, or visiting earth to bless the living. The lowest level was the floor of the church, where the faithful entered to worship, and "stood in God's garden on earth."[30]

24. Brock and Parker, *Saving Paradise*, 66.
25. Brock and Parker, *Saving Paradise*, 89.
26. Brock and Parker, *Saving Paradise*, 115.
27. Brock, "The Cross," 243.
28. Brock and Parker, *Saving Paradise*, 158.
29. Brock, "The Cross," 243. Also Brock and Parker, *Saving Paradise*, 87.
30. Brock and Parker, *Saving Paradise*, 86.

"The cross is a ubiquitous Anastasic symbol of resurrection," with Jesus absent from it until the fifth century. When he finally appears on it, he is depicted alive, in a position of prayer in paradise, and only on personal items. "None is a crucifix. Jesus on the cross is neither in agony nor dying." For the living, it was expected that they would display moral behavior which "demonstrated that baptism had reoriented Christians to ordinary life."[31]

Pictures of Jesus' crucifixion first appeared after Saxon Christians experienced severe violence at the hands of the Christian Carolingian Empire. The Saxons practiced a Christianity mixed with elements of pagan practice and had been the subject of missionary efforts to convert them to more correct belief and practice. One such effort was that of the English monk Boniface, who arrived in Saxony in 719 with a papal commission and whose efforts were enforced by the brutal work of Frankish king Charles Martel. Martel's grandson Charlemagne, crowned emperor by Pope Leo III on Christmas day of 800, amplified the terror tactics against the Saxons.

Charlemagne believed that religious conversion of the Saxons would make them submissive to the Carolingian Empire of the Franks, in which the sacred places of pagans were destroyed and after 797 refusing baptism carried the death penalty. Saxon resistance only provoked more brutality. For the Carolingians, the cross came to symbolize the power that protected them in battle and resistance from Saxons justified Carolingian violence. In other words, Charlemagne's preachers claimed that his assaults were justified as God's punishment for the pagan sinfulness of the Saxons. For the Saxons, the cross that was once a sign of life had become "a sign of terror." The first surviving crucifix, now residing in the cathedral of Cologne, is the Gero Cross. Produced about 960-70, it reflects the Saxon experience of suffering and violence — a dead Jesus in a form that expresses what they had experienced at the hands of the Carolingian Empire.[32]

The dispute concerning the Eucharist focuses the theological difference between Saxon and Carolingian Christianity. The Saxon Eucharist celebrated the risen Christ. Carolingian theologians saw the Christ celebrated in the Eucharist as "a pure victim, a holy victim, an unspotted victim." Where the Saxons had celebrated "the wondrous human body sanctified by Christ's incarnation," Carolingian worshipers faced a crucified Christ on the Eucharist table, who judged them according to their degree

---

31. Brock, "The Cross," 243-44.
32. Brock and Parker, *Saving Paradise*, 226-33, quoting p. 232.

of penance.[33] For the Carolingians, who forced their view of the Eucharist on the conquered Saxons, the crucified Christ justified violence against the Saxons since their sin had supposedly crucified Christ. But the Carolingians also faced judgment at the Eucharist table. Shedding of human blood was still sinful, and warriors faced continual guilt and need for penance.[34]

That shedding human blood was still considered sinful is quite visible in the limitations on warfare in the medieval era, described by John Howard Yoder. Fighting was limited to a small number of people. The prince was served by knights, who were relatively few in number, and by mercenaries, who were recruited when needed. In times of emergency, the prince could call a local militia for defense, but not on a large scale. The common people had no skills or weapons and were thus exempt from regular military obligations. Besides, these people were needed in the fields or in their trades, from which tax money could be raised for war. Other categories of people were forbidden from fighting. These included pilgrims, penitents, and both religious and secular clergy. "Thus the people allowed to fight in a just war were a small minority of the population." In addition, bishops or councils designated special places and certain times in which no fighting could take place. Finally, the sense that killing in even a just war was still wrong is visible in the fact that "just-war thinking was done in the confessional, and in the studies of the priests who developed canon law." The rules for just war were developed to enable priests to determine "the form and type of penance called for after killing."[35] Such items all indicate that killing in war was still considered sinful.

The shift to a dead or crucified Christ in the Eucharist separated believers from the living Christ and changed the understanding of salvation. In place of seeing the risen Christ as humanity's forerunner on a journey to paradise and toward divinity, Christ now "became a victim whose power lay in his suffering and judgment against sinful humanity." Instead of abundant life, he now offered "judgment to be feared." Where salvation had previously meant the enjoyment of community life in paradise, it now meant "escape from guilt and punishment."[36]

After the time of the Gero Cross, the attitude toward violence began to change. Some fraying of the idea that shedding human blood was sin oc-

33. Brock and Parker, *Saving Paradise*, 234-35.

34. Brock and Parker, *Saving Paradise*, 238.

35. John Howard Yoder, *When War Is Unjust: Being Honest in Just-War Thinking* (2d ed.; Maryknoll: Orbis, 1996), 9-12, quoting pp. 10, 12.

36. Brock and Parker, *Saving Paradise*, 238.

curred already when some ninth-century clerics began to say that penance was not required of soldiers.[37] Social conditions also contributed to the shift. As the Carolingian Empire declined in the eleventh century, local landlords plundered churches and countryside with impunity. To create some social order, bishops called peace councils and demanded that the local lords take oaths not to destroy church property. Church authorities then recruited soldiers to enforce such a Peace of God. With this step the eleventh-century church "accrued the authority to regulate violence and used armed force against enemies of the peace."[38] From such steps, Odo, abbot of Cluny, allowed monks to take up arms in defense of the church, and "Cluniac monks came to regard fighting for God as an aspect of holy vows." Gregory VII offered soldiers two paths to salvation — either give up arms completely or "employ their arms in the service of the church." From such moves, the idea developed that "military service was a way of imitating Christ and loving one's neighbors." Gregory even suggested that this military service might serve as penance for other sins.[39]

This sanctioned warfare became focused with the Peace Council of Clermont, France in November 1095. Pope Urban II declared a universal, binding Truce of God on Christians. At the close of council, he issued a call for an armed pilgrimage to Jerusalem. "Urban urged the crowd to take up arms and journey to Jerusalem to attack 'the bastard Turks' who held 'sway over our brothers.'" Christians were to stop fighting each other and to unite to free Jerusalem from the Muslims. For those who made the crusade, it would constitute penance for all sin. With the crusade, violence was now transformed from sin to a positive good. "Killing became a mode of penance, a pathway to paradise." Violence had become sanctified.[40]

John Howard Yoder listed several contrasts between justified war as still sinful and the sanctified violence of "holy war" or "crusade." For the sanctified violence of the crusade, there was "transcendent validation," which meant that commanders were free from political calculation of such criteria as "proportionality." This transcendent validation was known "by revelation" or "from beyond" rather than by careful analysis of the potential conflict. Further, in holy war, the enemy had no rights that needed to be respected, which meant that "genocide" could occur. The criterion of

37. Brock and Parker, *Saving Paradise*, 239.
38. Brock, "The Cross," 245.
39. Brock and Parker, *Saving Paradise*, 257-58, quoting p. 257.
40. Brock and Parker, *Saving Paradise*, 262-64, quoting pp. 263, 264.

"last resort" did not apply to crusade, and "success need not be probable." Thus dying in a hopeless cause could convey the "kind of immortality assigned to martyrs."[41]

Anselm's "*Cur Deus Homo* appeared during the first crusade and completed the theological developments that led to the Crusades." Anselm believed that the sins of humanity were serious enough that only God could undertake the necessary measures of compensation and that God "did so by becoming human to die on the cross." Unless the debt to God was paid, God would punish sinful humans and bar them from heaven. Since the debt was beyond any human capacity to pay, "God paid humanity's debt." "As God," Jesus could have chosen not to die, but as a human "he gave the gift of his death to his human kin."[42]

With this theology of atonement, "the Incarnation's sole purpose was to drive relentlessly to the act of dying." Although Anselm insisted that the atoning death was a free and willing act of God, humanity nonetheless could not be saved without it. "Christ's resurrection became irrelevant. Anselm fails even to mention it in *Why God Became Man*."[43]

Anselm was a friend of Urban II, and his atonement theology supported the pope's holy war. Although Anselm forbade his own monks to participate in the crusade, he wrote that dedication to God was demonstrated most fully by committing to die for God. He exhorted Christians "to imitate Christ's self-offering in the cause of God's justice." When church authorities "called for vengeance, they did so on God's behalf." As Brock and Parker quote Anselm: "When earthly rulers exercise vengeance justifiably, the one who is really exercising it is the One who established them in authority for this very purpose."[44] This view of God stands in sharp contrast to the image of God that earlier pages of this book have drawn out of the narrative of Jesus and the book of Revelation.

A generation after Anselm, Peter Abelard questioned Anselm's theory of atonement. But although Abelard rejected the idea that Christ gave satisfaction to God the Father, Abelard's view did not escape the implication "that we come to know love most fully by being moved by torture and execution as an act of self-sacrificing love for us, which then becomes the model for our own lives."[45]

41. John Howard Yoder, *When War Is Unjust*, 12-13.
42. Brock and Parker, *Saving Paradise*, 265, 266, 268.
43. Brock and Parker, *Saving Paradise*, 268.
44. Brock and Parker, *Saving Paradise*, 268.
45. Brock, "The Cross," 248.

Alongside the earlier correlation of narrative Christus Victor and Anselmian atonement to contrasting images of ecclesiology, the research by Brock and Parker traces a shift in Christian art and iconography from resurrected Jesus to images of a dead Jesus. This transition corresponds to the rise of church-sponsored, redemptive violence and thus mirrors the correlation of narrative Christus Victor with an early church that refused to shed human blood while Anselmian and satisfaction and substitutionary atonement reflect the church that had accommodated the sword. In a sense, satisfaction and substitutionary atonement participate in the same steps away from the nonviolent narrative of Jesus. Each portrays a role for violence — defined by justifiable war logic and operable in the feudal idea of satisfaction of the lord's offended honor, which is then elevated to the divine realm as an atonement image.

Responding to Challenges

It does not surprise that arguments for a new atonement motif and for nonviolent images of God have stimulated some challenges. Since some version of satisfaction atonement has been the dominant motif for centuries, it is to be expected that most challenges involved a defense of satisfaction atonement.

The Challenge of Paul

One challenge comes from those who appeal to writings of Paul. It has been long assumed that Paul's theology supports satisfaction atonement, which assumes the idea that God requires the death of Jesus in order to satisfy a divine need. That challenge was addressed above, in the section "Narrative Christus Victor: Round Three."

The Challenge of Newness

Christian theologians have been discussing theology and the meaning of Jesus Christ for more than two millennia. Supposedly standard, foundational statements of Christology were promulgated some seventeen centuries ago. Although a church council never proclaimed an official doctrine of atonement, some version of satisfaction atonement has been the predominant view for some eight centuries. With these facts in view, some observers no doubt find audacious a claim to present new insight and a new approach to the question of atonement and then to draw out implications for our understanding of God. Such challenges to newness may seem particularly appropriate when the author is self-identified as Anabaptist, an identity taken from a movement barely more than five centuries old that has always been a small minority and whose members in North America have joined the ranks of academic theologians only in the early to mid-twentieth century.

But a claim of new insight is not a claim to know more than previous generations. It is rather a claim based on the awareness of how context influences theology. It is an expression of the knowledge that our current context differs from previous contexts. The current chapter has made note of the feudal context that produced Anselm's satisfaction atonement image. Part II will sketch a number of instances of context. Chapter 6 sketches five New Testament Christological images that reflect five cosmologies or worldviews. These five images reveal ways in which the meaning of Jesus is restated when the Gospel narrative is carried into new contexts. That knowledge will then lead to a discussion of the reflection of yet another context in fourth- and fifth-century creedal statements. I am aware of our own context in the early twenty-first century. Much of Part II addresses issues of lived theology specific to our contemporary world. To be aware of context is to be aware of what has come before and then to recognize how proclamation of the Gospel will change in our contemporary context. A claim of newness is a claim to be aware of time and place. The claim to present something new is to express awareness that contexts change, that different contexts require new statements.

It is important to recognize with this claim of new insight in new contexts that the baseline of the discussion is the biblical text, and within the biblical text the norm for Christians is the narrative of Jesus' life, teaching, death, and resurrection. That baseline of the narrative of Jesus was sketched in Chapter 1 and will become visible again in the five Christological images discussed below in Chapter 6.

Equally as important as the reminder that the baseline is the biblical text is awareness of the continuing presence of the Spirit of God today. To claim to be able to say something new, that is, to bring new insight to our contemporary world, is a claim that God's Spirit is still present and working with us today, bringing that new insight into existence. The result is a gospel more fully present in our context than if it depended solely on refurbishing or updating past formulations.

The Challenges of Threefold Synthesis and of Keeping One Version but Not Another

As in the book in hand, satisfaction and penal substitutionary motifs have received the most serious challenges in recent decades, particularly from feminist, black, and womanist writers and from such new order evangelicals as Brian McLaren and Greg Boyd. These challenges have elicited defenses of satisfaction, which are given here in a schematic summary.[46]

A common approach of theologians to atonement theology is to propose an approach that in some way combines or holds together all three of the traditional motifs — classic Christus Victor, satisfaction, and moral influence. Suggestions vary. Some state that the issue of the work of Christ is too big to be contained in one theory and suggest keeping the three motifs without efforts at integration or synthesis. Such proposals may or may not recognize tension or dissidence among the three motifs. Others make an effort to articulate a comprehensive statement which is an integration or synthesis of motifs. Such efforts all make appeals to specific biblical texts. Common to this strategy of retaining all motifs is the assumption that they are compatible or are different but parallel ways to say the same thing.[47]

These efforts to claim all three motifs primarily constitute efforts both implicit and explicit to defend and preserve satisfaction atonement against various challenges. Purporting to keep all three motifs allows an advocate of satisfaction to acknowledge the validity of a particular critique against

---

46. For an extended discussion of such challenges, see my *Nonviolent Atonement*, 219-79.

47. In addition to numerous articles that argue some version of the case for integrating the three classic images into a larger whole, some book-length treatments are Peter Schmiechen, *Saving Power: Theories of Atonement and Forms of Church* (Grand Rapids: William B. Eerdmans, 2005); Boersma, *Violence, Hospitality and the Cross;* Robert Sherman, *King, Priest, and Prophet: A Trinitarian Theology of Atonement* (New York: T. & T. Clark, 2004). For a more extensive conversation with these and other statements as well as with the examples listed in note 48 following, see Weaver, *Nonviolent Atonement*, 220-28, 254-79. A recent critique of my approach that appeals to all three classic images is Ronald J. Sider, "A Critique of J. Denny Weaver's *Nonviolent Atonement*," *Brethren in Christ History and Life* 35 (2012): 214-41. For my specific response to Sider, see note 15 in Chapter 5 below.

one version, but to argue that no view is perfect or complete and then to point to supposed good points of satisfaction that allow it to be retained along with other equally incomplete motifs.

Other efforts to defend satisfaction atonement presume it as the given motif, but defend it by making use of the several versions of satisfaction, particularly the difference between penal substitution and classic satisfaction or another version of satisfaction. With two versions in view, it is then claimed that the negative critique applies only to one version. Most often the objection concerns the penal substitutionary version that emerged from the Protestant Reformers, followed by a claim that the objection does not apply to Anselm's version or to another version of satisfaction.[48] The idea from penal substitution that God would punish Jesus on the cross is called objectionable, for example, while some other version of satisfaction is acceptable because it does not include such punishment.

Because the answers to these strategies are similar and have one element in common, I treat these two challenges together — the defense of satisfaction by keeping all three motifs and the defense that plays one version of satisfaction off against another. It is a multitiered response.

First, historical observation displays the incompatibility of the three motifs and undercuts the effort to retain all three. Anselm specifically rejected the ransom motif. Then in turn, Peter Abelard supported the rejection of the ransom motif, but also rejected Anselm's view that Jesus' death satisfied God's honor. The claim to retain all three disregards this historical sequence of rejections. And in a further point along this line, Anselm certainly never considered that he was articulating an incomplete view that needed to be completed with elements from ransom and moral influence motifs. The same can be said for Abelard. The strategy of keeping all three motifs assumes that the motifs are intrinsically and transcendently true motifs separate from their historical contexts. In fact these motifs reflect historical contexts and personalities and cannot be simultaneously true.

---

48. For examples of this methodology, see Catherine Pickstock, *After Writing on the Liturgical Consummation of Philosophy* (Oxford: Blackwell, 1998); Daniel M. Bell, Jr., *Liberation Theology after the End of History: The Refusal to Cease Suffering* (London: Routledge, 2001). A popular statement is Bell's "God Does Not Require Blood," *Christian Century* 126 (February 10, 2009): 22-26. These authors are dealt with in Weaver, *Nonviolent Atonement*, 227-28, 259-63. An extended, book-length example of this methodology is Darrin W. Snyder Belousek, *Atonement, Justice, and Peace: The Message of the Cross and the Mission of the Church* (Grand Rapids: William B. Eerdmans, 2012). For a brief but comprehensive response to Belousek, see note 34 in Chapter 6 below.

Attempting to retain all three disregards arguments made by Anselm and Abelard, whose views are supposedly being defended.

Next, an observation based on the inner logic of the motifs arrives at this same conclusion. Consider the role for the death of Jesus in each motif. More precisely, consider where or what the death of Jesus is directed toward or aimed at for each motif. For the ransom motif Jesus or Jesus' death is directed toward or offered to Satan. For satisfaction motifs, Satan is out of the equation, and the death of Jesus is aimed Godward — toward God or God's honor or God's law or God's wrath, or it offers God obedience or worship or yet something else. Finally, Abelard rejected the idea that Jesus' death was aimed Godward and saw it as directed toward sinful humankind. It is logically untenable to make all three of these projections of the direction of Jesus' death simultaneously true.

The observation about the direction or object of the death of Jesus also reveals why it is logically untenable to keep one version of satisfaction while rejecting another. In any version of satisfaction, the devil or Satan has been removed from the equation. The only two possible objects of the death of Jesus are humankind or one or another version of the Godward direction. Thus if one rejects the idea of Jesus' death as penal substitution to satisfy a requirement of divine law, the death is nonetheless still aimed at some other Godward target, whether God's honor or restoration of God's creation or restoration of true worship to God or restoration of obedience to God on behalf of humankind or any other redefinition or rephrasing of divine need. In other words, however the divine direction is understood, all these various versions of satisfaction feature a divinely needed death as the basis for reconciling sinners to God.

With Satan removed from the equation, that only God or humankind remain as the objects of the death of Jesus leads to what is perhaps the greatest problem of all with satisfaction as well as moral influence atonement motifs. Jesus did not commit suicide. In order for Jesus' death to be aimed Godward or toward humankind — to satisfy divine honor or restore the created order or true worship of God or true obedience to God — people have to kill Jesus. And if reconciliation of sinners to God is a divine initiative, then the implication is that God sent Jesus to die in order to accomplish the divine end — either to satisfy God in some way or to demonstrate God's love to sinful humankind. In either instance, God arranges for the death of Jesus to accomplish the divine end, however defined. The result is the image of a God who uses or sanctions human violence as the way to accomplish divine ends. And it involves the people who kill Jesus as necessary to the purpose of securing the death in order to satisfy God's honor or restore the created order or offer obedience or restore true worship.

The result of this analysis brings into view a model of God that contradicts the image of the God revealed in the nonviolent story of Jesus Christ. Calling it a paradox or a demonstration of the power of God that both Jesus and those who killed Jesus were working within the will of God actually validates the argument that satisfaction atonement presumes a God who uses or sanctions violence. Thus the argument of this book calls for rejection of satisfaction and moral influence atonement motifs as appropriate images for Christians today. The same applies to any version of a ransom motif that features God knowingly offering the life of Jesus as a ransom.

However, rejecting these traditional or classic atonement motifs is in no way to reject the Bible. On the contrary, the motif proposed here, namely narrative Christus Victor, depends on the biblical witness, starting with the narrative of Jesus in the Gospels and concluding with a reading of the entire book of Revelation. Most importantly, between that material at the ends of the New Testament appear the writings of the Apostle Paul, whose compatibility with narrative Christus Victor has been demonstrated. This motif is thoroughly biblical. Given its reading of the Gospel narrative of Jesus, a reading compatible with Paul and then also found in Revelation, it is a better understanding of and makes use of a greater variety of New Testament writings than any version of satisfaction atonement, whose origins are in Anselm's assumption that the salvific working of God in Christ mirrored medieval feudal assumptions. And as the next chapter displays, narrative Christus Victor is also an extension of Old Testament writings.

The Challenge of Guilt

Some defenders of satisfaction atonement have argued that narrative Christus Victor does not deal with guilt, with the fact that individual sinners are guilty before God, guilty of having offended God. Narrative Christus Victor may deal with evil in a cosmic dimension, namely God's overcoming of the powers of evil, it is thought, but narrative Christus Victor does not deal with an individual sinner's personal guilt, the supposed objective guilt that accrues because of offending God. Neither, it is feared, does it deal with the feelings of inadequacy that accompany the awareness that human beings are born in sin and inevitably sin. For some people the claim of cosmic victory may even enhance an individual's own sense of guilt and inadequacy when confronted with the awesomeness of God's overcoming of the powers of evil in resurrection. Thus, it is important to discuss how narrative Christus Victor speaks to individual and personal guilt and feelings of inadequacy. The removal of guilt before God is discussed in the section on forgiveness in the following chapter. Here the analysis deals with an individual's personal feelings of guilt and inadequacy before God.

I have emphasized that the resurrection is an invitation from God to live in and participate in the life of Jesus and to continue the mission of Jesus to make the reign of God visible in the world. The resurrection is an invitation to every individual to experience reconciliation with God and the presence of the reign of God *now*, on earth, in our lives as human beings. Experiencing the reign of God *now* requires a choice on our part to leave the forces of evil and to join in the reign of God made present in the life of the resurrected Jesus. But our participation in the reign of God is also an act of God that happens apart from any contribution on our part. It must be an act of God because on our own initiative and power we cannot overcome the forces of evil. Earlier this combination of individual initiative and act of God was identified as the "paradox of grace," which is a description of Paul's "I worked harder than any of them — though it was not I, but the grace of God" (1 Cor. 15:10).

Here the concern is the side of the paradox that emphasizes God's act of grace to save. This act of God's grace puts on vivid display the value that the individual has in the eyes of God, regardless of the past life one has led. Feelings of guilt and inadequacy are addressed by the invitation of the resurrection. The fact that God addresses us demonstrates that we are worthy of God's call and God's act of grace. We are participating now in the reign of God because of what Jesus has done in making visible the reign of God and through our participation in the life of Jesus by the act of God's grace. What more value could one have as an individual than to be chosen by God? Rob Bell is certainly correct when he writes that in the loving call of God, we are "to trust that we are loved and that a new word has been spoken about us, a new story is being told about us."[49]

This life in the reign of God now is what Anabaptists called "walking in the resurrection." The well-known Anabaptist statement, the Schleit-

---

49. Rob Bell, *Love Wins: A Book about Heaven, Hell, and the Fate of Every Person Who Ever Lived* (New York: HarperOne, 2011), 195.

heim *Brotherly Union,* proclaims that baptism is to be given to those "who have been taught repentance and the amendment of life, . . . And to all those who desire to walk in the resurrection of Jesus Christ and be buried with Him in death, so that they might rise with Him."[50]

Walking in the resurrection means being cared for by God, even when we cannot completely overcome the sin in our lives or fix the abundant evil that still rules in the world. Living in the resurrection nonetheless enables us to address evils in the world under the power of God's grace. It enables us to feel like we are participating in the reign of God even as we are cognizant that we cannot do it ourselves and that our obedience to the rule of God always falls short.

In the Lutheran or Calvinist traditions, where it was understood that people cannot in any way accomplish their own salvation or overcome the rule of evil under their own initiative, an attempt or a claim to being or doing good was considered in itself to be a sign of depravity. In contrast, I would argue that a desire and an effort to accomplish good and confront evil is evidence of the grace of God working in an individual. The fact that narrative Christus Victor displays an impulse to overcome guilt and to participate in the body of Christ expresses precisely what God is doing in the world. Participating in the community created by and around Jesus Christ under the impulse of God's grace thus aligns our efforts with what Martin Luther King, Jr. famously called "the arc of the moral universe" that "bends toward justice."[51]

Narrative Christus Victor emerges from a reading of the New Testament. Chapter 4 carries the biblical discussion of nonviolent God even farther, namely through the Old Testament and then in the parables of Jesus. Violent images of God from these sources are frequently posed as a challenge to the claim that God rejects violence and should be depicted with nonviolent images. Demonstrating the nonviolence of God in Old Testament writings and in the parables is perhaps the most important dimension of the proposal for an atonement motif that features a God who rejects violence. The following chapter presents this material, with an extended response in Chapter 5.

50. Michael Sattler, "The Brotherly Union of a Number of Children of God Concerning Seven Articles," in *The Legacy of Michael Sattler,* trans. and ed. John H. Yoder (Classics of the Radical Reformation 1; Scottdale: Herald, 1973), 36.

51. Martin Luther King, Jr., *A Call to Conscience: The Landmark Speeches of Dr. Martin Lutgher King, Jr.,* ed. Clayborne Carson and Kris Shepard (New York: Warner, 2001), 199.

4 *Divine Violence: Bible versus Bible*

There can be no doubt whatsoever that much of the Christian tradition has assumed a role for divine violence and that an integral dimension of the traditional understanding of the omnipotence of God is the presumed prerogative of God to exercise violence. That divine exercise of violence appears in the Old Testament and the New Testament and is prevalent in theology at all levels today. This chapter and the next put these assumptions of divine violence on display and then fashion a response that defends the nonviolence of God.

Biblical Violence and Divine Violence

A serious challenge to the idea of a God who is nonviolent comes from those who appeal to the Old Testament. From Marcion in the second century to many theologians and biblical interpreters today, it is assumed that the God of the Old Testament sanctions and employs violence. Since the Old Testament belongs to Christian Scriptures, its view of God appears to challenge the idea that the God revealed in Jesus is a nonviolent God, a God who does not meet violence with greater violence. The Old Testament's narratives may be the most serious challenge of all to the idea of a nonviolent God both in the realm of theology and in the area of practical application. God is described there as one who uses great destruction as vengeance and punishment, who massacres large numbers of people through command of the natural order, and who commands God's followers to engage in killing on both large and small scales. A sketch of these violent images of God sets the scene for a response that highlights the nonviolence of God.

Divine Violence: Old Testament

Much of the violence of God in the Old Testament may be familiar. God used water to kill. A vengeful God, made sad by the wickedness of humankind, says "I will blot out from the earth the human beings I have created — people together with animals and creeping things and birds of the air, for I am sorry that I have made them" (Gen. 6:5-7). Noah built an ark, which saved him and his family from the flood that God used to destroy all other people and every living thing that was not on the ark.

In the exodus of enslaved Israelites from Egypt, God drowned the Egyptian army in the Reed Sea in order to allow the Israelites to escape. "The Lord drove the sea back" and the Israelites then passed between the walls of water. The Egyptian army followed, and when the waters returned to normal depths, "the Lord tossed the Egyptians into the sea" (Exod. 14:21, 27). In this way Israel learned to fear the Lord. "Thus the LORD saved Israel that day from the Egyptians; and Israel saw the Egyptians dead on the seashore. Israel saw the great work that the LORD did against the Egyptians. So the people feared the LORD and believed in the LORD and in his servant Moses" (Exod. 14:30-31).

Deuteronomy prescribes the death penalty for a range of sins. For example, 13:1-5 commands killing false prophets who speak "treason against the Lord your God." The next paragraph contains the injunction to kill anyone who tempts people to "worship other gods," even a family member. "Show them no pity or compassion and do not shield them. But you shall surely kill them; your own hand shall be first against them to execute them, and afterwards the hand of all the people" (vv. 8b-9). 21:18-21 gives the procedure for stoning a rebellious son to death: get a judgment against him from the elders of the city, and then "all the men of the town shall stone him to death." 22:22-24 prescribes the death penalty for adulterers.

The Israelite conquest of the land of Palestine conducted by Joshua under divine guidance (Joshua 1–12) was "sudden, bloody, and complete."[1]

---

1. John Bright, *A History of Israel* (4th ed.; Louisville: Westminster John Knox, 2000), 129.

It began with a miraculous crossing of the Jordan River, described in a fashion reminiscent of the crossing of the Reed Sea. The conquest of Jericho included the miraculous collapse of the city walls in response to the army's obedience, after which the Israelites entered the city and "devoted to destruction by the edge of the sword all in the city, both men and women, young and old, oxen and sheep, and donkeys," while "the silver and gold, and the vessels of bronze and iron, they put into the treasury of the house of the Lord" (6:2, 21, 24).

"Devoted to destruction" refers to the *ḥerem* in which all the inhabitants of a captured city were killed in order to dedicate them to God. Joshua 7 recounts what happened when there was a violation of the "devoted" booty from Jericho. Achan kept some of the treasure that was to go into the Lord's treasury, "the anger of the Lord burned against the Israelites" (v. 1), and God punished Joshua's army with defeat when they attacked the city of Ai. However, when Achan was identified as the guilty party, Joshua and the Israelites took Achan, his children, and all their possessions to the Valley of Achor. "And all Israel stoned him to death; they burned them with fire, cast stones on them, and raised over him a great heap of stones that remains to this day." With punishment exacted, "the LORD turned from his burning anger" (vv. 25b-26a). With order then restored, God commanded Joshua to "do to Ai and its king as you did to Jericho and its king." Joshua did so. He used a ruse to draw the forces of Ai out of the city into an ambush, where Israel slaughtered "all the people of Ai," twelve thousand men and women. And this time, the Israelites got to keep the spoils for themselves (8:1-29).

The book of Judges contains a number of accounts of killing blessed by God, both massacres of large numbers and graphic one-on-one violence. One such story tells of the collaborative team of Deborah and Barak (Judges 4). When Israel "did what was evil in the sight of the Lord," "the Lord sold them into the hand of King Jabin of Canaan," whose army commander was Sisera. Sisera had nine hundred iron chariots and "had oppressed the Israelites cruelly twenty years" (v. 3). Deborah, a prophetess who also acted as judge, summoned Barak to raise an army of "ten thousand from the tribe of Naphtali and the tribe of Zebulun." The plan was to station Barak's army in an ambush into which Deborah would draw Sisera's nine hundred chariots and his other troops. The strategy worked and "the Lord threw Sisera and all his chariots and all his army into a panic before Barak. Sisera got out of his chariot and fled on foot while Barak pursued the chariots and the army. . . . All the army of Sisera fell by the sword; no one was left" (vv. 15-16). Meanwhile, the fleeing Sisera approached the tent of Jael, the wife of a Kenite whose clan was at peace with King Jabin. Jael invited Sisera in, promising him safety. She covered him with a rug and, when he asked for a drink, gave him milk. He charged her to stand at the door of her tent and tell any pursuers "No" if asked whether anyone was inside. Sisera was obviously tired from his flight and fell asleep. Jael took a hammer and a tent peg "and went softly to him and drove the tent peg into his temple, until it went down into the ground" (v. 21). When Barak arrived in pursuit of Sisera, Jael called him in to see "the man whom you are seeking" (v. 22). The conclusion places God's guidance and blessing on this story: "So that day God subdued King Jabin of Canaan before the Israelites" (v. 23).

Following rule by judges, the Israelites asked for — and were eventually allowed to have — rule by a king. An incident with Saul, Israel's first king, described in 1 Samuel 15 continues the elements just observed. The prophet Samuel passed along to Saul a command from the Lord. Saul was to "punish the Amalekites for what they did in opposing the Israelites when they came up out of Egypt" (v. 2). The punishment was the *herem:* "attack Amalek, and utterly destroy all that they have; do not spare them, but kill both man and woman, child and infant, ox and sheep, camel and donkey" (v. 3).

Saul did most of what was ordered. He gathered an army of "two hundred thousand foot soldiers, and ten thousand soldiers of Judah" (v. 4) and defeated the Amalekites. He "utterly destroyed all the people with the edge of the sword," but Saul and his army "spared Agag, and the best of the sheep and of the cattle and of the fatlings, and the lambs, and all that was valuable, and would not utterly destroy them; all that was despised and worthless they utterly destroyed" (v. 9). In other words, Saul did not carry out *herem* as ordered.

The response from God came to Samuel: "I regret that I made Saul king, for he has turned back from following me, and has not carried out my commands." And Samuel informed Saul that as a result, "The LORD has torn the kingdom of Israel from you this very day, and has given it to a neighbor of yours, who is better than you" (v. 28). The one to whom the kingship was passed was David, the warrior king of Israel, whose name resonates through Israel's history and whose descendants include Jesus the Messiah (Matt. 1:1; Luke 3:23-31; Rev. 5:5-6).

The office of prophet arose in Israel as a response to the office of the king. Prophets offered critique of royal conduct and royal policies. Their messages often contain warnings of God's punishment on an unjust nation.

One example comes from the writings of Isaiah, who was active for some forty years at the end of the eighth century BCE, at the time of the full emergence of Assyria as a problem for Israel. A complete cycle of this divine punishment occurs in Isaiah 10:5-19, as the punisher becomes the punished. In vv. 5-11, the prophet gives voice to Yahweh, who says that he is sending Assyria, "the rod of my anger . . . against a godless nation." The godless nation is Israel, "the people of my wrath." Assyria is commanded "to take spoil and seize plunder and to tread them down like the mire of the streets." Since Yahweh's hand has already touched those whose idols are worse than Israel's, there is no reason to withhold judgment on Jerusalem and Samaria. But in vv. 12-19, Assyria in turn also falls under divine judgment because of "the arrogant boasting of the king of Assyria and his haughty pride." He vaunts himself, claiming that "by the strength of my hand I have done it," when it was actually the doing of Yahweh. "Shall the ax vaunt itself over the one who wields it, or the saw magnify itself against the one who handles it?" As a result,

> The Sovereign, the LORD of hosts,
>   will send wasting sickness among his stout warriors,
> and under his glory a burning will be kindled,
>   like the burning of fire.
> The light of Israel will become a fire,
>   and his Holy One a flame;
> and it will burn and devour
>   his thorns and briers in one day.
> The glory of his forest and his fruitful land
>   the LORD will destroy, both soul and body,
> and it will be as when an invalid wastes away. (vv. 16-18)

Almost a century later, in 612 BCE, Nineveh, the capital city of Assyria, fell to invaders. The prophet Nahum gives voice to God, who takes credit for the destruction of the ones who plagued Israel:

> A jealous and avenging God is the LORD,
> the LORD is avenging and wrathful;
> the LORD takes vengeance on his adversaries
> and rages against his enemies. (Nahum 1:2)

A variant reading of v. 8, "He will make a full end of her place," speaks of vengeance directed against Nineveh. Then comes vengeance against the king:

> Your name shall be perpetuated no longer;
> from the house of your gods I will cut off
> the carved image and the cast image.
> I will make your grave, for you are worthless. (v. 14)

Nahum's second chapter describes this vengeance as soldiers and chariots rampage through the city. "Devastation, desolation, and destructions!" (2:10). And the Lord takes full credit, for "restoring the majesty of Jacob, as well as the majesty of Israel" (v. 2) and for the destruction:

> See, I am against you, says the LORD of hosts, and I will burn your chariots in smoke, and the sword shall devour your young lions; I will cut off your prey from the earth, and the voice of your messengers shall be heard no more. (v. 13)

Not only the prophets proclaimed an angry God whose wrath was poured out on those who disobeyed, whether pagans or Israelites. Many Psalms, the worship music and the poetry of Israel, also appear to portray such a God. They praise or bow in awe before the majestic creator God, the God of Israel, who controls all things. This control includes the forces of nature active as the Israelites escaped from Egypt (e.g., Pss. 78:11-16, 43-48). It also includes the fortunes of nations where God expresses anger and wrath. When the people sin, God's wrath is poured out on Israel,

> For they provoked him to anger with their high places;
> they moved him to jealousy with their idols.
> When God heard, he was full of wrath,
> and he utterly rejected Israel. (78:58-59)

And again,

> Then the anger of the LORD was kindled against his people,
> and he abhorred his heritage;
> he gave them into the hand of the nations,
> so that those who hated them ruled over them. (106:40-41)

God's anger and wrath were also directed against Israel's enemies.

> He struck down many nations
> and killed mighty kings —
> Sihon, king of the Amorites,

and Og, king of Bashan,
and all the kingdoms of Canaan —
and gave their land as a heritage,
a heritage to his people Israel. (135:10-12)

These vignettes from throughout the Old Testament, whose number could be expanded greatly, picture a God who uses violence as punishment and judgment. At times God exercises violence directly, as in the stories of the great flood and the exodus. Other times it is Israel's leader or army that follows instructions from God to carry out the violence. And on occasion, when Israel needs punishing, it is the enemies of Israel who are directed to carry out God's violent punishment. The violence falls on those who disobey and oppose the will of God. When the Israelites disobey, the chosen people themselves experience this judgment. Being the chosen people means not only blessing; it also carries responsibility, with punishment for failure to obey.

Divine Violence: The Gospels

Following the display of violence attributed to God and violent images of God in the Old Testament, this section turns to images of a violent God in the Gospels. In particular, some of Jesus' parables feature a vengeful and powerful God who pronounces violent judgment on offenders. This section provides a sample.

Matthew recounts the parable of the unforgiving slave (Matt. 18:23-35). The parable likens the kingdom of heaven to a king who wished to settle accounts with his slaves. He called in one who owed ten thousand talents — a huge sum of money — and demanded payment. When the slave could not pay, the king ordered the slave and his family and all his possessions sold. When the slave begged for mercy, the king took pity and forgave the debt. As this slave departed the presence of the king, he came on a fellow slave who owed him a hundred denarii, a quite small sum of money. The one who had just experienced relief from the huge debt, seized his fellow slave and demanded payment. When it was not forthcoming, he threw the debtor into debtors' prison until he could pay what he owed. This action disturbed the other slaves greatly, who reported the action to the king. The king called in the unforgiving slave, accosting him with the words, "You wicked slave!" and charged that he should have shown the same mercy that he had been shown. As punishment, the angry king turned him over to be tortured until he could repay his entire debt. In his conclusion, Jesus uses the king as analogy for God. He says, "So my heavenly Father will also do to every one of you, if you do not forgive your brother or sister from your heart" (v. 35). In this parable God is pictured as one who tortures those who are not sincere in their forgiveness.

A similar image of God appears in the parable of the wicked tenants, which appears in all three of the Synoptics (Matt. 21:33-46; Mark 12:1-12; Luke 20:9-19). In this well-known parable, a landowner planted a vineyard, assembled the apparatus for a wine press, and hired tenants to run the operation while he was in a far country. When he then sent servants to collect on his investment, these servants were beaten and stoned, and finally one was killed. Thinking that the servants would respect his son, the owner sent the son to collect the fruits of his investment. But the wicked servants killed the son, thinking that with the son eliminated from the picture, they would be able to claim his inheritance. When Jesus then asked his hearers what the owner would do, the reply came, "He will put those wretches to a miserable death, and let out the vineyard to other tenants who will give him the fruits in their seasons" (Matt. 21:41). Jesus then made a messianic application, with a quotation from Psalm 118:22-23:

> The stone that the builders rejected
>   has become the cornerstone;
> this was the Lord's doing,
>   and it is amazing in our eyes. (Matt. 21:42)

The vineyard owner is analogous to God, including the harsh punishment, when Jesus says, "Therefore I tell you, the kingdom of God will be taken away from you and given to a people that produces the fruits of the kingdom. The one who falls on this stone will be broken to pieces; and it will crush anyone on whom it falls" (vv. 43-44). The Gospel writer adds that the priests and Pharisees wished to arrest Jesus because they knew themselves to be the subject of the parable.

Another parable compares the kingdom of God to a king who gave a marriage feast for his son (Matt. 22:1-14). But the invitees thought they had better things to do and even mistreated and killed the servants who carried the invitation. In response the angry king sent his soldiers to destroy the murderers and burn their city. Then he sent his servants out into the streets to "invite everyone you find to the wedding banquet" (v. 9). As a result the wedding hall was filled with guests. But the king became angry when one of those in attendance was not properly attired for a wedding celebration. The king commanded his servants, "Bind him hand and foot, and throw him into the outer darkness where there will be weeping and gnashing of teeth" (v. 13). Once again, God, comparable to the king in the parable, appears as a vengeful God who exercises great violence.

The details differ, but not the image of God, in the two versions of the parable of the talents (Matt. 25:14-30; Luke 19:12-27). In this parable, a wealthy man left on a journey and gave his slaves money to invest for him while he was away. In each version, one slave hid the talent he was given while the others followed orders and gained significant earnings. In Luke's version, it is also said that the nobleman was to acquire royal power on this journey. However, his citizens hated him and sent a delegation to protest his appointment. On the nobleman's return, the slaves were rewarded for the gains made with the talents entrusted to them. The slave who hid the talent returned it to the owner, saying that he had feared the owner as one who reaps where he has not sown. In Matthew's version, the angry owner commanded that the talent be given to the slave with the most talents, "for to all those who have, more will be given, and they will have an abundance; but from those who have nothing, even what they have will be taken away." And "as for this worthless slave, throw him into the outer darkness, where there will be weeping and gnashing of teeth" (Matt. 25:29-30). In Luke's version, the talent is also taken from the slave who did nothing and given to the one with the most talents, but nothing is said about the fate of this slave. However, for those who had protested the rule of the new king, he commanded, "Bring them here and slaughter them in my presence" (Luke 19:27). Again, God appears in Jesus' parable as a vengeful and violent God.

Matthew follows the parable of the talents with Jesus' statement of final, apocalyptic judgment (Matt. 25:31-46). Here one finds the rather well-known statement about dividing sheep from goats. The sheep on the right are those who gave food to the hungry, cold water to the thirsty, welcomed strangers, gave clothes to the naked, cared for the sick, and visited those in prison. These receive the invitation, "Come, you that are blessed by my Father, inherit the kingdom prepared for you from the foundation of the world" (Matt. 25:34). The goats on the left are those engaged in none of these activities. To these the word of judgment is, "You that are accursed, depart from me into the eternal fire prepared for the devil and his angels" (Matt. 25:41). Again, the God of the kingdom Jesus preached is a God who exercises violent judgment and punishment.

Divine Violence: Today's Version

The image of a vengeful and powerful God who offers blessing for obedience but who wreaks destruction and death to serve as warnings, judgments, or calls to repentance resonates throughout the history of the United States from the earliest settlers into the twenty-first century. God is said to act directly sometimes and at other times through compelling the violent deeds of people.

The English Pilgrims and Puritans who settled in Massachusetts beginning in 1620 had a belief in divine providence inherited from John Calvin. They believed themselves to be God's new chosen people, making an exodus from evil England parallel to ancient Israel's escape from Egypt and now destined by God to inherit the promised land of the new world.

They expressed the belief of being divinely chosen in compacts or covenants made with God to form a Christian society, in which the civil authorities would enforce church rules and regulations and only pious churchgoers could hold public office. (In modern language, it was a state church or an established church.) For example, in the Mayflower Compact the Pilgrims, the first settlers in New England, "covenant" themselves "for the glory of God, and advancement of the Christian Faith, and honour of our King and Countrey, . . . in the presence of God and one of another" to form a "civill body politike," that is, a political structure to govern their new society. This political body will enact laws for the general good, and the signers pledge "all due submission and obedience" to it.[2]

A well-known example of covenant appears in an often-quoted Puritan sermon. As Puritans on the ship *Arrabella* approached landfall, their leader Governor John Winthrop proclaimed, "Now if the Lord shall please to heare us, and bring us in peace to the place wee desire [the North American coast], then hath hee ratified this Covenant and sealed our Commission."[3] That is, Winthrop and his flock assumed that arriving safely at their destination would be God's ratification and blessing of their endeavor. Such covenants were characteristic of the Puritan settlers of New England.[4] The implication of these covenants is that their fulfillment would result in divine blessing on their endeavors while failure to live up to the

2. Williston Walker, *The Creeds and Platforms of Congregationalism* (Boston: Pilgrim, 1963), 92.

3. Conrad Cherry, ed., *God's New Israel: Religious Interpretations of American Destiny* (rev. ed.; Chapel Hill: University of North Carolina Press, 1998), 40.

4. See examples in Walker, *Creeds and Platforms.*

covenant would bring sanction in the form of violent punishment directed by God.

The covenanted intentions could not be sustained. By the 1640s already, aspects of this established, supposedly Christian society were declining. And then followed a string of disasters. There were shipwrecks and outbreaks of disease. In the years 1675-76 a series of Indian raids called King Philip's War devastated white settlements in southern New England. Huge fires occurred in Boston in 1676 and again in 1679. In the face of these disasters, their belief in a divine covenant led the church authorities to conclude that through these human disasters God was punishing them. They convened a synod to determine the causes of God's retribution. Beginning September 10, 1679, the synod met for ten days and developed a list of thirteen areas of sin and religious decay for which they thought God was punishing them. Among the sins listed were declining church attendance, swearing and taking God's name in vain, waning Sabbath observance, decline in the family and family values, excessive drinking, immodest dress by women, mixed dancing, and much more.[5]

Threads of the themes of societal and national chosenness accompanied by claims of divine blessing or punishment for transgressions have been woven through the American cultural mosaic ever since the colonial era. Here I mention only a few highlights of this history. Adherence to versions of these themes kept the Puritan worldview but restated the sense of being a divinely ordained society and nation in less religious and more secular language. In the Declaration of Independence of 1776, for example, the Christian God of the Puritans became Nature's God, the Creator, Supreme Judge of the world, and Divine Providence. Laws were no longer based on God's revealed word, but protected "inalienable rights," a secular-sounding way shaped by the rationalist, deistic thinking of the Enlightenment to identify innate rights without mentioning God. The ratification of the Puritans' divinely sanctioned covenant became an appeal "to the Supreme Judge of the world for the rectitude of our intentions" and then "a firm reliance on the protection of Divine Providence."

In the nineteenth century, the sense of being a predestined, divinely chosen people received a secular translation into a "manifest destiny" for

5. Sydney E. Ahlstrom, *A Religious History of the American People* (New Haven: Yale University Press, 1972), 160; H. Shelton Smith, Robert T. Handy, and Lefferts A. Loetscher, *American Christianity: An Historical Interpretation with Representative Documents*, vol. 1: *1607-1820* (New York: Charles Scribner's Sons, 1960), 204-16.

European settlers to possess the continent and to displace or kill off the native inhabitants. Thus under another name, a divine sanction accompanied the mass violence against Native Americans. Meanwhile, the suffering of the Civil War constituted punishment brought by God for the nation's sin of slavery, at least as Abraham Lincoln said in his second inaugural address: "If God wills that [the war] continue, until all the wealth piled by the bond-man's two hundred and fifty years of unrequited toil shall be sunk, and until every drop of blood drawn with the lash, shall be paid by another drawn with the sword, . . . it must be said that 'the judgments of the Lord are true and righteous altogether [Ps. 19:9].'"[6] In the twenty-first century the claim of divine blessing, stated in mostly secular terms and images but vouchsafed through success, remains strong. It appears in many forms — in the claims of American "exceptionalism," the pervasive and insistent American necessity and self-assigned mission "under God," in the popular mindset as well as in political rhetoric, to be "the best country in the world," to be and to remain the richest and strongest country both militarily and economically, to be first to the moon, to control space, to win the most Olympic medals, to be the only nation qualified to launch a preemptive strike to bring "freedom" to other nations, to function as the world's policeman, to be the leader of the free world, to possess the right to consume thirty or forty percent of the world's resources while possessing only about six percent of the population, and much more.

At the same time, other voices utter the rhetoric of divine judgment on a sinful nation. Pat Robertson and the late Jerry Falwell expressed that idea after the terrorist attacks of September 11, 2001. Falwell was a guest on Robertson's TV show, the 700 Club. In his introductory comments, Robertson said that the vulnerability of the United States demonstrated by the attacks of September 11 happened because "God Almighty is lifting his protection from us" because of developments like abortion and various kinds of sexual immorality. Falwell concurred, saying that the attacks of September 11 were the judgment by God brought on with the help of "the pagans, and the abortionists, and the feminists, and the gays and the lesbians . . . , the ACLU, People for the American Way" because they "have tried to secularize America."[7]

6. Abraham Lincoln, "Second Inaugural Address," in God's New Israel: Religious Interpretations of American Destiny, ed. Conrad Cherry (rev. ed.; Chapel Hill: University of North Carolina Press, 1998), 202.

7. "Transcript of Pat Robertson's Interview with Jerry Falwell Broadcast on the 700 Club, September 13, 2001," Appendix D in Bruce Lincoln, Holy Terrors: Thinking about Religion after September 11 (Chicago: University of Chicago Press, 2002), 106.

These comments angered many people, and Falwell and Robertson later apologized. However, their comments nonetheless reflected the early Puritan outlook, which assumed that success meant divine approval on their society while disaster signaled God's disapproval of the nation.

God was referenced again in late August 2005 after Hurricane Katrina inundated the Gulf coast and devastated the city of New Orleans, leaving nearly 1900 dead and hundreds of thousands without access to homes and jobs. Newspaper articles reported a variety of claimed reasons for which God was supposedly punishing either New Orleans or the United States: for shedding innocent blood through abortion, for the presence of gay bars and homosexuals on Bourbon Street and in the French Quarter, or as retribution on the United States for endangering the people of Israel by supporting the evacuation of Jewish settlers from the Gaza Strip.[8] New Orleans mayor Ray Nagin angered many Americans with a different charge, namely that Hurricane Katrina happened because "God is mad at America" for "being in Iraq under false pretenses." Nagin, who is African American, also said Katrina was a message from God to the black community for "not taking care of ourselves," for the "black-on-black crime" of young black men killing each other.[9] Again, in one way or another, these statements all reflect themes lingering from the Puritan beginnings of the United States, namely that hardship and disasters constitute divine punishment for religious sin and decay. Similar comments seem to appear in the news media following every disaster of national prominence, whether from human-produced or natural causes.

The intent here is not to adjudicate among these diverse claims. The point is rather to observe how smoothly such claims of a God who uses war and natural disasters as punishment seem to transition from the Old Testament accounts through the parables of Jesus to United States history to the present, and to see how prevalent the idea of a God who exercises violence is in North American society.[10] Those who disputed the claims of

8. Among many reports, see "Some See a Vengeful God amid Deadly Hurricane," *The Blade*, September 4, 2005, A4.

9. "Mayor: Hurricanes a Sign God Is 'Mad at America,'" *The Blade*, January 17, 2006, A5. Nagin later apologized for his "inappropriate" remarks.

10. The discussion has focused on the violence of God in the Bible and its links to American violence as tied to the themes of being a chosen people, a new Israel, a Christian nation, an innocent nation, and more. This discussion could be expanded greatly. Integral to the discussion is Robert Bellah's seminal article on civil religion, "Civil Religion in America," reprinted in *American Civil Religion*, ed. Russell E. Richey and Donald G. Jones (New York:

divine judgment expressed about September 11 or Katrina did so not because they thought God would not act in that way but because they disputed the idea that God was targeting the United States. Common to all these claims, on whichever side the observer stood, was the assumption that God was indeed a God who uses, sanctions, or commands violence.

Another kind of claim about divine violence occurs with the good intention of proclaiming comfort in the face of evil. A brother is killed in a traffic accident, and in following years well-intentioned people express the belief that God had "good reasons" for ordaining the death.[11] In a minor league baseball game, a line drive strikes the first base coach in the temple, and he dies almost immediately. Those closest to him believe "God plucked him," and his sons are told "God took him to heaven."[12] A person is killed by a drunk driver or a child dies, and often one hears, "I guess God needed an angel" or "I guess God needed her more than we did."[13] An uncle, whose beloved wife dies precipitously from cancer that was far advanced before symptoms appeared, reports being told "God had a plan for her." The people who voice such comments have the best of intentions. They want to bring comfort to the individual who has lost a loved one. However, these comments also imply something about the character of God, namely that God ordains the evils that kill people, whether the violence of an accident or the natural process of cancer.

Although those who have expressed these intended words of comfort are likely unaware of the relationship, their comments are in line with the

Harper & Row, 1974), 21-44. Recent literature that discusses the link between biblical and American violence includes Richard T. Hughes, *Myths America Lives By* (Urbana: University of Illinois Press, 2003); Robert Jewett and John Shelton Lawrence, *Captain America and the Crusade against Evil: The Dilemma of Zealous Nationalism* (Grand Rapids: William B. Eerdmans, 2003); Gregory A. Boyd, *The Myth of a Christian Nation: How the Quest for Political Power Is Destroying the Church* (Grand Rapids: Zondervan, 2005); Jeremy Young, *The Violence of God and the War on Terror* (New York: Seabury, 2008); Philip Jenkins, *Laying Down the Sword: Why We Can't Ignore the Bible's Violent Verses* (New York: HarperOne, 2011). For analysis from a nonviolent perspective of the role that the quasi-Christian civil religion of America played in the response to September 11, 2001, see J. Denny Weaver, "Responding to September 11 — and October 7 and January 29: Which Religion Shall We Follow?" *Conrad Grebel Review* 20 (2002): 79-100.

11. John Sanders, *The God Who Risks: A Theology of Providence* (Downers Grove: InterVarsity, 1998), 9.

12. S. L. Price, "A Death in the Baseball Family," *Sports Illustrated*, September 2007, 57, 61.

13. A Google search on such phrases finds many hits.

thought of John Calvin, who has had more impact on American theology than any other theologian. In the treatment of divine providence in his *Institutes of the Christian Religion,* his monumental systematic theology, Calvin wrote that if a traveler strays from his companions and is killed by robbers, or if a tree or a building falls and a man is killed, these deaths are due to "God's secret plan." Or if there is a drought and crops fail, "it is certain that not one drop of rain falls without God's sure command."[14] Although such statements are intended to provide comfort in the certainty of God, they share with the claims of divine vengeance the assumption that God is a God who can use violence, a God who kills or who ordains killing. Behind the loving God revealed in Jesus Christ is a God with a "secret plan" who ordains violence that kills people.

In the exercise of this violence, God is said sometimes to act directly — as in causing disease or withholding rain or guiding a hurricane or the flight of a baseball. Other times God is assumed to guide people to do evil things — whether the inhabitants of Ai who punish the disobedient Israelites, Indians who attack white settlements, armies that wreak devastation, drunk drivers who kill children, or angry men who fly planes into buildings, and whether directed against the enemies of the people of God or against the disobedient people of God. In every case, if God is indeed behind these events, then God exercises violence and leads people to execute violence.

Behind the claims about a "secret plan" or execution of divine judgment or God taking a beloved wife through cancer is the assumption that God controls all events great and small, including events wrought by violence and that cause suffering. Important historical advocates of this view were Augustine and John Calvin. In his book, *The God Who Risks,* John Sanders rejects this view of God. Sanders argues that God created human beings with free will. Since God cannot revoke this freedom, people can and do make choices that oppose the will of God. Thus God's creatures operate with certain boundaries. But because God did create human beings with free will, God has decided "not to control each and every event, and some things go contrary to what God intends and may not turn out completely as God desires. Hence, God takes risks in creating this sort of world."[15] Thus

---

14. John Calvin, *Institutes of the Christian Religion,* trans. Ford Lewis Battles (Library of Christian Classics; Philadelphia: Westminster, 1960), 198, 203-5, 208-9.

15. Sanders, *The God Who Risks,* 10-11. A similar argument appears in Gregory A. Boyd, *God of the Possible: A Biblical Introduction to the Open View of God* (Grand Rapids: Baker,

Sanders developed an image of a God who responds to the choices of free people, and from the side of human beings it is a God who responds to the prayers of God's people.

The key to dealing with this longstanding and prevalent challenge to the nonviolent character of God is to recall that God is revealed in Jesus Christ. And if God is truly revealed in Jesus Christ, then we should not attribute characteristics to God that do not find resonance in the story of Jesus Christ. As John Sanders wrote, "God in Jesus tabernacled among us, displaying God's way in the world. Jesus is *the* model for understanding God's relationship to the world. In Jesus we see what God is most truly like and what sort of relationship with us God desires. God is intimate and near, not remote or disengaged."[16]

Significant blocks of biblical material supposedly portray the violence of God. One of those blocks is the book of Revelation, which was already dealt with in Chapter 2. The Old Testament constitutes a second major group of materials frequently appealed to in support of a violent God. This chapter has provided a sample of such material. But the God fully revealed in Jesus is a nonviolent God. And if the God revealed in the story of Jesus who refused the sword is also the God of Abraham, Isaac, and Jacob, then we need another look at the Old Testament. Then a following section will respond to the violent images of God in Jesus' parables.

The Bible: Another Look

The Old Testament

Often overlooked with the claims about God's sanction of violence in the Old Testament are other, quite different strands of material as well as some alternative interpretations. In a challenge to the prevailing assumption that the Old Testament has a uniform picture of a God who uses and sanctions violence, I believe that the Old Testament actually displays a multi-faceted conversation about God and violence. Discovering this conversation about violence and the character of God in the Old Testament does not require new research and new academic specializations. It requires

2000). Additional discussion of human freedom and the existence of evil appears in Chapter 10 below on "Nature and Suffering."

16. Sanders, *The God Who Risks*, 115.

rather a willingness to look at familiar stories and what is already known with new eyes, or to bring a new question to familiar material. In fact, a pattern of both divine and human nonviolence and minimal violence and nonviolent resistance runs all the way through the Old Testament, beginning with the creation stories in Genesis 1 and 2.

The narrative in Genesis 1 walks the reader through six "days" of creation — "days" that show progress from chaos to order and from simple to the complex. The problems of reading this story as a scientific account are already well known. They involve the age of earth; alternating light and dark of "day" one without sun and moon, which do not appear until day four; green things growing in day three, doing their photosynthesizing, although the sun which powers photosynthesis does not appear until day four. The account in Genesis 2 poses still more problems if we read these two as scientific accounts. The order of the two stories is quite different — Genesis 1 has male and female at the end, as the culmination of creation. Genesis 2 has human being as male created at the beginning on a bare earth, followed by plants and animals, with human being as female created at the end. We need not resolve these issues in order to know what the accounts in Genesis 1 and 2 mean for the discussion of the nonviolence of God. In fact, however, seeing what these stories imply for the nonviolence of God provides a resolution for these other interpretative problems as well.

Important dimensions of these stories of creation appear when they are placed in conversation with creation as told in the Enuma Elish, a Babylonian creation myth from the same period as the early Old Testament. In the midst of Enuma Elish is the story of a rebellion of young gods against old gods.[17] Tiamat, female god, fought against Marduk the head god. Marduk killed Tiamat — he forced the wind into her mouth and blew her up like a balloon. And when she was thus distended, he shot her with an arrow. With Tiamat dead, Marduk took his sword and sliced her "like a shell fish into two parts." He set up the upper portion of her distended belly to become the big dome that makes the sky, parallel to the dome in Genesis 1:6, and established "stations" in this sky for each of the great gods. Finally, Marduk announced that he would "establish a savage; 'man' shall be his name. Verily, savage-man I will create. He shall be

---

17. For a translation of Enuma Elish, see "The Creation Epic," in *Ancient Near Eastern Texts Relating to the Old Testament,* ed. James B. Pritchard (3rd ed.; Princeton: Princeton University Press, 1969), 60-72, 501-3.

charged with the service of the gods that they might be at ease!" After conducting an investigation into which god had provoked Tiamat to rebel, Marduk identified Kingu as the guilty party. He "severed his blood (vessels)," and used the blood to create humankind to serve the gods and allow them freedom.[18]

Compare the violent story in Enuma Elish with the two accounts in Genesis. In Enuma Elish, creation of heavens and earth occurs as the spontaneous aftermath of violence — the lethal fight of Tiamat and Marduk followed by the mutilation of a corpse and divine vengeance — Marduk killing the god Kingu in punishment and using his blood to make humankind, who are called "savages." In contrast to this display of spontaneous responses to other spontaneous acts of the gods, the biblical accounts pose an entirely different scenario. They display purpose and order and creation without violence. In Genesis 1, God creates with a "word," while in Genesis 2 the creative image is of God as a sculptor, fashioning objects out of clay and then breathing life into them. Far from savages, human beings are made in the image of God and their appearance marks the high point of creation. When compared with the Enuma Elish, it should jump out that the Bible's stories picture creation as a product of divine intention and that it occurs entirely without violence.

Further analysis could develop a number of other significant differences between the Enuma Elish and the two accounts of creation in Genesis. For the moment, the important point to emphasize is that the differences occur in the realm of theology rather than science. In fact, if these accounts are made to speak to science, they reflect the same worldview and contain the same errors — flat earth covered by a dome, alternating day and night not related to sunlight and the rotation of the earth, green plants growing without benefit of sunlight. The differences are theological — creation as the unified intention of God in contrast to creation as spontaneous, random responses to other acts and a high view of humankind (made in the image of God) in contrast to a low view of humankind (savage, made for the service of the gods). Most important, creation in Enuma Elish is bloody and emerges from violence, while creation in Genesis is anything but violent — creation from God's word and from sculptures fashioned by God. These differences are *theological*.

The nonviolent creator God is also pictured as the God who became angry at humankind and in retaliation for their wickedness drowned all of

---

18. This summary of creation and the quotations are from "The Creation Epic," 68-69.

them in a great flood. John Sanders provides a helpful image for dealing with the violence attributed to God in the great flood, another story in the mythological chapters of Genesis. A strong motivation in Sanders's work is an understanding of God that invites prayer. For Sanders, prayer does not make sense if the unchanging, sovereign God of doctrinaire Calvinism has foreordained every event since before the creation, including the key strokes — and even deletions for spelling errors — as this sentence is typed. Sanders developed a different understanding of God, a God who responds to the prayers of God's people, a God who risks. The risk means giving human beings the freedom to oppose God, and in the midst of that freedom and risk God can work the divine will in the world. This idea of a God who responds is a helpful image for dealing with the accounts of the great flood — a God who became angry at the sin of humankind and who responded by wiping out all living things except one family of humans and either pairs or seven pairs of all animals and birds. When Noah emerged from the ark, he built an altar and offered burnt offerings to God. Perhaps God was moved by the previous destruction. In any case, the offerings pleased God, and God responded with a promise never again to destroy every living creature (Gen. 8:21; 9:11, 15).[19]

Alongside the arguments of Sanders, Walter Brueggemann noted the human, emotional characteristics attributed to God in the flood story. Yahweh is depicted as "sorry that he had made humankind," and "it grieved him to his heart" (Gen. 6:6). Brueggemann calls this a description "not of an angry tyrant, but a troubled parent who grieves over the alienation." Such a God can change intentions. "Israel's God is fully a person who hurts and celebrates, responds and acts in remarkable freedom." Thus even though the condition of humankind remains hopeless, God has decided to act with patience toward the rebellion of humankind. "I will never again curse the ground because of humankind, for the inclination of the human heart is evil from youth; nor will I ever again destroy every living creature as I have done" (Gen. 8:21). Brueggemann writes, "the flood has effected no change in humankind. But it has effected an irreversible change in God, who now will approach his creation with an unlimited patience and forebearance."[20] Thus Brueggemann can say in straightforward language that the story of the flood presents "the com-

19. Sanders, *The God Who Risks*, 9-13, 16, 53-54.

20. Walter Brueggemann, *Genesis* (Interpretation: A Bible Commentary for Teaching and Preaching; Atlanta: John Knox, 1982), 77, 78, 81.

plete reversal of Yahweh's mood and intention from the beginning to the end of the narrative."[21]

The idea of a God who risks, who responds to the prayers of God's people, and who can change attitudes challenges the hard edge of the idea of the vengeful God who wipes out virtually all living creatures. In their treatment of the flood story, the arguments of Sanders and Brueggemann thus contribute to the side of the conversation that reflects a nonviolent God.

The story of the children of Abraham happens under the oversight of the creator God of Genesis 1 and 2. God called Abraham and told him that his descendents would become a great nation in which all the families of the earth would be blessed (Gen. 12:3). How those descendants of Abraham understood and attempted to fulfill that calling constitutes the plotline that plays out through the rest of the Old Testament.

In *Yahweh Is a Warrior,* a groundbreaking book on violence in the Old Testament, Millard Lind noted the "essentially peaceful character" and the "pacifistic nature" of the narratives of the patriarchs. Their possession of land depended on the promise of God. "If one truly believes in the promise of grace that God will give the land, then one has no need to take the way of works by fighting for it."[22] Two examples display an explicit avoidance of conflict and a willingness to trust God.

Genesis 13 contains the story of Abram and Lot, both wealthy in livestock, who came from Egypt through the Negeb as far as Bethel in south-central Palestine. The land could not support the flocks and herds of both Abram and Lot living together, and their herders quarreled. Abram averted conflict by offering Lot his choice of land. "Let there be no strife between you and me, and between your herders and my herders; for we are kindred. Is not the whole land before you? Separate yourself from me. If you take the left hand, then I will go to the right; or if you take the right hand, then I will go to the left" (Gen. 13:8-9).

Another story depicts the patriarch Isaac's response when a dispute developed about the ownership of wells he had dug. He had grown wealthy with flocks and herds and a great household while living at Gerar in the territory of King Abimelech of the Philistines. This wealth provoked jealousy among the Philistines, who retaliated by stopping up his wells.

---

21. Walter Brueggemann, *The Theology of the Old Testament: Testimony, Dispute, Advocacy* (Minneapolis: Fortress, 1997), 363.

22. Millard C. Lind, *Yahweh Is a Warrior: The Theology of Warfare in Ancient Israel* (Scottdale: Herald, 1980), 35, 36, 38.

Abimelech asked him to leave the territory: "Go away from us; you have become too powerful for us" (Gen. 26:16). Isaac did move. Twice more he dug wells that were filled in by the Philistines, and two more times Isaac moved on rather than retaliating. Finally, for a third time they "dug another well, and they did not quarrel over it." Isaac called the place Rehoboth, saying "Now the Lord has made room for us, and we shall be fruitful in the land" (v. 22). When challenged, rather than fighting, Isaac's response was to move on and dig new wells. Eventually Abimelech recognized that God was blessing Isaac. He came to Isaac and proposed a nonaggression pact, a "covenant with you so that you will do us no harm, just as we have not touched you and have done to you nothing but good and have sent you away in peace." They exchanged oaths "and Isaac set them on their way, and they departed from him in peace" (vv. 28b-29, 31b). These stories of the patriarchs of Israel present a different view of God, of God's blessing, and of trust in God than do the stories described above of exodus and conquest directed by God.

In the previous section, note was made of the account of the crossing of the Reed Sea as a story of divine violence on behalf of Israel in which God killed the Egyptians. But that is not the only possible way to read this story. As the title of his book indicates, Millard Lind acknowledged that "Yahweh is a warrior," but he argued that what was distinctive was *how* Yahweh fought for his people. "Yahweh as God of war fought for his people by miracle, not by sword and spear."[23] Faith in Yahweh meant to trust God for safety, and that Israel could be led by a charismatic leader rather than a military ruler such as a king. Lind summarized:

> By miracle we mean an act of deliverance that was outside of Israel's control, beyond the manipulation of any human agency. This conviction was so emphatic that Israel's fighting, while at times a sequel to the act of Yahweh was regarded as ineffective; faith meant that Israel should rely upon Yahweh's miracle for her defense, rather than upon soldiers and weapons. The human agent in the work of Yahweh was not so much the warrior as the prophet.[24]

For Lind, the exodus from Egypt, and in particular the crossing of the Reed Sea, constitute the paradigm of Yahweh's fighting on behalf of Israel through miracle rather than an army.

23. Lind, *Yahweh Is a Warrior,* 23.
24. Lind, *Yahweh Is a Warrior,* 23.

Although Lind's account softens the image of a God who kills by having the deaths occur through natural occurrences, ultimately it is still God who is depicted as the origin of the forces of nature that kill. I add an additional layer of interpretation and carry Lind's important analysis a step further. It is not necessary to read an account such as the crossing of the Reed Sea as deliberate killing by Yahweh. The Egyptians could have refrained from pursuing the children of Israel and could have recognized the justness of the slaves' flight. When the heavily armored Egyptian army pursued the much lighter-traveling Israelites into the sea, the Egyptians were putting themselves in danger: they got themselves in trouble. Although the text says that the Israelites passed "on dry ground" (Exod. 14:22), it was soft enough to clog the wheels of the heavy chariots and make them difficult to maneuver. It was the Egyptian commanders who ordered their troops into an untenable situation. When the water returned to its natural course, the Egyptian army was done in because they were in a place they should not have been. Evil continues to provoke more evil; eventually evil suffers the consequences of its evil deeds.

Earlier we noted the stories of the violent, completed conquest of Palestine, and the *ḥerem*, in which everything and everyone from a conquered city was destroyed. But there is another side to the conquest.

After Joshua 1–12 presents the conquest as an accomplished fact, Joshua 13:1 states that Joshua "was old and advanced in years," and the Lord told him, "Very much of the land still remains to be possessed." There then follows a list of rulers and territories that still remain for conquest (13:2-6). Other texts as well in Joshua indicate an incomplete conquest: 13:13; 15:63; 16:10; 17:11-13, 16-18. The contrast to a sudden and complete conquest appears even more striking in the first verse of Judges. After the death of Joshua, the Israelites ask of the Lord, "Who shall go up first for us against the Canaanites, to fight against them?" (Judg. 1:1).

These mentions of territory yet to be conquered indicate a more complex picture of settlement than the sudden and complete victory pictured in Joshua 1–12. Archeological evidence indicates that a number of places in southern Palestine occupied by the Israelites were destroyed in the latter part of the thirteenth century, the century of the conquest. However, there are also significant indications of Israelite occupation by immigration, settlement, and amalgamation. Alongside the supposedly complete conquest, "the Bible presents another picture of the occupation of Palestine that makes it clear that it was a long process, accomplished by the efforts of individual clans, and but partially completed."[25] Or as another commentator wrote, as a literary piece, Joshua "is not quite the straightforward, smooth story the preceding basic plot summary above seems to imply."[26] These indications of occupation by settlement and amalgamation by no means cancel out the violent accounts that attribute military success to God. However, the settlement trajectory indicates that the accounts of violent conquest are stylized and programmatic descriptions, and they hold open the possibility of other understandings of God.

The book of Judges contains some counterparts to the violent stories. Judges 7 recounts the story of Gideon, who saved the Israelites from a big army of Midianites, described as "thick as locusts; and their camels were without number, countless as the sand on the seashore" (7:12). Gideon sent out a call and roused an army to meet the Midianites, but God told him that he had too many men, and that if they triumphed, then Israel would claim credit because of the large number of troops and "take credit away from" God (v. 2). Thus Gideon was instructed to inform his army that anyone who is "fearful and trembling" may return home — and twenty-two thousand went home. Ten thousand remained, but God told Gideon that that was still too many and gave instructions for a test that would reduce the number still further. Gideon brought the troops down to the water to drink. All that got down on their hands and knees and put their faces in the water to drink were put on one side, and on the other side he put the three hundred who scooped up water in one hand and lapped out of their hands like a dog. Gideon kept the three hundred and sent the rest home.

Gideon's instructions were that each of the three hundred carry a trumpet and a jar with a torch inside. In three clusters of one hundred, they surrounded the camp of the Midianites. At Gideon's signal, they all broke their jars, so that the flames burst out, they blew their trumpets, and began shouting, "A sword for the Lord and for Gideon!" (7:20). With the lights suddenly flashing, the trumpets blaring, and voices bellowing, the Midianites thought that they were surrounded by a huge army. They panicked and started fleeing and hacking at each other. The three hundred Israelites chased after them, but no slaughter is mentioned. Two captains were captured and killed.

---

25. Bright, *History of Israel*, 129. See also Donald Joseph Selby and James King West, *Introduction to the Bible* (New York: Macmillan, 1971), Old Testament 167.

26. James E. Bowley, *Introduction to Hebrew Bible: A Guided Tour of Israel's Sacred Library* (Upper Saddle River: Pearson Prentice Hall, 2008), 191.

This story of Gideon presents victory not through military means but by wits and a ruse carried out by a small handful of men who did virtually no killing. In other words, it is a story primarily of nonviolent resistance through creative imagination. That Gideon later engaged in military activity and one-on-one violence ought not detract from the point that Judges does feature an account of salvation of the Israelites that does not depend on military activity.

Following rule by judges, the Israelites asked for a king. The stories of the warrior kings of Israel, particularly David, are often told today as though God fully endorsed this kingship. However, the sanction of kingship was actually qualified. The office originated from lack of faith on the part of Israel and was granted by Yahweh only as an accommodation of that lack of faith.

Not having a king and rule by judges was a matter of faith in Yahweh, trusting Yahweh to raise up a leader in a time of crisis. Gideon based his refusal of the office of king on the kingship of Yahweh. "I will not rule over you, and my son will not rule over you; the Lord will rule over you" (Judg. 8:23).

But there came a time when the Israelites ceased trusting Yahweh and asked Samuel, a judge, to anoint a king who would rule them "like all the other nations" (1 Sam. 8:5b). Samuel prayed to Yahweh about this request. Yahweh told Samuel that the people wanted a king because "they have rejected me from being king over them" (v. 7). Samuel was to accede to their request but to accompany it with a warning. Because of the contemporary flavor and relevance of the warning, it merits hearing in its entirety.

> These will be the ways of the king who will reign over you: he will take your sons and appoint them to his chariots and to be his horsemen, and to run before his chariots; and he will appoint for himself commanders of thousands and commanders of fifties, and some to plow his ground and to reap his harvest, and to make his implements of war and the equipment of his chariots. He will take your daughters to be perfumers and cooks and bakers. He will take the best of your fields and vineyards and olive orchards and give them to his courtiers. He will take one-tenth of your grain and of your vineyards and give it to his officers and his courtiers. He will take your male and female slaves, and the best of your cattle and donkeys, and put them to his work. He will take one-tenth of your flocks, and you shall be his slaves. (vv. 11-17)

The parallels today to military domination of the national economy and usurpation of national resources by the Pentagon budget and wars are chilling. And just as people today refuse to say no to the Pentagon, in response to Samuel's warning the people said, "No! But we are determined to have a king over us" (v. 19). Yahweh's word to Samuel was to give them what they asked for. As a result, Saul was chosen as king.

The parable of the trees who sought a king in Judges 9:8-15 reflects similar skepticism about the office of king. Abimelech, a son of Gideon, killed all but one of his seventy brothers and procured the office of king from the lords of Shechem. In response, Jotham, the one surviving brother, gave the parable of the trees as a warning to Abimelech's followers. The olive tree, the fig tree, and the grape vine all refused the invitation to be king, saying that "gods and mortals" needed their produce. The bramble, who produces only shade, agreed to rule over the other trees, but threatened to devour those who refused to obey.

Walter Brueggemann analyzed the development of the monarchy and the ongoing tension between forces favoring and opposing the monarchy. "The pro-king opinion obviously prevailed, and the testimony of Israel is shot through with allusions to royal-Davidic-messianic claims that are regarded as fully legitimated."[27] Although having a king was a disobedient choice, God continued to work with Israel. For an analogy, one can perhaps compare God's continuing work with Israel to the attitude of a parent who continues to work with a son or daughter in spite of the young person's choices that displease or oppose the will of the parent. Evidence of this attitude is in the oracle of 2 Samuel 7, in which Nathan proclaims Yahweh's words of support for David as the father of a never-ending dynasty, along with promises of punishment of wrongdoing.

> When your days are fulfilled and you lie down with your ancestors, I will raise up your offspring after you, who shall come forth from your body, and I will establish his kingdom. He shall build a house for my name, and I will establish the throne of his kingdom forever. I will be a father to him, and he shall be a son to me. When he commits iniquity, I will punish him with a rod such as mortals use, with blows inflicted by human beings. But I will not take my steadfast love from him, as I took it from Saul, whom I put away from before you. (2 Sam. 7:12-15)

An element of God's continuing to work with Israel's desire to have a king was the rise of the role of the prophet. Prophets became prominent watchdogs and critics of the practices of kings. "When the prophets ap-

27. Brueggemann, *Theology of the Old Testament*, 602.

peared," Abraham Heschel wrote, "they proclaimed that might is not supreme, that the sword is an abomination, that violence is obscene."[28] The sword would be destroyed, as Isaiah wrote:

> they shall beat their swords into plowshares,
>   and their spears into pruning hooks;
> nation shall not lift up sword against nation,
>   neither shall they learn war any more. (Isa. 2:4)

The writer of Chronicles did not consider the wars of David wrong. But as is recounted in 1 Chronicles 28:1-6, "David's wars were regarded as a necessary evil, but the fierce doings David was involved in made him unfit to build the house for the Lord."[29] Thus Heschel could conclude, "The prophets were the first men in history to regard a nation's reliance upon force as evil." As an example he quoted Hosea's condemnation of militarism as idolatrous:

> Israel has forgotten his Maker,
>   and built palaces;
> and Judah has multiplied fortified cities;
>   but I will send a fire upon his cities,
>   and it shall devour his strongholds. (Hos. 8:14)

And as the alternative, Hosea wrote in the name of Yahweh, "I will not save them by bow, or by sword, or by war, or by horses, or by horsemen" (1:7).[30]

The point to draw from this discussion of kingship is that the institution of monarchy did not have unqualified divine support in Israel and that violence by kings in the name of God does not serve as unqualified evidence of divine support of violence. Further, when the office of king disappeared with the exile, Israel did not lose something that was intrinsic to its existence as the people of God.

As a counterpart to the stories of *ḥerem*, namely devoting the enemy and his possessions to God by massacring all the people and animals and destroying all the property, consider the story in 2 Kings 6. Here an enemy is overcome in an entirely different way. In this account, with God's help the prophet Elisha several times warned the king of Israel of places to

---

28. Abraham J. Heschel, *The Prophets* (New York: HarperPerennial, 2001), 203.
29. Heschel, *The Prophets*, 205.
30. Heschel, *The Prophets*, 212.

avoid in order to stay out of ambushes from the king of Aram. Finally, frustrated, the king of Aram sent his military officers and a large armed force to capture Elisha. But the eyes of this force were blinded so that they did not recognize Elisha. Elisha told them that the person they sought was not there, but he would lead them to him. Then Elisha led them into Samaria, where they were surrounded by the forces of the king of Israel. The Israelite king wanted to massacre the Aramean force, but Elisha told him instead to prepare food and drink for the Arameans. After they had feasted, the Israelite king sent them back to their own king. The story concludes, "And the Arameans no longer came raiding into the land of Israel" (2 Kgs. 6:23). This victory, if it should be called that, or this elimination of an enemy occurred with the help of a ruse, followed by kindness — most definitely a nonviolent conflict resolution.

Alongside the God who uses the nations for punishment as depicted in Isaiah, Nahum, and the Psalms, the Suffering Servant poems in the second section of Isaiah (particularly Isa. 42:1-4; 49:1-6; 50:4-9; 52:13–53:12) present another indication of a God who does not operate on the basis of violence. In these poems, the servant expresses his complete submission to the will of Yahweh, along with "the principle of righteous suffering as a positive good — not simply for the benefit of the sufferer, but of one man for another."[31] In frequently quoted words, it is said of the servant:

> Surely he has borne our infirmities
> and carried our diseases;
> yet we accounted him stricken,
> struck down by God, and afflicted.
> But he was wounded for our transgressions,
> crushed for our iniquities;
> upon him was the punishment that made us whole,
> and by his bruises we are healed.
> All we like sheep have gone astray;
> we have all turned to our own way,
> and the LORD has laid on him
> the iniquity of us all. (Isa. 53:4-6)

Considerable debate exists concerning the identity of the Suffering Servant — the servant as Israel, as an individual, a combination of the two, and including the traditional Christian interpretation that Jesus appropri-

31. Selby and West, *Introduction to the Bible*, Old Testament 345-46.

ated and fulfilled the servant's mission as the suffering Messiah. But we need not settle this debate to recognize that the God of the servant is a God who works through patient suffering, that is, a nonviolent God. The God of the servant poses a marked contrast to the God depicted in the violent God of conquest, judges, and kings.

Like Nahum, the book of Jonah also deals with Nineveh, the capital of the Assyrian Empire, which was noted for its cruelty. However, Jonah's conclusion differs greatly from that of Nahum. In the well-known story, when God called Jonah to preach to pagan Nineveh, the prophet ran away and ended up spending three days in the belly of the large fish. After being returned to land, Jonah agreed to preach, proclaiming "Forty days more, and Nineveh shall be overthrown!" The Ninevites responded. The inhabitants of the city "believed God; they proclaimed a fast, and everyone, great and small, put on sackcloth." When the king heard of these events, he also donned sackcloth and ashes and decreed, "All shall turn from their evil ways and from the violence that is in their hands." The hope was that God would change his mind about destroying the city. And God did indeed relent. "When God saw what they did, how they turned from their evil ways, God changed his mind about the calamity that he had said he would bring upon them; and he did not do it" (Jon. 3:10).

This display of mercy by God angered Jonah. After a discussion with God, Jonah built a booth outside the city wall to wait in the shade to see what would happen to the city. God sent a bush that grew to shade Jonah, and then a worm that killed the bush. Jonah declared himself angry enough about the bush to die. God's response: "You are concerned about the bush, for which you did not labor and which you did not grow; it came into being in a night and perished in a night. And should I not be concerned about Nineveh, that great city, in which there are more than a hundred and twenty thousand persons who do not know their right hand from their left, and also many animals?" (4:10-11).

This book is a parable. Jonah represents unfaithful Israel punished by captivity in Babylon (the great fish) and then returned to Palestine (spit up on the shore) for another opportunity. In spite of their repeated disobedience — Jonah's continuing anger — God continues to work with Israel as a merciful God, who shows mercy even to the enemies of Israel, represented by the city of Nineveh. Because of this juxtaposition of attitudes toward Nineveh, some commentators have suggested that Jonah constitutes a response to Nahum. Nahum writes that "The Lord is slow to anger but great in power, and the Lord will by no means clear the guilty" (Nah. 1:3). Jonah's prayer uses the same description of the Lord, but ends differently. Jonah fled to Tarshish and said to God, "I knew that you are a gracious God and merciful, slow to anger, and abounding in steadfast love, and ready to relent from punishing" (Jon. 4:2). Such words placed in Jonah's mouth, coupled with the mercy of God displayed in the parable, positions the book of Jonah as a prophetic softening of the divine justice in Nahum by a message of divine mercy.[32]

The monarchy in Israel came to an end some six centuries before Jesus, when the king and other leaders and numbers of people were taken to Babylon as captives. Exile was a defining moment for Israel in understanding what it meant to be the people of God. They lived in a setting where they did not hold the reins of control or determine the direction of society through government.[33] They lived without a political establishment and with no monarch, a situation certainly not unheard of in their history, but a decided change from rule by the dynasty of King David.

To these exiles in Babylon the prophet Jeremiah wrote that rather than pining after their lost life in Jerusalem, they should maintain their identity as God's people but settle down and decide to live in Babylon. "Build houses," "plant gardens and eat what they produce," get married and raise families and then encourage children to produce grandchildren. They should learn trades that benefited the society, and "seek the welfare of the city where I have sent you into exile, and pray to the LORD on its behalf, for in its welfare you will find your welfare" (Jer. 29:5-7). In other words, living as God's people Israel did not depend on having their hands on the means of political control. As John Howard Yoder wrote, "Jeremiah's abandoning statehood for the future is thus not so much forsaking an earlier hope as it is returning to the original trust in JHWH,"[34] that is, to the situation before Israel had a king. In this life in exile, they were to maintain their religious traditions and worship, which would serve as a witness to the way of Yahweh in the midst of a foreign nation. Nothing about this witness required that it depend on civil or government authorities or divinely sanctioned violence.

---

32. Klaas Spronk, *Nahum,* Historical Commentary on the Old Testament (Kampen: Kok Pharos, 1997), 9-10, quoting 9; Peter Machinist, "Nahum," in *The Harper Collins Bible Commentary,* ed. James L. Mays (rev. ed.; New York: HarperCollins, 2000), 665.

33. This line of argument follows material in John Howard Yoder, "Jesus the Jewish Pacifist," and "'See How They Go with Their Face to the Sun,'" in Yoder, *The Jewish-Christian Schism Revisited,* ed. Michael G. Cartwright and Peter Ochs (Grand Rapids: William B. Eerdmans, 2003), 69-92 and 183-202.

34. Yoder, "Jewish Pacifist," 71.

Stories in the book of Daniel illustrate this witness. The first chapter recounts the story of Daniel, Hananiah, Mishael, and Azariah, who were given new names by the palace master: Belteshazzar, Shadrach, Meshach, and Abednego. These young Hebrews were among the captives brought in for education that would enable them to enter the king's service. The young men were willing to learn the local language and a useful skill, but they refused the royal food and wine that was standard fare for trainees and asked instead for vegetables and water. This story is one of nonviolent cultural resistance. In other words, the young exiles maintained their own cultural and religious identity as Hebrews, which identified them as people who worshiped the God of Israel rather than the gods of Babylon. The outcome of the story is that the Hebrews thrived on their own kind of food and were allowed to continue with it as they worked for the king.

The third chapter of Daniel tells another story of Shadrach, Meshach, and Abednego. On intercession by Daniel they were appointed to be civil servants with responsibilities for the province of Babylon. After the three refused to worship the gods of King Nebuchadnezzar and the golden statue that he had set up, they were bound and thrown into a furnace. But when the three were not harmed in the fire, the king acknowledged the God of Israel and gave Shadrach, Meshach, and Abednego a promotion. Again, using contemporary terminology, this story is one of nonviolent cultural resistance. These stories portray ways that the Hebrews maintained their own religious and cultural identity, which was a witness to the God of Israel, even as they worked for the good of Babylon.

The story of Daniel and the den of lions in the sixth chapter has a similar outcome and meaning. Daniel was one of three presidents placed by King Darius over one hundred twenty satraps stationed throughout the kingdom to look after the king's affairs. Daniel's job performance earned him the favor of the king but jealousy from the other civil servants, who plotted against him. They persuaded the king to sign a proclamation that required worship and prayer to the king only for thirty days. The penalty for disobeying the decree was death in a den of lions, by which the other civil servants hoped to eliminate Daniel, who continued to pray three times daily to the God of Israel. However, after being left in the den of lions over night, Daniel said, "My God sent his angel and shut the lions' mouths so that they would not hurt me, because I was found blameless before him; and also before you, O king, I have done no wrong" (Dan. 6:22). As a result, the king issued a decree in support of Israel's God, and Daniel continued to prosper under King Darius.

These stories from the book of Daniel illustrate and put a theological blessing on the cultural resistance of the Hebrew captives. They maintained their identity as worshipers of Yahweh in a society where they had no control of political authority but nonetheless worked for the blessing of the culture in which they were captives. Their witness required courage and it could be confrontational, but the stories are told with a view to encouraging that witness. The stories of Queen Esther in the book bearing her name, as well as the earlier story of Joseph in Egypt, also portray this cultural resistance in exile.

After a sampling of texts on divinely sanctioned or practiced violence in the Old Testament, this second pass through the Old Testament reveals other strands of material. These texts reveal challenges to human violence, instances of nonviolent responses, and divinely sanctioned nonviolent resistance. With this second complex of materials in view, it becomes obvious that the Old Testament does not have a uniform picture of God. It truly features a conversation about violence and about the character of God. Walter Brueggemann recognizes such a conversation when he writes that Old Testament discourse "is not at all vexed about juxtaposing texts that explicitly contradict each other."[35] But the conversation does not end with the Old Testament. It continues in the New Testament.

Counters to Gospel Violence

Earlier note was made of the violent God in several of Jesus' parables, particularly in Matthew's Gospel. This section will make brief note of parables and sayings of Jesus that pose a nonviolent image of God. In other words, the conversation about the character of God made visible in the Old Testament is also evident in the Gospels.

In one instance, the contrast is explicit. The previous section described Matthew's version of the parable of the wedding banquet (Matt. 22:1-14). The first invitees who did not take the invitation seriously and killed a servant were in turn killed by the king's soldiers, and a poorly attired attendee was bound hand and foot and consigned to outer darkness. Luke's version omits the violent response of the man giving the banquet (not identified as

---

35. He further identifies the "theological articulation" of the Old Testament as "dialectical and dialogical" and notes that theodicy is the unresolved but "quintessential question of Jewish rhetoric." Brueggemann, *Theology of the Old Testament*, 82-83.

a king). The man is still angry at those who make light of the invitation. But the anger spurs him to send his slave to go "into the streets and lanes of the town and bring in the poor, the crippled, the blind, and the lame." And when there was still room remaining, the slave was to go out "and compel people to come in" to produce a full house. The judgment pronounced on those who refused the invitation: "None of those who were invited will taste my dinner" (Luke 14:21, 23, 24).

Luke's version of the parable thus still features judgment. But in this case, the people bring judgment on themselves by choosing not to attend the banquet. Jack Nelson-Pallmeyer called this "invitational judgment." This invitational judgment by God acknowledges self-exclusion. ". . . God's power cannot force us to live justly or punish us for being unjust. Our acceptance or refusal of the invitation to abundant life has consequences for ourselves and others, but God's invitational power excludes the punishing sanctions of a violent deity."[36] And thus with the alternative endings of this parable from Matthew and Luke in view, it is clear that the conversation about the character of God — violent or nonviolent — that was visible in the Old Testament is now also visible in the Gospels in the parables of Jesus. Other parables and sayings of Jesus also reflect the side of the conversation that has nonviolent images of God.

Invitational judgment is also visible in Jesus' conversation with the man frequently referred to as "the rich young ruler" (Matt. 19:16-30; Mark 10:17-31; Luke 18:18-30). He asked how to be saved. Jesus recounted the well-known commandments about not committing adultery, killing, lying, or stealing and then added one more: "sell your possessions, and give the money to the poor, and you will have treasure in heaven; then come, follow me" (Matt. 19:21). The young man went away grieving because he had great possessions.[37] Jesus' following comments concerned the difficulty that the rich have in entering the kingdom of God. There is nothing here of a violent, punishing God. The young man has selected himself out of the bounty of the kingdom that accrues to those who opt in.[38]

A most important parable to illustrate Jesus' use of a nonviolent image

36. Jack Nelson-Pallmeyer, *Jesus against Christianity: Reclaiming the Missing Jesus* (Harrisburg: Trinity, 2001), 315.

37. As will be discussed further in Chapter 9, Jesus was not asking the young man to give everything away and become destitute. It is likely that the disciples of Jesus had a common purse (see John 12:6). Jesus was asking the young man to live generously with his money and possessions and to trust the common purse for his daily needs.

38. Nelson-Pallmeyer, *Jesus against Christianity*, 316.

of God is the parable of the prodigal son (Luke 15:11-32). After having wasted his inheritance, the prodigal slinks home, hoping for the minimal acceptance of being treated like one of his father's hired hands. But the father has no consideration of making his son submit to such humiliation. He welcomes the prodigal with open arms, offering unmerited love and acceptance, and proclaims a great feast to celebrate his return home. The father, the stand-in for God in the story, is anything but the image of a vengeful God who must exact harsh but deserved punishment to uphold family honor. A more extensive analysis of this parable, its image of God and its application to the atonement discussion, will come in the discussion of forgiveness and atonement images in Chapter 8.

Some parables that have been assumed to feature a violent God have alternative interpretations. The parable of the wicked servants has such an alternative interpretation. In the most common understanding, God is represented by the vineyard owner who sent a troop of soldiers to kill the rebellious servants who had killed the owner's son, equated with the Messiah. Jack Nelson-Pallmeyer provides a different interpretation. In his alternative, it is suggested that Jesus' listeners would have been poor farmers who had firsthand experience with exploitative landowners. These laborers would know how brutal landowners could be and that rebellion was useless: it would only succeed in getting the rebellious laborers killed. Thus, in Nelson-Pallmeyer's view, the laborers would hear the parable as a statement by Jesus that warned them against rebellion. In an increase in the spiral of violence, rebellion would only bring down the greater violence of the landowner. In this view, Jesus is breaking with the common expectation that the coming Messiah would emerge from or provoke a violent revolution and that God would ensure victory through divinely engineered violence. If Jesus is warning against violent revolution, he is then also departing from the idea of a violent God who secures justice through violence.[39] This interpretation, of course, requires acknowledgement that different images of God do in fact appear in the Gospels. And, as with the Old Testament, it requires acknowledgment that the Gospel writers posed materials in ways that were comfortable with or assumed the idea of a violent God.

A further example not usually recognized is Jesus' reference to "the sign of Jonah" (Matt. 16:1). The Pharisees and Sadducees asked Jesus for "a sign from heaven." Nelson-Pallmeyer assumes that they were expecting Je-

---

39. Nelson-Pallmeyer, *Jesus against Christianity*, 256-58, 319-20.

sus to validate their view that a movement of apocalyptic violence was near. He refused to give a sign, saying only that this evil generation seeks a sign, "but no sign will be given to it except the sign of Jonah" (Matt. 16:4). His "conversation partners want assurance that with God's assistance, their enemies will fry. Jesus disappoints them with a story in which God's compassion thwarts the human desire for revenge."[40] The mercy of God in the book of Jonah was portrayed in an earlier section of this chapter.

The discussion in this section has focused on examples of parables and sayings of Jesus that imply or present nonviolent images of God. This material counters the image of a violent and vengeful God that is visible in a number of Jesus' other parables. This material from the parables in the Gospels puts on display that the conversation about the character of God that is so visible in the Old Testament continues in the New Testament as well. A section of this chapter also displayed the assumptions of a violent God that are prominent in the public ethos of the United States. As a whole, the book in hand intends to be the counter to these assumptions of a violent God in the contemporary public arena.

As a part of that counter to the common contemporary assumptions about a violent God, it is necessary to deal with the contrast of violent and nonviolent images of God that extends from the beginning of the Bible through the New Testament. Whether or not they recognize it, in one way or another, modern people are active participants in that discussion. This book engages on the nonviolent side of that discussion.

Chapter 5 takes that conversation further, using the narrative of Jesus as its primary reference point.

---

40. Nelson-Pallmeyer, *Jesus against Christianity*, 294.

5 *The Conversation about God*

Questions about the character of God and God's employment of violence emerged from the discussion of atonement images. The God pictured in the traditional atonement images was a God who used or sanctioned violence to accomplish the divine will. In contrast, the motif called narrative Christus Victor pictured a God who triumphed through resurrection — the restoration of life — rather than offering reconciliation after receiving a blood payment or a death whose satisfying character could be defined in a number of ways. The God who triumphs without violence through restoring life is specifically derived from the narrative of Jesus. Seeing the image of a God who triumphs without violence stimulated further discussion and analysis. For one, in contrast to the frequent assumption that Revelation portrays a violent God and a Jesus who will ultimately triumph through exercise of violence greater than that employed by the evildoers, Chapter 2 put the nonviolent orientation of Revelation on display. Chapter 3 then dealt with several additional challenges to the idea of a nonviolent God. Finally Chapter 4 exposed the conversation about God and violence that exists throughout the Old Testament as well as in the New Testament.

God versus God

The chapter in hand now responds to the imposing challenge posed by the entirety of Chapter 4, namely the challenge of what another large collection of materials from the Bible says. "What about the well-known images

123

in the Old Testament of a violent God or a God who employs violence?" And "What about the declarations of violent judgment attributed to Jesus in the Gospels?" Chapter 4 sampled a variety of materials to put these violent images of God on display, along with references to ways that that violent image of God has remained visible in the culture of the United States, from the earliest colonial times until the present.

But alongside these images of divinely sanctioned violence, Chapter 4 also presented a different picture of God. The analysis of Genesis 1 and 2 demonstrated that the Bible begins with nonviolent images of God. Then followed a discussion of a series of texts that depicted various nonviolent responses to conflict and alternative readings of some texts. What these contrasting accounts make clear is that the Old Testament does not present a uniform picture of God. As Walter Brueggemann was quoted earlier, the Old Testament is "not at all vexed about juxtaposing texts that explicitly contradict each other."[1] It actually contains an ongoing conversation with multiple perspectives and contradictory images of God. The writings of this Testament were produced over hundreds of years. They reflect a history of acts of God or views of God written from the limited, finite perspective of human beings. In the case of poetry, as in the Psalms and some writing by prophets, there is hyperbole and exaggeration. These writings portray multiple views of the character and the characteristics of the God of the Israelites — the Creator, the God of their Fathers Abraham, Isaac and Jacob, the God who saved them in the exodus from Egypt.

Claims of a violent God and contradictory images of God continue in the New Testament. Chapter 2 dealt with the book of Revelation. Chapter 4 extended the conversation to the Gospels, with descriptions of sayings attributed to Jesus that reflect a God of harsh judgment along with sayings that portray a merciful and nonviolent image of God.

The obvious question then arises: Which part of the conversation — the violent references and trajectory or the nonviolent images and trajectory — most truly reflects the character of God? Both trajectories are populated by people, whether the biblical writers themselves or characters in their stories, who claim to be inspired and guided by God. Putting a finger on one text or quoting one particular story will not resolve this apparent dilemma. Quoting these violent stories in the Old Testament or the conclusion of a parable attributed to Jesus in the New Testament is a time-honored method

---

1. Walter Brueggemann, *The Theology of the Old Testament: Testimony, Dispute, Advocacy* (Minneapolis: Fortress, 1997), 32.

used by those who want to preserve the idea of a God who uses or sanctions violence and war. But when these two trajectories or collections of texts are simultaneously in view, or when we hear the conversation between the two collections, no single story or text alone invalidates the alternative view as an authoritative biblical account. Neither trajectory alone, in and of itself, proves which more closely represents the character of God.

An Arbiter: The Narrative of Jesus

Finding a solution to the seeming dilemma posed by the parallel Old Testament accounts and elements of the Gospels requires identifying an arbiter, that is, a reference point that can serve as judge. That arbiter exists. Christians ought to recognize it, actually him. Christians profess that the most complete revelation of God is in Jesus Christ.

Here we do well to recall the brief sketch of the life of Jesus in Chapter 1. He confronted the injustices imposed by the temple leadership and the Roman authorities, but his confrontation was a nonviolent one. He crossed boundaries of race and gender forbidden by purity rules, he plucked grain and healed on the Sabbath counter to purity rules, he challenged the validity of the temple system, through which the priestly class controlled access to God's forgiveness and enriched themselves with the connivance of the Roman occupiers of Palestine. Although his actions were assertive and confrontational, they were done without violence. Such actions give reality to his suggestions for nonviolent challenges that will turn the tables on an aggressor: when insulted as inferior, turn the other cheek; when dunned for inability to pay an unjust debt, give the cloak with the coat; and when compelled to render service to the military, go the second mile. Jesus' principled rejection of violence was made clearly visible in the circumstances of his arrest and trial. He rebuked Peter for using his sword on the servant of the high priest. He chided the mob that arrested him for thinking that they needed to use weapons to capture him. His rejection of violence was clear in his response to Pilate that, since his kingdom was not oriented by the values of this world, his followers were not fighting for him. And finally, rather than starting a violent revolution, he submitted to the cruel execution of crucifixion. This outline makes clear that the nonviolence of Jesus was demonstrated by the way he lived his life. If God is revealed in Jesus, as Christian faith professes, then God should be considered nonviolent as a reflection of the nonviolence of Jesus.

John Howard Yoder locates Jesus' rejection of violence squarely within the historical experience of Israel. In an essay entitled "Jesus the Jewish Pacifist," Yoder reminded us that Jesus did not invent what is anachronistically called pacifism nor the idea that God's people could live in a land without controlling the reins of government.[2] Jesus added deeper and authentically Jewish reasons for pacifism and "not being in charge" of the government. In Yoder's argument, Jesus was carrying forward what was already found in the words of Jeremiah, "seek the welfare of the city where I have sent you into exile" (Jer. 29:7), and practiced in the stories of cultural resistance told in the book of Daniel. Since God was present in the life of Jesus, the life of Jesus reinforces the claim that these practices reflect the reign of God. Yoder's argument is thus applicable to the assertion that the nonviolence of Jesus indicates which side of the conversation in the Old Testament most truly represents the nature of God.[3]

The church that lives in the narrative of Jesus is a continuation of the people of God that began with Abraham.[4] Christians believe that the plotline of the Old Testament comes to fruition in the narrative of Jesus. If

2. John Howard Yoder, "Jesus the Jewish Pacifist," in Yoder, *The Jewish-Christian Schism Revisited*, ed. Michael G. Cartwright and Peter Ochs (Grand Rapids: William B. Eerdmans, 2003), 69-92. Yoder makes a different statement of the same argument in "'See How They Go with Their Face to the Sun,'" in *The Jewish-Christian Schism Revisited*, 183-202.

3. Although Yoder's argument that Jesus is the heir of centuries of Jewish pacifism is quite helpful, I do not follow Yoder's approach as a whole to violence in the Old Testament. Rather than picturing the conversation made visible in Chapter 4, Yoder attempts to appropriate the entire Old Testament for a pacifist faith. He shifts the focus from commands to war to a stress on obedience and argues that faith will no longer resort to such wars. For an in-depth description of this stance by Yoder, see John C. Nugent, *The Politics of Yahweh: John Howard Yoder, the Old Testament and the People of God* (Eugene: Cascade, 2011).

4. This should not be read as a statement of supersessionism, in which the Christian church replaces the descendents of Israel as the people of God. On this point, I follow the argument of Yoder, who wrote that the Jewish-Christian schism did not have to be. He argued that for several centuries, those who believed that the messianic age had begun in Jesus and those who rejected that claim worshiped together in synagogue or church without one side or the other being expelled from the community as heretical. Thus this disagreement need not result in a mutually exclusive schism. The belief that Jesus is the Messiah does not disfranchise Jews as God's people, and we could still be engaged in the discussion of this disagreement as an in-house, family argument among the people of God. See Yoder, *The Jewish-Christian Schism Revisited*. For a parallel argument from a Jewish scholar, see Daniel Boyarin, *Border Lines: The Partition of Judaeo-Christianity* (Philadelphia: University of Pennsylvania Press, 2004); idem, "Judaism as a Free Church: Footnotes to John Howard Yoder's *The Jewish-Christian Schism Revisited*," in *The New Yoder*, ed. Peter Dula and Chris K. Huebner (Eugene: Cascade, 2010), 1-17.

the God of Abraham, Isaac, and Jacob is truly revealed in Jesus and God is fully in Jesus, as Christian faith proclaims, then the God of Jesus cannot be a God who uses or sanctions violence.[5]

It seems clear that the narrative of Jesus, which testifies to the nonviolent character of God, continues the nonviolent side of the Bible's conversation about the character of God. The nonviolent side of the conversation most truly reflects the character of the God revealed in Jesus. As John Dominic Crossan said in his response to the two visions of God within the Bible, "We are bound to whichever of these visions was incarnated by and in the historical Jesus. It is not the violent but the nonviolent God who is revealed to Christian faith in Jesus of Nazareth and announced to Christian faith by Paul of Tarsus."[6]

Similar to Crossan, Jack Nelson-Pallmeyer argues that the narrative of the historical Jesus reveals a nonviolent God. Nelson-Pallmeyer notes that "although nobody can prove that Jesus' life and faith reveal a nonviolent, gracious God, it is possible to make a strong biblical case that this is true. No one can prove that Jesus was nonviolent and that his nonviolence was rooted in his experience of a nonviolent God, but no one can prove the opposite either." Thus he spends the last third of his book developing the case for Jesus' nonviolence and his nonviolent confrontation of the domination system put in place by the priestly class in cooperation with the Roman occupiers of Palestine.[7]

5. This resolution that I bring as a Christian is not the only way to deal with violence in the Old Testament. The leadership of the justice-seeking group Rabbis for Human Rights locates a pacifist orientation in the statement that humankind is made in the image of God (Gen. 1:26-27). It is then argued that human beings may not kill that which is made in the image of God. That beginning point would also stimulate a conversation about the various views of God and divine violence in the Hebrew Scriptures. For another statement of pacifism from a Jewish perspective, see Yoder's statements of the pacifism that Jesus inherited, in "Jewish-Christian Schism," 82-84, and "'See How They Go,'" 191.

6. John Dominic Crossan, *God and Empire: Jesus against Rome, Then and Now* (New York: HarperCollins, 2007), 95. Crossan's description of the two views of God throughout the Old Testament has significant parallels to the description here. However, I differ from Crossan at one crucial juncture. Crossan is concerned to display as equally balanced the violent and nonviolent images throughout the Bible. Thus he argues that Revelation depicts a violent God of judgment and the return of a violent Jesus as the counterpart to a nonviolent return of Jesus in the little apocalypse of Mark 13 (pp. 208-35). In contrast, as I argued in Chapter 2, since Revelation concerns the resurrected Jesus, as its first verse proclaims, its images depict the victory of the nonviolent reign of God through resurrection.

7. Jack Nelson-Pallmeyer, *Jesus against Christianity: Reclaiming the Missing Jesus* (Harrisburg: Trinity, 2001), chapters 19-25, quoting 229.

In dealing with violence in the Old Testament, Eric Seibert's argument is directed at a strongly evangelical audience. Nonetheless, in dealing with stories of violence in the Old Testament and the disturbing question of divine violence, his argument is parallel to that of Crossan and Nelson-Pallmeyer in appealing to the narrative of Jesus. Seibert develops a "christocentric hermeneutic" to address the problem of "disturbing divine behavior in the Old Testament." He argues that "the God Jesus reveals should be the standard, or measuring rod, by which all Old Testament portrayals of God are evaluated." Images of God that do not correspond to the account of Jesus "should be regarded as distortions." In reading the Old Testament stories Seibert suggests that the reader should distinguish between "the textual God and the actual God," and it is "the person of Jesus" that reveals the "moral character" of the actual God.[8]

Brian McLaren also expressed discomfort with the violent images of God in the Old Testament in light of the nonviolent story of Jesus. But rather than picturing two clusters of material throughout the Old Testament with contrasting images of God, McLaren described one stream with diverse images that are nonetheless evolving in an identifiable direction. He wrote that the Bible presents "an ongoing conversation about the character of God," which displays its evolution in the direction of less violence and toward mercy. People let go of their current "state-of-the-art understanding of God when an even better understanding begins to emerge." Such an evolutionary understanding provides one reason for the refusal of the Israelites to tolerate idols. "Idols freeze one's understanding of God in stone, as it were." The biblical culmination of this evolutionary trajectory

---

8. Eric A. Seibert, *Disturbing Divine Behavior: Troubling Old Testament Images of God* (Minneapolis: Fortress, 2009), 185. Jeremy Young also advocates discovering a nonviolent God, although a violent God appears throughout the Old Testament and also in the New. Young locates the nonviolent God in an interpretation of the cross, which reveals that God does not coerce obedience. He writes that a choice to follow Jesus in suffering can be "genuinely redemptive for both the individuals concerned and human communities," but can also become the basis for abuse. He thus cautions that following Jesus in accepting suffering can support oppression, unless "following Christ is the result of genuine self-awareness." He notes that in the face of distorted witnesses of both Testaments, nonetheless in both "there is a genuine, if often obscured, witness to a God who is non-violent and genuinely loving, and who is working to redeem the human race from the cycles of violence and abuse to which it is so often subject." Jeremy Young, *The Violence of God and the War on Terror* (New York: Seabury, 2008), quoting 196, 197. However, Young's argument displays very little of the nonviolent witnesses displayed in the book in hand and almost nothing of Jesus the nonviolent activist portrayed here.

is reached with Jesus. "We can only discern God's character in a mature way from the vantage point of the end of the story, seen in the light of the story of Jesus." McLaren concludes, "The images of God that most resemble Jesus, whether they originate in the Bible or elsewhere, are the more mature and complex images." "The character of the living God is like the character of Jesus." The process of a developing understanding still continues. "If we can look back and see the process unfolding in the past — in the Bible in theological history — then we have no reason to believe that the process has stopped unfolding now."[9]

The presuppositions one brings to the reading of the Bible most certainly shape what the reader will find. Here I have suggested what it might mean to read the Old Testament (as well as contradictory parables attributed to Jesus and the book of Revelation) with the presupposition in mind that the true character of God is revealed in the story of Jesus. Reading with that presupposition in mind reveals a lot of material that belies a violent God and that fits in one way or another with the nonviolent story of Jesus.

The idea of finding images of nonviolence and of a nonviolent God in the Old Testament still has a rather low visibility. Although readers likely recognized many of the stories mentioned in this conversation, newer perhaps is the idea of lining them up together to show a pattern, or at least a wide-ranging picture of a nonviolent God, a God who does not kill, and of practices that reflect that understanding of God. We have long been conditioned not to see a nonviolent God. The prevailing image of a violent God in both Testaments, and lack of familiarity with an alternative image in the same literature, reflect, I suggest, the prevalence of violence in our society and in our history, both as European immigrants and as North Americans.

The Authority of the Bible

Claiming the nonviolent images of God as the true representation of the character of God requires acknowledging that other views of God are distortions or even wrong judgments made by the biblical writers, whether in the Old Testament or in the Gospels. It is the narrative of Jesus, his actions,

---

9. Brian D. McLaren, *A New Kind of Christianity: Ten Questions That Are Transforming the Faith* (New York: HarperOne, 2010), 98-118, quoting 110, 111, 114, 118, 104.

that become the first-level norm for identifying the character of the God revealed in Jesus. But as stated above, use of this narrative requires acknowledging that not only Old Testament writers but also the Gospel writers distorted some of Jesus' teaching. In distinguishing the textual God from the actual God in the Old Testament, Eric Seibert puts it this way:

> I agree with the basic premise that some portrayals of Jesus in the Gospels do not reflect what Jesus actually said or did. It is unnecessary to assume that everything the Gospels say about Jesus accurately reflects the words and deeds of the historical Jesus. They clearly do not, a point that is quite evident when comparing a parallel account in two or more Gospels.[10]

Seibert adds that the distortion in the Gospels is less severe than in the Old Testament.

Jack Nelson-Pallmeyer offers a similar argument. He believes that the Bible "both reveals and distorts God. This opens up the possibility of discerning within scripture a nonviolent Jesus revealing a nonviolent God." Within this complex scripture, the life and faith of Jesus serve as the norm for discovering the character of God. "If we accept that the Gospels offer incompatible portraits of Jesus, then we must sift through diverse images in search of meaning. Jesus' life and faith can help us discern between revelation and distortion. This approach to scripture requires theology to deal with contradictions rather than the smashing of square pegs into round holes."[11] The earlier discussions of atonement imagery and those to follow on judgment, punishment, and forgiveness constitute the kind of theological discussion for which Nelson-Pallmeyer is calling.

Identifying distortions and contradictory images of God and siding with one set of images over the other raises the issue of how to read the Bible and the authority of the accounts that we discover in that reading. If some descriptions and images are declared to be distortions or errors, what kind of book is the Bible? And in what sense is the Bible an authoritative book for Christian readers?

A violent God appears from a supposed straightforward, "flat" or so-called "literal" reading of the Bible's accounts, that is, reading it as a timeless rule book whose injunctions and stories speak immediately to us over a time gap of several thousand years. If a particular story has a statement that God commanded war or a text has an image of a violent God, users of

---

10. Seibert, *Disturbing Divine Behavior,* 187.
11. Nelson-Pallmeyer, *Jesus against Christianity,* 225.

this method believe, then, that the question is settled: God is violent, God employs violent punishment, and God approves war.

Not only does such a reading ignore the presence of the nonviolent side of the conversation about God just described. It poses other problems as well. For one, it produces support not only for war. It also produces injunctions to execute rebellious sons (Deut. 21:18-21), adulterers (22:22-24), and "your brother, your father's son or your mother's son, or your own son or daughter, or the wife you embrace" if he or she entices you to worship other gods (13:6-10). It would rearrange our diets and cooking rules significantly (14:3-21). If we applied the "literal" reading to the examples of the patriarchs Abraham and Jacob and Kings David and Solomon and others, we would be living in polygamous marriages. There are injunctions against mixing types of cloth or planting a second crop in a vineyard (22:9, 11). Some have interpreted Deuteronomy 22:5 as an injunction that would forbid women to wear pants. A few groups have taken the injunction not to trim the edges of a beard (Lev. 19:27) to mean that beards are therefore required. Such examples can be multiplied several times over.

But the more important problem with the flat reading that supposedly applies directly to us across the centuries is that it does not recognize that we are dealing with a historical narrative that shows development over time. I suggest that we allow the Bible's character as a historical narrative to show us how to read it.

The unity of the Bible is provided by a historical narrative, the story of God's people that begins with Abraham and runs through the history of Israel to Jesus and the early church. Implicit throughout the description of both the violent and the nonviolent images of God in the Old Testament was the assumption that the history of the Israelites constitutes the orienting structure, the "backbone," that supplies the unity of the Bible. We read this long-running saga in Genesis, Exodus, Numbers, Joshua, Judges, 1 and 2 Samuel, 1 and 2 Kings, 1 and 2 Chronicles, Ezra, and Nehemiah. Close-up vignettes appear in Ruth, Esther, and parts of Daniel. The books of the prophets present commentary on events all along this history. Psalms presents the worship music of God's people, and Proverbs and Ecclesiastes review some of their wisdom. Leviticus and Deuteronomy contain their early law codes. In the New Testament, the story continues in the four Gospels and Acts. The Epistles provide commentary on the story for the early church. Apocalyptic writings in Daniel and Revelation present a view of events happening in the world from the perspective of the heavenly throne room. This description of the Bible's books could be greatly expanded, but the important point here is to see that it is the narrative of God's people that displays how the various books relate to each other and thus unifies the collection of writings that constitute the Bible.

Acknowledging the narrative character of the Bible is important. For one thing, this understanding makes the Bible's history *our* — that is, Christian — history. We who are self-identified as Christians, the church today, are a continuation of the story of God's people. The story that began with Abraham and goes through Jesus and the early church is the beginning of Christian identity as God's people. This reading displays not just the New Testament but the entire Bible as the Christians' book. When we see that the entire Bible is a history that culminates with Jesus, it becomes obvious that it is the beginning of a story in which we are still living. We are the current version of this long-running and ongoing saga of God's people. The Bible is important because it is *our* story.

Second, seeing the narrative as the unifying factor puts on display that the Bible should be read in terms of its context. Biblical material reflects the particular setting and times in which it was written. Thus it requires our theological discussion in order to determine how to stand in the line of the Bible's history today. All our contemporary statements of theology and ethics are also contextual — they start with awareness of the Bible's context and thus point to the contextual nature of our own theology.

Third, recognizing this story as the unifying element of the Bible impacts greatly how we understand what we find in the pages of the Bible. Seeing this story means that we should expect to see developments and changes, as the people of God grew in their understanding of what it meant to be God's people. We should expect to see instances where people got things wrong, without thereby seeing that recognition as a rejection of the truth of the Bible.

Stated boldly, we should get used to the idea that not all writings in the Bible speak with the same voice, and we can acknowledge that some ideas in it are wrong or misguided and can be abandoned. Thus the most important point of all is to see the direction of changes as the writers grew in their understanding of God. And since the important culmination of the story is in the narrative of Jesus, his story becomes the key to identifying the earlier voices in the story that most truly reflect the will of God.

An analogy may help clarify the difference between a "flat" or literal reading of the Bible and reading it as a historical narrative. What if we read the history of basketball in a flat, ahistorical way, as though the history dictated the rules for playing the game today? I am old enough to remember when basketball players were often called "cagers" and basketball was sometimes referred to as "the cage sport." The name came from the early years of basketball, when some teams played in a cage that separated rough play from spectators. The name stayed around long after the cages disappeared. Many more readers will recall when women played with different rules from men. There were six women per team, but only one woman per team was allowed to run the entire length of the floor. The other team members played only offense or defense and could not pass half-court. They stood at the line and watched, waiting for the action to come to their half of the court. Furthermore, women could only dribble twice, and then had to pass to a teammate. Evidently, behind these antiquated rules was the idea that women were rather delicate and should not exert themselves.

If we read the history of basketball in a flat, direct way, as a story whose past description would speak immediately to us and define the game today, it would condemn all contemporary versions of the game, which are played without cages and allow female players to run the floor and dribble. Of course we do not read the history of basketball in that way. Neither should we read the Bible as a book of transcendent rules and belief statements, existing above history and directly applicable today.

The intent of the analogy is only to show the difference between reading history as a rule book for the present and reading history as the beginning of a long-running story that we are still living. The analogy does not equate the importance of basketball with the Bible's story. Of course the Bible is much more important as a narrative than is the history of basketball. Make no mistake about that.

Acknowledging the narrative character of the Bible does mean that we no longer read it as a book that stands alone, above history and apart from a context, as though it speaks transcendent truth across the centuries and with direct application to our setting. No longer is it a book of examples of both good and bad behavior that apply immediately to our contexts. It is nonetheless the book that orients us in the world as Christians.

The Bible is a history book, but obviously a very important history book. It is by far the best source available on the origin of the people of God. It is this history that orients us and sets a direction for us in the world. It is in the history of origins that one discovers the ideas and practices that oriented what is now the Christian movement and continue to point the direction in which it should be going today. The task of the contemporary people of God is not to copy the earliest shape of the movement, as though it were possible to transport a movement over two or three thousand years and plant it again today. Rather the task is to continue the movement in a way and a direction true to its origins but also in conversation with the contemporary context, which differs greatly from the times of origin. Even though basketball players no longer play in cages and women run the full court, one can still clearly see that modern basketball is in continuity with the origins of the game. For Christians, the most defining moment of their story is the life, death, and resurrection of Jesus. It is in Jesus' life that the long-running saga that began with Abraham comes to its most definitive moment. We in the twenty-first century are now asking how best to continue this movement in a way that truly reflects the story of Jesus, which carries forward the story of the people of God that began with Abraham.

Understanding the historical orientation of the Bible brings to the fore the fact that the narrative implies and portrays development and change. The fact that movement and change are visible within the biblical narrative itself makes it possible to identify trajectories of change. By the time of the New Testament, for example, there had been a movement away from the polygamy practiced by the patriarchs and the kings of Israel. In another shift, there is a clear move toward less violence, which culminates with Jesus' rejection of violence. Changes occur in the way that Jesus is identified. Six times in the book of Acts the writer describes the brief narrative of Jesus used by the Apostles to identify Jesus in the months immediately after his death and resurrection (Acts 2:14-39; 3:13-26; 4:10-12; 5:30-32; 10:36-43; 13:17-41). Paul repeats that outline (1 Corinthians 15) but adds a point not made earlier, namely that the resurrection of Jesus requires belief in a general resurrection of the dead. Some decades later, as the eyewitnesses to Jesus began to die, the narrative outline visible in Acts was expanded by the four Gospel writers with their own input. New Testament interpreters took the story of Jesus into other worldviews and used the images from these diverse frames of reference to say that with his life, death, and resurrection Jesus was both above and below the cosmology of those worldviews — the Greek Logos (John 1), principalities and powers (Colossians 1), the high priest (Hebrews), a new Adam (Philippians 2), the slain Lamb (Revelation 4 and 5).[12] Meanwhile, the church in Acts expanded the circle of God's people to include Gentiles, abandoned the requirement of circumcision, allowed foods previously deemed unclean, and abandoned many other ancient laws.

These developments and changes all involved decisions about how to

12. This development in Christology will be discussed in more detail in Chapter 6.

communicate the gospel of Jesus Christ effectively in new contexts and to address new issues as the early church expanded beyond Jerusalem. Sometimes new insight was extracted from the story. Other times minds were changed about acceptable conduct.

With changes occurring, it should be obvious that different viewpoints appear in the Bible, and thus contemporary interpreters are not obligated to harmonize or synthesize everything the Bible may say on a particular question. In fact, with the changes along a trajectory made visible, contemporary interpreters should recognize that it is impossible to harmonize all views in the Bible. In the example just noted, it is not possible to harmonize the blessing of marriage to multiple wives with a clear endorsement of monogamous marriage. And in the argument of this book, if God (or the character of God) is revealed in Jesus, the violent and nonviolent images of God cannot be reconciled.

Changes have obviously continued in the Christian story in the centuries after the Bible. An example concerns slavery, which appears in several forms in the Bible. It was well into the nineteenth century before many Christians could accept a movement away from endorsement of slavery. More recently, another example comes from the status of women in the church. Beginning in the last century, challenges to long-held views on the status and role of women in the church began to appear. Since then there has been significant movement toward acknowledging the equal status of women and recognizing that women can and should have the right to hold any and all offices and to perform any function within the church. Although Christians still lack unanimity on this issue, movement is clearly in the direction of full equality for women in the church, even though the Bible contains a mixed message on this question.

Most recently, some Christians have come to believe that the church's longstanding opposition to homosexuality contradicts the welcoming stance of Jesus, who associated with a spectrum of diverse people. As a result, although the moves are still controversial, some congregations and denominations have taken steps to welcome gays and lesbians into membership, to allow their ordination, and most recently to provide blessings on committed relationships and marriages for same-sex couples. The Christian church generally may be in the midst of another historical change of direction. In light of the history of changes visible in the Bible and then in the history of Christianity, these moves to expand the church's welcome to gays and lesbians ought not surprise.

The primary focus of the book in hand concerns the Bible's presentation of divine violence and its violent images of God. The argument of the book is that longstanding views on the violence of God and God's sanction of violence should change. The key to understanding the direction of this particular conversation is the narrative of Jesus. In fact, it is the narrative of Jesus that puts on display that movement had occurred in the conversation about divine violence visible in the Bible, and that the particular conversation about divine violence has a culmination. When we observe that the Bible presents a narrative, a history, we can see the direction in which the story is developing. Seeing Jesus as the continuation of this narrative makes it obvious that the nonviolent side of the conversation is the part of the story that most truly reveals the character of God. If Christians put in practice what the idea of a nonviolent God means for the character of the reign of God made visible in Jesus, the face of Christianity in the world would change markedly.

The Bible is the church's book because it contains the story of the church's origins. Without this document, we would know very little about the beginning of the story that began with Abraham. But the Bible is the church's book for another reason as well. We are called *Christians*. The Bible is by far the best source to the life, teaching, death, and resurrection of Jesus. We read the Bible because it contains the story of the one who defines the primary identity of Christians, namely Jesus Christ, and displays his story as the continuation of the story that began with Abraham. It is in his story that we learn the nonviolent character of God. Stated differently, the words of the Bible are important, but they are not the primary authority. The ultimate authority for Christians is the narrative of Jesus that is contained in the words of the Bible. Or as Brian McLaren said in yet another way, "Look through the Bible to look at Jesus, and you will see the character of God shining radiant and full."[13]

The move of Christians to recognize the nonviolent character of God has been exceedingly slow. Until quite recently it was not even recognized that the Bible had a conversation on divine violence.[14] Although the conversation is engaged at the beginning of the twenty-first century, it is still a minority position. The hope and prayer for this book is that it moves

13. McLaren, *A New Kind of Christianity*, 118.

14. In addition to references to the arguments for the nonviolence of God cited throughout this book, the nonviolence of God was pointed to in the first edition (2001) of my book *The Nonviolent Atonement*. For other early arguments for a nonviolent God, see the components of a symposium on the subject: "Is God Nonviolent? A Mennonite Symposium," *The Conrad Grebel Review* 21 (2003): 5-55.

Christians in the direction of nonviolence, following the earlier movements away from polygamy, slavery, and patriarchy and toward recognition of the equality of women. In this movement toward accepting the nonviolence of God, when the Bible is read from the perspective of the nonviolence of Jesus, its story from Genesis to Revelation constitutes primary evidence for the nonviolence of God.

It should be emphasized that describing the conversation about divine violence and then appealing to the narrative of Jesus to identify the side of the conversation that most truly represents God is *not* a "picking and choosing" of preferred texts, nor is it discarding a part of the Bible. Nothing is being read out of the canon. Reading from the perspective of Jesus' life requires seeing the entire text of Scripture. Only with the complete text in view does the conversation in the text about divine violence become visible. No editor sanitized or harmonized the contradictions. The existence of the contradictions and unsavory accounts of divinely commanded massacres points to the authenticity of the ancient text. And only with this unexpurgated version in view do we see that there is an unfolding understanding that comes to fruition in Jesus and the view of God revealed in Jesus.[15]

---

15. Ron Sider vigorously disputes my atonement arguments as well as the arguments in this book for the nonviolence of God. See his "A Critique of J. Denny Weaver's *Nonviolent Atonement*," *Brethren in Christ History and Life* 35 (2012): 214-41. Sider claims biblical authority as the basis of his disagreement, which means little more than that he interprets the Bible differently than I do. He assumes that biblical accounts prove God's violence, while contradictions in the image of God are accounted for by claiming that we cannot know everything about God. The argument concerning the Trinity is dismissed by the claim that Jesus does not reveal everything about God. Sider assumes that all atonement motifs are unquestioned givens with the accompanying assumption that all theories are biblical. In essence, Sider's methodology fits individual biblical texts into the unquestioned atonement images, accompanied by the claim that any other interpretation violates biblical truth. In his conclusion, then, internal problems and contradictions within the motifs are ignored, and problems with one view are compensated for by another view. This approach means that Sider does not acknowledge the possibility of development within the biblical story and does not fathom alternative biblical interpretations such as those quoted from David Brondos. Sider also shows no evidence of understanding the feudal background from which Anselm developed the idea of satisfaction as an atonement motif, nor does he acknowledge the sequence in which Christus Victor was rejected by Anselm in favor of satisfaction, which was in turn rejected by Abelard. One can claim that these historically incompatible motifs are complementary rather than intrinsically incompatible only by ignoring the historical rejections and elevating the motifs to the level of unquestioned givens. Nonetheless, in spite of these major disagreements, Sider affirms my emphases on the nonviolence of Jesus and that nonviolence

Anger, Wrath, and Judgment

In view of the argument for the nonviolence of God, anger and wrath attributed to the God of Israel merit specific discussion. Divine anger is neither surprising nor inappropriate when people suffer injustice or rebel against the reign of God. The discussion, however, concerns not anger itself but the different views expressed by the biblical writers on how God expressed that anger. Some Old Testament writers depicted events — the exodus, successes in battle — as though God were directly involved in killing or in commanding armies to massacre. It is not surprising that prophetic writing rejoices at the thought of God's wrath descending on the perpetrators of injustice and attribute the death of enemies to God. These are authentic parts of the conversation. But other parts of the conversation depict conflict resolution without violence or depict a God who shows mercy. In some cases, we observed alternative interpretations of presumed violent texts. These differences become significant in light of the confession that God is revealed in the life, death, and resurrection of Jesus. Viewed from the perspective of Jesus, it is evident that images of a violent God were distortions or even errors by the biblical writers.

In and of themselves, expressions of God's anger and wrath are not contrary to the idea of a nonviolent God, that is, a God revealed in Jesus who acts not to destroy life but to restore life. Anger and wrath — which some might wish to restate as righteous indignation — directed against injustice is appropriate. Recall material referenced in Chapter 2 from Raymund Schwager, N. T. Wright, and Rob Bell. Schwager wrote that statements and threats of divine wrath were the equivalent of handing evildoers over to the consequences of their evil deeds. Wright provided a parallel argument. Following death and the restoration of all things, those who throughout their lifetime chose to worship that which is not God will become fully what they have chosen. They will not be consigned to a divinely run concentration camp or torture chamber, but by their own choice they

---

belongs intrinsically to Christian discipleship. In effect, Sider agrees with me in seeing the problems of violent images of God and of violence in traditional atonement motifs, but disagrees on how to respond. I suggested that the narrative of Jesus was the norm and that biblical exegesis and critique of the inherited images should proceed on the basis of that norm. In contrast, Sider assumes the classic images are unquestioned givens. They thus become the norm to which he conforms interpretation of the narrative of Jesus and the basis for his critique of my construction of atonement. In my view, his procedure is a de facto identification of an authority different from and higher than Jesus Christ.

will become creatures who no longer reflect the image of their Creator and are beyond hope and sympathy. Rob Bell made a similar claim in displaying God as a God of love. A loving God, Bell argues, desires the salvation of all people. However, even when their deeds anger that loving God, God respects the freedom of people to choose evil. The biblical writers correctly depict God's anger at those who continue in the way of evil, and they depict God's threatened wrath against such evildoers. But with that threatened wrath, God does not change character. God is always a loving God. The threatened wrath is the consequence, the "hell" that people create for themselves, Bell says, if they continue to choose evil. And the point of the harsh and threatening language is correction, the hope that making visible the consequences will lead people to repent and change their lives.[16] In this way, the "hell" that people create need not have the final word.

Note the tangible righteous anger in accounts of Jesus' speeches and his actions. In discussing the responses to John the Baptist and himself, Jesus accused the crowds of being like petulant children who complain regardless of the game suggested: "We played the flute for you, and you did not dance; we wailed and you did not weep" (Luke 7:32). Certainly some anger — righteous indignation — was behind the words when he blistered the scribes and Pharisees in Matthew 23 (and also lawyers in the parallel text in Luke 11). They lay "heavy burdens" on others, they love to be seen and to sit in the high places, and more. Then follows a series of declarations of "woe" on scribes and Pharisees, called "hypocrites," whom he accuses directly of expending great efforts in making a convert and then "you make the new convert twice as much a child of hell as yourselves." Jesus calls them "blind fools," and the epithet "hypocrites" appears four more times. They profess a false piety of hairsplitting interpretations of the law and detailed tithing while neglecting "justice and mercy and faith." This false piety gives them the appearance of dishes that are clean outside but dirty inside and of "whitewashed tombs, which on the outside look beautiful, but inside they are full of the bones of the dead and of all kinds of filth" (Matt. 23:13-28).

Then follow threats. "How can you escape being sentenced to hell?" Following their violent treatment of prophets who warn them, it is said

16. Raymund Schwager, *Jesus in the Drama of Salvation* (New York: Crossroad, 1999), 163-65; N. T. Wright, *Surprised by Hope: Rethinking Heaven, the Resurrection, and the Mission of the Church* (New York: HarperCollins, 2008), 182-83; Rob Bell, *Love Wins: A Book About Heaven, Hell, and the Fate of Every Person Who Ever Lived* (New York: HarperOne, 2011), chapters 3 and 4.

that "upon you may come all the righteous blood shed on earth, from the blood of righteous Abel to the blood of Zechariah son of Barachiah, whom you murdered between the sanctuary and the altar. Truly I tell you, all this will come upon this generation" (Matt. 23:33, 35-36). One can read these as threats of violence. However, one may just as well read them as statements that acknowledge the "hell" to which evildoers condemn themselves.

It is following these expressions of outrage at practices of the scribes and Pharisees that Jesus wept over Jerusalem. "Jerusalem, Jerusalem, the city that kills the prophets and stones those who are sent to it! How often have I desired to gather your children together as a hen gathers her brood under her wings, and you were not willing!" (Matt. 23:37). Such anger certainly fueled Jesus' protest in what is called the cleansing of the temple. "My house shall be called a house of prayer; but you are making it a den of robbers" (21:13)

The question is not whether injustice provokes anger. It is, rather, how that anger is expressed and by whom or through whom it is carried out. As a good observer of the scene, Jesus certainly knew of the growing sentiment for violent revolt against Rome. He counseled against that revolt, which would certainly produce devastating consequences for Jerusalem, which in fact happened with the invasion and destruction of the city in 70 CE. In particular, the alternative interpretation of the parable of the wicked tenants noted in Chapter 4 sees it as explicit counsel against violent revolution. The residents of Palestine encountered humiliating conditions and situations in which violent responses were certainly thinkable and understandable. But Jesus said not to return evil for evil and suggested ways to counter such insults with nonviolent but active responses: turn the other cheek, give the cloak with the coat, go the second mile. And as was noted earlier, Jesus' anger in the temple harmed no one but did expose corruption and offer the perpetrators opportunities for change.

An obvious contrast exists between the nonviolent statements of Jesus in Matthew 5–7 and the vehement rhetoric attributed to Jesus in Matthew 23. I have just argued that anger in and of itself is not wrong, but that the important point is how anger is expressed. From that view, I called the vehement language attributed to Jesus understandable expressions of anger, while emphasizing that Jesus expressed that anger through nonviolent action. John Dominic Crossan offers a different but convincing interpretation that falls within the approach to the Bible's violence outlined above. Writers who depicted a violent God in either the Old Testament or a Gospel, it is said, had a distorted image of God. Crossan attributes the violent rhetoric of Matthew 23 to the writer's increasingly vehement participation on the side of Christian Jews against Pharisaic Jews at the time that Matthew was written. Written in the 80s, the Gospel according to Matthew "represents an *intra*-familial clash *in Judaism* between Christian-Jewish scribes and Pharisaic-Jewish scribes." Such a family quarrel can be "extremely bitter." The unfortunate result of putting this rhetoric in Jesus' mouth, Crossan says, is that it opens Jesus to the charge of hypocrisy, given the contrast of Matthew 5 and Matthew 23. Thus Crossan concludes, "the Jesus of Matthew is regularly and rhetorically violent, but that is not Jesus himself; it is Matthew who is speaking."[17]

For some readers, portraying the God revealed in Jesus Christ as a nonviolent God or a God who does not kill may appear to threaten the sovereignty and omnipotence of God.[18] How can a God who does not kill and exercise violence have full sovereignty, it might be argued.

In actuality, however, the sovereignty and omnipotence of God are on display in what we know about the cyclical nature of violence and the ongoing legacy of oppression and exploitation passed from generation to generation. These evils that continue to oppress become visible and are pointed to when, as was just noted, evildoers are handed over to the consequences of their evil deeds.

Violence arouses hostility, which seeks an opportunity for revenge. Violence administered will eventually attract more violence in retaliation. Violence and oppression continue to cycle from one generation to the next, and it reaps its reward. The children of people who abuse alcohol and other chemicals inherit problems that can return to harm the parents as well as be passed on to another generation. This cycle is visible in the ongoing conflicts among nations. Rather well-known to historians is the observation that a humiliating peace treaty forced on the losing Germans after the First World War fostered resentment that would fester and become the soil in which the National Socialist party of Adolf Hitler could take root.

The oppression wrought by colonial powers in Africa produced angry rebellion and created conditions that continue to plague following generations after the countries have been freed from colonial rule. The United States is still suffering from the evil of slavery, the racism that supported it,

---

17. John Dominic Crossan, *The Power of Parable: How Fiction by Jesus Became Fiction about Jesus* (New York: HarperCollins, 2012), chapter 4, quoting 194-95, emphasis original.

18. See the arguments of John Sanders and Greg Boyd, referenced in Chapter 4, note 15.

and the injustice of abandoning freed slaves in poverty. That retaliation only provokes more retaliation appears many times over in the Middle East, whether the case of Israelis and Palestinians, or U.S. wars in Iraq and Afghanistan, where invasion and occupation are claimed to solve a problem caused by terrorism (which was already a response to perceived injustice), but have only produced new, alternating rounds of violent responses. This cyclical character of violent response is visible in the Bible's stories of Israel's interaction with her neighbors. Note the rise and fall of Egyptian, Syrian, Assyrian and Babylonian empires, their attacks on Israelites, alliances that provoke other alliances, and more.

It is not only pacifist or nonviolent Christians who observe this cycle of violence and retribution. It is visible in Mahatma Gandhi's oft-quoted dictum, "An eye for an eye and the whole world goes blind." Badshah Khan (1890-1988) constitutes a less well-known but equally striking example. Khan was a product of the vengeance-oriented culture of Pashtun Moslems in the region of the Afghanistan-Pakistan border. However, Khan came to the realization that his society's cycle of vengeance killings accomplished nothing. He swore off killing. In 1929, he organized the Khudai Khidmatgar or "Servants of God." It was a nonviolent "army" of 100,000 Pashtun Muslims, dedicated to social reform and to ending British rule in an as-yet undivided India. Khan came to live with Gandhi as an equal collaborator, and his 100,000-man movement played an important role in social reform and the drive for independence.[19] Like Gandhi, he was sorely disappointed by the separation between Muslims and Hindus after Indian independence.

That Hindus and Muslims as well as Christians can perceive the futility of continuing the cycle of violence brings to mind a comment from John Howard Yoder. He noted that discussions of moral theology intersect with debates in other disciplines about human nature and the shape of society. As one example, he suggested that if a religious spokesman says that "violence is always self-defeating," that is a claim "that a historian could verify or refute."[20] This intersection of disciplines must be true, if as Yoder said elsewhere, to align with the nonviolence of the reign of God made vis-

19. Eknath Easwaran, *Nonviolent Soldier of Islam: Badshah Khan, a Man to Match His Mountains* (Tomales: Nilgiri, 1999); Amitabh Pal, *"Islam" Means Peace: Understanding the Muslim Principle of Nonviolence* (Santa Barbara: Praeger, 2011), 97-123.

20. John Howard Yoder, "From the Wars of Joshua to Jewish Pacifism," in Yoder, *The War of the Lamb: The Ethics of Nonviolence and Peacemaking,* ed. Glen Harold Stassen, Mark Thiessen Nation, and Matt Hamsher (Grand Rapids: Brazos, 2009), 125.

ible in Jesus is to work "with the grain of the universe."[21] And since aligning with nonviolence does go with the grain of the universe, as is identifiable in the narrative of Jesus, it is possible for Hindus and Muslims also to sense and discover that grain.

Words invoking divine wrath and judgment function as warnings. They forewarn those who practice violence and oppression and injustice that their evil will eventually consume them. Unless they change their ways, they condemn themselves. The cyclical nature of violence and the ongoing legacy of racism and colonial exploitation are examples of this self-condemnation. They align with the biblical statements that threaten destruction on those who continue to choose the way of evil, violence, and destruction. The Old Testament writers rightly describe God's anger at human sin and disobedience, and those who offend God rightly fear the wrath of God. Meanwhile the God of those warnings allows evil the freedom to condemn and consume itself, sometimes on this earth, and most certainly in the eschaton. And as the discussion of forgiveness in the following chapter displays, the God of those warnings is a loving God who forgives and accepts those who repent. Throughout his book *Love Wins*, Rob Bell rightly argues that God does not change from loving to vindictive and judgmental at a person's death: God is always loving and waiting for individuals and groups to turn from evil and embrace the rule of God. And the Prophets and Psalmists rightly stand in awe and glorify the God who can bring the divine wrath to bear as well as reward the righteous while respecting the freedom of human beings to disobey God. The words of the Decalogue were not idle when they spoke of God "punishing children for the iniquity of parents to the third and fourth generation of those who reject me" (Exod. 20:5; also Num. 14:18 and Deut. 5:9).

This view of divine judgment does not threaten the sovereignty of God, but it does put on display that the sovereignty of God is ultimately eschatological. From the viewpoint of the nonviolence of God, the sovereignty and omnipotence of God are displayed in the ability of God to reverse the worst that human evil can accomplish, which is to destroy existence by killing. God's response is to reverse that evil with resurrection. The resurrection of Jesus is the guarantee that all people will one day be raised as Jesus was raised, as Paul proclaimed in 1 Corinthians 15:12-20. God's sovereignty is the capacity of God to accomplish the divine will de-

21. See note 28 below.

spite anything that the powers of evil can do to oppose the will of God, even including the killing of Jesus, God's anointed one.

This statement of omnipotence and sovereignty is a statement of eschatology. The ultimate victory of the reign of God awaits the final consummation with the return of Jesus. This victory and culmination are assured by the resurrection of Jesus. Meanwhile, in the interim, although evil has been defeated and evidence of that defeat appears in such things as the cyclical nature of violence, evil nonetheless still has freedom to cause harm. The image of the defeated dragon in Revelation 12 illustrates this freedom. Although defeated by the resurrection of Jesus, believers are warned that the dragon — the Roman Empire — still has the capacity to persecute. One can compare facing the ongoing but defeated evil in the world to being on the winning side in the fourth quarter of a football game in which the outcome has already been determined. The deciding moment of the game occurred at the end of the first half when the winning team — our team — capitalized on opponents' errors and scored a bundle of points to put the game out of reach. That scoring spree is like the resurrection. The game continues, players may be injured, perhaps even intentionally, but the outcome is determined.[22] The reign of God is victorious, God is sovereign, even as suffering and evil are still present.

What is at stake in this discussion is not the idea of divine judgment per se. The idea that God respects human freedom absolutely calls for the concept of judgment. The idea of divine judgment is a recognition that human beings can in fact choose against God. The same point can be made with the idea that a loving God respects the absolute freedom of human beings to make that choice. So judgment is an expression of God's love as a respect for that human choice.

What is being challenged in this discussion is the traditional understanding of last judgment as the time when God finally employs overwhelming violence to vanquish evil and sends sinners to a hell of eternal, never-ending torture in a lake of fire. Countless sermons, all with good intentions, have threatened sinners with this fire as a means of scaring them into accepting salvation in Jesus Christ. In the perspective of eternity, the time of a person's life is a mere speck when compared to never-ending tor-

22. I recall such an NFL playoff game a number of years ago. Playing in freezing rain, the winning team, already leading, capitalized on the other team's fumbles of a slick ball to score 17 points in 48 seconds at the end of the first half. The TV announcers proclaimed that, given the miserable playing conditions, the trailing team could not rally and that the outcome of the game was determined. It was.

ture. What I reject in this regard is the idea of a God with, as N. T. Wright put it, "a concentration camp" or a "torture chamber" in the restored heaven on earth.[23] The nonviolent God made visible in Jesus is, very simply put, not compatible with the idea that at the moment of death, a loving God becomes a God who condemns a soul to unending torture, the torture of unbearable pain forever.

No one really knows what happens after death. We have very few clues. The most important clue is the resurrection of Jesus, which means that God overcomes the annihilation of existence and that something follows physical death. Because Jesus preached the reign of God and called people to identify with it as the place that God is found, it is clear that how we live does make a difference. Observation of the world around us makes visible how evil deeds produce more evil responses, which continue to entrap people through the generations. Since resurrection will happen to all souls, it seems evident that those who are identified with the God made visible in Jesus in this life will continue in that status in the resurrected life. But how that status continues is more than we can know. (The conclusion of this book offers a suggestion.) And neither can we know specifically what transpires with those who rejected the reign of God in this life. What we can say is that the God revealed in Jesus is a nonviolent and loving God, who is always ready to forgive and receive those who repent.

It is obvious that the claim that Jesus' rejection of violence reveals that God is nonviolent and that God refuses to kill does not answer every question about God or say everything that we would like to know about God. That God is nonviolent is as much or more a claim about what *not* to say about God as it is a positive affirmation of the character of God. It is a statement that we should not make claims that God kills, however that killing might be sanitized with euphemisms. It must mean that God would not engage in torture, however comforting we might find the idea of violent, divine vengeance on evil and our most despised evildoers. That God is nonviolent has implications for our understanding of the sovereignty of God. It means that evil and destruction and killing in the world are the responsibility of sinful human beings rather than of God, which means that the sovereignty of God is understood as working the divine will in spite of sin that opposes the will of God. This sovereignty is revealed in the story of Jesus Christ and made manifest in the resurrection, which is the restoration of life where it had ceased to exist.

---

23. Wright, *Surprised by Hope*, 182.

The question of whether we should have nonviolent images of God may seem like an abstract question. But it is more than that. It has a profound impact on how we live, as the following section suggests.

Why It Matters

This book began with the stated intent of producing theology for living. More specifically, it presents theology that undergirds living in the nonviolent story of Jesus. With the assumption in mind that theology starts with the narrative of Jesus, I have argued that this narrative is a story of salvation whose culminating act is God's resurrection of Jesus. Resurrection constitutes God's invitation to us to live in that story as followers of Jesus, which makes the Christian life an extension of Jesus' presence in the world. Since Jesus rejected the sword, a call to live in Jesus' life becomes a call toward rejecting violence. Since the God of Abraham, Isaac, and Jacob is present in this story as the God who raised Jesus, the story arrives at the importance of picturing God with nonviolent images. And a nonviolent image of God thus requires a new reading of the Old Testament, which has traditionally been appealed to in support of the idea of a God who uses and sanctions violence.

Portraying theology for living in the story of Jesus as *Christian* theology is important. This Christian theology derived from the nonviolent narrative of Jesus highlights important characteristics of various forms of received, traditional Christian theology. This theology derived from the narrative of Jesus poses a contrast to the traditional atonement motifs, which say little or nothing of the life and teaching of Jesus, culminate with the death of Jesus, and place resurrection in a different section of the outline. At the least, such traditional theology does not seriously challenge or reject the violence that is contrary to the story of Jesus and the God revealed in Jesus' story, and at times it encourages violence. In Chapter 3, readers could follow the argument of Rita Nakashima Brock and Rebecca Parker that Anselm's satisfaction atonement encouraged people to join the first crusade. Feminists and womanists have argued that images of God and of the suffering of Jesus in satisfaction atonement encourage contemporary women to submit to abuse. The dispensationalist reading of Revelation features a violent God and a violent Jesus, who will use excessive violence to wipe out God's enemies in the end times. Many dispensationalists support a strong United States military force as well as military involvement in the Middle East because they believe that America's military forces will be involved in Armageddon, what they believe will be a future final conflagration in the Middle East. This belief not only assumes a violent God but also puts God on the side of the harassment and oppression administered to Palestinians. Then there are the attempts to interpret catastrophes today as divine vengeance on a sinful nation, which follow some accounts in the Old Testament.

Together these examples portray a consistent and comprehensive image of a God who uses and sanctions violence. Salvation for sinners comes through violence, the innocent death of Jesus that was needed to satisfy offended divine honor and restore order in the cosmos. Divine punishment is administered by the violence of marauding armies, whether those punishing Israel in the Old Testament or the planes of terrorists in North America. Other times, natural disasters are invoked as divine judgment, whether on the U.S. or its enemies. This biblical usage and these theological statements all place a divine seal of approval on violence at all levels from personal salvation to cosmic justice. Such biblical and theological claims concerning divine violence take on an extra sharp profile when they are juxtaposed with the profession that God is revealed in the Jesus who rejected the sword.

Now combine this multilevel divine sanction on violence with the easy references to war and war imagery in our everyday language. "War" has become a metaphor for opposition to anything that people oppose seriously, as in "war on poverty," "war on drugs," the "culture wars," the "war on cancer," "weapons in the war against HIV." Military metaphors abound in the sports world. A good athlete in any sport may be said to have a "killer instinct." A football player calls his teammates "the guys I go to war with." TV announcers burble about "the war in the trenches" or "the war on the glass." Good players are called "weapons in the coach's arsenal," quarterbacks throw "the bomb," and baseball players have "a gun" or "a cannon" for an arm. We are surrounded by easily accepted war metaphors and a theology that assumes that God approves of war and sanctions violence. This omnipresent, quasi-tangible, and visible violence makes violence appear normal, a commonsense given. It just seems to be the way the universe operates.

What is the potential impact of such a view of God accompanied by the continual, positive, metaphorical references to war? Timothy Gorringe has shown the correlation between satisfaction atonement and the practice of harsh penalties in the judicial system in European history since

Anselm.[24] Stanley Grenz wrote that when the law of the state replaced the honor of the feudal ruler as the basis of social order, theologians came to view sin as violation of civil law, with government as the avenger or means to exact penalty.[25] For one example, the image of God from substitutionary atonement has shaped the demands for justice of conservative Protestants in the conflict in Northern Ireland.[26]

In a different kind of imaging, recent news stories reported in the popular media recount research that points to an increase of violent behavior in children who spend time playing violent video games.[27] Saturday morning cartoons often picture violence among characters in humorous fashion, teaching children that violence can be fun and that it solves problems. Then there is the well-known impact of advertising — how through repetition and projection of images it works subliminally to create a need for a product where none previously existed. Advertising would not work and advertisers would not pay for it if people were not impacted by what they hear and see. Research findings clearly demonstrate the impact of images and practices on the minds of both children and adults.

With this data in mind, consider the potential impact on our minds of continual references to and images of an almighty God, who sanctioned massacres in the Old Testament, who brought salvation through sanctioned violence on Jesus, who uses human armies and terrorists and natural disasters to wreak judgment on evil people and evil nations, and who can and will turn to great violence in dealing with evil in final judgment. Does it surprise that through the centuries, people claiming a God of this stripe, with violence an intrinsic element of divine working, might end up justifying violence under a variety of divinely anchored claims and images, might become comfortable with a violence-based system of criminal justice and positive images of war in everyday society, and might enjoy violence in entertainment whether in cartoons, adult movies, or sports? It seems far from a mere conjecture that there may be a reciprocal relation-

24. Timothy Gorringe, *God's Just Vengeance: Crime, Violence and the Rhetoric of Salvation* (Cambridge Studies in Ideology and Religion 9; Cambridge: Cambridge University Press, 1996).

25. Stanley J. Grenz, *Theology for the Community of God* (Nashville: Broadman and Holman, 1994), 450.

26. Alwyn Thomson, *Fields of Vision: Faith and Identity in Protestant Ireland* (Belfast: Centre for Contemporary Christianity in Ireland, 2002), chapter 4.

27. A quick Google search reveals many such items.

ship between imaging a God who uses violence on the one hand and human comfort with a resort to violence on the other.

Theology that models violence (atonement motifs, image of God) in a sense is also theology for living. This theology, too, gives meaning to activities and claims a link between God and Christian behavior.

Since both violent and nonviolence-shaped theology confess the name of Jesus Christ, this situation might appear to pose a dilemma. At the least it poses a choice among theologies. One option is to continue to espouse theology from within the time-honored, multifaceted tradition that is comfortable with the idea that God exercises violence and with the exercise of violence by Christians in the name of God. I have attempted to give visibility to this theology.

The other option rejects violent images of God, and displays the victory of God through resurrection — the restoration of life — rather than through violence and the taking of life. These pages have presented such a theology. In choosing between these options, my view is obvious. I believe that living within the narrative of Jesus and extending the presence of Jesus in the world require a theology that puts on display Jesus' nonviolent way of making shalom visible against the injustices of the world. Living in this theology then is a lived expression of the belief that the character of God is revealed in the life and teaching of Jesus. And mention of the character of God brings us to the character of the universe that God created. Thus living within the story of Jesus is truly living and working with what John Howard Yoder called "the grain of the universe." It is to align with what Martin Luther King, Jr. famously called the long arc of the moral universe that "bends toward justice."[28] Do Christians believe in the resurrection of Jesus enough actually to accept the invitation it offers to live in his story, to work with the grain of the universe as it bends toward justice?

When compared with the traditional and prevalent theological options that espouse or model violence seemingly at all levels, this suggested theology does seem to indicate a new direction for living in the world. In the words of Brian McLaren, it is a "revolution of hope [that] makes radical demands of us. It requires us to learn new skills and habits and capaci-

---

28. John H. Yoder, "Armaments and Eschatology," *Studies in Christian Ethics* 1 (1988): 58. A parallel comment on "the grain of the cosmos" is in John Howard Yoder, *The Politics of Jesus: Vicit Agnus Noster* (2d ed.; Grand Rapids: William B. Eerdmans, 1994), 246. For King, see Martin Luther King, Jr., "Where Do We Go from Here?" in *A Call to Conscience: The Landmark Speeches of Dr. Martin Luther King, Jr.*, ed. Clayborne Carson and Kris Shepard (New York: Warner, 2001), 199.

ties: . . . a new way of seeing, . . . of thinking, . . . of living. . . . It is a new way of life that changes everything."[29] The theology presented here will not halt violence. That I know very well. But I do hope to show that violence is antithetical to Christian faith. Perhaps this thought will slow the easy association of Christian faith and the Christian God with violence. After all, if more Christians actually lived this theology, the world would be much more peaceful.

This chapter has established the basis for a lived Christian theology that is derived from the narrative of Jesus and points to the nonviolent God revealed in Jesus. To discuss the work of Jesus Christ is thus ultimately to point to the God who is revealed in Jesus. It becomes clear that the question of atonement is finally a question about the image of the God who is revealed in Jesus. I have argued that the nonviolent life and teaching of Jesus call for us to say that the God revealed in Jesus is a nonviolent God, or a God that we should identify with nonviolent images. Lived Christian theology appeals to this God. One encounters this God by living in the story of the one in whom this God is present, namely in Jesus Christ.

Part II focuses on the church as the continuation of the reign of God made present by Jesus in the world. The church is the embodiment of the reign of God. It constitutes a witness to the world that does not yet acknowledge the reign of God that will one day be the culmination of all things.

---

29. Brian D. McLaren, *Everything Must Change: Jesus, Global Crises, and a Revolution of Hope* (Nashville: Thomas Nelson, 2007), 283.

II The Reign of God Made Visible

6 *Christology and the Body of Christ*

Previous chapters pointed to the image of the God that is revealed in the narrative of Jesus and suggested how to read the Bible in light of that finding. Part II now turns more specifically to a living witness to God in the world. As the church has always professed, God was most fully present in the world in Jesus. The body of Christ, the church — those who live in the narrative of Jesus — continues the presence and the mission of Jesus in the world.[1] Stated another way, the church is the embodiment of and a living witness to the reign of God in those places in the world that do not yet acknowledge the reign of God. The goal of the chapters in Part II is to provide some sketches of what the church might look like whose mission is to continue the presence of Jesus Christ as a witness to the reign of God in the world.

To fill out the picture of Jesus as the witness to the reign of God in the world, this chapter begins with some additional theologizing about Jesus in the New Testament. This theology has a different orientation from that which emerged in place of the narrative in the centuries after the New Testament.

The shift in focus from the resurrected Christ to the dead Christ described by Rita Brock and Rebecca Parker and summarized in Chapter 3 is

---

1. For a book aimed at a broad audience and based on the premise that the church is "a flawed and broken body" but nonetheless "the presence of Jesus Christ in the world," see Gerald J. Mast, *Go to Church, Change the World: Christian Community as Calling* (Harrisonburg: Herald, 2012), quoting 35.

not the only historic change in the way the church has referred to Jesus. A pictorially less dramatic but nonetheless real transformation occurred from the first to the fifth centuries in the way that theologians depicted the person of Jesus. The transition involved the disappearance of the narrative identification of Jesus, described in Chapter 1, and its replacement with the philosophical category of ontology. With reference to "theology for living," the dropping away of the narrative in identifying Jesus meant loss of the element that serves as the basis of the Christian life lived in discipleship to Jesus. The indirect result of this loss was the emergence of ethics not based on the particulars of the narrative. As the following makes clear, the use of ontological categories was appropriate in its context. Nonetheless, when those new formulations became the norm of truth about Jesus, the narrative element that would link ethics to Jesus was absent. Understanding these changes contributes to the development of lived theology and understanding the church as a continuation of the presence in the world of the reign of God made visible in Jesus.

Five New Testament Christologies

Chapter 1 noted the beginning of the development of theology derived from the narrative of Jesus in Paul's comments on Jesus' resurrection. An essay by John Howard Yoder points to additional instances of theological development within the New Testament itself. The first version of Yoder's essay served as the keynote address for a conference[2] that asked whether there was or ought to be a Christology for the believers church that differed from or was distinguishable from the standard Christology inherited from Christendom.[3] Yoder responded to the conference question by point-

2. "Is There a Believers' Church Christology?" the sixth Believers Church Conference, Bluffton University, Bluffton, Ohio, October 23-25, 1980.

3. This ecclesiological motif emphasizes the voluntary character of the church, namely that people choose to join as believing adults rather than being born into a church community. Historically, adult versus infant baptism identified the two differing ecclesiologies by their contrasting points of entrée. A more important characteristic in recent history is whether the church identifies with or poses a witness to the social order. For a comprehensive synthesis of believers church motifs along with historical sketches of a number of believers church traditions, see Donald F. Durnbaugh, *The Believers' Church: The History and Character of Radical Protestantism* (Scottdale: Herald, 1985), and James Leo Garrett, Jr., ed., *The Concept of the Believers' Church: Addresses from the 1968 Louisville Conference* (Scottdale: Herald, 1969). For contemporary statements see chapter 5 of J. Denny Weaver, *Becoming*

ing to the moves of five New Testament writers and their five different Christological images.[4] Since the visible witness to the social order of believers church ecclesiology presumes a theology for living, sketching these five images serves the current proposal.

For each of these five images, Yoder identified an ancient worldview into which the New Testament author carried the story of Jesus, using the language of that worldview to describe Jesus in a way that surmounted or vanquished the supposed problem presented by the worldview. John 1 features a logos Christology against the backdrop of a Gnostic hierarchy. Rather than inserting Jesus into a slot in this hierarchy, John 1 eliminates the Gnostic ladder of divine beings that separated a spiritual God from contamination on material earth by identifying the Word with both God and human flesh. Identifying Jesus with the Word thus overcomes the separation as the incarnation "draw[s] all who believe into the power of becoming God's children."[5]

Hebrews discusses Jesus against a sacrificial cosmology, which has sacrifices mediated through priests at the bottom to angels who then carry the message to God. This hierarchy disappears and people are brought under the sovereignty of God when Jesus is pictured above the angels at the right hand of God as well as fully identified with human limits. "Fully assuming the priestly system, as both priest and victim, once for all he ends the claim of the sacrificial system to order the community of faith, putting in its place a new covenant, a new universalized priestly order, an unshakable kingdom."[6]

In Colossians the Pauline author discusses Jesus in terms of a cosmology held together by a system of principalities and powers both "visible and invisible" (1:16). But rather than finding a slot for Jesus in this network, Jesus is proclaimed Lord of the principalities and powers. They have

---

Anabaptist: The Origin and Significance of Sixteenth-Century Anabaptism (2d ed.; Scottdale: Herald, 2005), and Gerald J. Mast and J. Denny Weaver, *Defenseless Christianity: Anabaptism for a Nonviolent Church* (Telford: Cascadia/Herald, 2009).

4. Yoder's address for the conference contained four Christologies and carried the title "That Household We Are." It was first published, with the addition of a fifth Christological image, as "'But We Do See Jesus': The Particularity of Incarnation and the Universality of Truth," in *Foundations of Ethics*, ed. Leroy S. Rouner (Boston University Studies in Philosophy and Religion; Notre Dame: University of Notre Dame Press, 1983), 57-75. Yoder then reprinted it in *The Priestly Kingdom: Social Ethics as Gospel* (Notre Dame: University of Notre Dame Press, 1984), 46-62. Citations to follow are from *The Priestly Kingdom*.

5. Yoder, *Priestly Kingdom*, 51.

6. Yoder, *Priestly Kingdom*, 51.

"been subdued and broken" by his resurrection. "The believer risen with Christ has died to them and is no longer in their hold," because "as the image of the invisible creator" Jesus is "holding all things together, reconciling all things, head of the body."[7]

In Revelation 4 and 5, Jesus appears as the key to history, the slain Lamb who can "unroll the world's judgment and salvation."[8] As it was expanded in Chapter 2 above, the image of the slain but resurrected Lamb shows that appearances are deceiving. The powerful Roman Empire, seemingly victorious through its execution of Jesus and the eventual destruction of the holy city, has been defeated by the resurrection. And the crucified Jesus, defeated in the eyes of the world, has emerged victorious in his resurrection from the dead.

Finally, in the hymn fragment of Philippians 2:6-11, Jesus is pictured in the image of a new Adam or perhaps a primeval king. In contrast to fallen Adam in Genesis 3, Jesus accepted the limitations of his humanity and did not attempt to grasp after equality with God.[9] Thus on the basis of this "willing self-emptying," "he has been divinely exalted and given the name of Lord (Phil. 2:9), which fact all of the cosmos shall one day acknowledge."[10]

Yoder identified these five images as independent Christologies, but he also identified a "syndrome or deep structure" common to all five. This deep structure had six components. In each instance, he said, the Christology resulted when the New Testament writer had taken the narrative of Jesus into another culture or linguistic world, and used the language of that world to talk about Jesus. But rather than fitting the message of Jesus "into the slots the cosmic vision has ready for it, the writer places Jesus above the cosmos, in charge of it." Further, the New Testament writers each had "a powerful concentration upon being rejected and suffering in human form, beneath the cosmic hierarchy, as that which accredits Christ for this lordship." Thus salvation consists not of being integrated into a cosmic salvation system "through ritual or initiation," but of being called to "enter into . . . the self-emptying and the death — and only by that path, and by grace, the resurrection — of the Son." Most significantly, "behind the cosmic victory, enabling it, there is affirmed . . . what later confession called

---

7. Yoder, *Priestly Kingdom*, 52.

8. Yoder, *Priestly Kingdom*, 52.

9. For Yoder's expanded comments on these texts, as well as his discussion of the theological method of the biblical writers, see his *Preface to Theology: Christology and Theological Method* (Grand Rapids: Brazos, 2002), 81-137, esp. 81-87, 114-22, 130-32.

10. Yoder, *Priestly Kingdom*, 52.

preexistence, co-essentiality with the Father, possession of the image of God, and the participation of the son in Creation and providence." Finally, in this deep structure is the claim that "the writer and the readers of these messages share by faith in all that that victory means."[11]

This deep structure set the conditions for doing Christology that Yoder presented to the conference, which was asking whether there was or ought to be a Christology specific to the believers church. This church is a voluntary church composed of disciples to Jesus, a church whose visibility comes from living in the narrative of Jesus as a witness to the surrounding world. For the New Testament writers, Yoder showed, Christology began with the story of Jesus, a story that can be discussed in the terms of any culture into which it is carried. And in that culture, a valid Christology would be one that understood Jesus as identified with humanity in that culture but which also understood Jesus as surmounting that culture in terms understood by that culture. This surmounting or victory over that culture makes this a "high Christology," that is a Christology that clearly identifies God with the story of Jesus. In Yoder's words, this "high Christology is the natural cultural ricochet of a missionary ecclesiology when it collides as it must with whatever cosmology explains and governs the world it invades."[12]

For the moment, I draw four implications from Yoder's discussion. First, since a "high Christology," that is a Christology that identifies Jesus with God, is already visible in multiple forms in the New Testament, the later, classic creedal formulas are not intrinsically necessary as the guarantee of what came to be called the deity of Jesus, although they remain important historical references.[13] Second, it is apparent that theology and the task of theologizing are never finished. Theology is a process and is always in process. That it is in process does not mean uncertainty or lack of willingness to commit. Rather it means an awareness of the fact that contexts change. The idea of process signals the intent of the book in hand to state

11. Yoder, *Priestly Kingdom*, 53.

12. Yoder, *Priestly Kingdom*, 54.

13. Monika Hellwig also noted the "wide spectrum of Christologies [in the New Testament] which none of the authors tries to fuse into one." Monika K. Hellwig, *Jesus: The Compassion of God* (Wilmington: Michael Glazier, 1983), 44, 110-11. The argument of Hellwig's book (see pp. 121-23) has parallels to important elements of the book in hand. The parallels to Yoder are more than coincidence. He once recommended Hellwig's book to me as a good example of contemporary Christology. Like Yoder, she accepts the truth of Chalcedon in its context but also suggests a more meaningful way to talk about Jesus in our modern context.

the meaning of Jesus — to proclaim the whole gospel — for this time and place and a willingness to restate it again in other cultural contexts. The church should always be in a mode of asking how to express the meaning of Jesus in a changing context and in other cosmologies and worldviews.

Third, with reference to the discussion in Chapter 5 about continuing the story begun in the Bible, a contemporary theology that is "biblical" is a theology that struggles with the same issues as did the New Testament writers. These issues include the classic discussions of the relationship of Jesus to the God of Jewish monotheism and to the Spirit of God, and how Jesus could be discussed in the category of God at the same time that he is presented by the New Testament as a human being. And fourth, Christological statements that fit the characteristics of the "deep syndrome" are Christology for living. Each in its way carries forward the idea that identification with Jesus in the earthly realm links the believer to God in the celestial realm. It is sharing in Jesus' life that results in sharing in his resurrection.

Not at all surprisingly, theologizing about Jesus did not stop with these Christological images from the New Testament. Fierce debates about Christology went on for nearly five centuries before the Christian church attained what became accepted as the standard or normative answers of Christology to the questions about the relationship of Jesus to the one God, to the Spirit of God, and to the category of human being. The significance of the implications drawn from Yoder's discussion will become clear from the following analysis of the supposed normative or standard and perceived universal creeds and statements about Christology and Trinity. The results will reveal the accommodation of violence by these statements as a parallel to earlier analysis of the violence modeled in standard atonement images.

Nicea-Constantinople, Cappadocian Trinity, Chalcedon

One creedal statement and two formulas related to and derived from it have been recognized as the core and foundational norms of traditional, quasi-universally accepted theology. These three are the creed first proposed by the Council of Nicea in 325 CE and then restated in a lightly amended form by the Council of Constantinople in 381, the formula for the Trinity developed by the three Cappadocian Fathers around the time of the Council of Constantinople, and the christological formula proposed by the Council of Chalcedon in 451.

In answer to the question of Jesus' relationship to God, the Council of Nicea declared that Jesus is *homoousios* or "one in substance" or "one in being" with God. This phrase, which constitutes the heart of the creed, asserts the unity of Jesus with God the Father. In more modern language, it is a statement of the deity of Jesus. This formula, "of same substance," is a rejection of the claim by the priest Arius that Jesus was of similar substance *(homoiousios)* as God the Father. Nicea's answer, repeated fifty-six years later at Constantinople, is intended to safeguard the belief that salvation through Jesus Christ was of God.

The formula for the Trinity, "one God in three Persons" extends Nicea-Constantinople's language of "same substance" to include the Holy Spirit, who is declared equally divine with the Son Jesus Christ. The terminology is credited to Gregory of Nazianzus (c. 330-389), Basil of Caesarea (c. 330-379), and Basil's younger brother Gregory of Nyssa (c. 330-c. 395), who are often identified by their place of origin as the three Cappadocian Fathers. From them comes the idea of declaring that there is one divine substance *(ousia)* of God, which exists in three divine but distinct persons *(hypostaseis)*. The oneness and threeness of God are then held together in tension in the formula translated into English as "one God in three persons." This particular formula of Trinity was declared the official doctrine of the empire by Emperor Theodosius in 380 and 381.[14] In the Western theological tradition, it is also claimed that the person of the Holy Spirit "proceeds from the Father and the Son," while the Eastern church said "from the Father through the Son."

As a result of these formulas that equate Jesus as deity with God the Father, the question becomes acute of how the divine Jesus corresponds to the Jesus who exhibited such human characteristics as hunger, fatigue, and, most significantly, dying. The answer from the Council of Chalcedon was an additional application of the term *homoousios*. Jesus was declared *homoousios* with humankind as well as with the Father. In English according to the classic formula Jesus is "truly God and truly man," which was thus accepted as the formal proclamation of both the deity and the humanity of Jesus.

These formulas thus express Jesus' equality with God, describe the relationship of Father, Son, and Holy Spirit as a Trinity, and assert both the humanity and the deity of Jesus. They have been granted the status of be-

---

14. R. P. C. Hanson, *The Search for the Christian Doctrine of God: The Arian Controversy 318-381* (Edinburgh: T. & T. Clark, 1988), 804, 821.

ing general or universal statements that transcend historical particularity. As such they are proclaimed as what all right-thinking Christians everywhere, in all times and places, should espouse as the foundation or norm of Christian faith. I do not dispute the truth of these classic statements within the context in which they were given. However, a number of considerations bring me to challenge their status as universal statements of transcendent truth or norms of truth.

Interpretations of these creedal formulas figure in the discussion about the nonviolence of God. It is stated repeatedly throughout the book in hand that God is revealed in the narrative of Jesus, with the resurrection of Jesus as the ultimate testimony to the presence of God and the reign of God in his story. The creedal statements discussed here also identity Jesus with God. Nicea made that identification with the term *homoousios,* saying that Jesus is the same essence as God or one in being with God.

Frequently cited as a formal statement of Trinity is the "Quicunque vult" or "Athanasian Creed." It reflects the concerns of Athanasius, the opponent of Arius, but actually comes from the fifth or sixth Christian century. Included in it are the statements "Thus the Father is God, the Son is God, the Holy Spirit is God; and yet there are not three gods, but there is one God." And later, "Our Lord Jesus Christ, the Son of God, is equally both God and man. He is God from the Father's substance, begotten before time; and he is man from his mother's substance, born in time. Perfect God, . . . equal to the Father in respect of his divinity, less than the Father in respect of his humanity."[15]

Although traditional theology has presumed a God who uses violence, a straightforward reading of these classic formulas would align them with the argument of this book. If Jesus is "one in being" with God or "equally God" or "equal to the Father in respect of his divinity," these statements would certainly seem to support belief in a nonviolent God.[16] Traditional-

---

15. For the Athanasian Creed in Latin and English translation see "The Athanasian Creed: Quicunque Vult, 5th-6th C," in *Creeds and Confessions of Faith in the Christian Tradition,* ed. Jaroslav Pelikan and Valerie Hotchkiss (New Haven: Yale University Press, 2003), 1:675-77, quoting 676, 677.

16. As was noted in Chapter 2, Yoder used the argument that the incarnation and the ongoing life of the church under the Holy Spirit are all of one God to counter the claims of H. Richard Niebuhr, who wanted to relativize the nonviolence of Jesus by arguing that Jesus and God the Father revealed different things. John Howard Yoder, "How H. Richard Niebuhr Reasoned: A Critique of *Christ and Culture,*" in *Authentic Transformation: A New Vision of Christ and Culture,* by Glen H. Stassen, D. M. Yeager, and John Howard Yoder

ists who would preserve a prerogative of violence for God are put in the position of arguing for an interpretation of this language that applies Jesus' equality with God only to the incarnation and not to God in other settings and persons of the Trinity. Stated differently, they argue that there are attributes in the person of God that are not in the person of Jesus.[17]

Conversation on Christology

It is apparent that differences exist between the statements of Christology in the classic creedal statements and formulas and the identification of Jesus in Chapter 1 and in Yoder's description of five New Testament Christologies. The significance of these differences emerges in the light of the project to develop theology that is lived or in seeing the Christian life as one lived in the story of Jesus.

Historians have expended considerable effort in identifying first appearances of terms, lines of transmission of particular concepts or formulations, efforts at authoritative statements by bishops and popes, various theological arguments on one side or another, early theologians who either objected to or supported the terms eventually accepted, imperial declarations of official theological positions, and more.[18] This discussion reveals that these claimed general or transcendent terms and language have a line of development, a history. This history describes choices made and the po-

---

(Nashville: Abingdon, 1996), 61-65. See also Yoder, *The Politics of Jesus: Vicit Agnus Noster* (2d ed.; Grand Rapids: William B. Eerdmans, 1994), 17-18, and *For the Nations: Essays Public and Evangelical* (Grand Rapids: William B. Eerdmans, 1997), 242.

17. For an example of this argument, see Darrin W. Snyder Belousek, *Atonement, Justice, and Peace: The Message of the Cross and the Mission of the Church* (Grand Rapids: William B. Eerdmans, 2012), 427-29. For a comprehensive response to Belousek, see n. 34 below.

18. The literature is voluminous. The outline of developments from the post–New Testament era to Chalcedon is generally known, while details along the way change. A general introduction and survey is Jaroslav Pelikan, *The Emergence of the Catholic Tradition (100-600)* (The Christian Tradition: A History of the Development of Doctrine 1; Chicago: University of Chicago Press, 1971). Some revisionist treatments of this history are Hanson, *Search*, H. A. Drake, *Constantine and the Bishops: The Politics of Intolerance* (Baltimore: Johns Hopkins University Press, 2000), and Virginia Burrus, *"Begotten, Not Made": Conceiving Manhood in Late Antiquity* (Stanford: Stanford University Press, 2000). The fact that particular aspects change in this story of development does not detract from my overall argument. The point of comparison is with the end product of the historical development, but understandings of the way that endpoint was reached change.

litical involvements that shaped these choices. In other words, the classic terminology, which is not itself found in the Bible, is visible as a product of development in which some terms were accepted and others rejected. To accept the classic formulas as unquestioned givens means to accept a particular line of historical development and a particular set of conciliar decisions and statements and imperial decrees as authoritative or final decisions for now and for all future generations.

But observing the line of development can impact our understanding of the classic statements, which stand at the endpoint of the development. Awareness of this series of decisions removes the mantle of universalism and transcendence from these statements and locates them in their earthly contexts. Removing this aura of universalism or transcendence in no way denies the truthfulness of these statements in their contexts. They were undoubtedly the best or most truthful answers to the questions of the time in their particular settings. But that recognition raises one of the important questions that drives the theological enterprise of this book: In other contexts, might there be other truthful and appropriate ways to express the same concerns? Yoder's description of five christological images already in the New Testament that emerged from five different cultures clearly seems to indicate that the answer is "yes." In our contemporary context, the question becomes particularly acute in carrying the narrative of Jesus into non-Western cultures.

Another consideration, provoked by the impulse to produce theology for living, also points to the advisability — even the necessity — of developing additional statements about Jesus rather than accepting the classic formulas as unquestioned givens and norms. This point concerns the categories that the classic statements use to identify Jesus and to ensure the continuity of God and Jesus. The classic tradition gives one particular kind of answer to the questions raised by the New Testament. It answers the questions of the relationship of Jesus to God, and of the Father, Son, and Spirit to each other in terms of ontology, namely substance or being or essence. The being or substance of Son and Spirit is one being, the same being as God's being. Then, with those assertions in place, Jesus' ontology, his being, is also said to be the same being as that of humankind. Ontology was a category of the predominant philosophy of the early Christian centuries. This use of ontological categories reflects the cosmology or worldview of the early Christian centuries. It was a hierarchical cosmology of three layers — an underworld, the world we live in on earth, and then a far-off upper realm where God resides. Yoder referred to this cosmology as one with the "top open for transcendent validation," or as one "with the top open for God to manipulate things on the earth below."[19] To assert or accept the classic creedal tradition as authoritative and normative means to require the terminology that reflects this worldview. At the same time, our contemporary cosmology of an almost incomprehensibly large and expanding universe, which poses the hypothetical "big bang" behind the expansion, not to mention the possibility of evolution in the realm of biology, necessitates replacing ontology as the given with new assumptions.

As Yoder asserted, the fact that the classic christological terminology reflects an ancient worldview and a philosophical system no longer current does not in and of itself render the formulas of Nicea, the Cappadocians, and Chalcedon intrinsically wrong as statements about Jesus, nor does it invalidate their significant historic contribution to our understanding of Jesus. It is as appropriate to discuss the identity of Jesus in these fourth-century categories as in the worldviews used by the New Testament writers and described by Yoder. In fact, within the confines of the worldview and philosophical system assumed by the traditional statements, they are undoubtedly true answers and arguably the best answers.

However, identifying the Greek philosophical categories that they assume and indicating that the fourth-century world picture differs from our own already points to their particular historical specificity and the particular — not universal or general — character of those conciliar statements. And that particularity once again opens the door to possible use of other categories to discuss the continuity or unity of Jesus with God. For example, even as Yoder affirmed the correctness of the classic statements he also suggested the possibility of other categories and answers. "When, in the New Testament, we find the affirmation of the unity of Jesus with the Father," Yoder wrote, "this is not discussed in terms of substance, but of will and deed. It is evident in Jesus' perfect *obedience* to the *will* of the Father."[20]

19. Yoder, *Priestly Kingdom*, 57 as well as class lectures I heard when a student of Yoder's at what is now Anabaptist Mennonite Biblical Seminary.

20. John H. Yoder, *The Original Revolution: Essays on Christian Pacifism* (Scottdale: Herald, 1971), 136; idem, *The Royal Priesthood: Essays Ecclesiological and Ecumenical,* ed. Michael G. Cartwright (Grand Rapids: Wm. B. Eerdmans, 1994), 185, emphasis original. Similarly, at the time Yoder wrote those words, in a class lecture that I recall at now Anabaptist Mennonite Biblical Seminary, he suggested that in place of ontology as the category of continuity from God to Jesus, in our setting the category that linked God and to Jesus might be "ethics or history." Yoder suggested that for moderns discussing the relationship of Spirit, God, and Jesus, the question addressed by Trinity was not a problem of ontology but of time, namely how to say

Although our worldview and cosmology do not reflect the categories and world picture of the classic formulas, another dimension of these formulas actually presents a more problematic dimension for a lived theology. A most significant difference between the New Testament's identification of Jesus and that in the classic statements is the loss of the narrative dimension. Narrative is the basis for theology and ethics based on Jesus. That Jesus is "one substance with the Father," and that he is "truly God and truly man" provide little if any guidance for living in the story of Jesus and little that would shape the Christ-centered church as Jesus' body so that it can be a witness in the world. These formulas provide little that would enable the Christ-related person to shape the church as an extension of Jesus' presence in the world.

A wide variety of writers have noted the absence of narrative in the classic formulas. While affirming the Nicene formula's avoidance of the errors of Arius and Sabellius, Yoder wrote, "It is clear that *in form* we are moving farther and farther away from the Gospel story. The form of the confession is still used, but it has been so padded out with statements about the essence of Christ that one recognizes no narrative to it any more. One is not driven to think of the movement of time, of God doing something among humans in a given time and place, as being very important."[21] In seeking to recover Jesus from the hierarchical and patriarchal tradition that considered men to be the normative humans, feminist/liberationist theologian Rosemary Radford Ruether wrote, "A starting point for this inquiry must be a reencounter with the Jesus of the synoptic Gospels, not the accumulated doctrine about him but his message and praxis."[22] James Cone,

---

that the God of Israel was also the God who raised Jesus and the God who is still immediately present with us today. Echoes of Yoder's words appear in the book in hand.

21. Yoder, *Preface to Theology*, 202. In much the same vein as Yoder, Larry Rasmussen wrote: "The disabling and ultimately tragic development is that the focus soon shifts from Jesus and the particular way he incarnated with his community, the way of his God, to the metaphysical relationship of the individual figure, Jesus, to the church's God, now become also the empire's God. In the most un-Jewish of all possible moves, the Jew Jesus became a 'detached' Jesus at the hands of the great ecumenical councils. He was detached from his own historic community and its way, and found himself metaphysically fused to God alone. So one searches in vain in the classic creeds, those pure distillations of the faith, for anything at all about Jesus as the way in any moral sense, or of his community's way." Larry L. Rasmussen, *Moral Fragments and Moral Community: A Proposal for Church in Society* (Minneapolis: Fortress, 1993), 140.

22. Rosemary Radford Ruether, *Sexism and God-Talk: Toward a Feminist Theology* (Boston: Beacon, 1983), 134-38, quoting 135.

founder of the black theology movement, said that "Few, if any, of the early Church Fathers grounded their christological arguments in the concrete history of Jesus of Nazareth. Consequently, little is said about the significance of his ministry to the poor as a definition of his person."[23] A womanist scholar, Kelly Brown Douglas, notes that Nicene/Chalcedonian Christology establishes Jesus as Christ by focusing on God's incarnation in Jesus. But "in so doing, it diminishes the significance of Jesus' actions on earth. His ministry is virtually ignored." After quoting the Nicene Creed, Douglas adds, "This confession of faith moves directly from the act of the incarnation to the crucifixion and resurrection. The implication is that what took place between Jesus' birth and resurrection — the bulk of the Gospels' reports of Jesus — is unrelated to what it means for Jesus to be the Christ."[24] In seeking resources in the classic formulations to use in resisting empire today, Professor Joerg Rieger writes that including Jesus in the God-head as *homoousios* "needs to be seen in connection with the work of Jesus Christ — Christ's life in all its complexity, divine and human, including his resistance to the powers that be, . . . It is hardly an accident that the life of Christ is not mentioned in the creeds; . . . The challenge to empire posed by the life of Christ would have just been too great."[25]

The falling away of the narrative in the identity of Jesus did not happen as the result of any conspiracy to abandon the ethical dimension of Jesus. It was nonetheless real, and it has a historical correlation. In a parallel to the shift in atonement imagery that followed the ecclesiological developments symbolized by Constantine (described in Chapter 3), the falling away of the narrative from the identification of Jesus accompanies the ecclesiological shift to the church that came to identify with the social order.

With civil rulers assuming authority in churchly issues and treating the church as an institution of the empire, the rulers of the social order became presumed agents of God, and the political entities then became the bearers of God's providence.[26] This change concerns the identity of the institution that carries and makes visible God's providence or God's rule in history. Prior to Constantine, it was the church — the people of God — that wit-

---

23. James H. Cone, *God of the Oppressed* (rev. ed.; Maryknoll: Orbis, 1997), 107.

24. Kelly Brown Douglas, *The Black Christ* (Bishop Henry McNeal Turner Studies in North American Black Religion 9; Maryknoll: Orbis, 1994), 112.

25. Joerg Rieger, *Christ and Empire: From Paul to Postcolonial Times* (Minneapolis: Fortress, 2007), 96.

26. John Howard Yoder, "The Constantinian Sources of Western Social Ethics," in *The Priestly Kingdom*, 138; idem, "The Otherness of the Church," in *The Royal Priesthood*, 57, 60.

nessed to and made present God's rule in history. Since the church that consisted of a small, minority voice in a relatively inhospitable world could always feel itself in a precarious position and on the verge of extinction, it took faith to say that God was in control of history and that the reign of God had already triumphed in the resurrection of Jesus. It was very clear, however, that the church existed over against the social order or in a state of confrontation with the world. Revelation's picture of empire and emperors as dragon and beasts illustrates clearly this relationship of church to the social order. That relationship reversed itself in the course of the changes symbolized by Constantine and was fully consummated in following centuries. The end result was that it now seemed self-evident that God controlled history, a self-evidence linked to the empire's supposed embrace of Christianity and the eventual identification of the social order as "Christian." At the same time, the church as a faithful people of God became much less visible among the nominal faith of the majority of the supposed Christian social order. In fact, it required faith to say that a true and faithful church did exist in the midst of the society that was now Christian by imperial decree.

Parallel to the shift from church to empire as the institutional bearer of God's providence was the shift from Jesus to the ruler or emperor as the norm by which to judge the behavior of Christians. Stated in oversimplified fashion, the pre-Constantinian church looked to Jesus the Lord as the norm of faith and practice, and faithfulness to that norm constituted the decisive aspect of ethical discernment.[27] Being Christian meant to live the life modeled by Jesus, the head or lord of the church. Post-Constantine, the emperor symbolized the empire. Once Christianity became the religion of the empire and was embraced by civil rulers, the continuation of Christianity was linked to the success of the political order. Preservation of the political order and the institutions of the social order then became the decisive criterion for ethical behavior, and the emperor or ruler became the norm against which the rightness of a behavior such as killing or truth-telling was judged.[28] As one example of this alignment

---

27. The relationship between church and civil authorities did develop in different fashions in East and West, with the bishop in the West maintaining more independence vis-à-vis civil authorities than in the East. Nonetheless, albeit in different ways, both traditions came to assume that it was the political institutions which carried God's providence in history. The debate concerned not whether God worked through these political institutions but whether civil rulers or bishops had the most immediate divine authority over the political sphere.

28. Yoder, *Priestly Kingdom*, 138.

of success of church and empire, consider the empire's move against the dissident Christians called Donatists at Timgad in North Africa in 419. Already for more than a century the two sides, those eventually declared Catholics and the dissenters, had lobbied the imperial court for support. The emperor finally took military action against the dissenters after the Catholic side, with strong support from Augustine, argued successfully that the dissidents in Timgad were not only heretics but madmen who threatened the secular public order.[29] Suppressing a dissident Christian group was argued to be necessary in order to preserve the secular order of the empire that embraced Christianity.[30]

As the leader of the civil order that protected the Christian church, the appropriateness of the "Christian" emperor or ruler's behavior was judged not with reference to Jesus' teaching and example but by how it furthered the cause of the empire or any governing structure that protected the church. As a result of the shift in ethical reference point from Jesus to political authorities, there was a marked change in the ethical orientation of the church. The norm of "Christian" behavior became that which everyone could perform, with the emperor serving as the stand-in for "everyone." Being Christian came to mean adherence to a minimum standard of social behavior in the "Christian" empire. The idea was abandoned that the so-called hard sayings of Jesus (e.g., Matt. 5:38-44) applied to all Christians, and the teaching and example of Jesus were not thought to apply to the lives of ordinary Christians.[31] It seemed self-evident that the empire, and with it the church, would be endangered if everyone, starting with the emperor, acted by Jesus' teaching.

The exercise of the sword shows most clearly the change in the status of the church from contrast to accommodation with the social order. Whereas before, the majority of Christians did not wield the sword and

29. Brent D. Shaw, "State Intervention and Holy Violence: Timgad/Paleostrovsk/Waco," *Journal of the American Academy of Religion* 77 (2009): 853-94.

30. The complex interaction of suppression of dissident factions by imperial forces using violence with ecclesiastical officials opposing or appealing to imperial authorities as it suited their needs of the moment is well documented in Philip Jenkins, *Jesus Wars: How Four Patriarchs, Three Queens, and Two Emperors Decided What Christians Would Believe for the Next 1,500 Years* (New York: HarperOne, 2010).

31. Two differing institutional objections to the evolution of the church toward identification with the social order were the Donatist movement and the monastic movement. Donatism came to uphold a higher standard as a separatist movement. From a position within the church, monasticism gave visibility to a standard of Christian conduct higher than the minimal behavior of ordinary Christians.

pagans did, now Christians could wield the sword in the name of Christ.[32] The claim was that "Christian" concerns required use of the sword in order to defend society and the empire, which had transformed itself into a defender of the church and Christian faith. In a manner of speaking, *not* applying the teaching of Jesus became the "Christian" thing to do, and employing the sword became a way to extend Christian influence, even in holy war and crusade. In fact, it has been argued that early Muslim defenses of *jihad* appealed favorably to the use of the sword by Christian emperors to spread Christianity. Thus "early Muslim authors understood war waged on behalf of the one god of Abraham as just one of several ties that bound the character and history of the early Muslim *umma* [community] to that of the Christian Roman Empire of Constantine and his successors."[33] The actions of these emperors led to the classic Christological formulas becoming the official theology of the empire. Constantine had called the Council of Nicea. The Christological formula it produced was resurrected fifty-six years later at the Council of Constantinople. Emperor Theodosius proclaimed this new statement as well as the Cappadocians' trinitarian formula to be the official theology of the empire.[34]

32. The argument here challenges the contention of Peter Leithart that there was no fundamental change in church and ethics from Jesus and the New Testament to Constantine and after. Leithart argues that both Jesus and the New Testament generally are ambiguous on the use of the sword. Thus he can affirm Constantine's use of the sword and acknowledge Constantine's cruelty without seeing a change in ecclesiology and ethics. See comments throughout Peter J. Leithart, "Defending *Defending Constantine:* Or, the Trajectory of the Gospel," *Mennonite Quarterly Review* 85 (2011): 643-55. It is hoped that the arguments throughout the book in hand display that there is much more data on rejection of the sword in Jesus and the New Testament than Leithart is willing to see.

33. Thomas Sizgorich, "Sanctified Violence: Monotheist Militancy as the Tie That Bound Christian Roman and Islam," *Journal of the American Academy of Religion* 77 (2009): 897.

34. I can affirm much of the critique of retribution and penal substitutionary atonement and the intent to make Jesus' rejection of the sword integral to our discussion of the work of Christ in Belousek, *Atonement, Justice, and Peace.* However, based on a reading of the 2001 edition of *The Nonviolent Atonement* as well as some email exchanges, Belousek vigorously disputes the arguments concerning both atonement and Christology of the book in hand. He makes much of the claim that his views and critique are "orthodox." In his meaning, "orthodox" is the designation for the standard account of the creedal tradition, stated with a view to stifle further discussion. But who has the right to decide, both for today and for all future generations, that statements made by dominant males in the fourth and fifth centuries in historical contexts different from our own and presuming a cosmology and

As the church evolved in the direction of identification with the social order and came to accept imperial intervention, one result was that the church made peace with the sword. That is, it came to allow and eventually to support the spread of Christianity through the violence of secular rulers. Alongside of this development, the dropping away of the narrative was not missed in what became the classic formulas on the identity of Jesus with God. It is important to state that emperors did not cause this shift. It is much more the case that the rise of imperial Christianity paralleled the theological shift.

Presence of the narrative would have called much imperial activity into question. In words of Joerg Rieger just quoted about the absence of

---

philosophical system no longer current should be elevated above their contexts and installed as the transcendent or unquestioned given, the only acceptable norm of truth?

Meanwhile, from a list of problems that could be raised concerning Belousek's approach, consider the following. 1) He shifts the focus of the death of Jesus from satisfying the penalty of divine law to returning true obedience to God. But this argument then becomes a book-length example of the fact that redefining the "target" of Jesus' Godward-directed death camouflages but does not resolve any of the problems of satisfaction atonement, including the role of God behind the death and the need for both Jesus and those who kill Jesus to be working with the will of God (see the section titled "The Challenge of Threefold Synthesis . . ." in Chapter 3). 2) Making Jesus' nonviolence a dimension of Nicea means making such claims as "Under the phrase, 'For us humans and our salvation' comes not only the cross, but also Jesus' birth, resurrection, and ascension" (p. 14) (see the range of authorities quoted in this section who disagree). 3) Establishing the creedal tradition as the transcendent norm apparently makes it difficult to impossible to acknowledge the critiques made by feminist, black, and womanist theologies of both traditional atonement and Christology. By making visible elements missing from the standard account, these recent theologies add to the contextual identity of the classic formulas. These theologies merit only incidental references from Belousek, with footnote references to literature that rebuts them. 4) Belousek denies that the historical context influenced the Christological formulas. For only the most recent, seemingly total, refutation of such a claim, see Jenkins, *Jesus Wars,* as well as material in this section. 5) Belousek's doctrinal orientation means that he interprets Jesus through the lens of Paul, which means that Jesus is depicted primarily in terms of themes, rather than working from the narrative itself. 6) Therefore, Jesus' rejection of violence is defined as nonretaliation, which results in a tendency toward identifying a passive response to evil and an emphasis on righteous suffering. 7) To maintain the idea that resorting to violence is a divine prerogative not limited by the one person of the Godhead (pp. 427-29), Belousek employs an interpretation of *homoousios* and trinitarian theology in which Jesus' rejection of violence is excluded from equality with God, which in my view means that the character of God is not truly revealed in Jesus. In essence, Belousek and I agree that traditional theology has a God who can use or sanction violence, which he defends with scholastic logic, whereas I pose an alternative with reference to the narrative of Jesus.

the narrative of Jesus in the classic creedal formulas, "The challenge to empire posed by the life of Christ would have just been too great."

Lived Christology Today

The narrative of Jesus is integral to a lived theology. Chapter 1 developed that base. But to be emphasized again is that, although Christian theology is derived from the narrative of Jesus, Jesus was heir to a tradition running through the entire Old Testament, from accounts of nonviolent cultural resistance and conflict resolution and statements by prophets all the way to nonviolent accounts of creation in Genesis 1. Thus a theology derived from Jesus is a theology that encompasses the entire Bible.

In this chapter the discussion has pointed to additional Christological images in the New Testament. These also contribute to theology in which Christians live as disciples of Jesus, which forms the church as the body of Christ. The identity and location of Jesus in both upper and lower realms in the biblical texts just discussed express what was said in other ways in the narrative of Jesus' life, death, and resurrection. In terms of that hierarchical worldview, identification with Jesus overcomes the gap between God in the upper realm and human beings on earth. Alongside these christological images we have also observed the way that classic formulas for identifying Jesus did not eventuate in a Christian life that gave visibility to the narrative of Jesus.

This combination of observations stimulates the effort to chart a new theological trajectory. This trajectory does not define Christian faith by correct doctrine, as do the creedal Christian traditions, but nonetheless takes theology seriously. Neither is this new trajectory defined by inner experience or spirituality, although living life within the story of Jesus certainly has experiential dimensions. This trajectory of a lived theology has modern precedents, particularly in Anabaptist history. What makes it a lived theology is its beginning point in the narrative of Jesus and the idea that we relate to Jesus by being his disciples and living in his story. Depicting the narrative of Jesus and deriving implications from it in this way is to describe the way Christians should live. And to ask how Christians should live requires telling the story of Jesus and asking about its implications. That is, to talk about Jesus and the implications of the good news of his story is to portray a theology that is a way of life that brings the believer into fellowship with God through Jesus Christ and makes visible the gospel of Jesus Christ in the world today. Stated in traditional language, believers — the church as the body of Christ — who live in the story of the Jesus of this theology are an extension of the incarnation.

Along with his description of the five New Testament Christological images, Yoder drew implications from these images for theology in our context and for living in the story of Jesus. The implications included what should and should not be reproduced or translated from the New Testament images into our own worldview and contemporary experience. In particular, modern believers should not attempt to translate the ancient worldview and its answers into our very different context. Yoder's example of what not to translate were notions such as "preexistence or the participation of the Son in creation." In Yoder's view, that translation would be mixing the rules of two language worlds, akin to "asking whether with the bases loaded you should try for a field goal or use a number three iron."[35]

Rather than attempting to translate the ancient worldview and its answers into our context, Yoder argued that we should describe our context and then consider how the narrative of Jesus transforms that context. He suggested that the context of our time is "pluralism/relativism," which is the disappearance of the idea of absolute truth accessible to all rational persons.[36] He argued that we should not attempt to defeat pluralism/relativism by calling on a powerful political authority to validate one view, as occurred with the imperial church after the fourth century, nor should we continue to search for the impossible, namely an unchanging anchor or unassailable proof in a relativistic world. Rather, Yoder suggested, we should seek to understand how to make sense of the meaning of Jesus within the context of relativism.[37] In following this process we would be doing what the New Testament writers did, namely taking the story of Jesus into another context and using its parameters to explain how Jesus transcended or transformed that context.

Applied specifically in our contemporary context of relativism and pluralism, it means discovering how to witness to the ultimate truth of Je-

---

35. Yoder, *Priestly Kingdom*, 56.

36. This loss of the sense that there is an absolute truth accessible to all rational people has been called "postmodernity" or "the crisis of modernity." For some Anabaptist perspectives on this phenomenon, see the essays in Susan Biesecker-Mast and Gerald Biesecker-Mast, eds., *Anabaptists and Postmodernity* (C. Henry Smith Series 1; Telford: Pandora/Herald, 2000); J. Denny Weaver, *Anabaptist Theology in Face of Postmodernity: A Proposal for the Third Millennium* (C. Henry Smith Series 2; Telford: Pandora/Herald, 2000), 17-23.

37. Yoder, *Priestly Kingdom*, 60.

sus when there is no external source of appeal to guarantee the truth of Jesus. Yoder's suggestion is that choosing to live the story when it is not required and perhaps even dangerous demonstrates our commitment to the truthfulness of the story. "The real issue is not whether Jesus can make sense in a world far from Galilee, but whether — when he meets us in our world, as he does in fact — we want to follow him. We don't have to, as they didn't then. That we don't have to is the profoundest proof of his condescension, and thereby of his glory."[38] In the language we have used in this book, the confession that God was truly revealed in Jesus is expressed by a willingness to live in the story of Jesus, whose meaning is expressed in a lived theology.

Monika Hellwig reached a similar point with the suggestion that a relevant contemporary Christology is to identify Jesus as "the incarnate Compassion of God." This term causes us to confront human suffering, she wrote, along with "our own powerlessness and insignificance." But it then also brings Christians to the transforming power of "the living Risen Christ." Jesus as the Compassion of God bridges the potential schism between those who emphasize liberation "in concrete historical dimensions" and those who envision redemption "as primarily a matter of communion with and surrender to God in individual lives." The compassion of God makes God a participant in human history, "in solidarity with human suffering, history and destiny." And finally, Jesus as the compassion of God "allows for human initiative in Jesus in every phase of a redemptive incarnation without any denial of the divine initiative. It allows for the progressive human identification with the redemptive initiative of God" in Jesus.[39]

Along with setting up how to witness to the truth of Jesus in a pluralistic context, Yoder also gave some hints about what that lived witness might look like. It includes rejection of violence, the building of "forgiving community," and addressing realms of politics and culture.[40] Already in words published a decade earlier, when he wrote that unity of Jesus with the Father is discussed in the New Testament in terms of "will and deed" rather than "substance," Yoder also noted that this obedience makes visible that "God takes the side of the poor" and that when God is king "He rejects the sword and the throne, taking up instead the whip of

---

38. Yoder, *Priestly Kingdom*, 62.
39. Hellwig, *Jesus: The Compassion of God*, 121-23.
40. Yoder, *Priestly Kingdom*, 57.

cords and the cross."[41] The "whip of cords," of course, refers to Jesus' protest in the temple.

Yoder wrote that this brief list of areas of witness was a stand-in "for the longer list" of ways of being faithful to Jesus.[42] The following description of the church as the continuation of the presence of Jesus in the world expands the topics treated within Yoder's categories. I begin with discussion of the church as a believing community. Following sections and chapters deal briefly with violence, salvation and the practice of forgiveness, racial reconciliation, gender issues, economic issues, and the difficult question of suffering.

The Church as the Lived Narrative of Jesus

It is the commitment to live out of and within the specific story of Jesus found in the Bible — and not some abstract theological formula that one simply assents to intellectually — that gives the Christian expression of lived theology its particular identity as an ecclesiology, its particular non-controlling way of being a church in the world. Many religious groups could be said to have an ecclesiology that is distinct. What gives specific shape and content to the proposal in hand for the church is the intent to live within and be shaped by the reconciling and serving practices of Jesus found in his teaching and the events of his life. If most of the social order does not have this particular commitment to the nonviolent Jesus as an authoritative ethical and spiritual source, it follows almost as a matter of course that the church that accepts the Jesus found in the Gospel accounts as that source will produce a new social reality. This reality will be a new community visibly different from the society in which it lives, even as it interacts with and witnesses to that society on many levels and in a variety of ways.

Stanley Grenz's view of the church as an extension of Jesus' social mission has parallels to this view. The service dimension and concern for the needy in Jesus' mission were apparent, Grenz wrote, when he announced himself with the quotation from Isaiah in the synagogue in Nazareth: "The Spirit of the Lord is upon me, because he has anointed me to bring good

---

41. John Howard Yoder, *The Original Revolution: Essays on Christian Pacifism*, 136; idem, *Royal Priesthood*, 185.

42. Yoder, *Priestly Kingdom*, 58.

news to the poor. He has sent me to proclaim release to the captives and re-covery of sight to the blind, to let the oppressed go free, to proclaim the year of the Lord's favor" (Luke 4:18-19). Jesus' career enacted that declaration. Those he served included "the sick, the outcasts, the demon-possessed, the sinful, and the sinned against."[43]

Although Grenz's discussion of Jesus and the church lacks the visibility given here to the rejection of violence for Christians, I can agree when he writes that the church's involvement in social action — in service — "is a natural extension of Jesus' own ministry." That means that "in embarking on a ministry of service, the church is simply continuing the mission of Jesus himself." Following Jesus' example thus leads to a ministry of service that focuses on meeting the needs of those marginalized by society. This service includes the binding of wounds, as represented by the Good Samaritan. But it also involves more. And, according to Grenz, advocating for those in need can include "attempting to foster structural changes in society." Effecting structural changes will "lessen the likelihood of injury in the future," and in the process society may reflect to a greater extent the character of the reign of God.[44]

The following sections discuss a number of issues of service and witness that result from living in the narrative of Jesus.

Baptism: Creation of a New World[45]

To follow Jesus and to accept him as Lord involves a new way of life that expresses itself in redeemed attitudes and relationships among people both inside and outside the church. Baptism proclaims the existence of the community shaped by these redeemed relationships and incorporates new members into it.

Paul attributes the formation of the community to being "in Christ": "If anyone is in Christ, there is a new creation: everything old has passed away; see, everything has become new!" (2 Cor. 5:17). Or in the language of the New English Bible, "there is a new world." In Galatians 3:28 Paul states,

---

43. Stanley J. Grenz, *Theology for the Community of God* (Nashville: Broadman and Holman, 1994), 660.

44. Grenz, *Theology for the Community of God,* 660-62.

45. Discussion in this section of baptism as the creation of a new world or new human society follows John Howard Yoder, *Body Politics: Five Practices of the Christian Community Before the Watching World* (Scottdale: Herald, 2001), chapter 3.

"There is no longer Jew or Greek, there is no longer slave or free, there is no longer male and female; for all of you are one in Christ Jesus." And Ephesians 2 proclaims the tearing down of the wall that divided Gentiles and Jews: "For he is our peace; in his flesh he has made both groups into one and has broken down the dividing wall, that is, the hostility between us" (Eph. 2:14). In these texts, Yoder argues, Paul described the creation of a new social entity, the church, that transcends ethnic differences. The prior ethnicities do not disappear; rather, the new reality, the new world, transcends them. Cultural differences still exist but are no longer a cause for division. In speaking to Gentiles, Paul's message is "that the God of the Jews was inviting Paul's listeners — Gentiles — into the covenant story that God already had going."[46] John the Baptist in Matthew 3 and Luke 3 and Jesus in John 8 make the same point in other language.

Ethnic identity and ethnic differences clearly exist within the orders of God's providence. Rather than reifying these differences, the new community transcends them. Baptism incorporates a person into the community where those differences no longer divide.

This new entity, the church that transcends cultural differences, is not a theological version of the proverbial "melting pot" of Western individualism. In the melting pot, the individual leaves behind a particular cultural identity to join a new and supposedly better one. The whole is the sum of the parts, but formerly hostile cultures are not reconciled. They are merely abandoned as individuals "melt" into a new identity.

In contrast, in Paul's language, the formerly conflicting cultures are reconciled in a new humanity, a new creation. In this new creation, particular cultures may be retained, but their continuation no longer divides groups from each other. Because Christ died for all, there can no longer be discrimination. The new creation results in integrating the cultures into a new society that transcends their differences, even as they are retained and respected.

It is baptism that creates this new humanity, the church. Since social categories of class and ethnicity no longer constitute intrinsic differences that divide people, "baptism introduces or initiates persons into a new people." "The primary narrative meaning of baptism is the new society it creates, by inducting all kinds of people into the same people."[47]

When the meaning of baptism concerns the new community that it

---

46. Yoder, *Body Politics*, 31.
47. Yoder, *Body Politics*, 28, 32.

creates, the church thus formed becomes the model for the world that claims to be moving in the same direction. That model thus points to instances where the world has not lived up to its claims of equality. One example is the United States Declaration of Independence, which declared "all men are created equal," but actually meant only white, male property owners and excluded women both black and white, black men, Native American men, and poor men. Further, there was the segregated South of the United States, like apartheid in South Africa and Protestant-Catholic segregation in Northern Ireland. The nonviolent activism of Martin Luther King, Jr. keeps on display the continual need to work at overcoming racism in the United States.

The baptism of Paul following his conversion experience displays how the church created by baptism should transcend such differences. Still known as Saul, Paul had vigorously persecuted Jewish Christians when he was struck blind by a vision of Jesus on the road to Damascus. Although fearful of approaching Saul, who had a commission to arrest Jews who accepted Jesus as the Messiah, Ananias followed instructions given to him in a vision and went to pray with Saul. Saul's eyes were opened and he was filled with the Holy Spirit. "Then he got up and was baptized." Immediately afterward he began to "proclaim Jesus in the synagogues" and eventually engaged in a mission to bring the message of Jesus the Messiah to Gentiles. Thus in his person Paul displayed the transcending of differences between Jews and Gentiles in the church created by baptism.[48]

Yoder described steps in the turning away from this understanding of baptism. One step was the sharp separation of Jews and Gentiles sometime after the second century.[49] After that wall was erected, the lived meaning of Paul's message was impossible. Another turn came in the fifth century. After the empire became Christian by imperial edict, there were no more outsiders to convert. As a consequence, baptism became a celebration of birth, accompanied by a sacramental theology about baptism's impact on

---

48. On baptism into a new humanity that transcends differences, see Mast, *Go to Church, Change the World*, 68-70.

49. For Yoder's analysis of why that separation "did not have to be," see his *The Jewish-Christian Schism Revisited*, ed. Michael G. Cartwright and Peter Ochs (Grand Rapids: William B. Eerdmans, 2003). For a parallel argument from a Jewish scholar see Daniel Boyarin, *Border Lines: The Partition of Judaeo-Christianity* (Philadelphia: University of Pennsylvania Press, 2004). For Boyarin's supportive comment on Yoder, see Boyarin, "Judaism as a Free Church: Footnotes to John Howard Yoder's *The Jewish-Christian Schism Revisited*," in *The New Yoder*, ed. Peter Dula and Chris K. Huebner (Eugene: Cascade, 2010), 1-17.

the infant. Thus baptism lost its original meaning of breaking down barriers among classes. And without that social dimension, infant baptism could actually reify cultural and social differences, which were said to be intrinsic to the order of creation. Thus, within the church, classes and peoples stayed apart, men ruled over women, and Europeans assumed their right to rule the globe.[50] In the Reformation era, when radical Zwinglians, that is Anabaptists, developed the idea of baptism as a symbol for a conversion necessarily chosen by an adult, baptism was still focused on the impact on the individual and lacked the dimension of creating a new community that transcended cultural, ethnic, or gender differences.

Overcoming of social differences gives the church its distinct character. This communal or social orientation does not deny individuality or the personal nature of one's faith, but it does mean that the individual's faith attains its fullness through incorporation by baptism into the *believing community* which practices the love and mutual service embodied by Jesus and to which they are invited and empowered by his resurrection. Yoder expressed this concept of the church in terms of "liberation from the dominion of the mass." That is, the "Christian community is not Christendom. . . . It is the visible congregation of those who knowingly gather around the name, the teachings, and the memories of Jesus."[51]

The Church: A Community

A wide variety of writers depict the community dimension of the church, the way that the church is more than a collection of saved individuals. Rosemary Radford Ruether described this church as "a new family, a new community of Israel." In this new family those previously separated have been "overcome in an overflowing graciousness of God." Those included in this new community are all those previously marginalized within Israel, called "the poor" (Luke 4:18) along with an occasional Samaritan or Gentile. Ruether's list includes "the blind, the lame, lepers, those with bodily fluxes, those possessed by demons that caused madness and 'fits,' all those healed and restored to mental and physical health; also the 'sinners,' the prostitutes, tax collectors, and various impoverished people." These all, in-

---

50. Yoder, *Body Politics*, 40.

51. John Howard Yoder, "The Anabaptist Shape of Liberation," in *Why I Am a Mennonite: Essays on Mennonite Identity,* ed. Harry Loewen (Scottdale: Herald, 1988), 343-44.

cluding most specifically women in every category, are gathered together in feasting in which there is abundance left over (Mark 6:43; Matt. 14:20; Luke 9:17). It is such gatherings of the "unholy," in which there is "no separation of unclean persons, no careful distinction of holy and profane times," that scandalized those concerned with ritual purity.[52]

The understanding of the church that continues the presence of Jesus in the world has significant parallels with what Rita Nakishima Brock called "Christa/Community." In Brock's construction, Christa/Community includes the community around Jesus in which acts of healing, exorcism, and restoration become visible and it is clear that the extension of Jesus is "a lived reality expressed in relational images." These acts put on display that Christa/Community is "a relational event."[53]

Grenz wrote that the church is "a people brought together by the Holy Spirit" and "bound to each other through Christ." It is the "nation of God," a new reality consisting of people from the entire world who belong to God. "The church is an international fellowship comprising persons 'from every tribe and language and nation.'"[54] Grenz's stress on the international dimension parallels Yoder's emphasis that the reconciliation found in the church transcends cultural differences.

For Grenz, the fact that the church is a community is inherent in its divine mission. God's ultimate purpose is to move history to its culmination in the kingdom of God. But salvation in the kingdom occurs in relationships and includes creation. Ephesians 2 depicts this reconciled fellowship. The church is "far more than a collection of saved individuals." It is "the community of salvation." Thus the divine program establishes more than "individual peace with God in isolation; it extends as well to the healing of all relationships — to ourselves, to one another, and to nature."[55]

A Voluntary Church

The church that is a continuation of the presence of Jesus will be separate from or distinguishable within the social order. Stanley Hauerwas and Wil-

52. Rosemary Radford Ruether, *Women and Redemption: A Theological History* (Minneapolis: Fortress, 1998), 18.

53. Rita Nakashima Brock, *Journeys by Heart: A Christology of Erotic Power* (New York: Crossroad, 1988), 55, 72.

54. Grenz, *Theology for the Community of God*, 606-07.

55. Grenz, *Theology for the Community of God*, 626-27, quoting 627.

liam Willimon were correct when they wrote that the Christian's "commonwealth is in heaven," a variant reading of Philippians 3:20. Thus with their citizenship elsewhere, Hauerwas and Willimon wrote, Christians live on earth as "resident aliens."[56] Empowered by the Spirit of Christ and acting on their own volition,[57] individuals choose to accept baptism into the church as a new creation, a new community that reconciles differing social entities. That this new creation gives Christians "citizenship" elsewhere, which produces a church that is not identified with the social order, seems obvious when the host society is for example a Buddhist, Islamic, or Hindu-shaped culture. In such a context, the voluntary character of the church is clearly meaningful. The modern focus on the voluntary character of the church first appeared with Anabaptists in the sixteenth century, when they chose to separate themselves from the formally required, established church. However, in the pluralist society of the United States, where there is no established church and in a sense every church is a voluntary society, a stress on voluntariness as a characteristic of the church means little.

In another sense, the voluntary public witness of the church that continues the presence of Jesus Christ in the world carries great significance in the pluralist society of the United States. Although there is no established church and individuals are supposedly free to practice any religion or no religion, one frequently hears that the United States is a "Christian nation." Examples abound, from the relatives of a fallen soldier who might proclaim him "a warrior for Christ" to the unofficial but nonetheless unthinkable idea that a Muslim or even an avowed atheist could be elected president of the United States. In spite of the official separation of church and state written into the constitution of the United States, the notion of being a "Christian society" continues strong.[58] When one considers the history behind the claim to be a "Christian society" or a "Christian nation," the claim takes on the appearance of a modern version of an unofficial but real established church. In that context, the voluntary character of the church as understood here becomes significant.

56. Stanley Hauerwas and William H. Willimon, *Resident Aliens: Life in the Christian Colony: A Provocative Christian Assessment of Culture and Ministry for People Who Know That Something Is Wrong* (Nashville: Abingdon, 1989), 11-12.

57. See the comments in Chapter 1 on the paradox of grace that unites God's election with human freedom and responsibility.

58. The following paragraphs on distinguishing the church from the social order are revised from Weaver, *Becoming Anabaptist: The Origin and Significance of Sixteenth-Century Anabaptism,* 193-96.

A brief historical overview of the voluntary character of the church begins with the book of Revelation, which presents images of the church that was clearly distinguished from the Roman Empire. In the evolutionary series of changes in the third through fifth centuries of the Christian era described earlier, the church lost or abandoned its identity as an illegal minority movement. Christianity became the majority religion, and the church became established when emperors intervened in church affairs, bishops accepted that intervention and appealed to emperors for support, and emperors assumed the task of protecting the church. In effect, there was a quasi-fusion of church and society. It was assumed that everyone in the social order would conform to the Christian religion now backed by imperial decree, and that consequently the church thus served and represented the entire society.

Of course, this fusion of church and social order was never complete. The church maintained its own structures and hierarchy, while the monastic movement can be interpreted as a protest against this fusion of church and civil society from within the church. Throughout the Middle Ages the bishops and pope were in continual competition with secular rulers such as emperors and kings to see who had most power in the church — whether civil rulers could appoint church officials in their territories or if church authorities held the authority to invest civil rulers. Nonetheless, these conflicts and the less than total fusion of church and society did not call into question the assumption by officials on both sides that there was one faith that encompassed the entire social order. These competitions concerned which authority — church or civil — had ultimate jurisdiction over the one church that encompassed the social order.

The Reformation of the sixteenth century brought two changes to this picture. For one, the fracturing of the Roman Catholic Church meant that civil authorities now had a choice of religious preferences to establish. However, none of the new, major Protestant alternatives challenged the idea of an established church. The second change concerned a shift in the balance of power between church and civil authorities. By fostering reformation in their territories, Protestant civil authorities in particular gained ascendancy over church authorities in the struggle to control the one church that was assumed to encompass the social order of a particular ruler. Of the Reformation movements, only Anabaptists dissented from the established church and thus challenged the idea that the church encompassed the social order. Their choice to form a church independent of both civil authorities and established church authorities clearly identified theirs as a voluntary church.

The first English settlers to North America brought the idea of an established church along with them. The famed Puritan settlers in New England, whose name comes from their belief that the Church of England was not sufficiently purified of all vestiges of Catholicism, sought to establish what they considered the correct church order. Catholics and Anabaptists, for example, were not welcomed.

Official separation of church and state happened for the newly minted nation of the United States in 1791, when the first amendment was added to the U.S. constitution. It said, "Congress shall make no law respecting an establishment of religion, or prohibiting the free exercise thereof." That separation, however, was only at the federal level. The last vestige of official establishment at the state level disappeared in 1831,[59] when Massachusetts removed the favored tax status for Congregational ministers, the denomination that was the lineal descendent of the founding Puritans.

Many churches and churchmen opposed disestablishment. The response was that if the government would not make the United States "Christian," then Christians would have to "Christianize America voluntarily."[60] The host of parachurch organizations that arose by the mid-nineteenth century — Bible societies, tract societies, YMCA, YWCA, Sunday school societies, home mission societies, revival crusades, and more — had as a primary motivation the task of Christianizing America voluntarily. This struggle to Christianize America voluntarily is still going on, and the idea of a "Christian society" or of "Christian America" is a lineal descendent of the medieval state church, but without official government support. Many of those proclaiming "Christian America" in the twenty-first century would welcome a recovery of government coercion for their religious programs of choice, such as banning abortion and gay marriage or requiring the teaching of creationism or intelligent design in public schools.[61]

---

59. George C. Bedell, Leo Sandon, Jr., and Charles T. Wellborn, *Religion in America* (2d ed.; New York: Macmillan, 1982), 17-18, quoting 17.

60. For example, see Lyman Beecher, "On Disestablishment in Connecticut," in *Church and State in American History*, ed. John F. Wilson (Boston: D. C. Heath, 1965), 92-93; idem, "A Plea for the West," in *God's New Israel: Religious Interpretations of American Destiny*, ed. Conrad Cherry (rev. ed.; Chapel Hill: University of North Carolina Press, 1998), 122-30; Henry Ward Beecher, "The Tendencies of American Progress," in *God's New Israel*, 246-48.

61. For a book-length critique of the idea of a Christian nation and the harm that it does to the church because of the alliance with coercive power, see Gregory A. Boyd, *The Myth of a Christian Nation: How the Quest for Political Power Is Destroying the Church* (Grand Rapids: Zondervan, 2005).

The persistent claims about being a "Christian nation" in the midst of the legally secular, pluralist society provide a complex context in which it has meaning to say that the church described here is "voluntary." Vis-à-vis the secular society, of course the church is voluntary and visibly distinct as it would be in a society dominated by a different religion. But the church that continues the presence of Jesus in the world is also distinguishable from a "Christian society." Although it is unofficial, the idea of a "Christian society" encompassing the entire social order maintains the intent of an established church. Even if many individuals do not conform to "Christian" expectations, the expectation that the government of a "Christian society" will enforce specific Christian teachings is an established church legacy. And since the established church legacy has long ago made peace with the sword, it is not surprising that the name of Jesus Christ is associated with the nation's military endeavors. In contrast, the church I describe does not ask the government to enforce its beliefs or its practices, and it rejects the idea that believers participate in the military violence of a "Christian society." Since both the status of pluralism and the notion of being a "Christian society" are predominant claims, in this light it is meaningful to characterize the church described here as "voluntary." This church voluntarily chooses to be an alternative to both options.

A Peace Church[62]

If the particular story of Jesus is the norm that gives the church its distinct character and shapes its communal practices and its life together, then peacemaking and the rejection of violence are incipient as the privileged manifestation of discipleship or of following the example of Jesus. This place for rejection of violence should be clear from the account above, which does not separate nonviolent love from the core of Jesus' mission and life. Jesus' specific rejection of the violent option of the Zealots through his nonviolent confrontation of evil belongs in a central and necessary way to the peaceable nature of the reign of God revealed in Jesus' life and teaching. Yoder called this way of life, "liberation from the dominion of Mars."[63]

---

62. Material in this section is revised from paragraphs of Mast and Weaver, *Defenseless Christianity*, 76-79.

63. Yoder, "The Anabaptist Shape of Liberation," 339.

Since rejection of violence is intrinsic to the story and work of Jesus, I do not separate it from the confession of Jesus as Lord and norm. It may seem redundant to insist on explicitly attaching some version of nonviolence to the characterization of Jesus as Savior. But given the prevalence of faith in violence in North American society, a huge but sacrosanct Pentagon budget, the war-related national holidays, the linking of defense contracts to industry and civilian employment across the country, the defense of national violence by the majority of American Christians, and much more that could be listed, it is important to state explicitly again and again that rejection of violence belongs intrinsically to the church that lives in and from the story of Jesus and whose work is a continuation of the incarnation.

Central features of the Christ-following defenseless community include the enemy-loving servanthood of Jesus as the ethical norm, the nonviolent and peacemaking church as a witness to the social order, and the inherently peaceful nature of the community of Jesus' followers. Additional convictions or principles inseparable from such a noncoercive and Christ-loving community are baptism on confession of faith, absence of hierarchy, a biblical foundation, the practice of discipline, freedom of conscience, and economic sharing. These features and characteristics constitute more than a list of propositions and are not a creed or confession of faith to which Christians give assent. Living in a story shaped by these convictions is different from assenting to principles as parts of a creed. These convictions function together to structure a distinct way of life, a way of living in the world that begins by accepting the Prince of Peace as Lord and the New Testament as the authoritative repository of writings on the life and teaching of Jesus. They describe an outlook that begins to collapse if any of these aspects are compromised.

These central convictions deal with relationships between people, so that the church truly is a new and loving humanity and is authenticated by the way it lives as much as by what it believes. To live in this community means to put oneself inside this ongoing narrative or drama and to embody its convictions. It is not at all a copying of the early church or of selected historical ancestors. It is rather a continuation of and a carrying forward of this story in our own context. As an analogy, consider the way a baseball player does much more than assent to the rules of the game and agree that they are true. To be a baseball player means to put oneself inside the rules both formal and informal so that they shape that player's actions and activity. Even when he or she makes errors and transgresses the rules, wears modern styled uniforms, and uses much evolved equipment and playing strategy, it is still obvious that he or she is playing baseball and not ice hockey or field hockey, though these sports all employ sticks to hit round objects.

This depiction of an ecclesiology shaped by and continuing the narrative of Jesus does not describe a historical program to be imitated or transplanted.[64] This ecclesiology has had a number of manifestations and expressions throughout Christian history. Some have become separate structures, as the several Anabaptist groups. Others have remained in the dominant church, in the way of some monastic movements, the Base Community movement, or various clusters within the major Protestant denominations. Each has significance as a particular manifestation of the church that seeks to live out of the story of Jesus. Yet, for several reasons, none of these historical expressions can be canonized as an absolutized or normative form. No composite or summary of common elements gleaned from multiple expressions constitutes a definitive description. Neither is it possible to identify a modern normative form. Identifying a normative form carries several problems, some obvious, others more subtle. The only thing without which this church cannot exist is the presence and visibility of Jesus' loving and peaceful humanity in the lives of members.

One problem with describing a normative form on the basis of past history (tradition) is the implication that we have already known that some particular past forms also had the necessary answers to all new and future situations as well. But, most certainly, past forms cannot contain answers for all future situations and contexts. As much as one might revere ecclesiological forefathers and foremothers, presuming that their practices and theological formulations served our present and the future would mean that the future is already known, that it resembles the past. Further, forms that differ from the historical description would be intrinsically deviant rather than potentially new forms of faithful discipleship to Jesus Christ.

But there is another, more important and more profound reason for emphasizing that identifying an ongoing ecclesiology shaped by but extending the narrative of Jesus does not mean imitation or transplanting or recovery of a normative historical version. Rather than being a fixed image, living out the story of Jesus is a stance toward the world. It is a way to

---

64. The discussion here is a continuation of themes first raised in the section titled "The Authority of the Bible" in Chapter 5.

live in the world — a posture — shaped by the peaceful story of Jesus. As a posture, it can and does have multiple expressions. But more significantly, it is always in the process of becoming, a process of determining how to live in the world. It is never a fixed entity that has determined definitively the form that the church should take. We are always in the midst of figuring out what following Jesus looks like in our current context and where he will take us tomorrow. Or as Eugene Peterson wrote, "When we follow Jesus, it means that we don't know exactly what it means, at least in detail. We follow him, letting him pick the roads, set the timetables, tell us what we need to know but only when we need to know it."[65]

Already in the sixteenth century, Anabaptist leader Hans Denck foreshadowed these comments about the open-endedness of living in the story of Jesus. Denck wrote that one learns who Jesus is through following Jesus. One comes to knowledge of God through a means, he said. "But the Means is Christ, whom none can truly know except he follow him with his life. And no one can follow him except insofar as one previously knows him."[66]

These statements about the open-endedness of following Jesus reflect the way that human beings actually learn by doing. For example, a young couple has an idea what marriage may involve, but that idea will certainly evolve and grow in ways beyond their comprehension as they actually undertake marriage. In other words, we have the intention that the church is to live in and continue to reflect the presence of Jesus in the world, but what that means in practice becomes known only in actually living it out. The faithful church is always in the process of discerning what it means to live as a nonviolent, defenseless witness to the Prince of Peace in their current context.

If it appears that I am unable to discuss the meaning of the gospel of Jesus Christ without referring to the peace that he brings to the world, the impression is correct. The church that lives out of the narrative of Jesus will recover the intrinsically nonviolent and peacemaking qualities of the work of Jesus that the church as the body of Christ is called to make visible. This message of peacemaking is intrinsic to the story of Jesus. It is thus visible in theology derived from the narrative, and it is visible in the practices of church whose intention is to live out of that story. This is a lived theol-

---

65. Eugene H. Peterson, *The Jesus Way: A Conversation on the Ways That Jesus Is the Way* (Grand Rapids: William B. Eerdmans, 2007), 240.

66. Hans Denck, *The Spiritual Legacy of Hans Denck: Interpretations and Translation of Key Texts*, trans. Clarence Bauman (Studies in Medieval and Reformation Thought 47; Leiden: E. J. Brill, 1991), 113.

ogy of Jesus Christ. The gospel of peace is not a gospel if it does not make peace. It is time for Christians to work at giving greater credence to the nonviolent, peace-oriented message of Jesus, and to proclaim the peace of Christ without compromise or qualification. "Peace on earth, good will to all people!" sang the angels in announcing the birth of Jesus. That is the message I suggest Christians are called to proclaim in words and in deeds.

Alongside these assertions that Christians and the church continue Jesus' mission to make the reign of God visible, it is important to add some qualifiers. For one, this statement concerning the church is by no means a statement of perfection nor an implication that the church can fulfill this calling to perfection. The church is flawed, as are all human institutions, and whatever its best efforts might be, the church never fully or completely fulfills its mission. And not only do its best efforts fall short, even these best efforts carry with them elements of sinfulness and failure. Nonetheless, what the church is trying to accomplish, or what its orientation is, should be visible. As was stated once before, as one can determine that in spite of their errors a group of athletes is playing baseball and not ice hockey or field hockey, although these sports all use sticks to hit round objects, one should be able to identify that the church intends to live in and follow the narrative of Jesus rather than following a military general or a factory foreman.

Along a different line, it is also important to state that although the church has a calling to live as a witness to the reign of God in history, by no means are the presence and the working of God's rule in the world limited to the church. The church may have a privileged place as the visible representative of God's reign, but it most certainly does not have exclusive possession of it and the church is far from the sole place of God's working in the world. Wherever events happen that align with the rule of God, there God's rule is present regardless of the name in which it is done. Obvious examples might be the nonviolent movements of Mahatma Gandhi and Badshah Khan that were described in Chapter 5. When the long moral arc of the universe bends toward justice, as Martin Luther King, Jr. said, and when "the grain of the universe" aligns with the nonviolence of Jesus, as John Howard Yoder said, then others besides Christians can sense and discover that arc and that grain and align themselves with it.

Meanwhile, the following chapter adds some specificity to the practice of peace and nonviolence.

7 *Violence and Nonviolence*

In Part I it was argued that the God revealed in the narrative of Jesus should be understood as a God who does not use or sanction violence. Discussion of nonviolence occurs throughout this book. This chapter then fills in additional elements of nonviolence and expands further the discussion of nonviolent practices and of the violence confronted by the church that witnesses to the reign of God made visible in the life of Jesus. This discussion is by no means a primer on nonviolence. It is part of demonstrating that issues of violence and nonviolence occur in many settings. The following chapters develop some of these discussions still further.

The Nonviolence of Lived Theology

God in the Image of Humankind

The idea that God uses violence is a facet of an image of God made in the likeness of humankind. Human beings can lift a small weight, whereas the assumption goes, God can lift an ultimately heavy weight. But if lifting an ultimate weight defines a characteristic of God's omnipotence in contrast to human frailty, the result is a God pictured in the image of humankind.

When human beings commit evil, the impulse is to use the violence of retribution in punishment. Think of the schoolyard bully who picks on a small boy. This small boy threatens to call his big brother to beat up the bully. When human beings sin, it is claimed, God must exact punishment.

The bigger the evil, the more violence God must use in punishment. The final battle in the consummation at the end of time, in this view, is enormous beyond our imagination. For God to be God, God must employ the most violence of all, be the ultimate "big brother" to the "bully" who has threatened God's people. This is God in the image of human retributive justice.

The several versions of satisfaction atonement picture this need to punish in some fashion, while also picturing Jesus submitting to this retribution so that sinful humans who avail themselves of Jesus' death may avoid the punishment. Anselm envisioned God in the likeness of humankind in a different way. He projected the image of the feudal lord and his seeking the satisfaction of honor into the divine realm. God became the ultimate feudal lord. Although satisfaction atonement no longer makes the feudal overlay explicit, as its name indicates it continues the emphasis on death as that which is necessary to satisfy God. In the image of the God who must exact satisfaction or punish, we see an image in which divine and human practice mirror each other — God pictured in the image of humankind.[1] Criminal justice systems that operate under the philosophy of retribution for crime or paying a debt to society mirror the atonement idea of punishment or satisfying a debt in the divine realm, a point developed at length in the following chapter.

In this presumed need to retaliate with more violence to even the score, as Walter Wink says, "we become what we hate."[2] When a state executes murderers, the state has become a killer in order to demonstrate that killing is wrong. A country that decries the weapons build-up by another builds its own greater arsenal — thus becoming even more dangerous than the entity it hates. Atrocities committed in war are claimed as justification

---

1. Recall that in *Cur Deus homo* Anselm specifically projected the feudal idea of honor that must be satisfied into the divine realm, a clear modeling of the image of God on a human phenomenon. In one instance, as an aside while making another point, Anselm even used the example of a king whose entire population, save one innocent man, had sinned against the king and were in need of satisfaction. The example is found in Anselm of Canterbury, "Why God Became Man," in *The Major Works*, ed. Brian Davies and G. R. Evans (Oxford: Oxford University Press, 1998), 338. For a more complete discussion of Anselm, see Chapter 3 above and Joerg Rieger, *Christ and Empire: From Paul to Postcolonial Times* (Minneapolis: Fortress, 2007), chapter 3. Also recall from Chapter 3 above that changing or redefining what is satisfied or offered to God does not change the overall logic of the motif in which the salvation of humankind depends on Jesus' death going Godward.

2. Walter Wink, *Engaging the Powers: Discernment and Resistance in a World of Domination* (The Powers 3; Minneapolis: Fortress, 1992), 195-99.

for ever greater violence to overcome the enemy — and each side becomes what it decries in the other. A minority that has experienced oppression may enact the same kind of oppression when it comes into power. Under the claim of protecting itself from ever again experiencing oppression, it has become like the oppressor it feared and hated.

The idea that still greater violence is needed to overcome violence appears specifically in the discussion of eschatology. The idea that God will respond to evil with greater violence in the eschaton makes God into the ultimate purveyor of violence. The dispensational scheme of eschatology features Christ returning in vengeance to vanquish evil in the great battle of Armageddon, in which evil is finally defeated once and for all. This sequence is overwhelmingly violent, as David Kirkpatrick recently described the Left Behind Series of Tim LaHaye and Jerry Jenkins, the popular series of novels that portray a dispensationalist end to history. Writes Kirkpatrick, "Few have portrayed [Jesus] wreaking more carnage on the unbelieving world than Tim LaHaye and Jerry B. Jenkins. . . . Jesus eviscerates the flesh of millions of unbelievers merely by speaking."[3] But many writers of a different theological persuasion agree on the necessity of a violent component in eschatology. So writes Miroslav Volf, concerning the rider on the white horse of Revelation 19, which was interpreted in Chapter 2 above as a nonviolent image:

> The creation of the world involved no violence. . . . The chaos sets in as a distortion of the peaceful creation. Redemption cannot, therefore, be an act of pure positing but entails negation and struggle, even violence. First God suffers violence on the cross for the salvation of the world. Then, after God's patience with chaotic powers who refuse to be redeemed by the cross has come to an end, God inflicts violence against the stubbornly violent to restore creation's original peace.[4]

Jesus' Nonviolence

The idea of a nonviolent God poses an alternative to this violent image of God. Words and acts of Jesus display what a nonviolent God might look

---

3. David D. Kirkpatrick, "The Return of the Warrior Jesus," *New York Times,* April 4, 2004, 4-1.

4. Miroslav Volf, *Exclusion and Embrace: A Theological Exploration of Identity, Otherness, and Reconciliation* (Nashville: Abingdon, 1996), 300.

like in practice. In Matthew 5:39, Jesus says, "Do not resist an evildoer." This well-known but frequently misused statement is an injunction designed to change the situation, to interrupt the cycle of retribution and retaliation in human practice. I accept the interpretation that Jesus' words about not resisting an evildoer should be translated to mean "do not mirror evil" or "do not resist violently." The statement is thus an injunction against violent resistance, retaliation, or rebellion, all actions that would simply provoke more violence. With this interpretation, Paul then repeats the meaning of Jesus' words when he writes in Romans, "Do not repay anyone evil for evil," and "Do not be overcome by evil, but overcome evil with good" (Rom. 12:17, 21). 1 Thessalonians 5:15 and 1 Peter 3:9 convey this meaning as well.[5] In this context it becomes clear that Jesus' words about turning the other cheek, giving the undergarment with the outer garment, and going the second mile constitute three examples of how to resist without merely returning evil for evil. Chapter 1 explained their particular contexts. Here I note their capacity to change a situation or interrupt a cycle of abuse or violence.

Rather than retaliating against the slap, which would trigger a beating, turning the other cheek refuses to accept the insult and leaves the aggressor embarrassed. Refusing to obey the order to carry the soldier's pack risks precipitating violence, whereas cheerfully carrying it into a second mile puts the soldier in noncompliance with his own regulations and might even bring him to beg the peasant to put down the pack. Retaliating against the debt holder or refusing to surrender the garment for security would only provide more legal grounds for oppressing the poor debtor, whereas stripping naked and handing over the undergarment with the outer garment would shame the debt holder who exploits and harasses the poor debtor.[6] Jesus added an important injunction to these suggestions for nonviolent, nonretaliatory resistance, namely, "Love your enemies and pray for those who persecute you, so that you may be children of your Father in heaven" (Matt. 5:44-45). The object of the three examples of nonviolent resistance is to embarrass and expose evil, but it is not to belittle and humiliate the offender. Rather these tactics recognize the humanity of the offender and hold open the possibility of change. The injunction to "love your enemies" emphasizes that possibility and thus keeps alive the potential of converting the enemy into a friend.

---

5. Wink, *Engaging the Powers*, 185-86, quoting 186.
6. Wink, *Engaging the Powers*, 175-83.

In everyday speech, the term "love" has taken on connotations of romantic attachment and sentimentality. But here in Jesus' words, love means something else. It is closer to "act in such a way as to transform the enemy into a friend." Alongside this meaning of love, Walter Wink's warning is significant: "We become what we hate." Hating the enemy, retaliating in kind, turns the actor into precisely that which is hated. Retaliating in kind is imitation, mirroring evil. That mirroring is what Jesus and Paul warned against. And in the divine realm, the response of God in resurrecting Jesus is the divine act of changing the situation rather than responding to violence with more and greater violence. Jesus' followers who love their enemies are mirroring the response of God. Peacemaking means to love enemies, which is a way to say "interrupt the cycle of retaliation by acting in such a way as to convert an enemy into a friend."

Here in these injunctions not to mirror evil, to return good for evil, to love enemies, to change the situation is the basis of a lived theology of the church as the extension of Jesus' nonviolent, reconciling presence in the world. It stands as a counter to the God who uses the violence displayed in satisfaction atonement images and is mirrored in the prevailing systems of retributive justice. In contrast, the church proposed here is the continuation of the presence of the nonviolent narrative of Jesus in the world, and thus it gives a witness to the nonviolent God who was revealed in Jesus.

As Brian McLaren described living in the nonviolent narrative of Jesus, "Jesus uses the cross to expose Roman violence and religious complicity with it, while pronouncing a sentence of forgiveness on his crucifiers." The cross represents "God's willingness to accept rejection and mistreatment, and then respond with forgiveness, reconciliation, and resurrection. In this kingdom, peace is not made and kept through the shedding of the blood of enemies, but the king himself sacrifices his blood to make a new kind of peace, offering amnesty to repentant rebels and open borders to needy immigrants." If Rome's motto is "peace through the destruction of enemies, . . . for Jesus the motto is peace through nonviolent justice, peace through the forgiveness of enemies, peace through reconciliation, peace through embrace and grace." Thus

> To be a follower of Jesus in this light is a far different affair than many of us were taught: it means to join Jesus' peace insurgency, to see through every regime that promises peace through violence, peace through domination, peace through genocide, peace through exclusion and in-

timidation. Following Jesus instead means forming communities that seek peace through justice, generosity, and mutual concern, a willingness to suffer persecution but a refusal to inflict it on others.[7]

It requires faith, faith in the resurrection of Jesus, to live in this church that continues the mission of Jesus in the world. As John Howard Yoder suggested, we demonstrate our belief that Jesus Christ is Lord by living in his story when it is not required — and it is certainly not required in the secular and pluralistic world in which we live — and even when it may be costly or dangerous. And the more visibly this church that extends the presence of Jesus in the world makes clear its witness against the violence of American empire, the more risk it incurs because of its faith. But if God is fully revealed in Jesus, then living in his nonviolent story is living with what Yoder called "the grain of the universe,"[8] even if most of the world is blind to it. Do Christians believe strongly enough in the resurrection to live in the story of the one whom God raised?

The nonviolence of the church is a characteristic that qualifies all of its practices. This is simply another way of saying what the Apostle Paul said in his first letter to the Corinthians. No practice of faithfulness, not even the sacrifice of the body in martyrdom, is worth anything in the reign of God unless it is done in love (1 Corinthians 13). The way of love and nonviolence encompasses a wide range of issues and practices. The following provides a brief and schematic description, including some issues not commonly mentioned as problems of violence.

Nonviolence Applied

In the book *Teaching Peace,* Glen Stassen and Michael Westmoreland-White developed a twofold definition of violence. It is "(1) destruction to a victim and (2) by overpowering means. *Violence is destruction to a victim by means that overpower the victim's consent.*"[9] This definition includes the overt vio-

---

7. Brian D. McLaren, *Everything Must Change: Jesus, Global Crises, and a Revolution of Hope* (Nashville: Thomas Nelson, 2007), 158-59.

8. John Howard Yoder, "Armaments and Eschatology," *Studies in Christian Ethics* 1 (1988): 58.

9. Glen H. Stassen and Michael L. Westmoreland-White, "Defining Violence and Nonviolence," in *Teaching Peace: Nonviolence and the Liberal Arts,* ed. J. Denny Weaver and Gerald Biesecker-Mast (Lanham: Rowman & Littlefield, 2003), 18.

lence of war and the bodily harm that is done with weapons, but it also recognizes that systemic or structural injustices are also forms of violence.

Although systemic violence is clearly distinguishable from physical violence such as lynching or war, it is important to acknowledge the real harm done to people by the systemic violence of unjust structures and policies. Social structures and tax policies that enforce poverty do real harm to people. Practices of racism harm people. Laws and practices that discriminate against gays and lesbians harm people. Frustrations build under such violence, and eventually violent outbursts may occur, which harm more people and continue the cycle of violence begetting violence.

Direct violence also takes many forms. There is the direct violence that occurs with weapons, occurring at all levels from one individual harming another, then mob violence, through weapons-wielding police forces, to capital punishment and massive violence among nations at an international level. Related and contributing to this violence on a national and international level are the major industries that design and manufacture war materials, for use not only by the United States but for sale to many other nations around the world. Direct violence may also include words that belittle and demean — whether an adult repeatedly declaring a child's worthlessness or the words commonly used to denigrate and belittle classes of people because of ethnicity, skin color, disability, or sexual orientation, or words designed to deliberately insult another religion.

The theme of violence thus covers a wide range of issues. It is virtually self-evident that the church that lives out of the narrative of Jesus opposes these forms of both systemic and direct violence at all levels. That opposition can be passive — a refusal to participate in direct violence and seeking ways to minimize participation in the systemic violence of our society. But in keeping with the engaged, activist character of discipleship that results in a lived witness to Jesus in the world, the church can also engage in active opposition, either as an institution or in actions by groups of members. This opposition can include public demonstrations against war, refusal to pay that portion of income taxes that supports the war effort, active work against spousal abuse, public manifestations against capital punishment, public school teachers finding creative ways to insert nonviolent views of history into the school curriculum, churches sending counselors to high schools on military recruitment days to offer information on pacifism and service alternatives, support for women who have suffered or are suffering abuse, support for programs of restorative justice and Victim Offender Reconciliation Programs, participation in anti-racism projects, work to protect undocumented people from exploitation, protests against harmful cuts in the social safety net for the disadvantaged, public manifestations of respect for other religions, and much more. This opposition to violence is limited only by the imagination of those who live as disciples of Jesus, but the life and witness of the community should be living testimony to the futility of attempting to solve problems at any level with violence.

Such a list of suggestions on ways to witness against violence is not a blueprint for nonviolent activity. Many other examples could be listed. And further, in point of fact, the appropriate way to engage in nonviolent resistance to violence and injustice is not always clear. Only a few examples illustrate. For example, how should Harriet Jacobs, a nineteenth-century enslaved mother who wrote about herself under the name of Linda Brent, resist the sexual aggression of her owner, who will sell her children far away if she does not submit?[10] Although the example is old, no doubt the story has modern counterparts in the accounts that surface continually in our news — a young girl abused by a father or older relative who threatens great bodily harm if she tells, or an abused mother whose children are threatened if she reports the abuser. How do we resist the exploitation of poor laborers in other countries who sew clothes in sweatshops when virtually all the clothing we can buy in the United States is made in those shops, and poor people are trying to clothe themselves with the most affordable clothing available? How should one respond to a deranged individual who opens fire with automatic weapons in a theater or school or shopping mall? Should people who were hiding Jews during World War II have lied when questioned by the Gestapo? Today the question might be asked about people sheltering a person without legal papers whose deportation will cause great hardship to his or her family. Such examples could be expanded greatly. Answers to such questions are not easy or clear. Mistakes are made. But such mistakes ought not dissuade Christians from the effort to live nonviolently, any more than errors and fumbles in baseball or football result in abandoning all efforts to play.

Some readers may be tempted at this point to interject the question, "What would you do if a criminal threatened your wife/mother/daughter with a gun?" This question is always posed with the assumption that only two answers are possible — either do nothing and allow the loved one to be killed, or kill the intruder and save the loved one. Yoder's book *What*

10. For the story of Jacobs/Brent, see "Incidents in the Life of a Slave Girl," in Henry Louis Gates, Jr., ed., *The Classic Slave Narratives* (New York: Signet Classics, 2012).

Would You Do? provides an insightful and multifaceted answer to this question. He points out a number of assumptions behind the question, including the belief that there are only two answers and that the use of violence is the only way out. In fact, he says, the use of violence is not always successful, and there are actually seven possible outcomes. Two of those are escapes through either natural means or through God's providence. Yoder concludes, "I do not know what I *would* do if some insane or criminal person were to attack my wife or child, sister or mother. But I know that what I *should* do would be illuminated by what God my Father did when his 'only begotten Son' was being threatened."[11]

One example of the kind of escape Yoder mentioned is the story of 73-year-old Louise Degrafinried and her husband Nathan. When Mr. Degrafinried put the cat out early in the morning, he was confronted by a big man with a shotgun. The man forced his way into the house and pushed the couple against the wall. They recognized the intruder as one of five inmates who had escaped from a nearby state prison. Mrs. Degrafinried eyed the man and said, "Young man, I am a Christian lady. I don't believe in no violence. Put that gun down and you sit down. I don't allow no violence here." After a moment's hesitation he put the gun down and then told her he was very hungry. She made him a breakfast of bacon, eggs, toast, milk, and coffee. When the food was ready, she prayed with the intruder and then they ate together. When the police cars showed up, the intruder expressed fear that he would be killed. Mrs. Degrafinried responded, "No, young man, they aren't going to hurt you. You done wrong, but God loves you." She and her husband took him outside. When the police approached with guns, Mrs. Degrafinried shouted, "Y'all put those guns away. I don't allow no violence here." Mr. Degrafinried walked the prisoner to the car, and the prisoner was handcuffed and returned to prison. Soon after this event, I saw Mr. and Mrs. Degrafinried interviewed on the morning news show of a major national television network. It was a riveting experience for me. I still recall rather vividly how the news anchor tried to get Mrs. Degrafinried to talk about being a hero and her bravery in confronting an armed intruder. She wanted nothing of that. The suave news anchor was simply nonplussed when she insisted, "No, I was just acting like a Christian." There was a tragic counterpart to Mrs. Degrafinried's

11. John Howard Yoder, with Joan Baez, et al., *What Would You Do? A Serious Answer to a Standard Question* (expanded ed.; Scottdale: Herald, 1992), 11-42, quoting 42. Yoder discusses assumptions behind the question on 12-24.

actions. Later that same afternoon, two of the other escapees entered a backyard where a couple were barbecuing. When the husband went in the house and came out with a gun, he was shot and killed. His wife was taken hostage but released the next day.[12]

A similar challenge to nonviolence was posed by Malcolm X, who rejected the principled nonviolence advocated by Martin Luther King, Jr. Malcolm X was adamant that nonviolence left black people to be helpless victims in the face of brutality from white supremacists and a racist society. He claimed that black people had the right of self-defense in the face of brutality, a claim echoed by numbers of black militants and used by whites to denounce him as an extremist. He was renowned for the claim that black people could use "any means necessary" to defend themselves or to halt injustice. In a panel discussion of June 12, 1963, Malcolm asserted that Gandhi's program in India was successful because there the practitioners of nonviolence were the majority against the minority British occupiers, whereas nonviolence would not work in the United States where black people were the minority. Toward the end of his life, Malcolm had moderated his view on separation of black and white people and on occasion he could praise Martin Luther King, Jr.[13] However, he never wavered in his view of nonviolence and his advocacy of self-defense. He reiterated the right of African Americans to self-defense in the debate on extremism that he participated in at Oxford University on December 3, 1964, shortly before he was assassinated on February 21, 1965.[14] Like the question of "What

---

12. William H. Willimon, "Bless You, Mrs. Degrafinried," *Christian Century* 101, 9 (March 14, 1984): 269-70. A parallel story is Langston Hughes, "Thank You, M'am," in *The Best Short Stories by Negro Writers: An Anthology from 1899 to the Present,* ed. Langston Hughes (Boston: Little, Brown, 1967), 70-73. Several years ago I contacted the network that had broadcast the appearance of Mr. and Mrs. Degrafinried to see if I could obtain a video or a transcript of the interview. I was informed that they did not retain copies of material that far back.

A quite different story of escape by natural means through overcoming with kindness made national news several years ago. When an armed intruder walked into the living room of two women in their 60s who were watching television, they offered the man a ham sandwich, a bottle of rum, and a shower along with a disposable razor to shave off his beard for his getaway. They chatted amiably with the man and finally called a cab when he declared himself ready to leave. However, he fell asleep, apparently overcome by the rum, and the cab driver called police, who arrested the man. He was homeless. A Google search for "'Kindness' overwhelms armed intruder" brings up a number of references to this story.

13. On praise of Martin Luther King, Jr., see Manning Marable, *Malcolm X: A Life of Reinvention* (New York: Penguin, 2011), 405, 411-12.

14. For the views of Malcolm X on use of violence, see Marable, *Malcolm X,* e.g., 253,

would you do . . . ?" Malcolm's assertion assumed only two possible responses, namely practice passive nonresistance and be brutalized or resist with violence.

An important first point to make is that the impetus behind Malcolm's assertion of the right of African Americans to defend themselves was an expression of his sense of the hypocrisy of the many white people who controlled the political and social system that enforced the systemic violence of segregation but who counseled African Americans to be nonviolent and then blamed unrest on them when demonstrations exposed the injustice of the status quo. However, sympathetic critics of Malcolm X have pointed out that he misunderstood King's nonviolent activism and "the fundamental importance of the mainstream civil rights struggle to the large majority of black Americans."[15] King's nonviolence was not a passive stance but an activist effort to change the situation. In responding to the charge of passivism, King said that his stance was not "nonresistance," but rather one of "nonviolent resistance."[16] Certainly James Cone is correct when he says that "Martin's insight into the weakness of violence was much more profound than Malcolm's. On the issue of violence, Malcolm's value system was hardly different from that of the whites he criticized." And a bit later, Cone adds, "On this point, Martin seems to have history on his side, not only for African-Americans but for everybody. For unless humankind finds a way to put an end to violence, then violence will most certainly put an end to humankind."[17]

Recall the discussion of the cyclical nature of violence from Chapter 5. If the creator God revealed in Jesus is a nonviolent God, then in the words of John Howard Yoder, those who practice nonviolence are working with "the grain of the universe" or with what Martin Luther King, Jr. called "the long arc of the moral universe that bends toward justice." However, this "grain of the universe" is also visible to those with eyes to see apart from

---

303, 357, 405, 411-14, as well as "Malcolm X on Nonviolence," from panel discussion of June 12, 1963, http://www.youtube.com/watch?V=U1a_79xuzOE; "Martin Luther King and Malcolm X Debate," http://www.youtube.com/watch?V=h4PqLKWuwyU, which juxtaposes recorded statements of Malcolm and King; and "Malcolm X Oxford Union Debate — 1964," http://www.youtube.com/watch?v=jlx3v8RRqUU, which is a debate statement on extremism of December 3, 1964 at Oxford University.

15. Marable, *Malcolm X*, 406.

16. See video "Martin Luther King and Malcolm X Debate" in note 14.

17. James H. Cone, *Martin and Malcolm and America: A Dream or a Nightmare?* (Maryknoll: Orbis, 1991), 270.

Christian faith, as in the example just stated, namely the cyclical nature of violence. And Malcolm's assertion of the right to respond to violence with violence seems a clear example. Thus Christians may base a commitment to nonviolence on Jesus' words about not mirroring evil and loving enemies, but a Muslim can observe the futility of violence as well. An example is Badshah Khan,[18] who was described in Chapter 5.

Finally, a last point is to note examples where nonviolent struggles and struggles that came to recognize the futility of violence were successful. In addition to Gandhi's movement and the gains of the Civil Rights movement in the United States, many examples are described in the book *A Force More Powerful*.[19] Two other examples worthy of particular mention are the Revolution of the Candles that began in Leipzig, Germany, and the Singing Revolution in Estonia. What began as weekly prayer meetings in the Nikolai church in Leipzig grew into mass marches of hundreds of thousands of people that led eventually to the fall of the Berlin Wall.[20] The Singing Revolution that began in Estonia in 1987 was a series of mass demonstrations at music festivals that featured spontaneous singing, accompanied by Estonian rock musicians, of national songs and hymns forbidden during the years of the Soviet occupation. Eventually 300,000 Estonians, a quarter of the population, gathered to sing in Tallinn. There were various acts of defiance, including masses of people who served as human shields to protect radio and TV stations from Soviet tanks. In 1991 these actions led to Estonia achieving independence from the Soviet Union without bloodshed.[21]

Nonviolent confrontation does not guarantee a happy outcome. It can certainly fail. However, the possibility of failure or injury ought not in and of itself be a reason to abandon nonviolence. Applying the possibility of failure or injury equally means acknowledging that violent efforts also contain the potential for failure and injury. The Christian who intends to live out of the story of Jesus will thus find the norm for behavior in that story rather than in a calculus of so-called "real world" consequences or in

18. Eknath Easwaran, *Nonviolent Soldier of Islam: Badshah Khan, a Man to Match His Mountains* (Tomales: Nilgiri, 1999).

19. Peter Ackerman and Jack DuVall, *A Force More Powerful: A Century of Nonviolent Conflict* (New York: Palgrave, 2000).

20. Jörg Swoboda, *The Revolution of the Candles: Christians in the Revolution in the German Democratic Republic* (Macon: Mercer University Press, 1996).

21. For data on the Singing Revolution, see http://en.wikipedia.org/wiki/Demographic _threat.

the natural desire to retaliate in kind. Thus, as Yoder said, we may not always know what we might do, but we do know "what we should do," which is to confront the situation without violence, to avoid killing or doing great bodily harm even at the cost to oneself.

The goal of nonviolent confrontation and nonviolent action is to change harmful behaviors and ultimately to convert enemies to friends rather than to destroy them. In *Body Politics,* Yoder described baptism as the symbol of the conversion of the enemy to a friend. As was noted in Chapter 6, baptism celebrates the possibility of new life in Christ in the new creation. Nonviolent confrontation of an adversary is an expression of "our permanent readiness to see our adversary as able to change." Nonviolent techniques celebrate the dignity of the downtrodden and oppressed. However, it must also be recognized that violent confrontation can also engage such a celebration of the oppressed. What makes nonviolent techniques unique is that they also protect the dignity of the adversary and hold open permanently the possibility of change and reconciliation. Christian baptism celebrates the possibility that this change and reconciliation is indeed possible for all.[22]

Large numbers of people encounter systemic and structural violence. Tax structures and social systems that favor the wealthy enforce the violence of poverty on those at the bottom of the social hierarchy. A specific example of this tax and budgetary violence is allocating many millions of dollars for sports stadiums with luxury boxes while claiming lack of funds for inner city schools and services for poor people. Social practices of white privilege that silently hold back people of color and favor the white racial majority of the United States perpetuate the violence of racism. Social practices that favor men in the workplace perpetuate violence against women. The same applies to people who experience discrimination because of age or sexual orientation or disability. Both rhetoric and policies that blame "illegal aliens" for a host of domestic problems even as their labor is exploited by a number of industries enact violence on immigrants and on citizens who look like immigrants.

In terms of day-to-day living, most people in North America encounter such experiences of systemic violence more frequently than they do the direct violence of weapons. Since many of these issues of injustice are endemic to North American society, even people of nonviolent good will

---

22. John Howard Yoder, *Body Politics: Five Practices of the Christian Community before the Watching World* (Scottdale: Herald, 2001), 41-42.

participate in them. That reality gives impetus to specific acts of resistance that work toward justice and testify that such participation is involuntary.

The church that is a living presence of the life of Jesus has the potential to confront these issues of domestic and systemic violence. In fact, this confrontation may be one of the church's most visible witnesses to the presence of the reign of God made visible in Jesus. As a community of faith that lives out of the life and story of Jesus, it is concerned for those without power — the widows, orphans, and strangers of Jesus' time, who lacked political power in a world where political and economic status and power came through adult men. Today the people of particular concern to Jesus might include "illegal aliens," poor people, people without health insurance, people with AIDS, victims of discrimination of various kinds, and more. The internal structures and the governance of the church should reflect care for all members, regardless of social standing as defined by North American society. And as a natural extension of this caring, the life of churchly communities should witness against and confront these kinds of structural and systemic violence prevalent in North American society. This witness makes visible the true character of the reign of God. Continuing that witness, even in the face of relentless discrimination and disregard for the downtrodden, is necessary in order to keep visible the possibility of change celebrated by baptism.

This discussion of ways the church that lives in Jesus confronts multiple levels of violence and injustice is only schematic, a bare outline of a wide range of issues. The point here is not to mention all dimensions of violence and response but rather to say that confrontation of and witness against the multiple dimensions of violence in North American society is an intrinsic dimension of the church of Jesus Christ as I understand it. The following chapters sketch some of these issues in more depth.

The next chapter displays the nonviolence of God in the particular context of salvation and God's forgiveness of sin. The discussion displays the way that the narrative Christus Victor motif developed in Chapters 1 and 2 models God's forgiveness. This model of forgiveness and reconciliation, which is derived from the narrative of Jesus, then becomes the basis for understanding the practice of reconciliation in the context of conflict and injustice.

8   Atonement, Violence, and Forgiveness

Understandings of God and God's role in forgiveness differ significantly between narrative Christus Victor and the several versions of satisfaction atonement. Social practices then reflect these differences, which have profound effects on lived theology. Consider the following.

Forgiveness in Narrative Christus Victor[1]

How is forgiveness understood in the narrative Christus Victor atonement motif? Recall that the narrative of Jesus has no indication of any kind that the death of Jesus impacted God or is aimed at God or satisfies any kind of divine need, whether that need is punishment demanded by divine law, restoration of honor to an offended God, restoration of the distorted order of creation, restoration of worship wrongfully withdrawn from God, or restoration of true obedience to God. Such elements are simply not there when we rehearse the narrative of Jesus as given in the Gospels. Rather than being needed and directed by God, the death in this story is produced by the forces that oppose Jesus. If God is truly present in the life of Jesus as Christian faith proclaims, this death is clear evidence that the modus operandi of the forces of evil differs from the means of the nonviolent reign of God made visible in Jesus.

---

1. Parts of the material in this chapter are drawn from a longer discussion of forgiveness and atonement in J. Denny Weaver, "Forgiveness and (Non)Violence: The Atonement Connection," *Mennonite Quarterly Review* 83 (2009): 319-47.

All human beings are implicated in this narrative about Jesus. Although vanquished, the powers that crucified Jesus are still present and active in the world. The revelation of their defeat by the resurrection of Jesus does not hinder their continuing presence and activity.[2] The universality of sin means that every human being in some way is captive to and participates with the evil perpetrated by these powers. That universal participation makes every human in some way a collaborator with the forces that killed Jesus. Jesus did die because of the sins of each of us. He died while and because we are sinners. We cannot reverse that participation in Jesus' death or the impact of our ongoing participation with the power of evil. Nothing can undo or compensate for it.

However, when we acknowledge our complicity with the powers of evil, that is, when we confess our sin and switch sides — switch allegiance and loyalty — from the powers of evil to the reign of God, God accepts us as God's children. No prior compensation of God or satisfaction of divine anger or offended honor or restoration of worship or obedience makes that acceptance possible. God forgives — God lets go of justifiable anger against us — and we are accepted as God's children. In traditional terms, this is forgiveness of our guilt for having offended God. This forgiveness reveals what God always was, namely a loving God who was extending grace, acceptance, and communion to all (although some choose not to accept it). God's forgiveness is truly a gift, an unlimited and unmerited gift, offered before we respond and in spite of our participation with the powers of evil that crucified Jesus. God lets go of our offenses against God and responds to us as though we had not rebelled and participated with the forces that killed Jesus. This forgiveness and acceptance by God is an act of God's grace, unmerited grace.

It bears remembering that the process that involves both a choice to

---

2. The image of heavenly combat in Revelation 12 presents a visual way to understand the continuing presence of the defeated powers. Recall that the dragon with seven heads, ten horns, and seven crowns refers to Rome, the city built on seven hills with seven crowned emperors and three pretenders to the crown between the time of Jesus' death and resurrection and the writing of Revelation. The baby snatched to heaven is the resurrected Jesus. When the dragon is defeated and thrown down to earth, the heavenly voice proclaims, "*Now* have come the salvation and the power and the kingdom of our God and the authority of his Messiah, . . . But woe to the earth and the sea, for the devil has come down to you with great wrath" (12:10-12, emphasis added). In other words, the decisive victory has already occurred in the resurrection of Jesus. Nonetheless, Rome, representing the evil powers — the defeated dragon — may continue to threaten the church.

switch allegiance and unmerited forgiveness by God involves a paradox, as was explained in Chapter 1. Forgiveness by God includes both our responsibility and the grace of God. As Paul said, "But by the grace of God I am what I am, and his grace toward me has not been in vain. On the contrary, I worked harder than any of them — though it was not I, but the grace of God that is with me" (1 Cor. 15:10).

Being forgiven by God without compensation or satisfaction offered to God does not by any means ignore our complicity in sin. In order to experience God's freely offered forgiveness, the sinner must confess sin and make a change, namely switch to the side of the reign of God. In other words, receiving God's forgiveness means that the sinner has begun a lifelong process of learning to live in the reign of God. It is a lifelong process since evil is never fully overcome and God's forgiveness is therefore ongoing as well. Nonetheless, the fact or the intent to change is what demonstrates that the sinner is now on the side of the reign of God. Absence of the intent to align with the reign of God indicates a refusal to accept God's forgiveness. Meanwhile, God always remains the loving God, offering the gift of forgiveness. This is the forgiveness we are to model. It recalls Jesus' response to the woman taken in adultery: when she was left standing without an accuser, Jesus said, "Neither do I condemn you. Go your way, and from now on do not sin again" (John 8:11). Leaving the side of the forces of evil and joining with the reign of God is thus the lived version of the theology of divine forgiveness that emanates from narrative Christus Victor.

Jesus gave a parable that illustrates this divine forgiveness, namely the parable of the Prodigal Son (Luke 15:11-32). It might well be called the Parable of the Forgiving Father. In this well-known story, the prodigal asked for, received, and then squandered his inheritance in a distant land. His life spiraled out of control. When he hit bottom, the jolt moved him to return home with the intent to proclaim his unworthiness to be a son and then ask for a job as a hired hand. But even before the returning prodigal could make his speech, the father welcomed him back and proclaimed the grand celebration, while his older son sulked.

Richard Holloway interprets this parable as a statement of God's unmerited grace. For Holloway, the key interpretative indication comes from "the running of the father" to greet the returning prodigal, who comes into view at a great distance. Running, an abandonment of dignity, signifies that the father has broken the strict code of behavior expected for the patriarch of a family. This father had already been insulted when the son asked for the inheritance that was his legally only after his father's death.

Following that insult, the son sank even lower, namely to live with pigs. The son has thus placed himself outside the code of the community and merits banishment on his return. Meanwhile, the son's decision to return, in Holloway's view, is a dangerous but opportunistic effort to salvage something of his life. Since the son has already abandoned the code of the community, he has already made himself an outsider and should "be offered no succour, no food, no water, no shelter; he is already dead to them and they to him." His decision to ask the father to be treated as "a hired hand" is thus an effort to avoid the wrath of the community, a gauntlet he must run in order to reach his father. But before the prodigal could reach this dangerous stretch of his journey, the father spied him far off and abandoned all protocol and all dignity. He ran to greet the son, threw his arms around him and kissed him. In other words, the son is forgiven before he can make his prepared speech. And when he presented his speech, "there is a significant omission." "There is no opportunistic plea for a job on the farm." In Holloway's interpretation, this parable becomes a story of unconditional forgiveness, and it is the unconditional forgiveness that produced the change in the prodigal son.[3]

The response of the father in this parable mirrors the action of God depicted in narrative Christus Victor. The father, like God, maintains a consistent outlook of forgiveness and displays perpetual desire for the prodigal's return. When the son finally appears in the distance, the father runs to welcome him, proclaiming the celebration of the prodigal's return to the family, just as there is "joy in heaven over one sinner who repents" (Luke 15:7). This reception did not represent a change in the father's attitude but rather expressed the love and willingness to forgive that he had been feeling all along. Thus, when the son did return, the father, like God, let go of the anger that might justifiably be held against the son, who represents us sinners, and welcomed him with open arms as God welcomes us. And from the side of the wayward son, it was not a welcome that required nothing of him. In order for him to receive that forgiveness and welcome, he had to acknowledge the error of his ways and change the course of his life, as coming to the side of the reign of God requires a lifelong process.[4]

3. Richard Holloway, *On Forgiveness* (Edinburgh: Canongate, 2002), 80-82.

4. Although without the overlay of atonement theology given here, this interpretation of the parable is parallel to Donald B. Kraybill, *The Upside-Down Kingdom* (rev. ed.; Scottdale: Herald, 2003), 167-71.

Rob Bell interprets the parable in terms of God's response to two different ways to

Forgiveness in Satisfaction Atonement

Forgiveness in satisfaction atonement displays a markedly different picture of God from that portrayed in the parable of the Forgiving Father. It is said that God forgives and that God's forgiveness is without limits. But within the paradigm of satisfaction atonement, this limitless forgiveness depends on a prior act of God, who demands and exacts justice in the death of Jesus.

Within the image of satisfaction atonement, it is God who has been offended by human sin. In various versions of satisfaction atonement, this sin against God has been defined as an offense against God's honor, a disruption of the order of creation, a withholding of pure worship of God, or an offense against God's law or withholding obedience to God, and more. Because God is holy and just, sinful human beings cannot approach God unless and until the debt or damage to divine honor has been satisfied. Satisfying the divine need requires a death. Since human beings have no power to make that satisfaction to God for themselves, God sent Jesus to step in and die in their place. The death of sinless Jesus thus satisfies the honor of God or restores the order of creation or restores pure worship or satisfies the requirement of God's law or placates God's wrath or restores obedience. With the divine need satisfied, and God's honor or justice or order restored, God can then freely forgive all those sinful humans who accept the sacrificial death of Jesus on their behalf.

The underlying assumption of these several satisfaction atonement images is that pain on one side balances pain or offense on the other, that

---

choose to distance oneself from God. One is to stay away from God because of feelings of guilt and unworthiness — the prodigal proclaimed himself unworthy and requested to be treated as a "hired hand." The other way is to attempt to earn favor with God — the older brother, who refused to join the party, believing that he had been treated unjustly. In each case, the words of the son would place him outside the circle of the father. But in neither case does the father accept the distancing. He rejects the prodigal's story by welcoming him home. The father challenges the older brother's story, when he says, "Son, you are always with me, and all that is mine is yours" (Luke 15:31). For each son, the father is loving and accepting. In both cases, the son must decide whether to trust the word of the father, whether to accept the father's redefinition of their relationship. In terms of the narrative Christus Victor motif, Bell's telling of the parable reflects the offering of forgiveness by God without satisfaction. Either son can refuse the offer of grace and continue in the way of estrangement, but the father's love and invitation remain consistent throughout. Rob Bell, *Love Wins: A Book about Heaven, Hell, and the Fate of Every Person Who Ever Lived* (New York: HarperOne, 2011), 164-70.

the offense against God is balanced, satisfied by pain exercised against Jesus, namely his suffering and death. This intent to balance is true whether it satisfies honor, restores the distorted order of creation, restores true worship, or any other Godward intended result of the death of Jesus.[5] Suffering and death exerted on Jesus balances out — satisfies — the injury or injustice done to God by human sin. Further, however satisfaction is understood in these images, forgiveness consists of avoiding or forgoing the punishment that sinful humans deserve. Because Jesus' death has already satisfied the divine requirement of justice or order or obedience or true worship, God does not need to exact punishment on sinful human beings. The penalty they owe God has been paid by Jesus, which allows God to forgive them. Finally, however the image of satisfaction is defined, these atonement images picture a God who exacts violence or who sanctions violence — the death of Jesus — as that which upholds justice and consequently allows God to forgive. God establishes the scenario in which Jesus was sent to die in order to provide the death that would restore or satisfy the offended divine entity or attribute. However satisfaction is conceived, these images picture God as the one who exacts violence as the prerequisite for forgiveness of human sin. As was shown previously in Chapter 3, this image of a God who uses violence is contrary to the image of God revealed in the nonviolent narrative of Jesus.

Citation of the parable of the Forgiving Father focuses the contemporary conversation about forgiveness in atonement theology. Given the dominance of the satisfaction motif in the centuries since Anselm of Canterbury's articulation of the idea in *Cur Deus Homo,* what the father in the parable did *not* do is also important in understanding the implications of this story for atonement imagery. Satisfaction atonement in any of its forms assumes that forgiveness depends on satisfaction of some form of divine debt or need. But the father in the parable did not demand restitution or satisfaction as the prerequisite for restoring the prodigal to the embrace of the family. He did not demand repayment of the money wasted or

5. In order to defend some version of satisfaction atonement against charges of violence, a number of authors have made much of the differences between its several versions. It is argued, for example, that while visualizing violence done against Jesus in penal substitutionary motif is objectionable, the idea of restoring true worship to God does not assume the contractual arrangement of law and is therefore not based on violence. For examples see Chapter 3, n. 48. However, the analysis here and in Chapter 3 of the internal logic of any and all satisfaction images demonstrates that, however the divine target is defined, its satisfaction still depends on a Godward-directed death.

even a repayment schedule before he could pronounce forgiveness. There was nothing of the father as a stern judge demanding reparations in order to uphold justice or restore family honor or family order as the cost of the prodigal's return home. The father did not demand that the son first undergo punishment before returning. We do not see a father whose attitude changed from stern judgment to merciful acceptance *after* reparations were paid. But from the response of the older brother, who complains because no fete celebrates his own steadfastness, we might infer that such acts of reparation are the kind of move he thinks the father should require. In this case, responses of father and older brother then reveal the contrasting attitudes toward forgiveness in the differing atonement motifs, with the father imaging God's forgiveness as reflected in narrative Christus Victor and the elder brother mirroring the basis of forgiveness in satisfaction atonement.

The different understandings about the basis of forgiveness in the two atonement motifs have counterparts in human practice. Assumptions about forgiveness and punishment in satisfaction atonement are reflected in the practice of criminal justice. Forgiveness as pictured in narrative Christus Victor is mirrored in learnings in psychology and in the idea of restorative justice. Seeing these relationships underscores the importance of a lived theology.

The Practice of Forgiveness: Retributive Justice

Chapter 3 has noted the parallels between the philosophy of criminal justice and the underlying assumptions of the several versions of satisfaction atonement. Both assume that justice requires the balancing of the pain experienced by the victim with pain or violence or punishment exacted on the offender or his substitute. Although sinners avoid punishment for their sins — they are "saved" — the underlying assumption, namely that an offense is balanced or satisfied by punishment, is intact. God can forgive without exacting a penalty on sinners because the penalty required by God's justice has been previously met by the penalty-paying or divine-need-satisfying death of Jesus. In each case, whether we are talking of the criminal justice system or of satisfaction atonement, the underlying assumption is that the system depends on and even requires violence.

When an offense occurs and a suspect is apprehended, the purpose of the criminal justice system is to determine the guilt or innocence of the suspect. Procedures built into the system are intended to protect the accused by ensuring that evidence is collected and presented fairly, that the accused has a right to confront the accuser, that all laws are followed correctly in the process, and more. If the suspect is found innocent, then he or she is freed to function again in society. If the defendant is proved guilty, then punishment is administered — light punishment for a small offense, severe punishment for serious misdeeds. Capital punishment — killing the defendant — is reserved for the most heinous or egregious offenses. The theory is that pain balances pain. The scales of justice are balanced when the pain experienced by the victim is equal to pain administered to the offender. When the rules of the process have been followed and the pain administered is judged to be equal to the pain suffered by the victim, then, according to this system, justice has been done.[6]

This system that equates doing justice with administering punishment is called retributive justice. The punishment constitutes retribution for the offense. The practice of retribution ultimately depends on the exercise of violence. Punishment consists of pain — violence — exerted on the offender. The ultimate retribution is death — killing of the offender — but all punishments are administered with the intent of causing some level of pain to the offender, whether the pain of losing resources through a fine, or the pain of losing freedom via imprisonment, or, most severe, losing life through execution.

The application of the criminal justice system in the United States adds an additional layer of violence to the inherent violence of retribution. In her recent book, Michelle Alexander describes the silent racism present in the criminal justice system. At all levels of the system from the police presence on the street through the court system and prison sentences to the stigma placed on ex-prisoners for life, the systemic violence of the retributive system falls most often on people of color and in particular on African American men. As the system has developed since the 1960s, this disproportionate application of the system is presumed fair by the courts and in the public mind, but people of color nonetheless receive an extra application of the system's retribution.[7]

6. For a full description of this approach to justice under the heading of "retributive justice," see Howard Zehr, *Changing Lenses: A New Focus for Crime and Justice* (3rd ed., Christian Peace Shelf; Scottdale: Herald, 2005), 63-82.

7. Michelle Alexander, *The New Jim Crow: Mass Incarceration in the Age of Colorblindness* (rev. ed.; New York: New, 2012). This book receives additional comment in Chapter 9 to follow.

The philosophy undergirding the system of criminal justice reflects that of satisfaction atonement. Both assume that wrong is made right when pain or violence is administered to balance the offense. For both, the idea of "salvation" means to avoid or escape from punishment. In the atonement imagery, sinners avoid punishment because Jesus has already paid the price or borne the pain or undergone punishment or submitted to death to satisfy the divine need — thus forgiveness and salvation mean avoiding punishment by God. In the criminal justice system, the offender avoids punishment when a higher official issues a pardon, which cancels punishment.

For the criminal offender who has been punished as required by law for his or her offense, nothing remains to forgive. In theory, the offender has paid his or her debt to society. In practice the restrictions placed on ex-offenders can make the penalty endure for a lifetime, as Michelle Alexander showed is frequently the case for African Americans.[8] In theory an offender might refuse a pardon and choose to endure the retribution of punishment. In this case, enduring punishment would mean satisfying the penalty rather than receiving forgiveness. Similarly, sinners who refuse to accept the penalty-satisfying death of Jesus for themselves will suffer eternal punishment rather than receiving God's forgiveness and being saved from punishment.

A pardon issued by the authorities who administer the system allows an offender to escape the punishment required by the justice system. However, a pardon still functions within the system. The guilt of the offender remains, and a pardon does nothing for the victim of the offense. A pardon may provoke a public outcry — outrage if a pardon is granted to a grievous offender or if a pardon is not granted to a popular offender or to an offender whose offense was believed justified or judged minor in popular opinion. But these cries of outrage display clearly the assumption that "doing justice" means to balance an offense with appropriate pain or violence administered. Within the image of satisfaction atonement, this pardon is what forgiveness and salvation are all about. Because of Jesus' prior satisfaction of the divine need via his death, God issues a pardon to sinners who thus avoid the punishment they still merit.

For the motif of satisfaction, there is a correspondence between theology and practice. As recounted in Chapter 3, Rita Brock and Rebecca Parker's research into iconography demonstrated that the early church

---

8. See Alexander, *New Jim Crow*.

emphasized the resurrection of Jesus and that Anselm's articulation of the idea of access to God on the basis of suffering followed the introduction of the coercive and violent policies of Emperor Charlemagne.[9] Anselm's articulation of satisfaction atonement reflected the Norman feudal assumption of the need to satisfy honor in order to preserve societal order. In surveying the exercise of punishment in the criminal justice system of Europe since Anselm, the research of Timothy Gorringe reveals that the more stress a society placed on satisfaction or substitutionary atonement, the harsher the penalties meted out by its justice system.[10] In a more recent example, the image of God in substitutionary atonement, one of the contemporary forms of satisfaction atonement imagery, has shaped demands for justice from conservative Protestants in the political conflict in Northern Ireland.[11]

In my view, the practice of retributive justice, which reflects the theological assumptions of satisfaction atonement, is not practice that is developed or derived from the narrative of Jesus, who rejected violence. This exercise of violence and calls for retribution or vengeance as the exercise of justice do not reflect the image of God that is revealed in the story of nonviolent Jesus. These practices do constitute a lived theology, one that reflects satisfaction atonement, but this theology is not a lived version of the story of Jesus.

On the other hand, as the next sections demonstrate, there are practices that reflect the nonviolent narrative of Jesus and the image of the forgiving God in the Parable of the Forgiving Father.

The Practice of Forgiveness: Psychology

Forgiveness has become an object of both research and practice in the discipline of psychology. The emphasis is on the benefit of forgiving for the victim who forgives. In psychology, forgiveness is understood as choosing to let go of anger or hatred toward the offender. A victim is a person who is

9. Rita Nakashima Brock and Rebecca Ann Parker, *Saving Paradise: How Christianity Traded Love of This World for Crucifixion and Empire* (Boston: Beacon, 2008).

10. Timothy Gorringe, *God's Just Vengeance: Crime, Violence and the Rhetoric of Salvation* (Cambridge Studies in Ideology and Religion 9; Cambridge: Cambridge University Press, 1996).

11. Alwyn Thomson, *Fields of Vision: Faith and Identity in Protestant Ireland* (Belfast: Centre for Contemporary Christianity in Ireland, 2002), chapters 3 and 4.

both blameless and helpless before the offender; a victim lacks control and suffers through no fault of her or his own. When this powerless victim retains anger or hatred toward the offender, the victim continues to give the offender power and control over his or her life. By letting go of that anger or hatred, the victim ceases being a victim. With this decision, the person offended becomes an active performer, making a move to regain control of his or her life and to deny the offender power or control over the victim's attitudes or actions. Empirical research demonstrates the material benefit to an offended person who engages in the process of forgiveness.

In the practice of forgiveness as understood in psychology, the emphasis falls on the process of letting go of anger or hatred and on the benefit of this process for the one who forgives. This process of letting go, of forgiving, requires a decision to forgive, but it is an ongoing event, an attitude more than a one-time event. It may in fact continue for a lifetime. The ease of describing this process of letting go of anger ought not be allowed to mask its actual difficulty. The process of forgiveness may lead to reconciliation with the offender, but reconciliation is not necessary in order for the one who forgives to experience the benefits that result from the process of letting go of anger and hatred. From the perspective of Christian theology, it is important to note that psychologists maintain that both the process of forgiveness and the benefit to the one who forgives happen independent of any particular theological foundation. In other words, psychologists advocate forgiveness not out of Christian theological conviction but because it works and improves the mental health of the one who forgives.

An example of a prominent psychologist who advocates forgiveness is Robert Enright, a professor of psychology at the University of Wisconsin. Enright endorses a definition of forgiveness from British philosopher Joanna North, which he paraphrases as: "When unjustly hurt by another, we forgive when we overcome the resentment toward the offender, not by denying our right to the resentment, but instead by trying to offer the wrongdoer compassion, benevolence, and love; as we give these, we as forgiver realize that the offender does not necessarily have a right to such gifts."[12] In his book *Forgiveness is a Choice*, Enright describes four phases of the process of forgiveness. With twenty guidelines to mark progress, the phases are 1) uncovering one's anger, 2) deciding to forgive, 3) working on

12. Robert D. Enright, *Forgiveness Is a Choice: A Step-by-Step Process for Resolving Anger and Restoring Hope* (Washington: American Psychological Association, 2001), 25.

forgiveness, and 4) discovery and release from emotional prison.[13] Without passing over or forgetting the offense committed, forgiveness is for Enright a process that involves offering the wrongdoer compassion, benevolence, and love. This offering acknowledges the wrong committed but also invites the possibility of repentance and reconciliation. Stated differently, forgiveness is not a statement about the character or gravity of the offense, or about whether the offender merits forgiveness: the offense may be horrendous and the offender may not merit forgiveness. It is important to note that anger can play a healthy role in this process, when it motivates the wronged person "to take action, to right wrongs, to stand up and face problems, to fight for self-esteem."[14] Holding on to anger grants the offender continuing power over the victim, while letting go of anger — forgiving — empowers the victim to regain control of his or her life.[15]

It should be emphasized that offering the gift of forgiveness to an offender is not papering over, ignoring, or forgetting the offense or acting as though it never happened. On the contrary, the step of offering the unmerited gift of forgiveness is a frank acknowledgment that an offense occurred. And engaging in the process of forgiveness certainly does not preclude taking precautions to guard the safety of the victim against further offenses or taking steps to prevent the offender from further offenses.

I suggest that the offer of forgiveness can apply to great social evils as well. As a person committed to nonviolence, I admit that it is easy to harbor hostile thoughts toward administration members and to be angry about the thousands of lives needlessly lost on both sides and the billions of dollars consumed in only the most recent wars in Iraq and Afghanistan. Similarly, Native Americans might retain anger at the decimation of their numbers and the injustice they experienced in the course of settlement of North America by Europeans. African Americans can harbor anger about the his-

---

13. See Enright, *Forgiveness*, 78 for a chart of phases and guideposts.

14. Enright, *Forgiveness*, 104.

15. Considerable literature exists in the social sciences on the positive role that forgiveness plays in mental and physical well-being. Two examples with processes for forgiveness parallel to that of Enright are Sidney B. Simon and Suzanne Simon, *Forgiveness: How to Make Peace with Your Past and Get On with Your Life* (New York: Warner, 1990), and Fred Luskin, *Forgive for Good: A Proven Prescription for Health and Happiness* (New York: HarperCollins, 2002). Neither of these books, however, begins the forgiveness process with the offer of the unmerited gift mentioned by Enright, which has the potential to change the relationship between offender and offended. As stated below, this offer of the unmerited gift is parallel to God's grace in the narrative Christus Victor atonement motif.

tory of slavery and the continuing racism that undergirded it (racism is dealt with in more detail in the following chapter). But harboring anger and bitterness about such injustices accomplishes nothing while the offer of forgiveness empowers the one who forgives. And note again that the act of forgiveness toward these injustices is a forthright and open acknowledgement that injustice occurred. The injustices are not forgotten or ignored. On the contrary, awareness of the injustice and its legacy becomes data for clarifying what is necessary in order to pursue justice in the present, a pursuit that can occur without a thirst for vengeance and with a desire for reconciliation based on restorative justice. Thus forgiveness in the area of social injustice is far from a passive decision to accept the unjust status quo. It can actually be the beginning of seeking reconciliation based on justice.

Enright developed this process of forgiveness as a psychologist. He makes a point of saying that it can be practiced by a follower of any religion or no religion; it is "usable by theists and non-theists" alike.[16] He and his fellow researchers developed this process for the benefit of the one who needs to forgive, to assist "those who want to be free from the bondage of anger and resentment."[17]

However, beyond freeing the forgiver, the process may also benefit the offender. It is hoped that the gift of forgiveness will change the offender. Forgiving "is an act of mercy toward the offender, someone who does not necessarily deserve our mercy. It is a gift to our offender for the purpose of changing the relationship between ourselves and those who have hurt us."[18] When that change happens, reconciliation of offended and offender can result. In that case, the forgiver will have "in a real way conquered evil with good."[19]

Enright notes that working on forgiveness does not mean that the offended person is without fault. A part of preparation for the forgiveness process is to ask to what extent the offended person himself or herself may have and likely did contribute to the problem. When one begins the process of forgiving, the person frequently realizes "that he or she has been in the undesirable position of offender in the past."[20]

Another important point in Enright's proposal is the injunction to

16. Enright, *Forgiveness*, 77.

17. Enright, *Forgiveness*, 6 and elsewhere.

18. Enright, *Forgiveness*, 25.

19. Enright, *Forgiveness*, 37. Here, of course, good and evil refer to particular human actions and are not references to theological categories of sin and relationship to God.

20. Enright, *Forgiveness*, 175.

take a companion on the journey to forgiveness. Forgiving is hard work, and Enright writes: "You need to have someone you can talk with about each aspect of the forgiveness process. . . . Please don't do this alone."[21]

Important in Enright's model is its foundation in empirical science. "Our research group has conducted scientific tests using forgiveness as a form of therapy and education." Although he called their fifteen years of research "by no means completed," it is clear that a great deal of evidence in psychology demonstrates that forgiveness actually brings mental healing to offended persons.[22] Robert Enright believes in forgiveness because empirical evidence shows that it works.

Although Enright states that his approach to forgiveness works apart from any religious perspectives, I suggest that a theological overlay from the narrative Christus Victor motif provides validation for the model of forgiveness that Enright teaches.

An understanding of forgiveness derived from the narrative of Jesus features an image of God who lets go of anger without a prior satisfaction of a divine need by blood, suffering, and death. The God revealed in the story of Jesus is a God understood in nonviolent images. As depicted in narrative Christus Victor, God has a right to be angry with rebellious humankind, who all share in sin against God and in particular share in the death of Jesus. However, God is an ever-loving God who lets go of the anger against humankind and offers the gift of unmerited grace and forgiveness. Those who accept his gift are changed. They cease cooperation with the powers of evil and begin the process of learning what it is to live in the reign of God as made visible in the life, death, and resurrection of Jesus Christ. In other words, in this atonement image, forgiveness happens without a prior satisfaction of a divine requirement for blood or death. I suggest that narrative Christus Victor, with its image of a nonviolent God who offers the gift of forgiveness, does constitute a theological foundation for the practice of forgiveness developed by psychologists such as Enright. It proposes an image of "letting go" of anger by God in the transcendent realm as a theological model of forgiveness for the "letting go" of anger described by Enright in the discipline of psychology. And at the two levels, divine and human, there is the offer of the unmerited gift, which has the potential to change the situation.

Assumptions about the basis of truth differ between psychology and

21. Enright, *Forgiveness*, 80.
22. Enright, *Forgiveness*, 7.

theology. Enright believes in forgiveness because it works, but, while his research is convincing, Christians have another reason for practicing forgiveness. Forgiveness is true and should be practiced by Christians first of all because it emerges from the story of Jesus and what that story reveals to us about the character of God. Forgiveness works and is true because it is of God. The intersection of psychology and theology at the juncture of forgiveness is important. Theology does touch the world of human experience, and in this case evidence from empirical science validates a theological claim. The idea of a lived theology that expresses the nonviolence of Jesus has points of appeal in human experience as well as in biblical material and theological logic.[23] The exercise of restorative justice is an area where insights derived from the narrative of Jesus intersect with evidence derived from human experience.

The Practice of Forgiveness: Restorative Justice

Restorative justice is an alternative to retributive justice. Whereas retributive justice focuses on the end goal of administering punishment fairly, restorative justice has the end goal of restoring the relationship broken by the offense.[24] Although obviously some or even many shattered relationships can never be fully restored, the goal remains to restore them as far as possible. For restorative justice, justice is being done when the relationship between victim and offender is being restored, which involves healing of both victim and offender. This approach addresses needs not dealt with by the justice system, which focuses on determining guilt and meting out retribution as punishment.

23. This point reflects the view of John Howard Yoder who wrote: "We cannot discuss theology without interlocking with the human sciences that study the same phenomena from other perspectives. The believer says that faith in Jesus Christ makes love of the enemy imperative and possible. Could not a psychologist describe and measure this? If love leads one to go out and make peace with one's adversary, could not a sociologist describe this event? When a preacher claims 'Violence is always self-defeating,' is that not a claim that a historian could verify or refute? As we flesh out the realism of the message of reconciliation, it is therefore appropriate, even imperative, that we attend to those other disciplines." John Howard Yoder, "From the Wars of Joshua to Jewish Pacifism," in *The War of the Lamb: The Ethics of Nonviolence and Peacemaking*, ed. Glen Harold Stassen, Mark Thiessen Nation, and Matt Hamsher (Grand Rapids: Brazos, 2009), 125.

24. This discussion of restorative justice is based on Zehr, *Changing Lenses*. Howard Zehr is a major founder of the modern movement for restorative justice.

In the criminal justice system, which understands doing justice as applying the correct amount of punishment, the only role for the victim is to observe the process, along with the unofficial hope that the victim will "feel satisfied" when justice has been done. Within the judicial process, it is assumed that it is the society — "the people" — that has been offended. In a trial, the prosecuting attorney speaks in the name of "the people." When a fine is levied, it is paid to the state as representative of "the people." When an offender serves jail time, the offender is paying a debt "to society." Missing in this process is the fact that the offense did not concern society as a whole but a particular victim. The victim is a spectator to the process, and no part of the process addresses an effort to restore what was damaged or destroyed by the offender. Nor is there any mention of a process by which the victim can move beyond fear and anger, namely to experience release from anger — forgiveness — as described in the previous section.

In retributive justice, the idea is to punish the offender, that is, to apply pain that balances the offense. In contrast, the process of restorative justice envisions both victim and offender. For the offender, the goal is to bring the offender to recognize the harm committed and to begin to take steps to restore the harm done or to bring about restitution to the victim. And eventually, the goal is to change the offender so that further offenses will not happen. On the side of the victim, the process of doing justice involves the victim as an active participant. A part of the process focuses on the harm done to the victim. It involves moving the offender to perform restitution to the extent possible. Further, the goal is a healing of the victim, that is, enabling the victim to let go of anger and to live again without fear. The letting go of anger and living without fear is the process of forgiveness described earlier. Along with restoration to the extent possible of what was damaged, this process enables the victim to gain control of his or her life and may eventually lead to reconciliation with the offender.

The process of restorative justice can be long and difficult. An offender must be brought to recognize the harm done to the victim. Strange as it may seem, offenders often act out of a sense of injustice or anger, and they often do not recognize the damage they cause. Bringing an offender to recognize that hurt may be difficult. When the victim is ready, the offender may have a face-to-face meeting with the victim to hear about the hurt caused. Bringing the offender to take responsibility for his or her actions may involve sanctions that resemble the punishment of retributive justice, namely monetary fines or community service or incarceration. Although offenders might view them as punishment, administering such sanctions is not merely for the purpose of applying pain in retribution for the offense. Rather, such sanctions aid the offender to recognize the gravity of the offense, and to begin to accept responsibility for it. Fines collected and community service rendered should be directed to restoration of damage caused by the offense as well as to bring the offender to recognize harm caused. Rejecting the philosophy of tit-for-tat retribution as the basis of justice need not eliminate the role of sanctions administered with a view toward bringing an offender to accept responsibility and undertake restoration. In may also be the case that some offenders might prove incapable of real restoration and thus will require ongoing confinement.[25]

The goal of restoration applies even to the worst offenders. Every human being, even the worst offender, is made in the image of God. No person achieves perfect fulfillment of that potential — which is the meaning of what traditional theology has called "original sin." For some offenders, the image of God within may seem corrupted almost beyond recognition. Nonetheless, every human being is made in the image of God and is a potential child of God. The goal of restorative justice is to discover that spark of what makes an individual human and to do what is possible to actualize it. Christians demonstrate the belief that God loves everyone, not by how they treat the lovely people, but by how they treat the miserable and the unlovely.

Retribution has the meaning of retaliation. As an act of violence, retribution invites a violent response. Offenders often feel like outcasts in the society in which we live. Their offenses, although directed against individuals, are actually outbursts against society, which they believe has rejected them. When offenders with these feelings are punished by society, anger in the offender only grows. Eventually it will again find an avenue of expression, in an ongoing cycle of retaliation. That is, the cyclical nature of violence appears even within the framework of the justice system. Children inherit this violent orientation from parents who are caught in the cycle. The words in the Decalogue are not idle when they speak of God "punishing children for the iniquity of parents, to the third and fourth generation of those who reject me" (Exod. 20:5; also Num. 14:18 and Deut. 5:9). Violence does continue to cycle on from one generation to the next. In no way is the point here to justify offensive and criminal activity. However, understanding issues behind such activity is necessary in order to break the cycle of retribution and retaliation. It is this cycle of retribution and retaliation that restorative justice seeks to interrupt.

25. Zehr, *Changing Lenses*, 209-10.

The idea from restorative justice, of breaking the cycle of retaliation, can apply in the international realm as well. The universally abhorred attacks on the World Trade Center and the Pentagon on September 11, 2001 provide an example. For the overwhelming majority of Americans, those attacks created a need for punishment, for retribution, for retaliation and vengeance. In the public mind, the only questions were how soon and how large the retaliation would be. When it came two weeks later, it was a full-fledged invasion of Afghanistan.

This retaliation was based on the assumption that violence works — it produces justice — and that violent retaliation was necessary in order to balance the score. However, the terrorist attacks were already based on the idea of retaliation — payback to the United States for the nation's policies toward Palestinians. Somewhere, someone said that the only way to get Americans to see reason and change their behavior was to use violence. And the Americans responded with the same claim — that the only way to deal with the perpetrators of September 11 was to retaliate with violence.

Every war and violent conflict proceeds on the assumption that violence works and that retaliation will balance the offense and settle the conflict. But since each side believes in this formula, the cycle continues, always with the claim that violence is the only way to deal with the other side. The idea of retribution keeps a cycle of violence going.

The United States retaliation for the attacks of September 11 did not resolve the problem at all. Initially there was euphoria at the success of the invasion in expelling the Taliban from Afghanistan and the installation of a regime friendly to the United States.[26] But the cycle of violent retaliation — retribution — continued. The "defeated" enemy in Afghanistan withdrew to remote areas to regroup and then mounted a new, serious challenge to the United States occupation. This challenge is such that newly inaugurated president Barack Obama announced an increase in military involvement in the country beyond the levels of the initial retaliation. Clearly in this conflict, retribution produces more retribution.

When one actually acknowledges the reality of that cycle, it becomes obvious that the common assumption that violence works is wrong. Since both sides claim that the violence of retaliation will work, this violence is

26. Without attributing the idea to any particular spokesperson, newspaper accounts of the installation of the new Afghan president began "In the first peaceful transfer of power in Afghanistan for decades, . . ." Nowhere in the public accounts was there any recognition of the irony that extensive military action, massive bombing, and violent removal of the Taliban were the basis for this "peaceful transfer of power."

actually guaranteed to fail half the time. In fact, since the "winning side" also experiences losses and outcomes are often less than clear-cut, violence actually fails more than half the time. The Israeli-Palestinian conflict constitutes another obvious example. If violence and retaliation always worked, Israel would be the most secure state in the world. If violence and retaliation always worked, Palestinians would be free of Israeli occupation and enjoying an independent state.

Some minority voices have pointed to a different possible response to the tragedy of September 11, 2001. In an article published early in 2002, I asked rhetorically about the implications of a completely different response, a response shaped by the idea from restorative justice of acting to change the situation. At the time of the attacks on the United States, it was estimated that there were three million refugees in Afghanistan, left over from their earlier war against occupation by Russia. Using local supplies and hiring local labor, the United States could have paid to build houses for the entire refugee population with many fewer dollars than were spent on the military invasion, whose costs are now in the hundreds of billions of dollars.[27] It would seem obvious that building houses for refugees would create more goodwill for the United States — that is, change the situation — than does ongoing military retaliation, which costs much more money and many more lives. More recently, retired Senator and presidential candidate George McGovern expressed a similar idea. As the new administration of President Barack Obama was making the case for an escalation of United States involvement in the resurgent war in Afghanistan, McGovern suggested in an editorial in the *Washington Post* that, instead of spending money on more troops, funding a school lunch program would be a much more effective deterrent to more terrorism.[28]

Richard Holloway writes that nations cannot practice forgiveness, but can engage in the related concept of "magnanimity or political mercy." The goal of magnanimity, like that of forgiveness, is to "break the long chain of revenge."[29] The just suggested responses of building houses for refugees or funding a school lunch program in Afghanistan would constitute such acts of magnanimity.

With great impact, Holloway related the story of a missed opportunity

27. J. Denny Weaver, "Responding to September 11 — and October 7 and January 29: Which Religion Shall We Follow?" *Conrad Grebel Review* 20 (2002): 79-100.

28. George McGovern, "Calling a Time Out," *Washington Post*, January 22, 2009.

29. Holloway, *On Forgiveness*, 89-90.

for an act of magnanimity that had the potential to change the course of world history. His retelling comes from William Manchester's biography of Winston Churchill. When the hour arrived for the end of World War I, Churchill and his wife went to Downing Street to congratulate Lloyd George, the prime minister. Churchill interrupted a meeting already in progress and suggested that since the "fallen foe" was close to starvation, they should send "a dozen great ships crammed with provisions" to Hamburg. The suggestion received a cold rebuff. Six years later a soldier described his feelings at the time and wrote that "only fools, liars and criminals could hope for mercy from the enemy." His hatred grew for those responsible for the suffering. On observing the great misery, he wrote, "my own fate became known to me . . . I resolved to go into politics." That soldier was Adolf Hitler.[30]

Retributive justice prescribes retaliation as punishment for an evil deed done. When an evil deed has caused pain and suffering, retributive justice assumes that justice is done when an equivalent amount of pain and suffering is inflicted on the perpetrator. In this quid pro quo system, violence on one side requires violence on the other. In terms of the American "war on terror," this is a never-ending cycle with each side supposedly inflicting punishment on the other after each round. And since each side features itself as the right side, each side feels vindicated by inflicting violence on the other. In contrast, restorative justice would look for ways to change the situation so as to bring a halt to the violent cycle.

As was the case with forgiveness described in psychology, there are also intersections between theology and the practice of restorative justice. A specific intersection, I suggest, occurs with the idea from restorative justice of changing the situation or interrupting the cycle of retribution. As a biblical reference point, recall the earlier discussion of Jesus' words about not mirroring evil or not retaliating, followed by the three examples of how to do so (Matt. 5:38-41) and Paul's counsel not to "repay anyone evil for evil" or "be overcome by evil, but overcome evil with good" (Rom. 12:17, 21; cf. 1 Thess. 5:15; 1 Pet. 3:9). "Love your enemies" then appears as another statement about changing the situation by returning good for evil. As Walter Wink warned, "we become what we hate."[31] And it becomes clear once again that the practices of forgiveness and restorative justice are

30. Holloway, *On Forgiveness*, 90-92.

31. Walter Wink, *Engaging the Powers: Discernment and Resistance in a World of Domination* (The Powers 3; Minneapolis: Fortress, 1992), 195.

not injunctions to a passive acceptance of injustice nor a mere agreement to live and let live. Expressing love of enemy as a means to change the situation is an active process of seeking restoration and reconciliation.

In language used in the discussion of restorative justice, the injunctions from Jesus and Paul tell us to act in such a way as to change the situation, to act so as to interrupt the cycle of violence and violent retribution. There is thus a clear biblical and theological warrant for the active practice of working for restoration rather than for retribution. When the practice of forgiveness begins with the offer of an unmerited gift to the offender, that could be called an act of love for the enemy or an effort to overcome evil with good. When reconciliation is achieved, it becomes a validation in the realm of social science of the words of Jesus. When the process of restorative justice succeeds in changing an offender so that he or she does not offend again, it demonstrates the truthfulness of the injunctions not to mirror evil. As was the case for forgiveness in psychology, significant data in the social sciences supports the practice of restorative justice. Although results vary by population studied and length of time between offenses, there is considerable statistical data that suggests that the practice of restorative justice lowers recidivism.[32] Parallel to the comments on theology and the practice of forgiveness in psychology, I can say that I believe in the practice of restorative justice because it reflects the teaching of Jesus, but also because it works.

In this section on the practice of forgiveness, it is noted that an important part of the process is to offer the offender an unmerited gift. One aspect of this gift is for the victim to begin letting go of anger and to begin the process of regaining control of his or her life. Another goal for this gift, a goal not always achieved, is to effect a change in the offender, which will open the possibility of reconciliation between victim and offender. In the practice of restorative justice, one particular focus is to interrupt the cycle

32. An internet search brings up many websites and writings. For an overview of studies see the Resources page of the Center for Restorative Justice and Peacemaking (http://www.cehd.umn.edu/ssw/RJP/Resources/default.asp). See also Jeff Latimer and Steven Kleinknecht, "The Effects of Restorative Justice Programming: A Review of the Empirical" (http://www.justice.gc.ca/eng/pi/rs/rep-rap/2000/rr00_16/rr00_16.pdf); and Lynette Parker, "Restorative Practices and Reoffending" (http://www.restorativejustice.org/editions/2002/July02/recidivism). Helpful is Marty Price, "Mediated Civil Compromise — A Tool for Restorative Justice" (http://www.vorp.com/articles/civil.html). Discussion of an entire state's success with rehabilitation of juveniles is in Todd Lewan, "Missouri Rehabilitates Juveniles," *Wisconsin State Journal*, December 30, 2007, A1, A11.

of retaliation and to change or rehabilitate the offender so that he or she does not offend again. This offering of an unmerited gift resembles Jesus' words, "love your enemies." And offering an unmerited gift and working to rehabilitate the offender certainly comprise two actions that correspond to Jesus' injunction not to mirror evil and to Paul's words about overcoming evil with good.

Unmentioned to this point is the Golden Rule: "Do to others as you would have them do to you" (Luke 6:31; also Matt. 7:12). Since this would mean treating the enemy well, this rule also reflects the words of Jesus and Paul about not mirroring evil and about overcoming evil with good.

These injunctions all reflect God's forgiveness. The discussion shapes a way of living that reflects analysis derived from the narrative of Jesus and what that narrative reveals for an understanding of God. Living in that narrative is what Christians are about. It most certainly includes addressing the sin of racism.

9 Race, Gender, Money

Neither the narrative of Jesus' life nor his teaching provides a blueprint for addressing the social issues that face much of the world today. Nonetheless, materials in these accounts do give some indications and provide some markers for evaluating the society in which we live. There is no best social structure or economic organization. What we can learn from the narrative of Jesus and his teachings are guidelines for evaluating the particular contexts in which we find ourselves.

Jesus and Racial and Ethnic Reconciliation

Jesus' parables and his acts display challenges to racial and ethnic stereotypes and discrimination.[1] There is the well-known parable of the Good

1. As used here, race refers to physical characteristics, primarily skin color, and ethnicity refers to cultural practices. In what follows, discrimination on the basis of either race or ethnicity is treated as one thing. However, the terms are complex and neither should be assumed to say everything important about a person identified by it. There is a growing body of literature on the different functions of these two categories, and some scholars have begun to question the viability of race as an essentialist category. For a beginning of this conversation, see Elliott Butler-Evans, "Beyond Essentialism: Rethinking Afro-American Cultural Theory," in *Cultural and Literary Critiques of the Concepts of "Race,"* ed. E. Nathaniel Gates (New York: Garland, 1997), 178-79; Victor Anderson, *Beyond Ontological Blackness: An Essay on African American Religious and Cultural Criticism* (New York: Continuum, 1995), 11-12; Bell Hooks, *Yearning: Race, Gender, and Cultural Politics* (Boston: South End, 1990), 51-55;

Samaritan, the man who helped an injured man found lying in the road after leaders of the religious establishment passed by on the other side. From this parable, the term "good Samaritan" has passed into the English language as an expression for a helpful person.

Less often recognized, however, are the anti-racism implications of this parable. Jews of Jesus' day regarded Samaritans as of mixed ethnic origin rather than truly Israelite. As a result, Samaritans were despised and experienced discrimination. According to the strict purity code, they were considered unclean. It was a challenge to this discrimination and these attitudes when Jesus' parable made the Samaritan out to be the good person in contrast to the failures of the perceived religious and social leaders of society. The good neighbor, the hated Samaritan, had become the object of love, the one whom the lawyer has just been told to love as himself (Luke 10:27). If the parable were told today, it might feature any of several examples of discrimination in our society. The Samaritan might be an African American woman employed in a hotel, invisible to a white mayor and city council president, visiting in town to recruit a new industry but concerned about how to ensure that the new business will hire employees of "the right kind" — that is, white ones. Or perhaps it puts a so-called illegal alien in the role of the Samaritan, with the priest and Levite played by members of Congress in coat and tie who are known to demand loudly that measures be instituted against undocumented people. Or perhaps the role of the Samaritan is taken by a person from a country accused of terrorism with the other roles played by the political leaders who call for ever tougher sanctions and military measures against that country.

Recall from Chapter 1 the story in John 4 of Jesus' encounter with the Samaritan woman at the well at Sychar, which adds an additional element to his challenge of discrimination based on race or ethnicity. In this encounter, Jesus not only used a Samaritan as a good example and as the enemy to be loved. He actually traveled in Samaria and interacted with a Samaritan woman. In contrast, those who wished to avoid ritual contamination from the supposedly unclean Samaritans avoided traveling through Samaria. They walked out of their way to the east side of the Jordan River and made their way on that side of the Jordan when traveling from Judea in the south of Palestine to Galilee in the north. In making this journey

---

Patricia Williams, "The Ethnic Scarring of American Whiteness," in *The House That Race Built: Black Americans, U.S. Terrain*, ed. Wahneema Lubiano (New York: Pantheon, 1997), 258.

Jesus crossed a geographic boundary that was also an ethnic boundary, and his interaction with the Samaritan woman put this crossing of racial or ethnic boundaries on display. Later we will look at the feminist dimension of this story.

As the one who makes the reign of God visible in his person and his acts, Jesus' parable and travel put the reign of God on the side of confronting racial and ethnic discrimination. The parable and the journey through Samaria exemplify that confronting this evil requires a change in attitudes and practices. His example in the parable challenged prevailing attitudes, and his trip through Samaria showed the need for prevailing practices to change.

These boundary crossings are more than an example for Christians in the twenty-first century. Crossing of boundaries and racial or ethnic reconciliation are also visible in theological formulation. When Jesus confronted discrimination against Samaritans, that became another item of offense for those who maintained the strict purity code. Thus racism and ethnic discrimination should be listed with the powers that killed Jesus. The resurrection's victory over the powers of evil is thus a victory over racism. The resurrection shows that Jesus' making present of the reign of God includes overcoming racism. Our participation in the reign of God requires us to "change sides," to switch loyalties from whatever is opposed to God to the side of the reign of God. This participation thus calls for racial and ethnic reconciliation, and to refuse or deny or ignore this reconciliation is to place ourselves outside the reign of God. Resurrection is then the invitation to identify with Jesus and to participate in the ethnic and racial reconciliation that is present in Jesus and that God is now already accomplishing in the world.

The church that displays this ethnic and racial reconciliation is the new creation and the new humanity initiated by baptism. Jesus' transcending of barriers between Jews and Samaritans makes visible this reconciliation. Paul discussed it in terms of reconciliation between Jews and Gentiles. In the United States, the long history of slavery, segregation, lynching, and discrimination on the basis of race brings the issue of reconciliation among African Americans and white people to the fore. Alongside this history are the racist overtones of such continually hot political issues as "illegal aliens" and the expressed need to erect fences and ensure secure borders, and the lack of acceptance of immigrants of differing ethnicities as expressed in "English only" requirements and the hostility to cultural diversity courses in some schools. Given the presence of many ethnicities in the United States, transcending ethnic differences, that is, true reconciliation among ethnic groups, should be an important dimension of the church's witness to the world.

It is important to state specifically that confronting and overcoming racism and ethnic discrimination and the subsequent reconciliation testified to by baptism are explicit dimensions of the reign of God. Drawing on elements of Jesus' story concerning his teaching and interaction with Samaritans gives racism and ethnic discrimination an indisputable place in theology derived from the narrative of Jesus. James Cone was certainly correct when he wrote that lack of attention to the particular history of Jesus in Palestine and focus on the abstract issue of Jesus' deity produced a mainstream or standard theology in which the sin of racism was invisible or ignored. When Christological discussion took place within the context of Christianity as the favored religion of the Roman Empire, Cone wrote, it "became easy to define Jesus as the divinizer (the modern counterpart is 'spiritualizer') of humanity. When this happens Christology is removed from history, and salvation becomes only peripherally related to this world."[2] In another context, Cone wrote that since the church fathers of the time of Constantine "were not slaves, it did not occur to them that God's revelation in Jesus Christ is identical with the presence of his Spirit in the slave community in struggle for the liberation of humanity." Thus they "could ask about the Son's relation to the Father . . . without connecting the question to the historical freedom of the oppressed."[3] These same factors make it possible today for Christians to appeal to Jesus Christ but to ignore his teachings about Samaritans and his concern for the "stranger" (Matt. 25:35-46). In contrast, the intent here with a lived theology derived from the narrative of Jesus is to put on display that confronting and overcoming racism belong to salvation in the reign of God that is made visible in the person of Jesus.

Since living in the story of Jesus requires a change in loyalty to the reign of God, it is clear that racial and ethnic reconciliation is no easy declaration of tolerance or merely claiming to like everyone or to be colorblind or pretending that color does not matter. Attitudes and practices need to change. It is necessary to confront racism actively, to become antiracist. Not to challenge the systemic injustice of racism is to condone it. In North America, racial and ethnic reconciliation requires those who belong

2. James H. Cone, *God of the Oppressed* (rev. ed.; Maryknoll: Orbis, 1997), 107.
3. Cone, *God of the Oppressed*, 181.

to the dominant, white culture to take specific steps to challenge the attitudes and practices that surround us — our own attitudes as well as the structures and philosophies of the institutions in which we participate. This specific action to counter racism and to enact race reconciliation makes this a lived theology. If this dimension of the story of Jesus is not lived, then the telling of the story is not Gospel.

This lived theology has significant parallels to points emphasized by Cone. As noted, for Cone Christian theology begins with the Jesus of history. It is in the story of Jesus in history that one sees liberation from oppression taking place. And the God who is present in Jesus is the liberating God who saved Israel in the exodus. For Cone, as for the lived theology of this book, theology that does not deal with the reality of liberation — salvation — in history is not true theology. "Fellowship with God is made possible through God's activity in history, setting people free from economic, social, and political bondage. God's act of reconciliation is not mystical communion with the divine; nor is it a pietistic state of inwardness bestowed upon the believer. God's reconciliation is a new relationship with *people* created by God's concrete involvement in the political affairs of the world, taking sides with the weak and the helpless."[4]

Progress has been made. We can be glad that today, legal segregation has disappeared and that individual expressions of prejudice and overt racism are almost universally condemned. However, the legacy of racism still colors — or perhaps better stated, whitewashes — aspects of American society. Some elements of racism are silent but present under other names. It is present in the way that the abomination of slavery has been glossed over in school textbooks and in popular understandings of American history.[5] It has managed to erase the history of lynching from the public memory of white people, even though in the era of lynching (1880-1940, with some continuing until 1968) nearly five thousand African Americans were lynched as a means of terrorizing black people into submission.[6]

---

4. Cone, *God of the Oppressed*, 209.

5. For example, see James W. Loewen, *Lies My Teacher Told Me: Everything Your American History Textbook Got Wrong* (New York: Simon & Schuster, 1995), chapters 5 and 6; Tim Wise, *Dear White America: Letter to a New Minority* (San Francisco: City Lights, 2012), 99-110.

6. For photos that portray the unspeakable horror of lynching, see James Allen, et al., *Without Sanctuary: Lynching Photography in America* (Santa Fe: Twin Palms, 2000). For additional bibliography on lynching, see James H. Cone, *The Cross and the Lynching Tree* (Maryknoll: Orbis, 2011). Cone's book is a powerful meditation on the relationship between

Racism shapes perceptions of reality through "white privilege," the assumption of many people that the United States is a "white" society and that wherever one goes, one should be able to carry on all daily affairs with white people, accompanied by the assumption that one need make no effort to understand or know about any other culture and how it differs from white culture.[7] Racism is present in the common perception that since the disappearance of legal segregation and discrimination, and now the election of an African American president, the problem of racism has been solved and thus racism now involves only the commission of specific acts judged to have a racial bias. This perception is reinforced repeatedly by the way the news media report incidents, as though a perpetrator acts individually with no reflection of or reinforcement from the social ethos. The assumption that racism applies only to individual incidents renders invisible, for example, the fact that for the overwhelming majority of people, whether black or white, the first thing to register when meeting a person for the first time is race. The assumption that racism involves only individual acts applies to the silent prejudice behind the assumption of white privilege, as well as to the mostly unacknowledged but real systemic racism that produces higher unemployment among African Americans and other minorities, de facto segregation in housing, an achievement gap in schools, lower average wages for non-white workers, and more. Many observers believe that a kind of racism drives the efforts to undo gains of the Civil Rights movement under the cover of a presumed color-blind society in which consideration of race and ethnicity in college admissions and hiring practices would not be allowed and in new restrictions on voter IDs, hostility to "illegal aliens," and opposition to multicultural education that welcomes diversity.

One of the most disturbing instances of racism in a supposedly color-blind society is the operation of the criminal justice system in what Michelle Alexander has called a "new Jim Crow." In the "war on drugs," which proceeds under the guise of race-neutral policies, at all levels of the system from the police on the street through the court system and prison to the stigma placed on ex-prisoners for life, the system functions to con-

---

the cross of Jesus as a Roman terror tactic and the lynching tree as a terror tactic employed by white supremacy.

7. Wise, *Dear White America*, 71-74. Although not without occasional satirical references, Wise's book is an extended discussion of white privilege and the impact that indirect racism continues to exert on the culture, politics, and economic policies of the United States.

trol large numbers of young African men while ignoring or giving much lesser sentences to white people, who commit the same offenses at the same rate as African Americans. It is particularly disturbing that rulings of the Supreme Court have rendered it virtually impossible to challenge the racial bias of this system at any level, despite widespread awareness that statistical evidence reveals overwhelming bias against African Americans.[8]

In *The Souls of Black Folk,* a well-known book on racism in the United States published in 1903, W. E. B. Du Bois wrote, "The problem of the Twentieth Century is the problem of the color line." In a new preface to a 1953 reprinting, Du Bois wrote that the color line was still "a great problem of this century," but that behind it stands the even greater problem that "so many civilized people are willing to live in comfort even if the price of this is poverty, ignorance and disease of the majority of their fellowmen; that to maintain this privilege men have waged war until today war tends to become universal and continuous, and the excuse for this war continues largely to be color and race."[9] Most disturbingly, what Du Bois says is still true. In 1994, Cornel West wrote about "how much race *matters* in the American present."[10] And the story just summarized from Michelle Alexander displays the truth of these words today, as this book is written.

True reconciliation requires confession of past injustice, whether by individuals or the church or the national culture. And it means acknowledgment of current injustice, which is the heir to past discrimination. The beginning of reconciliation means recognition of the injustice that exists and making changes to achieve reconciliation.

It is not as though only those who belong to the dominant culture are guilty of participation in the evil of racism. James Cone writes that God is on the side of the oppressed who struggle for justice, which means that God enters history to break down the hostility and racism of white people. From their side, the oppressed people must accept this new existence wrought by God "by struggling against all who try to make us slaves."[11] The implication of Cone's position is that not engaging in the struggle for liberation is to accept the oppression practiced by the dominant society,

8. Michelle Alexander, *The New Jim Crow: Mass Incarceration in the Age of Color-blindness* (rev. ed.; New York: New, 2012). The racist practices of the criminal justice system described by Alexander are noted in Wise, *Dear White America,* 34-35.

9. W. E. Burghardt Du Bois, *The Souls of Black Folk: Essays and Sketches* (Greenwich: Fawcett, 1953), v, xiv, also 23.

10. Cornel West, *Race Matters* (New York: Vintage, 1994), xvi, emphasis original.

11. Cone, *God of the Oppressed,* 215-18.

which is to participate in the evil — the sin — of oppression. In remarks of Garth Kasimu Baker-Fletcher, a second-generation black theologian, this implication becomes explicit.

Baker-Fletcher writes of the need to be delivered from the desire to conform to white societal expectations and values. Through hearing the word of Jesus Christ there is a deliverance that results in one becoming a Christian. And there is a second deliverance that is an extension of the first. It is "hearing the word of Blackness, which is a cry to leave Euro-dominated Space and return to God's affirmation of your Afrikan self. . . . It is a deliverance because after it occurs, one is no longer bound by the mental, cultural, and spiritual shackles of Euro-dominators."[12] Baker-Fletcher also wrote that it is easy for African Americans to use this domination to claim the status of victims, but he also emphasized the problem of "self-imprisonment." "We are not wholly innocent." he writes. Self-imprisonment comes from accepting the views that white society has placed on black women's bodies and the abusive system of patriarchy as well as the inheritance of "generations-long intertribal hatred" from Africa. Self-imprisonment also involves an inherited subordination of women, and the "sin of irresponsibility, abusiveness, and sexist behavior" by African American men, including the black on black violence of gang warfare.[13]

Although in different ways, racism is a sin that touches all people. True reconciliation occurs when people recognize their particular kinds of accommodation and participation in it and then consciously chart a new direction of confronting racism. Their individual acts will not immediately change the systemic racism of the society that surrounds us, but with this change their participation becomes involuntary. And true reconciliation is achieved because from their several sides, all these participants in racism are now joined together in a common bond to confront it. This is the racial and ethnic reconciliation to which the resurrection of Jesus Christ calls every Christian.

---

12. Garth Kasimu Baker-Fletcher, *Xodus: An African American Male Journey* (Minneapolis: Fortress, 1996), 86.

13. Karen Baker-Fletcher and Garth Kasimu Baker-Fletcher, *My Sister, My Brother: Womanist and XODUS God-Talk* (Bishop Henry McNeal Turner/Sojourner Truth Series in Black Religion 12; Maryknoll: Orbis, 1997), 124-26. Cornel West was writing as a social commentator rather than as a theologian and thus did not make the application to "sin" noted here. However, West's references to "self-loathing" and "self-hatred" point to the same problem that Baker-Fletcher addressed theologically. West, *Race Matters*, 27, 97-98, 122.

Resurrection is the invitation to participate in this reconciliation. Baptism initiates those who accept the invitation into the new creation that is the reconciled people as the body of Christ. Their mission is to put on display the nature of reconciliation in the reign of God and to provide a vision of the future reign of God. Racial and ethnic reconciliation is a part of what the church is about. If the church does not put this racial and ethnic reconciliation on display it is not living in or making a living witness to what Jesus was about.

Jesus and Women

The role and status of women in church and in society in North America has been an important topic of discussion since the nineteenth century. In the United States, women began working for the right to vote already in that century. Other issues have concerned the advisability or the necessity of women working outside the home, equal pay for equal work, and access to the same kind of privileges and responsibilities that men take for granted in the workforce. These discussions have had their counterparts in the church, with women claiming the right to ordination and full participation in all aspects of church teaching, life, and governance.

Progress toward full equality of women has not been uniform in either society or church. One example is that of Elizabeth Cady Stanton and Susan B. Anthony, who are renowned for their work in gaining the vote for women. Less well-known is the fact that both Cady Stanton and Anthony entered alliances with male white supremacist groups — the men would support the vote for white women in exchange for support in preventing black men from voting.[14] It is not surprising therefore that African Ameri-

14. Delores S. Williams, "The Color of Feminism: Or Speaking the Black Woman's Tongue," *Journal of Religious Thought* 43 (1986): 44-46; Susan Brooks Thistlethwaite, *Sex, Race and God: Christian Feminism in Black and White* (New York: Crossroad, 1991), 35-41; JoAnne Marie Terrell, *Power in the Blood? The Cross in African American Experience* (Bishop Henry McNeal Turner/Sojourner Truth Series in Black Religion 15; Maryknoll: Orbis, 1998), 60.

The implication of the action by Cady Stanton and Anthony is that voting was a matter of only a social issue such as economic or political power. However, womanist theologians see their action at a much deeper level, as an offense against the very humanity of black women and thus an affront to all humankind made in the image of God. For a theological statement that begins with the experience of black women and goes on to discussion of what it means to be human in the image of God, see M. Shawn Copeland, *Enfleshing Freedom: Body, Race, and Being* (Minneapolis: Fortress, 2010).

can women have not felt included in writing on feminist issues by white feminists.

Alongside feminist theology African American women have produced womanist theology. These theologies have different agendas. Feminist theology, for example, has concerned itself with "liberation" of women from "traditional" roles in the home, has advocated for the right of women to work outside the home and to engage in the professions on an equal basis with men. Within the church, feminists have worked for an end to male dominance, patriarchy, and hierarchy and have sought the right for women to be ordained and to hold any church office. Womanist writers had other concerns. They have stressed a threefold agenda of opposition to racism, sexism, and poverty. They have protested both male dominance of some elements of the black church and claims of feminists to speak for all women. The poorer economic status of black women has meant that they have long worked outside the home, womanists said, often as domestics and serving people in white homes and establishments. Prominent womanist Delores Williams includes this difference in her description of "surrogacy," the numerous ways in which black women have been forced to fill roles properly belonging to white men and women and black men.[15] Although the most recent writing by both feminists and womanists has sought to address these differences, they are evident in early womanist writings that respond to feminist writing.[16]

Ideas can be drawn from the narrative of Jesus to address this complex of issues that confront women both black and white. In the description of Jesus' encounter with the woman at the well at Sychar in Samaria, the previous section noted Jesus' crossing of racial and ethnic boundaries. That story also pictures Jesus crossing another boundary defined by the purity code, the boundary of gender. During her time of menstruation, a woman was considered ritually unclean. A man who touched her thereby also rendered himself ritually unclean. Since one could not know if a woman was menstruating, she was always assumed to be in an unclean state, and a man concerned for ritual purity would never touch a woman other than his wife. The unclean state also extended to vessels used by a

---

15. See Delores S. Williams, *Sisters in the Wilderness: The Challenge of Womanist God-Talk* (Maryknoll: Orbis, 1993), 22-29, 62-74, 178-203 and throughout.

16. For example, Katie G. Cannon, *Black Womanist Ethics* (Atlanta: Scholars, 1988); Jacquelyn Grant, *White Women's Christ and Black Women's Jesus: Feminist Christology and Womanist Response* (American Academy of Religion Academy Series 64; Atlanta: Scholars, 1989); Williams, *Sisters in the Wilderness*.

woman, such as a pitcher. That is, a man would not drink from a vessel handled by a woman.

In his interaction with the woman at the well, Jesus crossed these boundaries related to supposed female impurity. He not only talked to her, but he asked to drink from her pitcher. That he did indeed cross boundaries in a surprising manner is clear from the reaction of the woman, who asked, "How is it that you, a Jew, ask a drink of me, a woman of Samaria?" (John 4:9). The astonishment of the disciples, namely "that he was speaking with a woman," (v. 27) similarly points to these boundary crossings.

One of Jesus' most remarkable crossing of boundaries concerning women appears in the event reported in Matthew 15:21-28 and Mark 7:24-30. His interlocutor in this story is usually identified as "the Syrophoenician woman," from the account in Mark. In Matthew she is called a Canaanite. In other words, she is a Gentile and therefore unclean according to purity rules. The designation Syrophoenician identifies her with the minority Greek upper class in the empire, a contrast to Jesus' identity with the poor Jewish population exploited by the empire.[17]

Just prior to the exchange with this woman, in a conversation with the disciples Jesus had set aside the rules on ritually unclean foods and "declared all foods clean." "Do you not see that whatever goes into a person from outside cannot defile, since it enters, not the heart but the stomach, and goes out into the sewer?" (Mark 7:18-19). Immediately following this declaration about food, Jesus is pictured putting aside additional strictures on ritual purity as he crosses a geographical boundary into Gentile territory, where he interacts with another woman outside the bounds of ritual purity, this time a Gentile.

Jesus had hoped to stay in the region incognito, but the woman recognized him. She pleaded for him to cast the demon out of her daughter. He ignored her, and the disciples begged him to send her away to stop the harassment. Finally Jesus told her that he was not sent to Gentiles but "only to the lost sheep of the house of Israel" (Matt. 15:24). The woman persisted in her plea, humbling herself at Jesus' feet.

Jesus' reply to the woman reflected the feelings of Jews toward

17. For the following understanding of the story of the Syrophoenician woman, see Gerd Thiessen, *The Open Door: Variations on Biblical Themes,* trans. John Bowden (Minneapolis: Fortress, 1991), 40-46; David Rhoads, "Jesus and the Syrophoenician Woman in Mark: A Narrative-Critical Study," *Journal of the American Academy of Religion* 62 (1994): 343-76; Reta Halteman Finger, "How Jesus Learned about Ethnic Discrimination," *The Mennonite,* December 26, 2000, 6-7.

Gentiles. "Let the children be fed first, for it is not fair to take the children's food and throw it to the dogs" (Mark 7:27). Dogs were scavengers, and the term was an insult, derogatory and perhaps even racist.

The woman was not deterred. Her answer turned the tables on Jesus: "Lord, even the dogs under the table eat the children's crumbs" (Mark 7:28). And Jesus changed his mind, the only instance in the New Testament where an interlocutor got the best of him in an argument. He said, "For saying that, you may go — the demon has left your daughter" (v. 29). And it was so.

Accepting correction from a Gentile man would already have been a statement about crossing boundaries. The story takes on an added dimension because the Gentile is a woman, and she is pleading on behalf of a daughter. The story pictures a clash of three kinds of barriers — rich versus poor, Jew versus Gentile, and finally male versus female. The woman prevails and Jesus revises his inherited prejudice toward Gentiles. In the Gospel of Mark, this story puts on display the fact that the reign of God has no ethnic boundaries but is open to all peoples. "In this episode, Mark seeks to attack the very heart of human resistance to the universality of the gospel and in so doing calls his hearers to sow the seeds of the kingdom everywhere."[18]

In this instance, it is a woman who leads to this opening of the gospel. If the church is truly an extension of the mission of Jesus in the world today, as I believe it is, then to live in this story means most certainly to accept women as full participants in that work. Men have no privilege or status afforded by anatomy. Living out of this story means abandoning the tradition of hierarchy and patriarchy of men over women. And if Jesus could learn from a woman, that is the case for men today as well.

The resurrection of Jesus is God's call to embrace the equality of women in this community around Jesus. And most specifically, it is a call to accept and value the status of women as coworkers in dimensions of the making present of the reign of God on earth. Baptism initiates people into this new creation that transcends sex and gender, or, in Paul's words, "there is no longer male and female, for you are all one in Christ Jesus." And as womanists have made clear, this acceptance includes not only ordination of women to leadership positions. The call of resurrection also invites us to address issues of poverty and social status that have created divisions within the community of God's people, the church. The following section addresses issues of economics.

18. Rhoads, "Jesus and the Syrophoenician Woman," 371.

There are of course some New Testament texts, as well as significant material from the Old Testament, that give men authority over women and that appear to prohibit leadership offices for women within the church. In response, I again refer to Paul's declaration about transcending cultural and sexual differences in the new humanity: "There is no longer Jew or Greek, there is no longer slave or free, there is no longer male and female; for all of you are one in Christ Jesus" (Gal. 3:28). But perhaps more importantly, note again the narrative of Jesus and its role in understanding the conversations within the Bible. Chapter 4 exposed the conversation about the character of God in both Old and New Testaments. Chapter 5 then argued that the narrative of Jesus shows that the sides of that conversation that reject violence more accurately depict the character of God. In a similar way, one can also uncover a conversation about the role of women throughout the Bible. Again, when one sees the boundaries that Jesus crosses in his interactions with the Samaritan woman and the Syrophoenician woman, it seems clear that the changes in the Bible's story are in the direction of equality of women and that living into the equality of women and a rejection of hierarchy and patriarchy is the way for the church today to live in and extend the presence of Jesus in the world.

Jesus and Economics

Jesus did not propose a specific economic system. He did, however, make a number of comments about wealth, its acquisition, and its uses. These comments provide criteria by which modern Christians and the modern church can evaluate their use of resources, and also evaluate the adequacy and the justness or fairness of whatever economic system rules the particular society in which they live.

In his address to the synagogue when he announced his ministry, Jesus included the claim "The Spirit of the Lord . . . has anointed me to bring good news to the poor" as well as to relieve other forms of oppression and "to proclaim the year of the Lord's favor" (Luke 4:18-19). It has been suggested that with "the year of the Lord's favor," Jesus was placing his mission within the prophetic idea of the Jubilee year.[19] Leviticus 25 establishes ev-

---

19. André Trocmé, *Jesus and the Nonviolent Revolution,* ed. Charles E. Moore (Maryknoll: Orbis, 2003), 13-15; John Howard Yoder, *The Politics of Jesus: Vicit Agnus Noster* (2d ed.; Grand Rapids: William B. Eerdmans, 1994), 30.

ery fiftieth year as a year of Jubilee, and in that year property is to revert to its original owners. It is not necessary to resolve the question definitively of the extent to which Jesus' words proclaim or are shaped by the Jubilee principle. Even without advocating a specific economic philosophy, it is apparent that good news for the poor signals that concern for poor people belongs integrally to Jesus' mission.

That Jesus began his mission with a quotation from Isaiah shows that what Christians today call the Old Testament was Jesus' Scripture, and that he saw himself as a continuation of the spirit of the prophets of Israel. In fact, apart from the text of Isaiah 61 that Jesus quoted, there is in the Old Testament a prophetic tradition of critique of economic exploitation and oppression. Amos condemned those who became rich by exploiting the poor. "They sell the righteous for silver, and the needy for a pair of sandals" (2:6), take grain from the poor through levies, bribe judges (5:11-12), and generally build a rich lifestyle on the backs of poor people (6:1-7). Jeremiah castigated those whose exorbitant lifestyles are built on exploitation of the poor and vulnerable (5:26-29), words echoed in Psalm 10:8-11. Isaiah also warned about exploitation of the poor by the wealthy, those

> who make iniquitous decrees,
> who write oppressive statutes,
>   to turn aside the needy from justice
> and to rob the poor of my people of their right,
>   that widows may be your spoil,
> and that you may make the orphans your prey! (Isa. 10:1-2).[20]

When Jesus proclaimed "good news for the poor," along with release of captives and freedom for the oppressed, he was not rejecting the idea of wealth per se. He was rather continuing in the tradition of condemning ill-gotten wealth, wealth that was gained through exploitation of the poor and vulnerable. Earlier I noted Jesus' suggestion for the poor person to engage in economic protest by giving the undergarment with the outer garment when hauled into debtor's court (Matt. 5:40). The action Jesus recommended exposes the exploitation of a poor man by a wealthy debt holder, and thus falls in line with the words of Amos, Jeremiah, and Isaiah that condemn exploitation of poor people.

Jesus did not condemn wealth or acquisition of wealth in and of them-

---

20. Texts in this paragraph are suggested by Ronald J. Sider, *Rich Christians in an Age of Hunger: A Biblical Study* (rev. ed.; Downers Grove: Intervarsity, 1984), 55-66.

selves. The problems concerned attitudes toward wealth and how it was obtained. On the one hand, wealth was not to be acquired through exploitation and oppression. In the Scriptures that Jesus read are injunctions against usury and prophetic critique of the exploitation of workers (e.g., Lev. 25:35-37; Deut. 23:19-20; 24:10-15; Ps. 15:5; Isa. 58:3; Amos 4:1; Mal. 3:5). If ill-gotten wealth is condemned, the implication is that wealth obtained in a just manner is acceptable. But it was important how wealth properly obtained was used. It was to be shared and shared generously. "When you give a luncheon or a dinner, do not invite your friends or your brothers or your relatives or rich neighbors, in case they may invite you in return, and you would be repaid. But when you give a banquet, invite the poor, the crippled, the lame, and the blind. And you will be blessed, because they cannot repay you, for you will be repaid at the resurrection of the righteous" (Luke 14:12-14).

A dimension of generosity with wealth depends on recognizing where ultimate worth resides. Followers of Jesus are to live generously rather than simply accumulating earthly wealth. "Do not store up for yourselves treasures on earth, where moth and rust consume and where thieves break in and steal; but store up for yourselves treasures in heaven, where neither moth nor rust consumes and where thieves do not break in and steal. For where your treasure is, there your heart will be also" (Matt. 6:19-21). In other words, one should not be identified by or bound by earthly possessions.

> Consider the ravens: they neither sow nor reap, they have neither storehouse nor barn, and yet God feeds them. Of how much more value are you than the birds! . . . Consider the lilies, how they grow: they neither toil nor spin; yet I tell you, even Solomon in all his glory was not clothed like one of these. But if God so clothes the grass of the field, which is alive today and tomorrow is thrown into the oven, how much more will he clothe you — you of little faith! And do not keep striving for what you are to eat and what you are to drink, and do not keep worrying. For it is the nations of the world that strive after all these things, and your Father knows that you need them. Instead, strive for his kingdom, and these things will be given to you as well. (Luke 12:24, 27-31)

Living generously, living without worrying about food, clothing, and possessions seem like rather strange sayings, even irresponsible ones, in our modern context. It has been suggested that Jesus' comments about sharing among individuals and living without attachment to personal possessions is an application of the common purse kept by Jesus and his disciples. Sharing equally would exclude keeping individual accounts but would also mean that an individual was never left stranded. Further, the idea of contributing generously from what is not needed appears in Judas's insincere words about selling the costly perfume that Mary used to anoint the feet of Jesus. He said aloud that the perfume should have been sold and the money given to the poor, but in actuality he wanted to steal the money when it was added to the common purse (John 12:5-6). And the assumption of a common purse may also clarify Jesus' words to the rich young man who asked Jesus what he needed to do to have eternal life. In addition to obeying all the commandments, Jesus told the young man, "Sell your possessions, and give the money to the poor, and you will have treasure in heaven; then come, follow me" (Matt. 19:21). In the context of a common purse, this would not be a requirement that the man become destitute. It was rather an invitation to join the followers of Jesus, who supported each other and lived loosely to earthly wealth and possessions.[21]

There are numerous historical examples of groups that choose to live with a common purse. Modern-day Hutterites, whose roots go back to sixteenth-century Anabaptists, come immediately to mind. In the nineteenth century in North America, many religious groups — some within the broad stream of traditional Christianity, others outside it — attempted to live with a common purse. Some groups of recent origin but with ties to historic Anabaptism and with some form of common purse include Reba Place Fellowship in Chicago, the Plough Creek Fellowship in Tiskilwa, Illinois, and New Covenant Fellowship in Athens, Ohio.

I do not believe that a common purse is required for followers of Jesus. However, the ideas of being generous with wealth, seeing wealth as a means to do good, and living loosely to earthly possessions and wealth — not allowing material possessions and wealth to define one's identity and not making their accumulation an end in and of itself — are incumbent upon all who live out of the story of Jesus.

In Luke 19, the story of Zacchaeus's encounter with Jesus illustrates several of the issues just raised. Zacchaeus was a wealthy tax collector, which meant that he worked for the Roman occupiers of Palestine. As a result of Jesus' recognition of him, Zacchaeus volunteered to give half of his possessions to the poor. That giving reflects the idea of living generously and holding loosely to wealth and possessions. Further, the job of tax col-

21. Sider, *Rich Christians*, 87-88.

lector gave opportunity for embezzlement and ill-gotten wealth. Evidently Zacchaeus had indeed gained some of his wealth dishonestly because he also volunteered, "and if I have defrauded anyone of anything, I will pay back four times as much" (Luke 19:8).

The encounter of Jesus and Zacchaeus fits the idea of restorative justice discussed earlier in Chapter 8. It might have been possible to pursue punishment for Zacchaeus's ill-gotten gains. But rather than seeking punishment Jesus acted to "change the situation," to use a phrase suggested earlier. He met Zacchaeus as a respected Jewish man. In response Zacchaeus acknowledged his thievery and offered to make restitution. And with that restitution, he was restored to the community. Jesus declared, "Today salvation has come to this house, because he too is a son of Abraham. For the Son of Man came to seek out and to save the lost" (Luke 19:9-10). None of this restoration would have come about as a result of efforts merely to seek punishment.

The words of Jesus about living generously and living loosely to wealth and possessions apply to more than individuals. They also apply to groups and even nations. In often-cited comments from Matthew 25:31-46, Jesus talked of giving food and water to hungry and thirsty people, shelter to strangers, clothing to the naked, and healing to sick people, as well as comforting those in prison. This aid to "the least of these" (v. 40) is often cited as the basis for charitable work. Virtually always overlooked, however, is that the assembled people addressed in Jesus' statement of judgment are "the nations." "When the Son of Man comes in his glory, and all the angels with him, then he will sit on the throne of his glory. All the nations will be gathered before him, and he will separate people one from another" (vv. 31-32). That is, it is nations and large economic structures as well as individuals that are judged on how they treat those in need.

But this is not a blueprint that establishes a particular economic philosophy, capitalist or socialist or mixed, as most systems are today. It is, nonetheless, an important criterion by which to judge any economic system on the basis of how well it cares for all of its citizens. Nations are not judged on how well they take care of the rich and powerful but on their care for those without political influence, those on the margins — poor people, homeless people, immigrants and aliens, and people in prison.

By this criterion many modern nations are failing the test. On paper, the old Soviet Union promised jobs and security to everyone. However, millions of dissenters were killed or sent to harsh labor camps, which was the virtual equivalent of a death sentence. And it was a well-known fact that in spite of the words about equality, government and party leaders enriched themselves far beyond the level of working people. Many of the countries trying to recover from colonial occupation come up short by this criterion. Of course they are free from the colonial oppressor. But in any number of cases the indigenous rulers continued to rule in the way they had learned from the colonial occupiers. As a result, the lives of people in the street remain in large part unchanged while government leaders continue to enrich themselves.[22]

The free society of the United States also fails by this criterion. Large numbers of people encounter systemic and structural economic violence. Tax structures and tax policies favor the wealthy. The more money one makes the easier it is to find "loopholes" in which to shelter income from taxes, and lower income people pay a greater percentage of their income in taxes than do wealthy people. This tax structure does not work for poor people, whose numbers are increasing. However, it works well for the wealthy at the top of the economic ladder, where wealth continues to accumulate and the gap between rich and poor continues to widen.

Another example of policy and practice that favor the wealthy is the allocation by a number of cities and states of hundreds of millions of dollars for sports stadiums with luxury boxes while claiming lack of funds for inner-city schools and services for poor people.[23] It is claimed that the money spent for stadiums to retain teams in host cities will bring economic benefits to the entire communities. In fact, aside from the wages

22. As one example, consult Adam Hochschild, *King Leopold's Ghost: A Story of Greed, Terror, and Heroism in Colonial Africa* (Boston: Houghton Mifflin, 1998). This book describes the cruelty and exploitation in The Congo from the stage of personal ownership by Belgium's King Leopold through colonial rule by Belgium to independence after 1960. Exploitation changed little from one system to the next, with the profiteering by government officials after independence happening with support of the United States.

23. I am particularly aware of the case of Cleveland, Ohio, the state where I lived for thirty-one years. At least $300 million in public money acquired through taxes and other schemes was allocated for stadiums for the Indians and Browns while there is little help to rescue the school system which is at least $200 million in debt. There are also academic studies that show that the huge dollars spent on sports teams are a drain rather than economic gain for a city. For a sample of literature, see Joanna Cagan and Neil deMause, "A Tale of Two Cities," *The Nation* 267.5 (August-October, 1998): 24; Mark S. Rosentraub, "Why Baseball Needs New York to Just Say No," *The Nation* 267.5 (August-October, 1998): 20-24, 26; Neil de Mause and Joanna Cagan, *Field of Schemes: How the Great Stadium Swindle Turns Public Money into Private Profit* (rev. ed.; Lincoln: University of Nebraska Press, 2008); Dave Zweifel, "Poor Kids Strike Out as Greed Wins," *The Cap Times*, April 21-27, 2010, 30.

paid to park employees, the economic benefits accrue primarily to the few privileged owners. This practice at the local level for sports teams occurs at the national level as well. For example, virtually limitless billions of dollars are allocated yearly for the Pentagon generally and for wars in Afghanistan and Iraq in particular, in spite of well-known overspending and waste in military procurement. In response to a banking crisis in 2008, Congress allocated $7 billion to bail out the banking industry. In response to an economic downturn, the next year Congress allocated another $787 billion as an economic stimulus package. Yet there are complaints that there is no money to help the many individuals whose homes were foreclosed because they lost jobs and could not keep up loan payments. In 2010 Congress claimed the necessity of budget restraint in not extending unemployment benefits and in refusing to pass a "bailout" to support public education.[24]

Brian McLaren, pastor, author, activist, and leader in the emerging church movement, certainly knows and critiques the destructive dimensions of the current capitalist system. In line with comments above, he stresses that money and the economy are not bad in and of themselves. It is rather how they are used. "For Jesus, the economy isn't a bad thing at all. He frequently uses business images to describe the kingdom of God, and entrepreneurship symbolizes for him the work of God's kingdom." Although I wrote a few paragraphs ago that Jesus did not establish a particular economic system, I do not object when McLaren goes a step farther to suggest an alternative approach to economics based on "laws" derived from Jesus' teaching. In place of an unsustainable system of progress through continual, rapid growth, an economy shaped by Jesus offers doing "good deeds for the common good." Instead of attempting to attain "serenity through possession and consumption," a system shaped by Jesus "envisions satisfaction through gratitude and sharing." Rather than seeking salvation through competition that divides the world into winners and losers, Jesus seeks "a hunger and thirst for justice." And finally, rather than the freedom of unaccountable corporations that become wealthy on the basis of labor by the poor, Jesus offers the alternative of "the rich and poor joining their labor for the building of a better world by the building of better communities." The result would be an economic order that pro-

24. Now, as this is written in spring of 2012, when Congress did approve some funds for a national settlement related to foreclosure abuses, including a minuscule $2000 for those who lost homes, the governor of Wisconsin, where I live, appropriated some $26 million of Wisconsin's $140 million earmarked for threatened homeowners and applied it to the state budget deficit.

moted economic, environmental, and social sustainability. In this system, all would work together for the common good. Through the medium of money, individuals would exchange the fruits of their labor for what others produced.

> Together they are deeply grateful for all they earn and have, and they are careful to share with those who are in need. Where there are systemic injustices that privilege some and disadvantage others, they work for justice so the system becomes more of what it can and should be. Those who are more prosperous, believing that more is expected from them, seek to use their advantages to help those who are less prosperous, and together rich and poor seek to build better communities that, in turn, build a better world. This collaborative pursuit, they discover, brings the co-liberation of true prosperity.[25]

Recent immigrants and immigrants without official documents correspond approximately to the "strangers" mentioned by Jesus (Matt. 25:35, 38, 43-44). Their exploitation is another example of social policy and practice that does not care for "the least of these." These people have little power in the political system. Yet both rhetoric and policies blame "illegal aliens" for a host of domestic problems even as their labor is exploited by a number of industries and various local communities and some states enact measures that impose structural violence on immigrants and citizens who look like immigrants. The health care debate in the United States constitutes one more example.

Living out of the story of Jesus — a lived theology — has the potential to confront these issues. Living out of this theology produces concern for those without power in the system — the widows and orphans and strangers of Jesus' time, who lacked political power in a world where political and economic status came through adult men. Today "the least of these" might include "illegal aliens," poor people, people without health insurance, people with AIDS, victims of discrimination of various kinds, and more. It is more than obvious that one individual cannot confront all these problems at once. However, the internal structures of both local Christian communities and their national denominations should practice care for all members, regardless of social standing as defined by North American society. That practice will serve as a critique of and a witness to the structural im-

25. Brian D. McLaren, *Everything Must Change: Jesus, Global Crises, and a Revolution of Hope* (Nashville: Thomas Nelson, 2007), chapters 25 and 26, quoting 206, 209, 217, 219, 223.

balance that favors the already wealthy and privileged at the expense of those without political power. And as resources permit, the social and outreach programs of the church at all levels — local, national, international — can work specifically to alleviate such problems.[26]

The political and economic system of the United States and other nation states are certainly not the only modern structures that promote economic policies that favor the wealthy at the expense of "the least of these." Wes Howard-Brook and Anthony Gwyther, the authors of *Unveiling Empire*,[27] interpret the book of Revelation as an anti-imperial response to Rome, the pervasive empire of the first century. Applying the message of Revelation to the present then means identifying the structure today that corresponds to the pervasive Roman Empire of the late first century. A candidate, of course, would be the United States. Although the United States would never admit to being an empire, the review of its history reveals the "imperial earmarks that accompanied the growth of the nation: slave labor; demonization, genocide, and displacement of indigenous people; colonization of distant lands (e.g., Hawaii, Alaska, the Philippines, Guam); cultural arrogance; and global military power." However, Howard-Brook and Gwyther suggest that the United States is no longer the dominant imperial force in the world. Their suggestion for the largest, current manifestation of empire is "global capital." They accept a definition of "imperialism" as "a mechanism for transferring income from the middle to the upper classes."[28] This transfer of wealth at the service of global capital has functioned in recent decades under the idea of "free trade." The notions of free market and free trade are treated as ultimate and intrinsically true values. It is claimed that they benefit everyone. However, in fact, these ideas serve the interests of the wealthy and powerful to the detriment of the poorer countries, labeled "underdeveloped." Through controls operating under the International Monetary Fund (IMF) and the World Bank (WB) to produce free trade, the wealthy nations pursued policies that produced enormous, unpayable debt among the poorer countries. In re-

---

26. This discussion is similar to that of Stanley Grenz. He noted that Jesus' message was addressed to the marginalized, "the disadvantaged, the outcast, the 'sinners,'" and that it challenged the rich and privileged "to solidarity with the poor and outcasts." Jesus was the "great leveler. The God he reveals acknowledges no socioeconomic distinction." Stanley J. Grenz, *Theology for the Community of God* (Nashville: Broadman and Holman, 1994), 373-75.

27. Wes Howard-Brook and Anthony Gwyther, *Unveiling Empire: Reading Revelation Then and Now* (Maryknoll: Orbis, 1999).

28. Howard-Brook and Gwyther, *Unveiling*, 236-37.

sponse, the IMF and WB have forced "restructuring" on the local economies, which eliminates any preference for locally produced goods. This process of "free trade" allowed cheap imported goods from North America and Europe to flow into the local economies. Sale of these goods under the banner of "free trade" then benefited the wealthy countries, while putting thousands of local workers and farmers out of business.[29]

James Harder noted this destructive capacity of free trade in the specific case of Mexico. The North American Free Trade Act of 1994 opened Mexico to the sale of agricultural products grown in the United States. The local Mexican farmers could not compete with the megafarms and agribusiness of their northern neighbor. As a result, thousands of Mexican farm families were devastated. Many moved to already overcrowded Mexico City, where they joined the swelling ranks of poor people hoping desperately to survive as day laborers.[30]

A Warning: The Unholy Troika

The images of dragon and two beasts in Revelation 12 and 13 symbolize the empire and emperor. Their appearance constitutes a warning to first-century readers not to become complacent and allow themselves to be deceived by an empire not currently engaged in oppression of Christians. Christians in the twenty-first century need to heed this warning as well.

These three figures represent an unholy troika. From Chapter 2 above, recall the seven heads, ten horns and seven crowns that identify the dragon as an evil symbol of imperial Rome. This dragon appears again in Revelation 12:3, "with seven heads and ten horns, and seven diadems on his heads," and then takes "a stand on the sand of the seashore" (v. 18). The first beast rose from the sea. Like the dragon, it had multiple heads and "horns with the diadems" (13:1). The dragon gave it power and authority. One of the beast's heads apparently recovered from a "mortal wound" (v. 3), which amazed the population so that they worshiped the dragon and the beast. This first beast was allotted forty-two months "to make war on the saints and to conquer them" (v. 7). Meanwhile, the second beast arose out of the

---

29. Howard-Brook and Gwyther, *Unveiling*, 236-45.

30. James M. Harder, "The Violence of Global Marketization," in *Teaching Peace: Nonviolence and the Liberal Arts*, ed. J. Denny Weaver and Gerald Biesecker-Mast (Lanham: Rowman & Littlefield, 2003), 179-93. This article provides an excellent short look at the violence of the global market and the control of local economies by multinational corporations.

earth. It had "two horns like a lamb," but "it spoke like the dragon" (v. 11). This second beast "exercises all the authority of the first beast on its behalf, and it makes the earth and its inhabitants worship the first beast" (v. 12).

This troika stands as an evil caricature and a counterfeit parallel to God, Jesus Christ, and the Holy Spirit. In this mimicry, the dragon parallels God the Creator and Father, who gives authority to Jesus Christ. In its exercise of the authority of the dragon, the first beast is a caricature of the emperor and thus stands as a parallel to Jesus Christ, who exercises the authority of God. The beast's head that recovered from a mortal wound is a reference to the legend by which Nero was said to return from the underworld to plague the earth once again, which is a caricature of the resurrection of Jesus. Finally, as the Spirit of God leads to Christ and God, the second beast leads people to worship the first beast. This set of images is thus a warning to Christians not to be deceived and to place their loyalty with empire and emperor, who claim ultimate divine authority over all peoples, but to remain loyal to the reign of God, which is present in Jesus Christ.[31]

When Revelation was written late in the first century or early in the second, Rome was not persecuting Christians in Asia Minor and the church was becoming comfortable with the empire. Revelation was written to remind the churches of Asia Minor of the true character of empire — it is like a dragon with beastly rulers — and to call the churches again to their first loyalty, the resurrected Christ. This warning and admonition apply equally well to Christians in the twenty-first century. We have national and international structures that claim ultimate loyalty but engage in economic and political policies that exploit and oppress the vulnerable, which is the opposite of what living in the narrative of Jesus calls for. We have leaders who claim the name of Jesus Christ but wage war in Jesus' name — a parallel to the beast that looks like a lamb but speaks like the dragon. These leaders proclaim the rhetoric of free trade and the international market system, which promise riches to all but actually benefit only a few to the detriment of the many whom Jesus called "the least of these."[32] The message to first-

---

31. On the counterfeit trinity and the Nero myth, see M. Eugene Boring, *Revelation* (Interpretation: A Bible Commentary for Teaching and Preaching; Louisville: John Knox, 1989), 154-57, and Mitchell G. Reddish, *Revelation* (Smyth and Helwys Bible Commentary; Macon: Smyth and Helwys, 2001), 154-60.

32. For an article-length discussion of the dragon and the two beasts and the modern relevance of the text, see J. Denny Weaver, "The Dragon Lives Still," in *Compassionate Eschatology: The Future as Friend*, ed. Ted Grimsrud and Hardin Michael (Eugene: Cascade, 2011), 134-51.

century Christians to beware the nature of empire still applies today. Our ultimate loyalty as Christians lies not with national entities but with the kingdom of God. As Mitchell Reddish wrote, "Revelation 13 is a reminder that no person or institution deserves our ultimate allegiance."[33]

The Lord's Supper: An Economic Model

These issues of generosity and economic justice appear in John Howard Yoder's description of the Lord's Supper as a practice of the church that is a model for the watching world.[34] In the well-known words of institution of what today is called "The Lord's Supper," Jesus said, "Do this in remembrance of me" (Luke 22:19). Yoder's first point is that the meal Jesus blessed was the ordinary meal of the band of disciples eating together. The reference to "breaking bread together" designates their ordinary shared meal, a common table.

That it was an ordinary meal is seen, Yoder argues, when we observe the connection in the Gospels between food or eating and the appearances of the risen Jesus. An example is Jesus' appearance to the two disciples on the road to Emmaus, as depicted in Luke 24. They did not recognize Jesus until he "took bread, blessed and broke it and gave it to them." Then their eyes were opened — they recognized a common occurrence from previous meals together. The words Jesus spoke with these two disciples were the words of institution from the Last Supper, where Luke wrote, "Then he took a loaf of bread, and when he had given thanks, he broke it and gave it to them" (22:19). Paul repeats these words when he quotes Jesus in 1 Corinthians 11:24. Yoder's point is that the mention of "breaking bread together" refers not to a special ritual but to the ordinary shared meal of the roving band of disciples with Jesus.

This ordinary common meal displays sharing among members of the community. According to Yoder, the ideas of sharing money and possessions and social leveling are actually an extension of the common shared table, the sharing of sustenance.

This idea of the common meal continued after Jesus was no longer

---

33. Reddish, *Revelation*, 265.

34. The following discussion of the Lord's Supper follows John Howard Yoder, *Body Politics: Five Practices of the Christian Community before the Watching World* (Scottdale: Herald, 2001), chapter 2.

bodily present with the disciples. When the event of "breaking bread together" appears in Acts in the stories of the first Christians, it is a continuation of the practice begun with Jesus and his disciples. It is not an accident that the story of Pentecost in Acts 2 ends with four activities: teaching, fellowship, prayer, and breaking bread together (2:42). That is, those who accepted Jesus as Messiah continued the practice of eating together in a common meal.

In Acts 6 is a story of organizing the sharing of food so that all are treated equitably. There were in the church some widows who were Hellenists, that is, Greek-speaking Jews who had lived outside Palestine, who complained that they were not getting their fair share. In response to the complaint of these women, seven Hellenist members were chosen to help in distribution in order to be sure that all were treated equally. Yoder notes that accommodating the Hellenist members was the transition from a local network in Palestine to the beginning of what could become a worldwide network.

The church is like a new family, with Jesus as the head of the family, the one who insists on the equal status of each member. As noted earlier, baptism initiates new believers into this new creation, this new family that transcends differences of class, gender, and ethnicity. Calling this new creation a family emphasizes the leveling function of breaking bread or the common meal together. This family crosses and reconciles across previous boundaries of wealth, class, hierarchy, education, royal birth, ethnicity, and sexual orientation. Since rich and poor eat together as equals, social classes no longer exist in this family. Together all share equally in the "breaking of bread."

The shared meal, the "breaking of bread" is itself a thanksgiving. Jesus' words of institution and the descriptions of the common meal all have a prayer of thanksgiving to accompany the breaking of the bread. The meal is equal fellowship and sharing and is also a time of thanksgiving.

Since bread is sustenance, Yoder emphasizes that the meal of sharing and thanksgiving has economic implications. It is an economic act, an act of sharing the daily material things that sustain life. Practicing the shared meal properly is an act of economic ethics. Development of the idea of sharing other material possessions and money was an extension of the economic act of breaking bread together.

The previous section put on display the way that this kind of economic justice was front and center in Jesus' ministry from the beginning. It is already visible in the quotation from Isaiah at the beginning of his ministry when he talked about good news for the poor, release of captives (who were primarily economic prisoners), and freedom for the oppressed. And his deeds and teaching made it visible. Items mentioned include the suggestion for a protest by a poor man in debtor's court, those to invite to a banquet, the injunctions to live loosely and generously with wealth, the disciples' practice of a common purse, the response to Jesus by Zacchaeus, and the cup-of-cold-water saying. When the church breaks bread together, it should be giving a public witness to the idea of economic justice that was integral to Jesus' ministry and continued in the early church.

Yoder contrasted the Lord's Supper as a model of economic sharing with the practice of the Lord's Supper as a special ritual that has prevailed since the early Middle Ages. As Yoder defined the problem, when it became a special ritual with the focus on how Jesus was present in the bread and wine, the idea of sharing, the economic dimension of the supper, fell away. In Yoder's view, considering it a special ritual has enabled the church to avoid the economic implications of breaking bread together. His point is not to critique the claim that Jesus is present in the bread and wine but to argue that the focus on the special status of the ritual led to turning the focus away from the early emphasis of the meal as an experience of sharing.

Posing the Lord's Supper as an act of economic justice, as Yoder does, adds weight to its observance. It is a ritual of remembering the life of Jesus. But its meaning goes far beyond the church. It is an enactment of being the family of God, in which all are equal children of God around Jesus the head of the church. And that enactment extends beyond the church. As the subtitle of Yoder's *Body Politics* says, it is a practice "of the Christian community before the watching world."

The Lord's Supper as a model of economic sharing can lend theological significance to other practices of the church. Many congregations have potluck suppers. The Mennonite congregation I attend in Madison, Wisconsin has a potluck every Sunday after worship. As part of the routine, regular attenders bring extra food so that visitors who have come without food may participate in the community meal. It is an enactment of the idea that all are welcome in the family of God. Other congregations put on weekly or monthly suppers to which all members of the local area are invited. Such congregational or community meals are not a substitute for the ritual service of communion. However, the idea of the Lord's Supper as a model of economic justice in which all comers participate equally adds theological significance to the congregational meals. They become an extension of "breaking bread together" in the common meal blessed by Jesus.

Whether congregations have formal Communion as Lord's Supper every Sunday or every few weeks or months, they should recover the idea that it is a common meal with significant economic implications. All are welcome without regard to gender, wealth, occupation, sexual orientation, ethnicity, or birth status. If practiced as it should be in the life of the church, it is a display for the watching world of what the future reign of God looks like.

Understanding the economic witness of the practice of the Lord's Supper thus situates the church in the world. Truly acting on the economic implications will shape the church's witness. As observed in Jesus' words and deeds and as spelled out by Yoder, the economic implications of the common meal mean that as God's people we are concerned about people without clout, people without power, people who do not have enough, people without adequate resources, people on the margins. These concerns call Christians to advocate for just economic policies and to oppose economic policies and tax structures that harm those whom Jesus called "the least of these."

Along with this advocacy for "the least of these," Yoder offered an important point of caution. Being concerned about the poor and marginalized and those without clout does not mean becoming an advocate for a particular political philosophy, whether socialism or democracy. Recall that the church defined by faith in Jesus as the Messiah transcends all ethnic groups and political boundaries and is not identified with the social order or by political boundaries, nor with any particular culture, ethnicity, or economic or political philosophy.

But with that caution, Yoder makes clear that all economic orders, whatever combination of capitalist and socialist policies they practice, have provisions that *if applied in good faith* can protect poor people, people on the margins. One example he noted in our society is publicly funded education for all. In principle a person does not have to be wealthy to get an education in our society. Publicly funded roads and public transportation are another example, although public transportation is sadly lacking in many areas of the United States. Although they are endangered, we have government programs that assist with medical care for poor people and with the additional expenses that come when caring for people with special needs. Although the previous section pointed to numerous instances of economic injustice carried on in American society, here are examples suggested by Yoder of programs in our society that if adequately funded and applied would serve the interests of disadvantaged people.

Thus the Christian calling is not to try to replace one system with another. Our calling as Christians is not to join a revolution to overthrow a capitalist system in favor of a socialist system, or in other places to assume that working for economic justice means replacing a socialist system or a tribal system with a market economy. Rather our calling as Christians is to use the available mechanisms of the system we are in to advocate for the poor and less advantaged. And in instances of grave injustice — a few examples are race segregation, treatment of undocumented people, legislation that cuts already inadequate funding for medical care for poor people — the available mechanisms can include acts of public protest and civil disobedience. Previous chapters have mentioned nonviolent activism in several contexts. Here it is sufficient to say that such expressions of protest are extensions of the economic implications of the "breaking bread together" blessed by Jesus.

Yoder raised one other implication from the economic sharing that is an extension of the Lord's Supper. It concerns the way that vocations are practiced. Some theologies, particularly in the Calvinist and Lutheran traditions, have defined vocation on the basis of presumed orders of creation. According to this argument, orders of creation determine social location and how people function in various vocations. In South Africa during the apartheid era, for example, the order of creation was claimed to place white people over black people. Barely more than 150 years ago in our country, it was said that the orders of creation established superior white people to rule inferior black people with slavery. Martin Luther said that one's Christian calling was to exercise the vocation in which one found oneself: rulers rule and exercise the sword, executioners execute people for the rulers, bankers accumulate money, soldiers fight, bakers bake bread, and women stay home and become mothers. In every instance the vocation or station in life defines the Christian service one renders.

The problem Yoder identified with vocation defined by the orders of creation is not only disapproval of the killing involved with the vocations of hangman and soldier. It is the prior question of the criteria with which to judge whether a vocation is being exercised appropriately. If the practice is defined by presumed "orders of creation," it is actually the common conventions of a given society that define the exercise of the vocation. In this case, Christian service is defined by the conventions of the social order. In contrast, in Yoder's perspective, and I believe that he is correct, the practice of a vocation should rather be shaped by criteria developed from an understanding of the narrative of Jesus. Any vocation that is honorable and necessary is open to Christians. The important question concerns how the chosen vocation is practiced. Is it practiced simply as an end in itself, or is it used in some way to make the host society more just or to serve people in need?

For example, rather than just accumulating money, bankers can pursue practices that further economic justice. People with a gift for making money can use it to support worthy causes. Lawyers can do some pro bono work and take cases that have justice implications. Realtors can work on ways to house people according to their needs. Developers can do some of their work on so-called "affordable housing," rather than focusing on lucrative high-end building. Medical doctors can direct some of their practice to people without medical insurance. Judges and court officials can work with programs of restorative justice. Public school teachers can work examples of nonviolence into the standard curriculum. And more. This list could be extended at great length.

Talking about how one exercises a vocation may seem to have moved a great distance from Jesus' words "do this in remembrance of me." But exercising a vocation in a way that promotes equality and advocates for the marginalized is an extension of the economic implications of the common meal that Jesus blessed.

Support for Yoder's suggestions on economic sharing comes from an unexpected source, namely Frans de Waal's book *The Age of Empathy*.[35] De Waal has spent three decades studying animal behavior, with a particular focus on primates. He uses observations about animal behavior to challenge the common assumption about "nature red in tooth and claw," and the belief that the competitive and violent behavior of human beings reflects that view of nature.[36] He notes that while primates do engage in some fights over territory, they also engage in a great deal of cooperative and empathetic behavior. In fact, their survival as well as that of numbers of herd and pack animals depends on such cooperation. De Waal applies those observations to human beings as well. "What we need is a complete

35. Frans De Waal, *The Age of Empathy: Nature's Lessons for a Kinder Society* (New York: Harmony, 2009).

36. The source of the phrase "red in tooth and claw" is apparently a poem penned by Alfred Lord Tennyson titled "In Memoriam A.H.H." The phrase appears in canto 56, which reads:

Who trusted God was love indeed
And love Creation's final law
Tho' Nature, red in tooth and claw
With ravine, shriek'd against his creed.

overhaul of assumptions about human nature. Too many economies and politicians model human society on the perpetual struggle they believe exists in nature, but which is a mere projection."[37] In Chapter 10 I will deal with some implications of de Waal's research for the discussion of nonviolence and nature. Here I will consider a few of de Waal's findings that have implications for economic policy.

De Waal writes that given the financial collapse and the crisis in health care in the United States, "reliance on the profit principle has proven disastrous." Societies need a "balance between selfish and social motives."[38] Allowing unfettered economic domination by the wealthy leads to disaster. Individual initiative needs to be balanced by empathy, with incentives for people to work both for themselves and for others. Perceptions of fairness and empathy or concern for others are both important. Animal behaviors provide de Waal with examples. A chimpanzee who receives a large amount of food may eat first, but eventually all are allowed to share in the bounty. Individual chimpanzees may trade favors of food and grooming.[39] Monkeys will cease performing an activity and become agitated if another receives a better reward for the same activity. Public anger at the huge bonuses paid to CEOs of companies who sought government bailouts are hardly surprising.[40] When one of a pair of capuchin monkeys was offered a choice of a reward for itself alone or another that included the partner as well, the monkeys "overwhelmingly preferred the prosocial option, thus demonstrating that they care for one another."[41]

De Waal's major thesis derived from observations of animal behavior is that empathy that builds cooperation is necessary for a healthy society. He noted Adam Smith's "'invisible hand,' according to which even the most selfish motives will automatically advance the greater good." However, de Waal says, "a society based purely on selfish motives and market forces may produce wealth, yet it can't produce the unity and mutual trust that make life worthwhile." There is, de Waal says, the need for "a second invisible hand, one that reaches out to others. The firmest support for the common good comes from enlightened self-interest: the realization that we are all better off if we work together."[42] Acting with compassion is not

---

37. De Waal, *Age of Empathy*, 7.
38. De Waal, *Age of Empathy*, 37-38.
39. De Waal, *Age of Empathy*, 173-74.
40. De Waal, *Age of Empathy*, 187-89.
41. De Waal, *Age of Empathy*, 193.
42. De Waal, *Age of Empathy*, 222, 221, 223.

merely a matter of personal sacrifice of time and money to relieve the plight of others. It is also furthering a political agenda that recognizes the dignity of every person and thus benefits society as a whole. Society at large fragments and is weakened when some individuals are allowed to flounder.

De Waal is a primatologist who deals with animal behavior, not with theology. Nonetheless, his conclusions support Yoder's theological claims. This is another example of interdisciplinary linking, alongside earlier notice of historical and sociological demonstrations of the futility of pursuing violence, the observation of reduced recidivism rates for the practice of restorative justice, and the well-being produced by the practice of forgiveness.

Baptism and Lord's Supper as "Sacraments"

In traditional understanding, a sacrament is an act that accomplishes what it signifies. Yoder indicates that baptism and the Lord's Supper as he has developed them are still sacraments. Baptism relativizes prior differences and creates the new, egalitarian community. The Lord's Supper is economic sharing. In both instances, ordinary performance of the ritual enacts a new reality, and the body of Christ — the church as the continuation of Jesus' mission in the world — is present in the performance of the ritual.[43] Those who want a "high" view of sacrament but without joining one of the sacramental Christian traditions can have it in this view articulated by Yoder.

The discussions of race, gender, and economics all picture the church that poses a witness or a challenge to the surrounding society. Mention was made of nonviolent activism. Such advocacy is not always popular, and it can be costly or even dangerous. This brings the discussion to the issue of suffering.

---

43. Yoder, *Body Politics*, 33.

10 *Nature and Suffering*

Discussion of questions about nature and suffering could expand virtually without limit. The sketch here can only begin this particular conversation.

Jesus and Nature

Christian theology has long carried the affirmation that the incarnation hallows the natural world that is God's creation. Jesus' existence as a human being, subject to the conditions of human existence, makes gloriously clear that the physical and material world is not evil in and of itself. In the person of Jesus, the reign of God is present in the material world and puts on display that the reign of God encompasses physical life and that God loves the earth. These things are of course true. But there is more to say about the natural and material world than that God has hallowed it.

In his teaching, Jesus took examples from nature. God's care even for sparrows implies God's greater care for people (Luke 12:6). God's care for ravens and lilies and grass that soon withers makes visible God's even greater care for God's people (vv. 22-28). Jesus was familiar with the cultivation of fruit and fig trees to produce fruit (6:43-44; 13:6-9). Parables of sowing in fields showed familiarity with other dimensions of agriculture (Matt. 13:3-9; 13:24-30). These references in Jesus' teaching display comfort and familiarity with the natural world.

The many accounts of healings and exorcisms go beyond familiarity with nature to show that nature exists within the purview of the reign of

God. That power of the reign of God over nature is given yet more visibility as Jesus raises people from the dead — a widow's son (Luke 7:11-15), Jairus's daughter (8:40-42, 49-55), and Lazarus (John 11:38-44). But the most important indication concerning the power of the reign of God over the natural order is God's resurrection of Jesus. The end of life in the natural world is death. Death means the cessation of existence in the physical world. Jesus' resurrection displays the capacity of the reign of God to overcome even this final ending, namely the cessation of existence.

These observations are not a blueprint for incorporating an approach to nature into a lived theology developed from the story of Jesus. Other elements come into play. For one, the accounts of creation in Genesis 1 and 2 provide two points that are relevant in discussing an attitude toward the created order. The created order is not divine: it is created by God. Therefore, it is not to be worshiped. That is a theological observation, not a scientific assertion. It is true for any view of the science of origins that a reader may hold.

A complementary point is the fact that we are part of the order created by God. Whether the image of creation by spoken word in Genesis 1 or the anthropomorphic image of God as sculptor in Genesis 2, human beings are pictured coming into existence in the same way that other living beings come into existence. Thus whatever view one may hold of the science of human origins, it is clear that human beings belong to and are part of the created order. Out of respect for the world that originated with God, people should live in harmony with it rather than assuming that it can and should be dominated and used up. As womanist theologian Karen Baker-Fletcher said, "We ought to practice Christianity in such a way that we reclaim our need for spiritual and physical healing and wholeness of earth and humanity." As beings who came into existence in the same way as other of God's created beings, "Our task is to find ways to share this land fairly, to live in greater harmony with it, and to respect environments that have served as shelter for other creatures besides ourselves."[1]

The respect for the environments that Baker-Fletcher mentioned has been frequently eroded by the misapplication of the term "dominion" in Genesis 1:28. It has long been read as a license to dominate, control, exploit, and use up the earth's resources. The term needs to be understood as a facet of humankind made in the image of God (v. 27). In this light, domin-

---

1. Karen Baker-Fletcher, *Sisters of Dust, Sisters of Spirit: Womanist Wordings on God and Creation* (Minneapolis: Fortress, 1998), 19, 33.

ion identifies humankind as God's representative on earth to carry out God's intent to care for and nurture the earth. As described by Walter Brueggemann, this means to exercise power "as God exercises power." It thus follows that "there is nothing here of coercive or tyrannical power, either for God or for humankind." The dominance of dominion "is that of a shepherd who cares for, tends, and feeds the animals. Or, if transferred to the political arena, the image is that of a shepherd king. . . . Thus the task of 'dominion' does not have to do with exploitation and abuse. It has to do with securing the well-being of every other creature."[2] Elsewhere, Brueggemann writes that those given dominion must practice "wisdom."

> Wisdom is the critical, reflective, discerning reception of Yahweh's gift of generosity. That gift is not for self-indulgence, exploitation, acquisitiveness, or satiation. It is for careful husbanding, so that resources should be used for the protection, enhancement, and nurture of all creatures. Wisdom is the careful, constant reflective attention to the shapes and interconnections that keep the world generative. Where those shapes and interconnections are honored, there the whole world prospers, and all creatures come to joy and abundance. Where those shapes and interconnections are violated or disregarded, trouble, conflict, and deconstructiveness are sure. There is wisdom in the very fabric of creation. Human wisdom consists in resonance with the "wisdom of things," which is already situated in creation before human agents act on it.[3]

It can go without saying that past efforts to use nature to justify men's domination of women or white people's rule of people of color is fundamentally antithetical to wisdom that seeks the enhancement, nurture, joy, and abundance of all.

A specific instance of harmful exploitation of land and destruction of the environment has a link to the racism challenged in the previous chapter. The problem is sometimes called "environmental racism," which touches both people and the environment. The term applies to the fact that hazardous waste sites, garbage and trash dumps, and industries that pollute are most often concentrated "in black and Hispanic urban com-

2. Walter Brueggemann, *Genesis* (Interpretation: A Bible Commentary for Teaching and Preaching; Atlanta: John Knox, 1982), 32.

3. Walter Brueggemann, *The Theology of the Old Testament: Testimony, Dispute, Advocacy* (Minneapolis: Fortress, 1997), 531-32.

munities" and "southern black rural communities."[4] In other words, the people who benefit least from the economic gain of industrial pollution are those most subject to the environmental hazards.

It is commonly assumed that nature is violent, as portrayed in the well-known phrase "nature red in tooth and claw." The argument about the nonviolence of God (see Chapters 4 and 5) comes into play at this juncture. One might ask, for example, whether a God whose nonviolent character is revealed in Jesus would create a world based fundamentally on violence.

Several kinds of observations concerning the natural order indicate that it is not as violent as is commonly assumed. When biologist Todd Rainey analyzed available primate data from a nonviolent perspective, a number of observations suggest that while apes and monkeys have conflicts, they also have means of settling those conflicts without resorting to bloodshed. What appear to be violent arguments and confrontations are ways that animals who lack verbal ability learn about each other, communicate boundaries for territory and mates, determine distribution of food, and deal with newcomers to the group. Few conflicts result in serious injury, and many primates have practices of conflict resolution and reconciliation.[5] The human species is the only one that routinely fights to the death and kills its own kind in large numbers. It appears, Rainey concludes, that "many human observers have read their own violent assumptions into their observations of animal behavior," which should in turn challenge humans to consider their "assumptions about both the inevitability and the effectiveness of violence."[6]

Renowned primatologist Frans de Waal agrees that observers have projected their own biases about violence and competition onto nature. He supplies many examples that counter the image of "nature red in tooth and claw." I mentioned his book *The Age of Empathy* in Chapter 9 in discussions of economic policy and of the importance of social structures that treat all members of society fairly. Although de Waal does not make the application himself specifically to nonviolence, numbers of his illustrations throughout the book also fit in that context. He notes that while

4. Baker-Fletcher, *Sisters of Dust,* 61. For literature on environmental racism, see *Sisters of Dust,* 134, nn. 1 and 4.

5. W. Todd Rainey, "Nature's Tooth-and-Claw Conflict Resolution," in *Teaching Peace: Nonviolence and the Liberal Arts,* ed. J. Denny Weaver and Gerald Biesecker-Mast (Lanham: Rowman & Littlefield, 2003), 235-45.

6. Rainey, "Nature's Tooth-and-Claw," 243.

monkeys and apes have disputes among themselves and that chimpanzees, for example, do occasionally wage war on other bands and can be vicious, for the most part these primates do not fight to the death. They perform acts of reconciliation through such activities as grooming or bringing food to share. They have processes by which food is shared. Most apes want to be the first to put their hands on food, and ownership is respected, but eventually food is shared and even low-ranking individuals eat. "It is a rather peaceful scene even though there is also quite a bit of jostling for position." De Waal rejects the idea that nature is based on a struggle for life. "Many animals survive not by eliminating each other or keeping everything for themselves, but by cooperating and sharing." He applies these observations to American society, which emphasizes individual acquisition at the expense of society. Rejecting the idea of a bloody, competitive view of nature means rethinking competition as the basis of human society. "What we need is a complete overhaul of assumptions about human nature. Too many economists and politicians model human society on the perpetual struggle they believe exists in nature, but which is a mere projection" of their own ideology of individualism and cutthroat competition onto nature. Projecting perpetual violent struggle from nature onto human behavior "is a trick we have fallen for for too long. Obviously, competition is part of the picture, but humans can't live by competition alone."[7]

The Age of Empathy contains numerous illustrations of cooperative rather than competitive behavior. Various species of primates practice empathetic and cooperative, group-oriented behavior. They develop alliances for protection, and have mechanisms for resolving quarrels. A few examples will illustrate. Among Chinese golden monkeys the dominant male steps between quarreling females and calms them by turning to each in turn for stroking or friendly expressions. Both male and female chimpanzees "actively broker community relations," with females removing rocks or branches from the hands of angry males. Females also reconcile males after a fight. While dominant leaders attain status from their roles in the group, the group as a whole benefits from having fewer quarrels, and the leader benefits from a more harmonious society. These societies would not thrive with leaders who acted only in their own interests. De Waal's point is that the work of mediators involves enlightened self-interest.[8] Such ob-

---

7. Frans De Waal, *The Age of Empathy: Nature's Lessons for a Kinder Society* (New York: Harmony, 2009), 6-7.

8. De Waal, *Age of Empathy*, 34-37.

servations align with the idea that the nature created by God revealed in the nonviolent story of Jesus is not fundamentally "red in tooth and claw" as commonly assumed.

Observations at the level of cell biology produce similar conclusions. Immunologist Angela Horn Montel argues that the prevalence of violent metaphors in immunology — "deliver a lethal blow," "arsenal of weapons," secretion of cells that "attempt to bludgeon the enemy," "battles against foreign invaders," "a patient assassin"[9] — not only reflects assumptions about the acceptance of violence among the general public but has had unintended and undesirable consequences. For example, such terminology has contributed to the idea that germs must be wiped out, which has resulted in the production of antibacterial soaps and many other products "impregnated with antibacterial agents." Such products have sometimes destroyed the protective layer of helpful organisms on our bodies, rendering people more rather than less vulnerable to disease and may also "actually exacerbate the already troublesome emergence of strains of harmful bacteria that are resistant to some, or even all, the known antibiotics."[10] It is also recognized that some cells are necessarily destroyed in the development of a healthy fetus in the same process that is elsewhere described as a "violent conflict." Montel thus suggests that changing the image of the interaction of host and pathogen away from violence and toward images such as "dance between microbe and host" can better enable Christians "to feel one with the great circle of life," and to move closer to the nonviolent God who is made visible in the suffering of Jesus Christ.[11]

Furthermore, some devastation for which a supposedly violent God is blamed should more properly be attributed to human activity. There are several examples. Hurricane Katrina devastated the city of New Orleans as well as portions of the Gulf Coast in August 2005, killing nearly 1900 people and leaving hundreds of thousands without access to homes and jobs. As was mentioned in Chapter 4, a number of religious spokesmen and politicians linked the destruction to God.[12] Often ignored in the reporting on the impact of the storm and flooding was the extent to which decisions by

9. Angela Horn Montel, "Violent Images in Cell Biology," in *Teaching Peace: Nonviolence and the Liberal Arts,* ed. J. Denny Weaver and Gerald Biesecker-Mast (Lanham: Rowman & Littlefield, 2003), 223-24.

10. Montel, "Violent Images," 227.

11. Montel, "Violent Images," 233.

12. For remarks attributing the devastation of hurricane Katrina, see notes 8 and 9 in Chapter 4. That chapter also provides arguments against such a view of God.

human beings contributed to the devastation. More than two centuries of decisions about dikes, dams, and draining of marshlands, actions taken for the benefit of large farming interests, industrialization, and urbanization, halted the silt buildup from the river and drained wetlands. As a result, much of the barrier that would have absorbed the force of the storm was long gone. Such decisions, coupled with a lack of willingness to spend money on dikes for protection of poor residential areas, added greatly to the damage.[13] When the tsunami killed more than 200,000 people in Southeast Asia in 2004, damage inland was most severe where natural coastal barriers had been removed to build hotels and vacation resorts.[14] New, exclusive residential developments in southern California are subject to mudslides. It is well known that cutting of mountainside trees to make way for houses removes the vegetation that holds the land in place. Rain then softens the earth which has the potential to slide down the mountain. When the real contribution of human decisions is factored into these instances of devastation, it appears that nature as well as the God of nature are not as destructive as commonly perceived. Destruction is multiplied when and where people have sought to dominate nature and have not made sufficient efforts to live within it.

Writings in the philosophy of science by theologian Nancey Murphy make a quite different argument for the nonviolence of God based on observations of the natural world.[15] Murphy describes a hierarchy of scientific methodologies that begins at the atomic level and moves through chemistry and biology. Above biology the hierarchy has two branches. The natural science branch has cosmology, while the social science branch has psychology, the social sciences, and ethics. Finally theology is the discipline that tops both branches. Murphy argues that each mode of inquiry answers questions about the world and about human functioning, but eventually there come "boundary questions" that must be answered by the next discipline higher in the hierarchy. Ultimately, at the top of the pyramid, theology answers ultimate questions about the nature of reality. For exam-

13. Michael Grunwald and Susan B. Glasser, "The Slow Drowning of New Orleans," *Washington Post*, 9 October 2005: http://www.washingtonpost.com/wp-dyn/content/article/2005/10/08/AR2005100801458.html.

14. http://en.wikipedia.org/wiki/2004_Indian_Ocean_earthquake_and_tsunami.

15. For a summary statement of her argument, see Nancey C. Murphy, *Reconciling Theology and Science: A Radical Reformation Perspective* (Scottdale: Herald, 1997). A longer discussion is Nancey Murphy and George F. R. Ellis, *On the Moral Nature of the Universe: Theology, Cosmology, and Ethics* (Minneapolis: Fortress, 1996).

ple, the science of cosmology can explore the immense expanse of the expanding cosmos and posit that its expansion is due to a "big bang." However, it cannot explain why the big bang happened or where it came from, which are questions that theology has an answer for — namely that the so-called big bang originated with God. This answer does not prove the existence of God, but the answer is as plausible as positing something else such as the eternality of the universe and Evolution with a capital E. Thus according to Murphy there need not be a conflict between science and Christian theology. Rather, Christian theology provides "an extra layer of explanation . . . for the physical world we see around us."[16]

One concern of Murphy is to provide an understanding of God that is in accordance with the revelation of God in the nonviolence of Jesus and that also envisions God's providential control of all reality while preserving human freedom and the freedom of creation. If creation and human beings are genuinely to have freedom, then God must not use coercion and must be nonviolent. Murphy's argument assumes and works with modern scientific observations, but encompasses them within the reign of God. At the subatomic level of quantum physics, the location and movement of any one particle is random and entirely unpredictable while the behavior of matter as a whole is predictable. Murphy uses this randomness within predictability to construct an image of God as Creator who allows the freedom of creation.[17] Murphy describes some of the characteristics of the expanding universe after the so-called big bang — the total mass of the universe that impacts gravity and electromagnetism, the strong and weak nuclear forces within atoms — that allowed life to develop on our planet. Minute variations in these entities would have rendered impossible life as we know it. Murphy calls the exactness of these cosmic constants the "cosmological fine-tuning" after the initial big bang that would indicate "divine creation." If theology is the top level of the hierarchy of ways of knowing, then divine creation is the "ideal explanation" from a Christian perspective of the source of the universe. The fine-tuning does not prove the existence of God, but it adds weight to traditional arguments and is thus a kind of "confirmation for God's existence and creative role."[18]

The enormous, almost unfathomable age of the cosmos and the fine-tuning that was present almost from the beginning allowed for human be-

16. Murphy and Ellis, *Moral Nature of the Universe*, 218.

17. Murphy, *Reconciling Theology and Science*, 74.

18. Murphy, *Reconciling Theology and Science*, 35-37.

ings to evolve with "the capacity to 'image' God."[19] The God of this process is the God who limited God's own power in order to allow the freedom of creation. The noncoercive, nonviolent character of God is thus intrinsic to the process that created human beings. It is also the case that God has to "suffer" the consequences, sometimes deadly consequences, of the freedom given to creation and to human beings. Those consequences include the just-noted devastation of hurricanes and tsunamis, which is exacerbated by human choices. The ultimate demonstration of God's acceptance of suffering is allowing Jesus, the Messiah, to suffer and die. To imitate Jesus and to have the "image of God" is to imitate the "moral character of God," which means to refuse to participate in coercion. This imitation of Jesus and the moral character of God can and does mean suffering. But God is not the cause of the suffering. Rather, God is on the side of those who suffer in a life of sacrifice.[20] However, the power of God is also demonstrated in that death does not have the last word. The resurrection of Jesus is the guarantee that the reign of God will ultimately prevail. "God's plans for creation do not end with the world as we know it. They will be fulfilled in a transformation prefigured in the resurrection of Jesus."[21]

In Chapter 6 it was noted that the classic creedal statements use a fourth-century worldview and ontological categories from Greek philosophy to explain how Jesus is both of God and identified with humankind. It appears that Murphy has made a parallel argument in terms of a modern cosmology and a modern philosophical and scientific outlook. In a way that differs significantly from the classic statements, her language and imagery also portray Jesus as a revelation of God and as one who suffers the same conditions as humankind. Murphy is also beyond the classic statements in that her formulations appeal to a characteristic not visible in the classic formulas, namely the nonviolence of Jesus, which is seen in the narrative of his life, and also in that her image of Jesus is posed as the model that Christians can and do follow as disciples of Jesus in imitation of the moral character of God.

The discussion in this section has ranged far — from Jesus' familiarity with and participation in nature to the character of the God who created

---

19. Murphy, *Reconciling Theology and Science*, 74.

20. Murphy, *Reconciling Theology and Science*, 69-71.

21. Murphy and Ellis, *Moral Nature of the Universe*, 193; Murphy, *Reconciling Theology and Science*, 72-74, quoting 74. It is also the case that the approach in this book has a greater theological role for resurrection than does Nancey Murphy's construction of theology and science.

the cosmos. Jesus experienced the ultimate in identifying with humanity by dying, and his life and manner of submitting to death reveal the character of God. Working out from the belief that God is revealed in Jesus, in Part I of this book I pointed to the nonviolence of God made visible in the Old Testament as well as in the often-presumed violent book of Revelation. In this chapter, I have summarized how Murphy provides a confirming argument for the nonviolence of God on the basis of observations in the natural world.

This discussion does have implications for a lived theology derived from the narrative of Jesus. This theology would challenge us to live in harmony with the created order rather than seeking to dominate and exploit it. Looking at nature with a nonviolent image of the Creator has the capacity to reorient research at the cellular level and to point to reinterpretations of primate behavior. Applying such changes can contribute a worldview in which nonviolence makes sense. It further establishes the idea that living out of the story of Jesus means living in line with the character of God, and that nonviolent character is shown to be visible in the created world itself. It is what John Howard Yoder called "the grain of the universe."[22]

Most importantly, the resurrection hallows this view of God in creation. God's resurrection of Jesus puts on display the capacity of the reign of God to overcome the freedom of creation to annihilate life. The resurrection of Jesus is the beginning of the restoration of humanity and of creation. Thus resurrection goes beyond an invitation to enter into the nonviolent life of Jesus. It is also an invitation to live in harmony with the grain of the universe, to participate now in God's restoration of the created order in the eschaton.

Rita Nakashima Brock and Rebecca Parker's *Saving Paradise* emphasizes the need for a Christianity that sees paradise not as a pristine past nor a distant future hope but as "already present." Seeing God's paradise present now will underscore the need to protect God's creation and to experience an "ethical grace" that brings our lives and our cultures into accord with the paradise of God's creation. This insight will bring "sustaining communities to the forefront of our work," since communities are what sustain human relationships "that require us to share responsibility, act

---

22. John Howard Yoder, "Armaments and Eschatology," *Studies in Christian Ethics* 1 (1988): 58. "Grain of the universe" is Yoder's phrase most often cited. Elsewhere he wrote of "the grain of the cosmos." John Howard Yoder, *The Politics of Jesus: Vicit Agnus Noster* (2d ed.; Grand Rapids: William B. Eerdmans, 1994), 246.

generously toward one another and resist oppressive and dominating forces that separate human beings from each other and deny our powers of love and friendship."[23] The focus in this volume on living in the narrative of Jesus supports Brock and Parker's call to experience paradise in the present. Belief in the resurrection gives reality to the idea of paradise present. As the church and our lives exhibit the future reign of God breaking into the present, the idea of paradise present expresses the beginning of God's restoration of creation. When we live in harmony with God's creation, we participate in that restoration.

Two Kinds of Suffering

We may participate now in the beginning of God's future restoration of the created order and celebrate the experience of paradise in the present. Nonetheless, dealing with the destructive force of nature, along with discussions of practicing nonviolence that can result in hostile responses when confronting injustice based on gender issues or racism or economic oppression, brings to the fore the issue of suffering. I discuss two kinds of suffering, one involuntary and one voluntary or chosen.

Involuntary suffering occurs apart from any activity or choice made by the one who suffers. It is not chosen but comes from a variety of sources. It is, for example, the suffering imposed by poverty, imposed by the economic systems that operate for the benefit of the rich and powerful while keeping the poor poor. It is the suffering imposed by discrimination against people because of race, gender, or sexual orientation. Involuntary suffering is caused by disease and accidents that cause hardship to self or loved ones and that take the lives of loved ones. Another kind of involuntary suffering is that caused by natural disasters such as floods and hurricanes. Sometimes this suffering caused by natural disasters is made worse by human choices, as when the rich and the powerful control much of the land and make choices that leave poor people the most vulnerable to flooding. And finally, there is the suffering caused by war, which touches many innocent people. This list of suffering could be made much longer. Earlier sections discussed these causes of suffering and how the followers of Jesus may confront them.

23. Rita Nakashima Brock and Rebecca Ann Parker, *Saving Paradise: How Christianity Traded Love of This World for Crucifixion and Empire* (Boston: Beacon, 2008), 418.

Another kind of suffering may result from efforts to confront these injustices. In a sense, it is voluntary suffering — voluntary in the sense that one knows that the chosen justice-seeking activity may result in suffering. Loving enemies and confronting injustice is not always easy. In fact, loving enemies and confronting injustice can be very difficult and dangerous. Engaging in such activities can easily result in suffering. These activities are not undertaken in order to suffer, but confronting injustice requires awareness that the struggle might result in suffering. Thus in a manner of speaking, the suffering that results from the pursuit of justice is suffering that an individual undertakes voluntarily.

How we understand suffering in the life of Jesus, and how we understand human suffering, both voluntary and involuntary, are very important discussions. Atonement theology informs these discussions, whether one opts for the traditional satisfaction imagery or the nonviolent image of narrative Christus Victor.

Recall briefly the analysis of satisfaction and substitutionary atonement images from Chapter 3. In these images, Jesus' suffering and death were the purpose and the culmination of his mission. He was sent to die — to offer a death to God — because God needed his death to balance or satisfy the offense against divine honor, however that divine need is defined. For these atonement images, it is possible to say that Jesus' suffering was salvific. His suffering and death constitute the foundation of our salvation.

In these satisfaction atonement images, Jesus' primary saving activity is suffering and dying. If Jesus is taken as a model for the Christian life, these atonement images appear to hallow suffering and even death in and of themselves. Suffering in and of itself is likened to Christ's suffering. As was displayed in Chapter 3, it is this point concerning the salvific quality of suffering and its implication for following the example of Jesus that has led many feminist and womanist theologians to reject the idea of atonement. And by the same token, it has led defenders of the several versions of satisfaction atonement to reject the idea that Jesus, at least specific dimensions of Jesus' life, is the model for the Christian to follow.

Now contrast this necessary suffering and death in satisfaction and substitutionary atonement with Jesus' death as it appears in narrative Christus Victor. There death is not the focus or purpose of Jesus' mission, and death is not the saving element. Jesus' mission was to *live,* to live in a way that made present the reign of God and invited people to share in it. His mission was life-bringing and life-giving. It was not organized around an elaborate plot to get Jesus killed in order to fulfill a divine need. When we understand that Jesus' death did not supply a divine need or pay a debt to God, it is possible to say within the framework of narrative Christus Victor that God did not need the death of Jesus. From another perspective, in the sense that God desired for Jesus to fulfill his mission, it is possible to say that Jesus' death was desired, desired in the sense that saving his life would mean failing his mission. And from yet one more perspective, since the ultimate character of Jesus' mission provoked an ultimate response from the powers of evil, namely depriving Jesus of his life, it is possible to say that Jesus' death was inevitable. However, for none of these statements from within narrative Christus Victor is death God's saving action. On the contrary, God's saving action is the restoration of life, the resurrection. Resurrection is the basis of salvation. Or stated just a bit differently by womanist Delores Williams, "the resurrection does not depend upon the cross for life, for the cross only represents historical evil trying to defeat good. The resurrection of Jesus and the flourishing of God's spirit in the world as the result of resurrection represent the life of [Jesus'] ministerial vision gaining victory over the evil attempt to kill it."[24] Because salvation as understood within narrative Christus Victor does not depend on a death initiated or sanctioned by God, viewed from the side of God's saving act, I designate narrative Christus Victor as a nonviolent atonement image.

It is important to see that although suffering and death occurred in the story of Jesus as depicted in narrative Christus Victor, suffering and death are not the focus or purpose of Jesus' life. Rather, suffering and death are the *result* of Jesus' living faithfully and faithfully carrying out his God-given mission. Jesus could have avoided suffering and saved his life. But saving his life in that fashion would have meant failing his God-given mission to live fully for and in complete obedience to the reign of God. Jesus refused to fail his mission. He chose obedience to his mission, which meant choosing to suffer and die. But that suffering and death in and of themselves were not redemptive. Suffering and death were not the purpose of his mission; they were rather the result of his faithful obedience to his mission to live for the reign of God.[25]

---

24. Delores S. Williams, *Sisters in the Wilderness: The Challenge of Womanist God-Talk* (Maryknoll: Orbis, 1993), 165.

25. The view I advocate rejects redemptive suffering and finds the locus of God's saving activity in the resurrection of Jesus. However, since for Jesus to live fully meant choosing to die, I can appreciate James Cone's choice to emphasize the cross. Cone recognizes that ultimate hope resides in the resurrection, in which "God is giving people meaning beyond history." Nonetheless, because the cross of Christ has been a deeply meaningful source of en-

Jesus' choice to face death rather than surrender his mission has contemporary parallels in individuals who chose to face death rather than withdraw in order to safeguard their lives. Two who come immediately to mind are Martin Luther King, Jr. and Oscar Romero.

Claiming Jesus as the norm for the Christian life as pictured by narrative Christus Victor has a much different feel than it does for satisfaction atonement. Rather than focusing on the salvific quality of suffering through identifying with Jesus' suffering and death, the emphasis falls on how to live in the reign of God. When we live in the story of Jesus, we know that just as suffering was a reality for Jesus, suffering is a possibility for us. But suffering in and of itself is not what makes us "like Christ." While suffering may occur, it is sharing in his life and thus continuing his mission to witness to the rule of God in the world that make us "like Christ."

The idea of suffering for our Christian confession may seem far removed in the tolerant society of North America,[26] which professes freedom of religion. But North Americans need to keep in mind the message of the book of Revelation about perseverance in the face of empire. The story of early Christian martyrs belongs to the heritage of every Christian. *Martyrs Mirror* from the Anabaptist Christian tradition both inspires faithfulness and reminds the faithful that persecution is possible. Other Christian traditions also treasure martyr books. Suffering is an important element of the history of African Americans. The suffering of enslavement and the subsequent racial suffering imposed by segregation, lynching, Jim Crow laws, and the factors of white privilege is involuntary and is not

---

couragement for African Americans, Cone can emphasize with Martin Luther King, Jr., that the importance of the cross is "the hope that emerges out of terrible circumstances," and in particular the circumstances of lynching, which has deeply impacted Cone's thought. Although there is "nothing redemptive about suffering in itself," Cone retains a focus on the cross. "The gospel of Jesus," he says, "is not a rational concept to be explained in a theory of salvation, but a story about God's presence in Jesus' solidarity with the oppressed, which led to his death on the cross. What is redemptive is the faith that God snatches victory out of defeat, life out of death, and hope out of despair, as revealed in the biblical and black proclamation of Jesus' resurrection." James H. Cone, *The Cross and the Lynching Tree* (Maryknoll: Orbis, 2011), 36, 91, 150. For a similar perspective from a womanist theologian, see JoAnne Marie Terrell, *Power in the Blood? The Cross in African American Experience* (Bishop Henry McNeal Turner/Sojourner Truth Series in Black Religion 15; Maryknoll: Orbis, 1998), 124-25, 139-43.

26. Of course, as mentioned in other parts of this book, suffering from other causes is present — the suffering caused by economic policies that favor the wealthy at the expense of the poor, discrimination because of race, ethnic origin, or sexual orientation, and more.

caused by Christian commitment. But it has often attained religious connotations.[27] Meanwhile, in several countries of the world suffering because of being Christian is a reality. Thus, even for Christians in North America who do not personally suffer for their faith, facing the reality of persecution should be a part of Christian commitment.

At the same time, it is important to emphasize that suffering per se, suffering as an end in and of itself, is not desired for us by God. As I understand the God revealed in Jesus Christ, God does not desire that we suffer. Suffering is not the means by which we are saved. We may suffer because we are Christians, but that suffering is the result of faithfulness to our calling to live for the reign of God. We may suffer as a result of choosing to confront injustice and oppression, but such suffering is the result of the confrontation and is not redemptive.

Responding to involuntary suffering builds on what is learned about the character of God as revealed through Jesus Christ and given expression in narrative Christus Victor. First of all, it is important to repeat that from the perspective of the reign of God, suffering is not the will of God. The God who declared creation "good" and created humankind for fellowship with God does not desire that people suffer. The incarnation, the act of God in Christ to bring salvation to a fallen creation, provides eloquent testimony that God desires only the best for God's creation.

With this understanding of the character of God, it is clear that God is not the cause of involuntary suffering. Suffering caused by such tragedies as car accidents or disease or natural catastrophes is not a means by which God punishes or teaches individuals or societies. The suffering and oppression caused by economic injustice or by discrimination on the basis of race, ethnicity, gender, or sexual orientation are not God's chosen tools for teaching patience or any other virtue. Such evils appeared in Chapter 4 as examples of references or appeals to violent acts of God in both historical and contemporary theology. These evils are often claimed as part of a supposed "secret plan" identified by such historical figures as Augustine and John Calvin. But I agree with the conclusion of theologians such as John Sanders and Gregory Boyd that although the reasons for bad happenings cannot be known, the revelation of God in Jesus Christ shows that these events should not be blamed on or attributed to God.[28]

---

27. For two efforts to derive theological meaning from this suffering, see Terrell, *Power in the Blood* and Cone, *The Cross and the Lynching Tree.*

28. John Sanders, *The God Who Risks: A Theology of Providence* (Downers Grove: Inter-

Boyd discussed this kind of suffering and the Christian's response to it under the traditional, long-standing question of evil, namely how a loving and all-powerful God can allow evil and suffering to exist in the world. There are two prevailing traditional answers: either reject a God who causes evil, or claim that a loving God causes evil for mysterious and unknown reasons. As I do here, Boyd rejects both answers. There is indeed a mystery surrounding the question of evil, he says, but when we see the character of God as revealed in Jesus Christ, we can know that "this mystery doesn't surround God's character, will or purpose. Rather, it's a mystery that necessarily surrounds an unimaginably complex creation, that has become a war zone," that is, a scene of struggle and confrontation between the reign of God and the rule of evil.[29]

A combination of factors contribute to the ambiguous nature of the world. Boyd lists one factor as the irrevocable freedom that God gave to human beings. "God created the world out of love and for the purpose of expanding his love."[30] But love involves risk. For love to be genuine, it "must be chosen. And choice means that a person can say no." As a result, people make choices that oppose the will of God. However, the divine grant of freedom is irrevocable. It is logically impossible to claim that God can both grant free will and override it. "In deciding to create something as it is, God *can't* decide to create it other than it is." "If God decided to create a world where love is possible, he thereby ruled out a world in which his will is always done."[31] God's capacity to influence events in the world is thus limited by the choices of human beings who exercise their irrevocable, God-given freedom. Of necessity God works with rather than overriding these choices. And the generations of choices that oppose the will of God comprise one significant contribution to the ambiguous character of the world.[32]

Varsity, 1998), chapters 4 and 6; Gregory A. Boyd, *Is God to Blame? Moving Beyond Pat Answers to the Problem of Evil* (Downers Grove: InterVarsity, 2003), especially chapter 3.

29. Boyd, *Is God to Blame?* 106.

30. Boyd, *Is God to Blame?* 62.

31. Boyd, *Is God to Blame?* 112, emphasis original.

32. John Sanders expresses the same understanding that for love to be genuine, it cannot be coerced, which in turn means that people can oppose God. "What God desires is a reciprocal relationship of love. Love is vulnerable and does not force itself on the beloved. Thus there is the risk that the beloved may not want to reciprocate love. In creating such conditions God takes the implausible yet possible risk that his creatures may reject him." Sanders, *The God Who Risks*, 258. Sanders's primary concern in this book is to develop an image of God in which prayer matters and God responds to the free choices of human beings whether they work with or oppose the will of God.

The second factor that contributes to the ambiguous character of the world is the complexity of the natural world. Boyd refers to chaos theory, and the idea that in some way every event is linked to every other event. A well-known example is the claim that the flapping of a butterfly's wing in South America can supposedly lead several years later to a hurricane in the North Atlantic Ocean. "Every decision we make affects other agents in the same measure." Short-term effects may be obvious, but the long-term impact may continue long after the initial decision is forgotten and "in ways we could never have anticipated."[33] In the earlier section on nature, for example, I noted the centuries-long, human contribution to the devastation caused by a hurricane and a tsunami.

Boyd locates the cause of involuntary suffering, not with God, but in the ambiguity of the world, a product of the unfathomable complexity of the natural world interacting with generations of human decisions.[34] We can make these assertions, Boyd says, because of what we know about the character of God revealed in Jesus Christ. We know the character of God — that God is love — by observing the self-giving of God in the life, death, and resurrection of Jesus. We do not determine the character of God on the basis of "our experience, our independent philosophizing or even our interpretation of the Bible apart from Christ." But on observation of Jesus' life, death, and resurrection we can know with certainty that God desires only the best for God's people. "Our picture of God must be centered unequivocally and unwaveringly on Jesus Christ." That is where God is "decisively revealed."[35]

The two factors — the accumulation of free decisions by people and the unfathomable complexity of the interconnected natural world — make it fundamentally impossible to identify the cause of any particular event. Yet order does exist in the world. In order for people to develop loving relationships with each other, the function of creation must be dependable. "If God wants a world in which agents can relate to one another, he must create a world that is very stable and thus quite predictable. In deciding to create this kind of world, God ruled out a world in which the laws of nature could be altered every time someone was going to be harmed."[36] A world with frequent suspensions of rules would be chaos. God does not

---

33. Boyd, *Is God to Blame?* 97.
34. Boyd, *Is God to Blame?* 80-84.
35. Boyd, *Is God to Blame?* 39.
36. Boyd, *Is God to Blame?* 114.

change the rules by which the world functions nor override the irrevocable freedom given to humans. That dependability means that characteristics of large groups and large natural entities are predictable, while it is impossible to determine the causes of individual events. Thus one cannot say why a baby is stillborn to a woman who desperately wants a child while in the same hospital a healthy baby is born unwanted. Or why because of a traffic delay one person was late getting to work and missed dying when the World Trade Center was bombed on September 11, while perhaps another person decided at the last minute not to take a scheduled vacation day and consequently died when the building collapsed. The cause of such tragedies and the reasons for the suffering caused by natural disasters and the conditions of systemic oppression are not knowable: they are mysteries. But in the face of such mystery, I fully agree with Boyd on what is knowable. Because of what we know about the character of God revealed in the story of Jesus Christ, we know that this suffering is not the will of the God of love, nor is it caused by this God. The mystery behind such events resides in the nature of the world.

Earlier I noted Nancey Murphy's discussion of science. Like Boyd and Sanders, Murphy's view of God was shaped by what is revealed of God in Jesus Christ. Thus she articulated a view that described God's overall control of the natural order while particular events remain unpredictable, which is coupled with the understanding that human freedom requires the image of a nonviolent God who does not coerce obedience. Murphy's acceptance of a nonviolent God who does not coerce corresponds to Boyd's and Sander's description of the God who grants irrevocable freedom to humankind.

Although one can grow stronger through dealing with adversity, God does not intentionally bring suffering on us as a teaching tool or a saving medium. The God of Jesus, the God who raised Jesus from the dead, wants us to overcome this suffering. The resurrection of Jesus shows that God will ultimately overcome suffering with the return of Jesus as the culmination of the reign of God. In the meantime, as Boyd wrote, we are to live "with our eyes on Jesus" and "remember that God is with" us.[37] That comment aligns with Murphy's similar assertion that God does not bring suffering but rather is with us in that suffering, providing the strength to endure.[38]

37. Boyd, *Is God to Blame?* 153-54.

38. This argument is also consonant with womanist Delores Williams's rejection of efforts to use Mary as an example of "social motherhood" that would bless the suffering of Af-

That God does not cause suffering leads to a most important point for Christian behavior. Since evil and suffering are the result of human activity, they can and should be opposed. Accompanying the belief that God provides strength to endure is the message of the resurrection. The resurrection is God's call to live — to live for the reign of God. In the context of suffering, the resurrection is a call to confront suffering and to confront the causes of suffering — tax policies that favor the wealthy and oppress the poor, national political policies that lead to war and support war, environmental policies that desecrate God's good creation, the racism — often silent but real — that manifests itself in many ways in our society, and more. As has been demonstrated throughout this book, Jesus' life manifests resistance to the evil in the world. Being a living witness to the reconciling love of God made visible in the life, death, and resurrection of Jesus is a call to an active life, an activist faith of continuing the mission of Jesus to witness to the reign of God breaking into the world even now.

Greg Boyd stresses this activist response to evil and suffering. If we accept the picture of God revealed in Jesus, "then we must conclude that much of what transpires in this world is against God's will. Rather than accepting it as coming from the Father, we ought to resist it in the power of the Father."[39] This activism constitutes our efforts to align ourselves with the way that God will ultimately restore the world. Those who follow Christ, that is, the church, are following the will of God to "expand the kingdom of God, and his promise is that the kingdom of Satan will not be able to withstand the expansion." "The church is the vehicle for finishing off the work Jesus began. Christians can't do this on their own, of course, Jesus is present in and with them to accomplish this task."[40]

Boyd contrasts this activist stance with the "blueprint view," namely the idea that everything that occurs has already been laid out before creation in a great divine "blueprint" with a "secret plan" that God follows in controlling both good and evil. Boyd points out that the blueprint view leads to passivity and resignation. If evil is a product of God's will, the assumption is that little can be done to oppose it. People "pray for the ability

---

rican American women. "And given the kind of critique the content of this womanist book [*Sisters in the Wilderness*] directs to Christian notions of atonement, womanist theology cannot affirm the suffering of 'social motherhood' or the suffering of any other kind of motherhood." Nonetheless, Williams adds, it is important to recognize "that *both* Mary and Jesus are active in the work of redemption." Williams, *Sisters in the Wilderness*, 183.

39. Boyd, *Is God to Blame?* 54.

40. Boyd, *Is God to Blame?* 73.

to accept things more than the ability to change things." In contrast, "Jesus taught a *piety of revolt,* not resignation." This activism results in the peace God gives. "It's an abiding tranquility we experience even while resisting and revolting against circumstances contrary to God's plan."[41] The focus of this book on a lived theology echoes Boyd's vision.

Black and womanist theology have parallel arguments that call for active resistance. Recall the comments from James Cone and Garth Kasimu Baker-Fletcher in Chapter 9 on race and ethnic reconciliation. Cone wrote, "God's act of reconciliation is not mystical communion with the divine; nor is it a pietistic state of inwardness bestowed upon the believer. God's reconciliation is a new relationship with *people* created by God's concrete involvement in the political affairs of the world, taking sides with the weak and the helpless."[42] Resisting the efforts of white society to define black identity along with the "self-imprisonment" Baker-Fletcher mentioned, implies a call for active resistance.[43] Womanist Delores Williams wrote that "Black women also participate in sin when they do not challenge the patriarchal and demonarchal systems in society defiling Black women's bodies through physical violence, sexual abuse, and exploited labor." Again, such a statement calls for active resistance.[44]

The people of God live with faith in the resurrection. To be "in Christ" is to live with the faith to struggle against suffering and injustice. It is our lives as Christians in the midst of suffering that give witness to our faith in God. Living with this faith is sometimes difficult. But having this faith in the midst of suffering and injustice is a witness to the power of God that works in the life of every Christian. This faith is a witness to the presence of the reign of God in our world and in our lives as Christians. Do we truly believe in God's resurrection of Jesus strongly enough to live in the story of Jesus who makes God's rule visible?

---

41. Boyd, *Is God to Blame?* 74-75, emphasis original.

42. James H. Cone, *God of the Oppressed* (rev. ed.; Maryknoll: Orbis, 1997), 209.

43. Karen Baker-Fletcher and Garth Kasimu Baker-Fletcher, *My Sister, My Brother: Womanist and XODUS God-Talk* (Bishop Henry McNeal Turner/Sojourner Truth Series in Black Religion 12; Maryknoll: Orbis, 1997), 124-26.

44. Delores S. Williams, "A Womanist Perspective on Sin," in *A Troubling in My Soul: Womanist Perspectives on Evil and Suffering,* ed. Emilie M. Townes (Bishop Henry McNeal Turner/Sojourner Truth Series in Black Religion 8; Maryknoll: Orbis, 1993), 146.

Conclusion

This book has given visibility to the nonviolent character of God made especially visible in the life, death, and resurrection of Jesus. The argument has dealt with the image of God in the several atonement motifs, in the book of Revelation, and in the Old Testament. It has also discussed practices of Christians who live in the narrative of Jesus. By living in that story, Christians continue the presence of Jesus in the world, which witnesses to the presence of the reign of God around us. The result is a theology of discipleship to Jesus, a lived theology of the reign of God made visible in Jesus.

In the course of the discussion of the character of God revealed in Jesus, this book also reached conclusions about the character of the Bible and the way a book written over a span of centuries more than two millennia ago is authoritative for Christians today. It does not stand as a transcendent source of rules that dictate theology and behavior for the twenty-first century. It is rather a book that contains the origins of the people of God. Believers today continue to carry this history forward. The lived-out version of the reign of God made visible in Jesus is the continuation of the history that began with Abraham, and what I have written in this book about the character and activity of God continues a conversation begun in the pages of the Bible. The result is a statement for our time of theology that is specific to Jesus, who made and makes the reign of God visible in the world.

I conclude with three different vignettes of this lived theology. The first describes a tangible vivid, personal experience of the presence of the reign of God.

The Reign of God Today

A few simple words brought the tangible reality of the reign of God present in the world to my senses. The elderly gentleman said only, "When I hear you praying, I have hope. When I hear you praying, I have hope." But his words filled me with a sense of the presence of the reign of God that still moves me deeply some twenty years later.

An elderly Haitian gentleman spoke the words. It was in December 1992 and I was in Haiti with a delegation from Christian Peacemaker teams. CPT, as it is commonly called, is a nonviolent, activist violence-reduction project sponsored by Mennonite, Brethren, and Quaker churches. CPT carries out nonviolent peace actions and violence reduction programs in places such as Hebron in the occupied West Bank, with native Americans in Canada, and in Colombia.

My CPT delegation was in Haiti to confront the violence perpetrated on much of the populace by the military junta that seized control of the government in a coup that ousted the democratically elected president Jean-Bertrand Aristide. Rumor had it that this coup likely had the tacit support of the United States government. At that epoch Aristide had been a justice-seeking, wildly popular president. In an election certified by foreign observers, he received something like 65 percent of the vote. The second-place candidate, the one backed by the United States, had received 15 percent.

The rule by the junta that ousted Aristide was repressive. Haitians were forbidden to meet in groups of more than four without an army permit. It was government policy to obliterate Lavalas, the movement that had brought Aristide to the office of President. It was illegal to say the name of Lavalas, and people who mentioned Lavalas or Aristide in public were subject to arrest. Or they just disappeared in the night. More than once our small group of North Americans was cautioned not to mention Aristide or Lavalas when walking in the street, lest we bring suspicion on the Haitians walking with us.

From a total population of six million, an estimated 250,000 Aristide supporters were living in the underground rather than risk death at the hands of the army. Most of those in the underground had come to the attention of the army, either because they had worked publicly for Lavalas or in social programs organized by Lavalas to address such needs as literacy or the fair sale of crops. Many had left their homes precipitously, slipping out a back way when friends or family came to warn them of army personnel approaching their houses.

Our delegation spent a bit more than a week talking with people in the underground in order to hear their stories and to give them a voice. One part of our mission was to gather stories that we could tell back in the U.S. to give visibility to the problems. The hope was that exposing this violence to the light of day might unleash forces of change.

Another part of our mission was to engage in public action that would speak for the suppressed and oppressed people of Haiti. On the particular day in question, we had gone to the U.S. embassy carrying a statement that described the oppression of the population being carried out by the coup government that the U.S. appeared to support. We handed the statement through the iron bars of a locked gate to a low-level functionary who assured us that her superiors would give it careful consideration.

Our status as foreigners protected us, and we could say things Haitian nationals could not. Part of our mission was to speak for them. Thus Haitian TV stations were invited to film us outside the U.S. embassy. Protected by our status as foreigners, in full view of Haitian TV cameras, we read statements from people hiding in the underground. One was an eloquent call for Haitians and foreigners alike to continue to struggle nonviolently for justice in Haiti. I took great satisfaction from helping to give a public voice to the suppressed Haitian voices. But I did not suspect that the best was yet to come.

From the embassy, we walked perhaps a half mile in the heart of Port-au-Prince to a statue that served as a symbol of Haitian freedom. From this statue, we could see in full view a hundred meters away the two buildings that housed the government powers of Haiti: its army headquarters and its capitol building. (This capitol was the white, heavily damaged government building frequently featured in TV news reports of the earthquake that devastated Port-au-Prince in January 2010.) These buildings housed the oppressive forces whose policies our delegation was in Haiti to protest against. We gathered in an uneven circle around this statue that symbolized freedom. In that circle our delegation recited a liturgy, sang songs, and prayed together.

One member of our circle prayed aloud. It took a couple moments before I realized that another voice was also speaking just at my right hand. I turned and saw the elderly Haitian, who had to repeat his quiet, labored English words a couple times before they sank in. He said only, "When I hear you praying, I have hope. When I hear you praying, I have hope." As this elderly gentleman's words penetrated my consciousness, that is when I sensed the presence of God. I have never felt nearer to God than at that moment.

The elderly gentleman's experience of hope in our circle revealed to me in a profound way the significance of our action. I had gone to Haiti to engage in political protest, and the public performance of worship, song, and prayer had seemed secondary or even a distraction. And this protest against injustice and oppression was important: I would eliminate none of our political activity. But the elderly gentleman opened my eyes to see the importance of performing these actions as Christians, as God's people. Our actions were a symbolic protest against violence and injustice. But when I heard this man's words, I realized that it was also much more than a political protest. For a brief moment, in our circle the reign of God actually *was* present. Our group was the shalom community of God's people, making visible and present God's peace and salvation — the reign of God — in contrast to the oppressive powers resident in the capitol building and army headquarters. For a brief moment, our circle was *more* than a symbol: in the hope expressed by this elderly Haitian man, I sensed that the future peaceable reign of God *was* tangibly present and breaking into our world and I experienced it. The elderly man had felt that peace and in his words I experienced it too. It was glorious.

Those of us gathered in that circle were there because we were Christians committed to nonviolence. Our gathered circle expressed our solidarity with suffering people. But our gathering witnessed to another way as well, to the peaceable reign of God. While the vision is not yet realized, standing in that circle, we were acting out for a brief moment the peaceable kingdom of Isaiah 11. Gathered in that circle, we were making a protest against violence and injustice on the doorsteps of those who perpetrated violence and injustice.

This gathering was what the church should be: a lived, visible expression of God's future salvation breaking into the present. In the church people should experience this inbreaking. The church is a community where peace, justice, and reconciliation are visible and real. Although not always as vivid as my experience in Port-au-Prince, the reign of God is present when the congregation gathers for worship or meets to consider how to spend its budget for the coming year. Daily activities of a congregation and its individual members make present the inbreaking of the reign of God into the world — in welcoming to the congregation new people who want to experience a peace church, in providing mental health services, healing the sick, working with Habitat for Humanity, working with homeless people, teaching students, participating in public demonstrations on behalf of justice and workers' rights and against war and for preserving health care for needy families, and much more. This is salvation experienced in the church whose life is a continuation of the story of Jesus. It is giving a lived expression of the narrative of Jesus, who is the presence of the reign of God in the world.

Trinity

Another way of describing the presence of God and the reign of God in the world uses a more traditional image. This book has observed the God of Israel and pointed to the nonviolent character of God visible in the Old Testament. God's presence in the life of Jesus and in the resurrection of Jesus have appeared prominently throughout, and I have mentioned the presence of God with Christians today. That presence occurs in the experience of the grace of God referred to by Paul in 1 Corinthians 15:10. It is manifest in the presence and support of God in the experience of suffering as noted by Nancey Murphy and Greg Boyd. It was present in the circle of peace witness around the statue in Port-au-Prince.

These references to the presence of God bring to mind a comment by John Howard Yoder in his class lectures later published as *Preface to Theology*.[1] The discussion concerned the Trinity. Yoder explained that for the early church fathers, the Trinity was an ontological problem. It was a question of how to have three substances also be one substance and also occupy one location. That was a valid discussion, and the traditional answer was a valid statement in its context. That analysis appeared in the discussion of Chapter 6 of the book in hand. However, in our different context and worldview, we might formulate the answer differently. For us, Yoder suggested, the Trinity was an answer to a time problem — a way to say that the God of Israel was the same God that was present in Jesus and had raised Jesus from the dead and who is also immediately present to us today.

The three manifestations of God — the Trinity in time — that Yoder mentioned are present in this book's statement of lived theology — God present in Israel and in Jesus and immediately to us today. Living in this story when it is not required and even if it is costly is our witness that the story of Jesus is true. As Yoder said in another place,

1. These lectures were available in an informal publication as John H. Yoder, *Preface to Theology: Christology and Theological Method* (Elkhart: Goshen Biblical Seminary, distributed by Co-op Bookstore, 1981). As a formal edited edition they were published posthumously as *Preface to Theology: Christology and Theological Method* (Grand Rapids: Brazos, 2002).

The real issue is not whether Jesus can make sense in a world far from Galilee, but whether — when he meets us in our world, as he does in fact — we want to follow him. We don't have to, as they didn't then. That we don't have to is the profoundest proof of his condescension, and thereby of his glory.[2]

The lived theology of this book depicts a way to testify to the truth that the God of Israel who was present in Jesus is immediately present to us today.

The New Jerusalem

The New Testament closes with a vision of how glorious it is to live in the church that is the earthly witness to the reign of God. It is the vision of the New Jerusalem in Revelation 21. I present two related and overlapping interpretations of the meaning of New Jerusalem for today.

Version One

In one perspective, the vision of the New Jerusalem (21:10-27), the true culminating image of Revelation, presents an intrinsically nonviolent view of the reign of God and the church today that lives in and gives witness to the reign of God. As the New Jerusalem descends from heaven, the heavenly announcer proclaims "the home of God is among mortals, he will dwell with them as their God; they will be his peoples, and God himself will be with them" (v. 3). Thus the New Jerusalem is where God is, and one would expect it to be run as the reign of God is governed, without violence.

It is more than obvious that the description of the city employs highly symbolic imagery. Twelves abound, which is the number that symbolizes God's people. The city has twelve gates, three on each side, with twelve angels at the gates, and the names of the twelve tribes inscribed on the gates. And the city has twelve foundations, inscribed with the names of the twelve apostles. The city is a cube of 12,000 stadia per side. With one stadium being 600 to 660 modern feet, the cube that is the city would be about 1500 miles per side — a huge cube with one side about the size of the

2. John Howard Yoder, "'But We Do See Jesus': The Particularity of Incarnation and the Universality of Truth," in *The Priestly Kingdom: Social Ethics as Gospel* (Notre Dame: University of Notre Dame, 1984), 62.

United States east of the Mississippi River. But recall that one thousand means "very big number." Thus 12,000 emerges as a huge, symbolic number involving the divine twelve — and it becomes obvious that the number is symbolic and does not define a real dimension. The walls are built of jasper, the foundations adorned with precious gems, the gates made of enormous pearls, and the streets paved in gold. Construction of these precious objects points to the value of the city. It may also convey another message as well, namely that these precious materials are mere building materials when compared to the real content of the city. This city is where God resides — the glory of God replaces the light of sun and moon and the Lamb is the lamp of the city.

The important point concerning the vision of the New Jerusalem is to know what it signifies. Since it follows a judgment scene in ch. 20 and features an enormous city constructed of fantastic materials, the seemingly obvious and traditional answer is that the New Jerusalem is a vision of heaven. But I accept a different answer, one that emphasizes both the intrinsically nonviolent orientation of Revelation and also the story of Jesus as theology for living. The New Jerusalem is a symbolic representation of the church living in the midst of the world. The cheering throngs in Revelation 7 portray the supremacy of the reign of God over the worst that the powers of evil can generate. As the culmination of the book, the reader encounters a vision of the gloriousness of living as an inhabitant of the church that gives witness to the victory of the reign of God over against the evil powers of the world.

To see that the New Jerusalem, the church, exists in the midst of the present world, note that the powers and expressions of evil continue to exist right alongside the New Jerusalem.[3] In words attributed to the one seated on the throne,

> It is done! I am the Alpha and the Omega, the beginning and the end. To the thirsty I will give water as a gift from the spring of the water of life. Those who conquer will inherit these things, and I will be their God and they will be my children. But as for the cowardly, the faithless, the polluted, the murderers, the fornicators, the sorcerers, the idolaters, and all liars, their place will be in the lake that burns with fire and sulfur, which is the second death. (Rev. 21:6-8)

3. On the New Jerusalem as an image of the church in present time, see Wes Howard-Brook and Anthony Gwyther, *Unveiling Empire: Reading Revelation Then and Now* (Maryknoll: Orbis, 1999), 184-95.

The point here is that even in the presence of the New Jerusalem, evildoers are still around. Since the traditional view pictures the wicked already judged and vanquished in the previous chapter, the presence of evildoers outside the New Jerusalem should jump out boldly. Since they are there, it is apparent that the New Jerusalem is not a post-judgment vision of heaven but a vision of how glorious it is to live in the church that participates now in the life of the resurrected Jesus even in the face of the threat from Rome.

Other comments reinforce the view that the New Jerusalem is not post-judgment heaven but a vision of the church in time and in the world. Following the statement that the glory of God provides the light of the city, one reads about who does and does not enter the open gates of the city that are never shut.

> Its gates will never be shut by day — and there will be no night there. People will bring into it the glory and the honor of the nations. But nothing unclean will enter it, nor anyone who practices abomination or falsehood, but only those who are written in the Lamb's book of life. (21:25-27)

In other words, those who follow God exist side-by-side with those who do not, but only the children of God belong to the New Jerusalem, that is, enter its always-open gates. Entering or remaining outside does not concern physical boundaries and geographical movement. It is a statement of belonging, belonging understood in terms of loyalty and adherence to the rule of God. It is a statement about living in the resurrected Jesus versus being defined by loyalty to Rome. Those who live within the rule of God are in the city and those who do not are outside the city.

A similar observation applies to a sentence in the book's epilogue.

> Blessed are those who wash their robes, so that they will have the right to the tree of life and may enter the city by the gates. Outside are the dogs and sorcerers and fornicators and murderers and idolaters, and everyone who loves and practices falsehood. (22:14-15)

The idea is clearly expressed here that the faithful and faithless exist together in time, and those who wash their robes — apparently in the blood of Jesus — may enter the city. This interpretation receives additional clarity in light of the reading of some ancient manuscripts which replace "wash their robes" with "do his commandments." The import of the text, and of the vision of the New Jerusalem, is to portray the joy and the glory of living today in the reign of God in face of the threat of Rome.

The New Jerusalem in this interpretation is the church, which reflects the reign of God made victorious in the death and resurrection of Jesus. To experience the work of Jesus Christ is to live in the New Jerusalem, which is to live as a disciple of Jesus. To describe the New Jerusalem is to portray a vision of what it means to live today as a disciple of Jesus and as a part of the earthly structure that continues his mission to give visibility to the reign of God. The New Jerusalem clearly portrays this mission since its temple is "the Lord God the Almighty and the Lamb." In other words, the New Jerusalem, the church, has the task of living so as to witness to the presence of the reign of God. Or as Brian McLaren has said, the New Jerusalem is "not a different space-time universe, but a new way of living that is possible with this universe, a new societal system that is coming as surely as God is just and faithful." It represents "a new spirituality, a new way of living in which the sacred presence of God is integrated with all of life and not confined to temples (v. 22)."[4] And, as has been emphasized throughout, the New Jerusalem with "the Lamb" as temple cannot be other than nonviolent.

The nonviolent character of the New Jerusalem corresponds to God's rule of history. The outcome of history does not depend on the earthly function of the church as the New Jerusalem. The reign of God becomes visible when the church lives in such a way as to continue the incarnation, but the outcome of history does not depend on human effort in the church. God has already determined the outcome of history, and the resurrection of Jesus is the ultimate indicator of that outcome. It is that outcome which the multitudes of Revelation 7 celebrate and that is the victory of Michael in Revelation 12 and the presence of the New Jerusalem in Revelation 21. The Bible reaches its climax with this invitation to live in the resurrected Jesus in the church as the New Jerusalem. With the New Jerusalem, the one seated on the throne, that is, God, announces, "See, I am making all things new" (21:5). In the church as the people of God, as disciples of Jesus Christ, we participate in that renewal. It is indeed glorious.

---

4. Brian D. McLaren, *Everything Must Change: Jesus, Global Crises, and a Revolution of Hope* (Nashville: Thomas Nelson, 2007), 296.

Version Two

N. T. Wright sees the New Jerusalem in a different way but one that overlaps with Version One. Wright believes that God's salvation will be a restoration of earth and all its systems, human and otherwise. Since resurrection occurred on earth in the midst of God's creation, salvation as the restoration of all things will occur on earth. Thus Wright sees the New Jerusalem in Revelation 21 as a vision of that future restoration, God and the church becoming present on earth. The saints do not go off to a distant heaven, but rather "it is heaven that comes to earth." Wright calls this the final answer to the Lord's Prayer, "that God's kingdom will come and his will be done on earth as in heaven." It is not a wiping the slate clean and starting over. If it were a starting over, "there would be no celebration, no conquest of death, no long preparation now at last complete."[5] Rather this is a restoration of all things, human and otherwise.

The pre-restoration version of earth featured a temple as a symbol of the presence of God. In the New Jerusalem of the restoration, such a symbol is no longer necessary because the reality, "the presence of God himself" is here. "The living God will dwell with and among his people, filling the city with his life and love and pouring out grace and healing in the river of life that flows from the city out to the nations." And in this New Jerusalem with the presence of the living God, the redeemed people of God have a role in the new world. They will be "the agents of [God's] love going out in new ways, to accomplish new creative tasks, to celebrate and extend the glory of his love."[6]

In Wright's view, this vision of the future reign of God in a restored earth has important meaning for the church today. The future is also a continuation of the present. Thus the church today is preparation for and an advance edition of the New Jerusalem. The church today is important because it makes visible "the plan of redemption revealed in action in Jesus Christ."[7]

Wright also pointed to a problem posed by his interpretation of the New Jerusalem as the future restoration on earth of all creation. As was noted above in Version One, there are categories of people who still exist

---

5. N. T. Wright, *Surprised by Hope: Rethinking Heaven, the Resurrection, and the Mission of the Church* (New York: HarperCollins, 2008), 104-5.

6. Wright, *Surprised by Hope*, 105-6.

7. Wright, *Surprised by Hope*, 97.

outside the city, "the dogs and sorcerers and fornicators and murderers and idolaters, and everyone who loves and practices falsehood" (22:15). Even though there has been judgment and all things have been restored, there are still the unredeemed present outside of the city. And furthermore, "the river of the water of life flows *out of* the city."[8] And on the banks of the city stands the tree of life, "and the leaves of the tree are for the healing of the nations" (22:2).

How can it be that even after final judgment and the restoration of all things there are still the wicked, the unredeemed outside the restored city, as well as a healing of the nations that continues? We simply cannot know, Wright says.

> There is a great mystery here and all our speaking about God's eventual future must make room for it. This is not at all to cast doubt on the reality of final judgment for those who have resolutely worshipped and served the idols that dehumanize us and deface God's world. It is to say that God is always the God of surprises.[9]

In these two interpretations of the New Jerusalem, we are confronted with two interpretations of the ending of Revelation and thus of the Bible. Both endings emphasize the importance of the church in the world today as a making visible of God's future restoration of all things. Both interpretations make that point, even though one understands New Jerusalem as the church in the present and the other as a vision of the future restoration. But Wright's conclusion can stand for either view.

> Heaven and hell are not, so to speak, what the whole game is about. This is one of the central surprises of the Christian hope. . . . The question of what happens to me after death is *not* the major, central, framing question that centuries of theological tradition have supposed. The New Testament, true to its Old Testament roots, regularly insists that the major central, framing question is that of God's purpose of rescue and re-creation for the whole world, the entire cosmos. The destiny of individual human beings must be understood within that context — not simply in the sense that we are only part of a much larger picture but also in the sense that part of the whole point of being saved in the present is so that we can play a vital role . . . within that larger picture and pur-

---

8. Wright, *Surprised by Hope*, 184 emphasis original.
9. Wright, *Surprised by Hope*, 184.

pose. . . . The question ought to be, *How will God's new creation come?* and then, *How will we humans contribute to that renewal of creation and to the fresh projects that the creator God will launch in his new world?*[10]

Wright's words return us to the beginning goal of this book, namely to produce a theology for living the reign of God made visible in Jesus. May it be so.

---

10. Wright, *Surprised by Hope*, 184-85.

Works Cited

Ackerman, Peter, and Jack DuVall. *A Force More Powerful: A Century of Nonviolent Conflict.* New York: Palgrave, 2000.

Ahlstrom, Sydney E. *A Religious History of the American People.* New Haven: Yale University Press, 1972.

Alexander, Michelle. *The New Jim Crow: Mass Incarceration in the Age of Colorblindness.* Rev. ed. New York: The New Press, 2012.

Allen, James, Hilton Als, John Lewis, and Leon F. Litwack. *Without Sanctuary: Lynching Photography in America.* Santa Fe: Twin Palms, 2000.

Anderson, Victor. *Beyond Ontological Blackness: An Essay on African American Religious and Cultural Criticism.* New York: Continuum, 1995.

Anselm of Canterbury. "Why God Became Man." In *The Major Works,* ed. Brian Davies and G. R. Evans, 260-356. Oxford: Oxford University Press, 1998.

"The Athanasian Creed: Quicunque vult, 5th-6th c." In *Creeds and Confessions of Faith in the Christian Tradition,* vol. 1, ed. Jaroslav Pelikan and Valerie Hotchkiss, 675-77. New Haven: Yale University Press, 2003.

Aulén, Gustaf. *Christus Victor: A Historical Study of the Three Main Types of the Idea of Atonement,* trans. A. G. Herbert. New York: Macmillan, 1969.

Baker-Fletcher, Garth Kasimu. *Xodus: An African American Male Journey.* Minneapolis: Fortress, 1996.

Baker-Fletcher, Karen. *Sisters of Dust, Sisters of Spirit: Womanist Wordings on God and Creation.* Minneapolis: Fortress, 1998.

Baker-Fletcher, Karen, and Garth Kasimu Baker-Fletcher. *My Sister, My Brother: Womanist and XODUS God-Talk.* Bishop Henry McNeal Turner/Sojourner Truth Series in Black Religion 12. Maryknoll: Orbis, 1997.

Barrett, C. K. *The Gospel According to St. John: An Introduction with Commentary and Notes on the Greek Text.* New York: Macmillan, 1962.

Bedell, George C., Leo Sandon, Jr., and Charles T. Wellborn. *Religion in America.* 2d ed. New York: Macmillan, 1982.

Beecher, Henry Ward. "The Tendencies of American Progress." In *God's New Israel: Religious Interpretations of American Destiny,* ed. Conrad Cherry, 235-48. Rev. ed. Chapel Hill: University of North Carolina Press, 1998.

Beecher, Lyman. "On Disestablishment in Connecticut." In *Church and State in American History,* ed. John F. Wilson, 92-93. Boston: D. C. Heath, 1965.

————. "A Plea for the West." In *God's New Israel: Religious Interpretations of American Destiny,* ed. Conrad Cherry, 122-30. Rev. ed. Chapel Hill: University of North Carolina Press, 1998.

Beker, J. Christiaan. *Paul the Apostle: The Triumph of God in Life and Thought.* Philadelphia: Fortress, 1980.

Bell, Daniel M., Jr. "God Does Not Require Blood." *Christian Century* 126 (February 10, 2009): 22-26.

————. *Liberation Theology after the End of History: The Refusal to Cease Suffering.* London: Routledge, 2001.

Bell, Rob. *Love Wins: A Book About Heaven, Hell, and the Fate of Every Person Who Ever Lived.* New York: HarperOne, 2011.

Bellah, Robert N. "Civil Religion in America." In *American Civil Religion,* ed. Russell E. Richey and Donald G. Jones, 21-44. New York: Harper & Row, 1974.

Belousek, Darrin W. Snyder. *Atonement, Justice, and Peace: The Message of the Cross and the Mission of the Church.* Grand Rapids: William B. Eerdmans, 2012.

Biesecker-Mast, Susan, and Gerald Biesecker-Mast, eds. *Anabaptists and Postmodernity.* C. Henry Smith Series 1. Telford: Pandora and Herald, 2000.

Boersma, Hans. *Violence, Hospitality and the Cross: Reappropriating the Atonement Tradition.* Grand Rapids: Baker Academic, 2004.

Boring, M. Eugene. *Revelation.* Interpretation: A Bible Commentary for Teaching and Preaching. Louisville: John Knox, 1989.

Bowley, James E. *Introduction to Hebrew Bible: A Guided Tour of Israel's Sacred Library.* Upper Saddle River: Pearson Prentice Hall, 2008.

Boyarin, Daniel. *Border Lines: The Partition of Judaeo-Christianity.* Philadelphia: University of Pennsylvania Press, 2004.

————. "Judaism as a Free Church: Footnotes to John Howard Yoder's *The Jewish-Christian Schism Revisited.*" In *The New Yoder,* ed. Peter Dula and Chris K. Huebner, 1-17. Eugene: Cascade, 2010.

Boyd, Gregory A. "Christus Victor View." In *The Nature of the Atonement: Four Views,* ed. James Beilby and Paul R. Eddy, 23-49. Downers Grove: InterVarsity, 2006.

————. *God of the Possible: A Biblical Introduction to the Open View of God.* Grand Rapids: Baker, 2000.

————. *Is God to Blame? Moving beyond Pat Answers to the Problem of Evil.* Downers Grove: InterVarsity, 2003.

————. *The Myth of a Christian Nation: How the Quest for Political Power Is Destroying the Church.* Grand Rapids: Zondervan, 2005.

Bright, John. *A History of Israel.* 4th ed. Louisville: Westminster John Knox, 2000.

Brock, Rita Nakashima. "The Cross of Resurrection and Communal Redemption." In *Cross Examinations: Readings on the Meaning of the Cross Today*, ed. Marit Trelstad, 241-51. Minneapolis: Augsburg Fortress, 2006.

―――. *Journeys by Heart: A Christology of Erotic Power*. New York: Crossroad, 1988.

Brock, Rita Nakashima, and Rebecca Ann Parker. *Saving Paradise: How Christianity Traded Love of This World for Crucifixion and Empire*. Boston: Beacon, 2008.

Brondos, David A. *Paul on the Cross: Reconstructing the Apostle's Story of Redemption*. Minneapolis: Fortress, 2006.

Brown, Joanne Carlson, and Rebecca Parker. "For God So Loved the World?" In *Christianity, Patriarchy and Abuse: A Feminist Critique*, ed. Joanne Carlson Brown and Carole R. Bohn, 1-30. New York: Pilgrim, 1989.

Brueggemann, Walter. *Genesis*. Interpretation: A Bible Commentary for Teaching and Preaching. Atlanta: John Knox, 1982.

―――. *The Theology of the Old Testament: Testimony, Dispute, Advocacy*. Minneapolis: Fortress, 1997.

Burrus, Virginia. *"Begotten, Not Made": Conceiving Manhood in Late Antiquity*. Stanford: Stanford University Press, 2000.

Butler-Evans, Elliott. "Beyond Essentialism: Rethinking Afro-American Cultural Theory." In *Cultural and Literary Critiques of the Concepts of "Race,"* ed. E. Nathaniel Gates, 171-84. New York: Garland, 1997.

Cagan, Joanna, and Neil deMause. "A Tale of Two Cities." *The Nation* 267/5 (August-October 1998): 24.

Calvin, John. *Institutes of the Christian Religion*, ed. John T. NcNeill, trans. Ford Lewis Battles. Library of Christian Classics. Philadelphia: Westminster, 1960.

Cannon, Katie G. *Black Womanist Ethics*. Atlanta: Scholars, 1988.

Carroll, James. *Constantine's Sword: The Church and the Jews: A History*. New York: Houghton Mifflin, 2001.

Carter, Craig A. "The Liberal Reading of Yoder: The Problem of Yoder Reception and the Need for a Comprehensive Christian Witness." In *Radical Ecumenicity: Pursuing Unity and Continuity after John Howard Yoder*, ed. John C. Nugent, 85-105. Abilene: Abilene Christian University Press, 2010.

Cherry, Conrad, ed. *God's New Israel: Religious Interpretations of American Destiny*. Rev. ed. Chapel Hill: University of North Carolina Press, 1998.

Cone, James H. "Black Spirituals: A Theological Interpretation." *Theology Today* 29 (1972): 54-69.

―――. *The Cross and the Lynching Tree*. Maryknoll: Orbis, 2011.

―――. *God of the Oppressed*. Rev. ed. Maryknoll: Orbis, 1997.

―――. *Martin and Malcolm and America: A Dream or a Nightmare?* Maryknoll: Orbis, 1991.

―――. *The Spirituals and the Blues: An Interpretation*. Maryknoll: Orbis, 1992.

Copeland, M. Shawn. *Enfleshing Freedom: Body, Race, and Being*. Minneapolis: Fortress, 2010.

"The Creation Epic." In *Ancient Near Eastern Texts Relating to the Old Testament*, ed.

James B. Pritchard, 60-72, 501-3. 3rd ed. Princeton: Princeton University Press, 1969.

Crossan, John Dominic. *God and Empire: Jesus against Rome, Then and Now.* New York: HarperCollins, 2007.

———. *The Power of Parable: How Fiction by Jesus Became Fiction about Jesus.* New York: HarperCollins, 2012.

de Mause, Neil, and Joanna Cagan. *Field of Schemes: How the Great Stadium Swindle Turns Public Money into Provate Profit.* Rev. ed. Lincoln: University of Nebraska Press, 2008.

Denck, Hans. *The Spiritual Legacy of Hans Denck: Interpretations and Translation of Key Texts,* trans. Clarence Bauman. Studies in Medieval and Reformation Thought 47. Leiden: E. J. Brill, 1991.

De Waal, Frans. *The Age of Empathy: Nature's Lessons for a Kinder Society.* New York: Harmony, 2009.

Douglas, Kelly Brown. *The Black Christ.* Bishop Henry McNeal Turner Studies in North American Black Religion 9. Maryknoll: Orbis, 1994.

Drake, H. A. *Constantine and the Bishops: The Politics of Intolerance.* Baltimore: Johns Hopkins University Press, 2000.

Du Bois, W. E. Burghardt. *The Souls of Black Folk: Essays and Sketches.* Greenwich: Fawcett, 1953.

Durnbaugh, Donald F. *The Believers' Church: The History and Character of Radical Protestantism.* Scottdale: Herald, 1985.

Easwaran, Eknath. *Nonviolent Soldier of Islam: Badshah Khan, a Man to Match His Mountains.* Tomales: Nilgiri, 1999.

Eller, Vernard. *The Most Revealing Book in the Bible: Making Sense of Revelation.* Grand Rapids: William B. Eerdmans, 1974.

Enright, Robert D. *Forgiveness Is a Choice: A Step-by-Step Process for Resolving Anger and Restoring Hope.* Washington: American Psychological Association, 2001.

Finger, Reta Halteman. "How Jesus Learned about Ethnic Discrimination." *The Mennonite,* December 26, 2000, 6-7.

Garrett, James Leo, Jr., ed. *The Concept of the Believers' Church: Addresses from the 1968 Louisville Conference.* Scottdale: Herald, 1960.

Gates, Henry Louis, Jr., ed. *The Classic Slave Narratives.* Reprint. New York: Signet Classics, 2012.

Gorringe, Timothy. *God's Just Vengeance: Crime, Violence and the Rhetoric of Salvation.* Cambridge Studies in Ideology and Religion 9. Cambridge: Cambridge University Press, 1996.

Grant, Jacquelyn. *White Women's Christ and Black Women's Jesus: Feminist Christology and Womanist Response.* American Academy of Religion Academy Series 64. Atlanta: Scholars, 1989.

Grenz, Stanley J. *Theology for the Community of God.* Nashville: Broadman and Holman, 1994.

Grunwald, Michael, and Susan B. Glasser. "The Slow Drowning of New Orleans."

Washington Post, October 9, 2005. http://www.washingtonpost.com/wp-dyn/content/article/2005/10/08/AR2005100801458.html.

Hanson, R. P. C. *The Search for the Christian Doctrine of God: The Arian Controversy 318-381.* Edinburgh: T. & T. Clark, 1988.

Harder, James M. "The Violence of Global Marketization." In *Teaching Peace: Nonviolence and the Liberal Arts,* ed. J. Denny Weaver and Gerald Biesecker-Mast, 179-93. Lanham: Rowman & Littlefield, 2003.

Hauerwas, Stanley, and William H. Willimon. *Resident Aliens: Life in the Christian Colony: A Provocative Christian Assessment of Culture and Ministry for People Who Know That Something Is Wrong.* Nashville: Abingdon, 1989.

Hays, Richard B. *The Moral Vision of the New Testament: Community, Cross, New Creation: A Contemporary Introduction to New Testament Ethics.* New York: HarperCollins, 1996.

Hellwig, Monika K. *Jesus: The Compassion of God.* Wilmington: Michael Glazier, 1983.

Heschel, Abraham J. *The Prophets.* New York: HarperPerennial, 2001.

Heyward, Carter. *Saving Jesus from Those Who Are Right: Rethinking What It Means to Be Christian.* Minneapolis: Fortress, 1999.

Hochschild, Adam. *King Leopold's Ghost: A Story of Greed, Terror, and Heroism in Colonial Africa.* Boston: Houghton Mifflin, 1998.

Holloway, Richard. *On Forgiveness.* Edinburgh: Canongate, 2002.

Hooks, Bell. *Yearning: Race, Gender, and Cultural Politics.* Boston: South End, 1990.

Hopkins, Julie M. *Towards a Feminist Christology: Jesus of Nazareth, European Women, and the Christological Crisis.* Grand Rapids: William B. Eerdmans, 1995.

Horsley, Richard A. "Ethics and Exegesis: 'Love Your Enemies' and the Doctrine of Nonviolence." In *The Love of Enemy and Nonretaliation in the New Testament,* ed. Willard Swartley, 72-101. Louisville: Westminster John Knox, 1992.

———. *Jesus and Empire: The Kingdom of God and the New World Disorder.* Minneapolis: Fortress, 2003.

Howard-Brook, Wes, and Anthony Gwyther. *Unveiling Empire: Reading Revelation Then and Now.* Maryknoll: Orbis, 1999.

Hughes, Langston. "Thank You, M'Am." In *The Best Short Stories by Negro Writers: An Anthology from 1899 to the Present,* ed. Langston Hughes, 70-73. Boston: Little, Brown, 1967.

Hughes, Richard T. *Myths America Lives By.* Urbana: University of Illinois Press, 2003.

Jenkins, Philip. *Jesus Wars: How Four Patriarchs, Three Queens, and Two Emperors Decided What Christians Would Believe for the Next 1,500 Years.* New York: HarperOne, 2010.

———. *Laying Down the Sword: Why We Can't Ignore the Bible's Violent Verses.* New York: HarperOne, 2011.

Jewett, Robert, and John Shelton Lawrence. *Captain America and the Crusade against Evil: The Dilemma of Zealous Nationalism.* Grand Rapids: William B. Eerdmans, 2003.

Kelly, J. N. D. *Early Christian Doctrines.* Rev. ed. New York: Harper & Row, 1978.

King, Martin Luther, Jr. *A Call to Conscience: The Landmark Speeches of Dr. Martin Luther King, Jr.*, ed. Clayborne Carson and Kris Shepard. New York: Warner, 2001.

———. "Where Do We Go from Here?" In *A Call to Conscience: The Landmark Speeches of Dr. Martin Luther King, Jr.*, ed. Clayborne Carson and Kris Shepard, 171-98. New York: Warner, 2001.

Kirkpatrick, David D. "The Return of the Warrior Jesus." *New York Times,* April 4, 2004, 4-1, 4-6.

Kraybill, Donald B. *The Upside-Down Kingdom.* Rev. ed. Scottdale: Herald, 2003.

Kreider, Alan. "'Converted' but Not Baptized: Peter Leithart's Constantine Project." *Mennonite Quarterly Review* 85 (2011): 575-617.

Krieg, Robert A. *Story-Shaped Christology: The Role of Narratives in Identifying Jesus Christ.* New York: Paulist, 1988.

Leithart, Peter J. *Defending Constantine: The Twilight of an Empire and the Dawn of Christendom.* Downers Grove: InterVarsity, 2010.

———. "Defending *Defending Constantine:* Or, the Trajectory of the Gospel." *Mennonite Quarterly Review* 85 (2011): 643-55.

Lewan, Todd. "Missouri Rehabilitates Juveniles." *Wisconsin State Journal,* December 30, 2007, A1, A11.

Lincoln, Abraham. "Second Inaugural Address." In *God's New Israel: Religious Interpretations of American Destiny,* ed. Conrad Cherry, 201-2. Rev. ed. Chapel Hill: University of North Carolina Press, 1998.

Lind, Millard C. *Yahweh Is a Warrior: The Theology of Warfare in Ancient Israel.* Scottdale: Herald, 1980.

Lindsey, Hal. *The Late Great Planet Earth.* Grand Rapids: Zondervan, 1970.

Loewen, James W. *Lies My Teacher Told Me: Everything Your American History Textbook Got Wrong.* New York: Simon & Schuster, 1995.

Luskin, Fred. *Forgive for Good: A Proven Prescription for Health and Happiness.* New York: HarperCollins, 2002.

Machinist, Peter. "Nahum." In *The Harper Collins Bible Commentary,* ed. James L. Mays, 665-67. Rev. ed. New York: HarperCollins, 2000.

Marable, Manning. *Malcolm X: A Life of Reinvention.* New York: Penguin, 2011.

Mast, Gerald J. *Go to Church, Change the World: Christian Community as Calling.* Harrisonburg: Herald, 2012.

Mast, Gerald J., and J. Denny Weaver. *Defenseless Christianity: Anabaptism for a Nonviolent Church.* Telford: Cascadia and Herald, 2009.

"Mayor: Hurricanes a Sign God Is 'Mad at America.'" *The Blade,* January 17, 2006, A5.

McDonald, H. D. *The Atonement of the Death of Christ in Faith, Revelation, and History.* Grand Rapids: Baker, 1985.

McGovern, George. "Calling a Time Out." *Washington Post,* January 22, 2009.

McLaren, Brian D. *Everything Must Change: Jesus, Global Crises, and a Revolution of Hope.* Nashville: Thomas Nelson, 2007.

———. *A New Kind of Christianity: Ten Questions That Are Transforming the Faith.* New York: HarperOne, 2010.

Montel, Angela Horn. "Violent Images in Cell Biology." In *Teaching Peace: Nonviolence and the Liberal Arts,* ed. J. Denny Weaver and Gerald Biesecker-Mast, 223-34. Lanham: Rowman & Littlefield, 2003.

Murphy, Nancey C. *Reconciling Theology and Science: A Radical Reformation Perspective.* Scottdale: Pandora and Herald, 1997.

Murphy, Nancey, and George F. R. Ellis. *On the Moral Nature of the Universe: Theology, Cosmology, and Ethics.* Minneapolis: Fortress, 1996.

Nelson-Pallmeyer, Jack. *Jesus against Christianity: Reclaiming the Missing Jesus.* Harrisburg: Trinity, 2001.

Neufeld, Thomas R. Yoder. *Killing Enmity: Violence and the New Testament.* Grand Rapids: Baker Academic, 2011.

Nugent, John C. *The Politics of Yahweh: John Howard Yoder, the Old Testament and the People of God.* Eugene: Cascade, 2011.

———. "A Yoderian Rejoinder to Peter J. Leithart's *Defending Constantine.*" *Mennonite Quarterly Review* 85 (2011): 551-73.

Olson, Roger E. *Reformed and Always Reforming: The Postconservative Approach to Evangelical Theology.* Grand Rapids: Baker Academic, 2007.

Pal, Amitabh. *"Islam" Means Peace: Understanding the Muslim Principle of Nonviolence.* Santa Barbara: Praeger, 2011.

Paul, Robert S. *The Atonement and the Sacraments: The Relation of the Atonement to the Sacraments of Baptism and the Lord's Supper.* New York: Abingdon, 1960.

Pelikan, Jaroslav. *The Emergence of the Catholic Tradition (100-600).* The Christian Tradition: A History of the Development of Doctrine 1. Chicago: University of Chicago Press, 1971.

Peterson, Eugene H. *The Jesus Way: A Conversation on the Ways That Jesus Is the Way.* Grand Rapids: William B. Eerdmans, 2007.

Pickstock, Catherine. *After Writing on the Liturgical Consummation of Philosophy.* Oxford: Blackwell, 1998.

Price, Marty. "Mediated Civil Compromise — a Tool for Restorative Justice." http://www.vorp.com/articles/civil.html.

Price, S. L. "A Death in the Baseball Family." *Sports Illustrated,* September 24, 2007, 54-62.

Rainey, W. Todd. "Nature's Tooth-and-Claw Conflict Resolution." In *Teaching Peace: Nonviolence and the Liberal Arts,* ed. J. Denny Weaver and Gerald Biesecker-Mast, 235-45. Lanham: Rowman & Littlefield, 2003.

Rasmussen, Larry L. *Moral Fragments and Moral Community: A Proposal for Church in Society.* Minneapolis: Fortress, 1993.

Ray, Darby Kathleen. *Deceiving the Devil: Atonement, Abuse, and Ransom.* Cleveland: Pilgrim, 1998.

Reddish, Mitchell G. *Revelation.* Smyth and Helwys Bible Commentary. Macon: Smyth and Helwys, 2001.

Rhoads, David. "Jesus and the Syrophoenician Woman in Mark: A Narrative-Critical Study." *Journal of the American Academy of Religion* 62 (1994): 343-76.

Rieger, Joerg. *Christ and Empire: From Paul to Postcolonial Times.* Minneapolis: Fortress, 2007.

Rosentraub, Mark S. "Why Baseball Needs New York to Just Say No." *The Nation* 267/5 (August-October 1998): 20-24, 26.

Ruether, Rosemary Radford. *Sexism and God-Talk: Toward a Feminist Theology*. Boston: Beacon, 1983.

—————. *Women and Redemption: A Theological History*. Minneapolis: Fortress, 1998.

Sanders, John. *The God Who Risks: A Theology of Providence*. Downers Grove: Inter-Varsity, 1998.

Sattler, Michael. "The Brotherly Union of a Number of Children of God Concerning Seven Articles." In *The Legacy of Michael Sattler*, trans. and ed. John H. Yoder, 34-43. Classics of the Radical Reformation 1. Scottdale: Herald, 1973.

Schmiechen, Peter. *Saving Power: Theories of Atonement and Forms of Church*. Grand Rapids: William B. Eerdmans, 2005.

Schwager, Raymund. *Jesus in the Drama of Salvation*. New York: Crossroad, 1999.

Seibert, Eric A. *Disturbing Divine Behavior: Troubling Old Testament Images of God*. Minneapolis: Fortress, 2009.

Selby, Donald Joseph, and James King West. *Introduction to the Bible*. New York: Macmillan, 1971.

Shaw, Brent D. "State Intervention and Holy Violence: Timgad/Paleostrovsk/Waco." *Journal of the American Academy of Religion* 77 (2009): 853-94.

Sherman, Robert. *King, Priest, and Prophet: A Trinitarian Theology of Atonement*. New York: T. & T. Clark, 2004.

Sider, J. Alexander. "Constantinianism before and after Nicea: Issues in Restitutionist Historiography." In *A Mind Patient and Untamed: Assessing John Howard Yoder's Contributions to Theology, Ethics, and Peacemaking*, ed. Ben C. Ollenburger and Gayle Gerber Koontz, 126-44. Telford: Cascadia, 2004.

Sider, Ronald J. "A Critique of J. Denny Weaver's *Nonviolent Atonement*." *Brethren in Christ History and Life* 35 (2012): 214-41.

—————. *Rich Christians in an Age of Hunger: A Biblical Study*. Rev. ed. Downers Grove: Intervarsity, 1984.

Simon, Sidney B., and Suzanne Simon. *Forgiveness: How to Make Peace with Your Past and Get On with Your Life*. New York: Warner, 1990.

Sizgorich, Thomas. "Sanctified Violence: Monotheist Militancy as the Tie That Bound Christian Roman and Islam." *Journal of the American Academy of Religion* 77 (2009): 895-921.

Smith, H. Shelton, Robert T. Handy, and Lefferts A. Loetscher. *American Christianity: An Historical Interpretation with Representative Documents* 1: 1607-1820. New York: Charles Scribner's Sons, 1960.

"Some See a Vengeful God amid Deadly Hurricane." *The Blade*, September 4, 2005, A4.

Southern, R. W. *Saint Anselm: A Portrait in a Landscape*. Cambridge: Cambridge University Press, 1990.

Spronk, Klaas. *Nahum*. Historical Commentary on the Old Testament. Kampen: Kok Pharos, 1997.

Stassen, Glen H., and Michael L. Westmoreland-White. "Defining Violence and Nonviolence." In *Teaching Peace: Nonviolence and the Liberal Arts,* ed. J. Denny Weaver and Gerald Biesecker-Mast, 17-36. Lanham: Rowman & Littlefield, 2003.

Stewart, Robert B., ed. *The Resurrection of Jesus: John Dominic Crossan and N. T. Wright in Dialogue.* Minneapolis: Fortress, 2006.

Swoboda, Jörg. *The Revolution of the Candles: Christians in the Revolution in the German Democratic Republic.* Macon: Mercer University Press, 1996.

Terrell, JoAnne Marie. *Power in the Blood? The Cross in African American Experience.* Bishop Henry McNeal Turner/Sojourner Truth Series in Black Religion 15. Maryknoll: Orbis, 1998.

Thiessen, Gerd. *The Open Door: Variations on Biblical Themes,* trans. John Bowden. Minneapolis: Fortress, 1991.

Thistlethwaite, Susan Brooks. *Sex, Race and God: Christian Feminism in Black and White.* New York: Crossroad, 1991.

Thomson, Alwyn. *Fields of Vision: Faith and Identity in Protestant Ireland.* Belfast: Centre for Contemporary Christianity in Ireland, 2002.

"Transcript of Pat Robertson's Interview with Jerry Falwell Broadcast on the 700 Club, September 13, 2001." In Bruce Lincoln, *Holy Terrors: Thinking about Religion after September 11,* 104-7. Chicago: University of Chicago Press, 2002.

Trocmé, André. *Jesus and the Nonviolent Revolution,* ed. Charles E. Moore. Maryknoll: Orbis, 2003.

Volf, Miroslav. *Exclusion and Embrace: A Theological Exploration of Identity, Otherness, and Reconciliation.* Nashville: Abingdon, 1996.

Walker, Williston. *The Creeds and Platforms of Congregationalism.* Boston: Pilgrim, 1963.

Weaver, J. Denny. *Anabaptist Theology in Face of Postmodernity: A Proposal for the Third Millennium.* C. Henry Smith Series 2. Telford: Pandora and Herald, 2000.

———. *Becoming Anabaptist: The Origin and Significance of Sixteenth-Century Anabaptism.* 2d ed. Scottdale: Herald, 2005.

———. "The Dragon Lives Still." In *Compassionate Eschatology: The Future as Friend,* ed. Ted Grimsrud and Michael Hardin, 134-51. Eugene: Cascade, 2011.

———. "Forgiveness and (Non)Violence: The Atonement Connection." *Mennonite Quarterly Review* 83 (2009): 319-47.

———. *The Nonviolent Atonement.* 2d ed. Grand Rapids: Wm. B. Eerdmans, 2011.

———. "Responding to September 11 — and October 7 and January 29: Which Religion Shall We Follow?" *Conrad Grebel Review* 20 (2002): 79-100.

West, Cornel. *Race Matters.* New York: Vintage, 1994.

Williams, Delores S. "The Color of Feminism: Or Speaking the Black Woman's Tongue." *Journal of Religious Thought* 43 (1986): 42-58.

———. *Sisters in the Wilderness: The Challenge of Womanist God-Talk.* Maryknoll: Orbis, 1993.

———. "A Womanist Perspective on Sin." In *A Troubling in My Soul: Womanist Perspectives on Evil and Suffering,* ed. Emilie M. Townes. Bishop Henry McNeal Turner Series 8, 130-49. Maryknoll: Orbis, 1993.

Williams, Patricia. "The Ethnic Scarring of American Whiteness." In *The House That*

Race Built: Black Americans, U.S. Terrain, ed. Wahneema Lubiano. New York: Pantheon, 1997.

Willimon, William H. "Bless You, Mrs. Degrafinried." *Christian Century* 101/9 (March 14, 1984): 269-70.

Wink, Walter. *Engaging the Powers: Discernment and Resistance in a World of Domination.* The Powers 3. Minneapolis: Fortress, 1992.

Wise, Tim. *Dear White America: Letter to a New Minority.* San Francisco: City Lights, 2012.

Wright, N. T. *The Resurrection of the Son of God.* Christian Origins and the Question of God 3. Minneapolis: Fortress, 2003.

————. *Surprised by Hope: Rethinking Heaven, the Resurrection, and the Mission of the Church.* New York: HarperCollins, 2008.

Yoder, John Howard. "The Anabaptist Shape of Liberation." In *Why I Am a Mennonite: Essays on Mennonite Identity,* ed. Harry Loewen, 338-48. Scottdale: Herald, 1988.

————. "Armaments and Eschatology." *Studies in Christian Ethics* 1 (1988): 43-61.

————. *Body Politics: Five Practices of the Christian Community before the Watching World.* Scottdale: Herald, 2001.

————. "'But We Do See Jesus': The Particularity of Incarnation and the Universality of Truth." In *Foundations of Ethics,* ed. Leroy S. Rouner, 57-75. Boston University Studies in Philosophy and Religion. Notre Dame: University of Notre Dame Press, 1983.

————. "'But We Do See Jesus': The Particularity of Incarnation and the Universality of Truth." In *The Priestly Kingdom: Social Ethics as Gospel,* 46-62. Notre Dame: University of Notre Dame, 1984.

————. "The Constantinian Sources of Western Social Ethics." In *The Priestly Kingdom: Social Ethics as Gospel,* 135-47. Notre Dame: University of Notre Dame, 1984.

————. *For the Nations: Essays Public and Evangelical.* Grand Rapids: William B. Eerdmans, 1997.

————. "How H. Richard Niebuhr Reasoned: A Critique of *Christ and Culture.*" In Glen H. Stassen, D. M. Yeager, and John Howard Yoder, *Authentic Transformation: A New Vision of Christ and Culture,* 31-89. Nashville: Abingdon, 1996.

————. "Jesus the Jewish Pacifist." In *The Jewish-Christian Schism Revisited,* ed. Michael G. Cartwright and Peter Ochs, 69-92. Grand Rapids: William B. Eerdmans, 2003.

————. *The Jewish-Christian Schism Revisited,* ed. Michael G. Cartwright and Peter Ochs. Grand Rapids: William B. Eerdmans, 2003.

————. *The Original Revolution: Essays on Christian Pacifism.* Scottdale: Herald, 1971.

————. "The Otherness of the Church." In *The Royal Priesthood: Essays Ecclesiological and Ecumenical,* ed. Michael G. Cartwright, 53-64. Grand Rapids: William B. Eerdmans, 1994.

————. *The Politics of Jesus: Vicit Agnus Noster.* 2d ed. Grand Rapids: William B. Eerdmans, 1994.

————. *Preface to Theology: Christology and Theological Method.* Elkhart: Goshen Biblical Seminary, distributed by Co-op Bookstore, 1981.

————. *Preface to Theology: Christology and Theological Method.* Grand Rapids: Brazos, 2002.

————. *The Priestly Kingdom: Social Ethics as Gospel.* Notre Dame: University of Notre Dame Press, 1984.

————. *The Royal Priesthood: Essays Ecclesiological and Ecumenical,* ed. Michael G. Cartwright. Grand Rapids: William B. Eerdmans, 1994.

————. "'See How They Go with Their Face to the Sun.'" In *The Jewish-Christian Schism Revisited,* ed. Michael G. Cartwright and Peter Ochs, 183-204. Grand Rapids: William B. Eerdmans, 2003.

————. *The War of the Lamb: The Ethics of Nonviolence and Peacemaking,* ed. Glen Harold Stassen, Mark Thiessen Nation, and Matt Hamsher. Grand Rapids: Brazos, 2009.

————. *When War Is Unjust: Being Honest in Just-War Thinking.* 2d ed. Maryknoll: Orbis, 1996.

Yoder, John Howard, with Joan Baez, Tom Skinner, Leo Tolstoy, and others. *What Would You Do? A Serious Answer to a Standard Question.* Rev. ed. Scottdale: Herald, 1992.

Young, Jeremy. *The Violence of God and the War on Terror.* New York: Seabury, 2008.

Zehr, Howard. *Changing Lenses: A New Focus for Crime and Justice.* A Christian Peace Shelf Selection. 3rd ed. Scottdale: Herald, 2005.

Zweifel, Dave. "Poor Kids Strike Out as Greed Wins." *The Cap Times,* April 21-27, 2010, 30.

Index